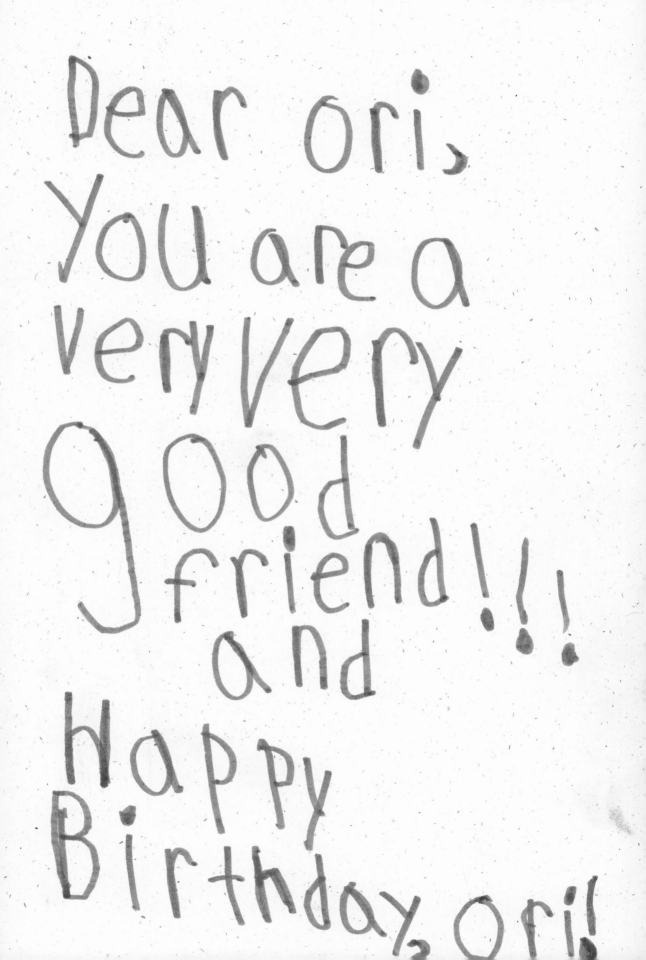

Dear ori,
You are a
very very
good
friend!!!
and
Happy
Birthday, ori!

WRITER
PAUL JENKINS

ARTIST
PAOLO RIVERA

LETTERER
VIRTUAL CALLIGAPHY'S JOE CARAMAGNA

ASSISTANT EDITORS
MOLLY LAZER, AUBREY SITTERSON
& THOMAS BRENNAN

ASSOCIATE EDITOR
ANDY SCHMIDT

EDITORS
TOM BREVOORT & STEPHEN WACKER

COLLECTION EDITOR: JENNIFER GRÜNWALD
EDITORIAL ASSISTANT: ALEX STARBUCK
ASSISTANT EDITORS: CORY LEVINE & JOHN DENNING
EDITOR, SPECIAL PROJECTS: MARK D. BEAZLEY
SENIOR EDITOR, SPECIAL PROJECTS: JEFF YOUNGQUIST
SENIOR VICE PRESIDENT OF SALES: DAVID GABRIEL
PRODUCTION: JERRY KALINOWSKI
BOOK DESIGNER: SPRING HOTELING

EDITOR IN CHIEF: JOE QUESADA
PUBLISHER: DAN BUCKLEY

MYTHOS. Contains material originally published in magazine form as MYTHOS: SPIDER-MAN, HULK, FANTASTIC FOUR, GHOST RIDER, CAPTAIN AMERICA and X-MEN. First printing 2008. ISBN# 978-0-7851-1597-7. Published by M
PUBLISHING, INC., a subsidiary of MARVEL ENTERTAINMENT, INC. OFFICE OF PUBLICATION: 417 5th Avenue, New York, NY 10016. Copyright © 2006, 2007 and 2008 Marvel Characters, Inc. All rights reserved. $24.99 per copy in the U.S. and
in Canada (GST #R127032852); Canadian Agreement #40668537. All characters featured in this issue and the distinctive names and likenesses thereof, and all related indicia are trademarks of Marvel Characters, Inc. No similarity betwe
of the names, characters, persons, and/or institutions in this magazine with those of any living or dead person or institution is intended, and any such similarity which may exist is purely coincidental. **Printed in the U.S.A.** ALAN FINE, CE
Toys & Publishing Divisions and CMO Marvel Characters, Inc.; DAVID GABRIEL, SVP of Publishing Sales & Circulation; DAVID BOGART, SVP of Business Affairs & Talent Management; MICHAEL PASCIULLO, VP of Merchandising & Commun
JIM O'KEEFE, VP of Operations & Logistics; DAN CARR, Executive Director of Publishing Technology; JUSTIN F. GABRIE, Director of Editorial Operations; SUSAN CRESPI, Editorial Operations Manager; OMAR OTIEKU, Production Manager; S
Chairman Emeritus. For information regarding advertising in Marvel Comics or on Marvel.com, please contact Mitch Dane, Advertising Director, at mdane@marvel.com. For Marvel subscription inquiries, please call 800-217-9158.

10 9 8 7 6 5 4 3 2 1

MYTHOS

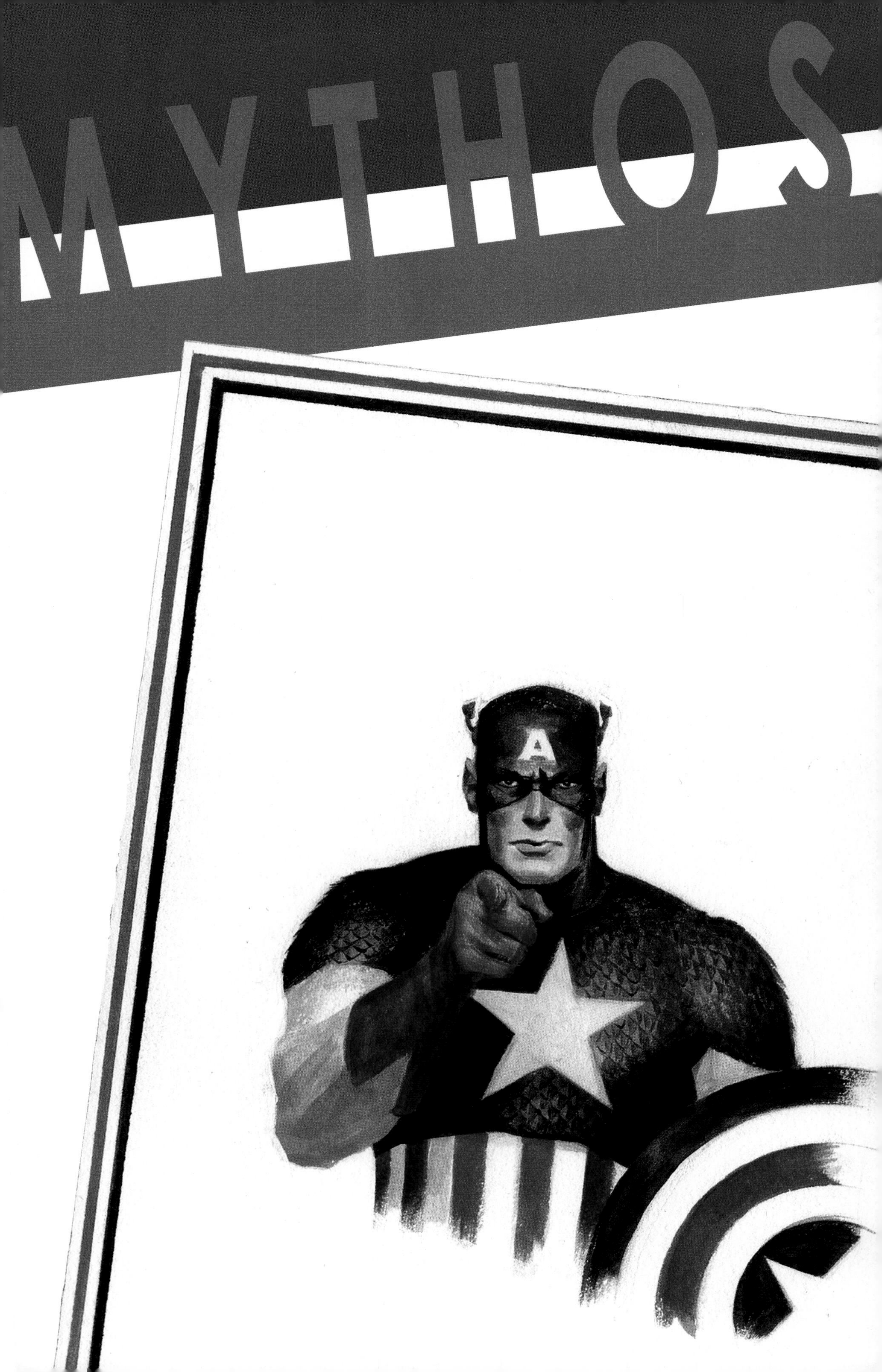

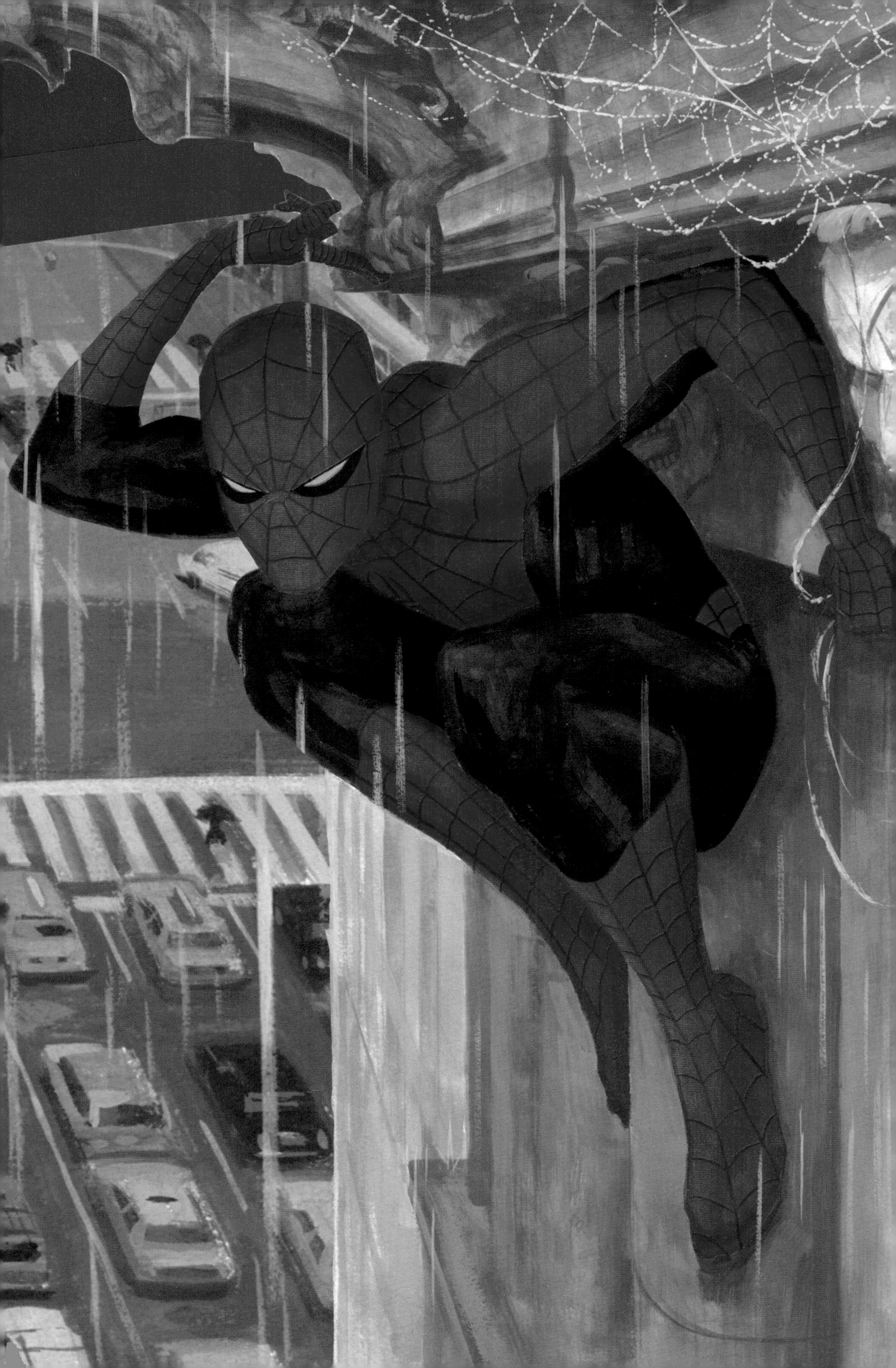

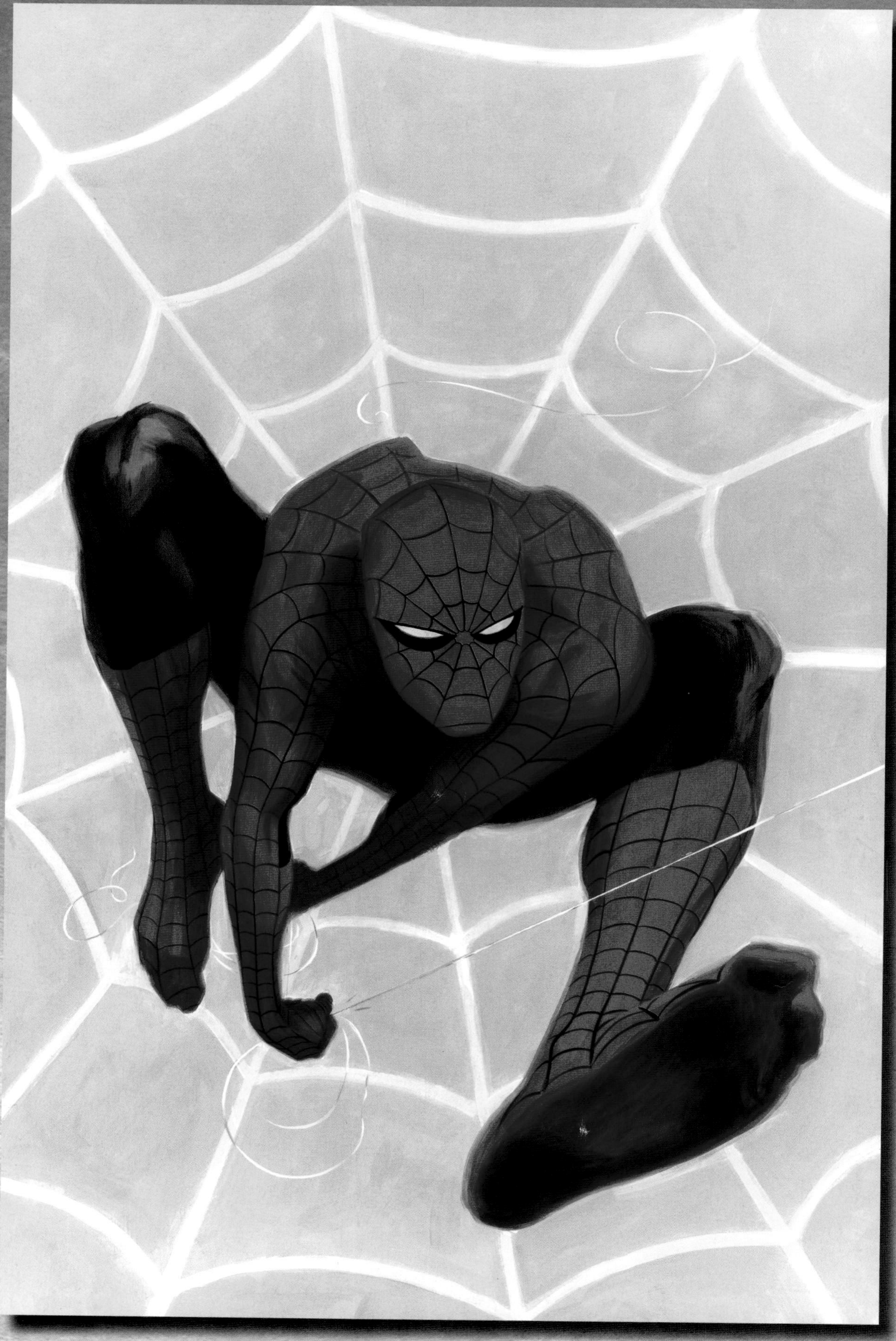

- Spider-Man -

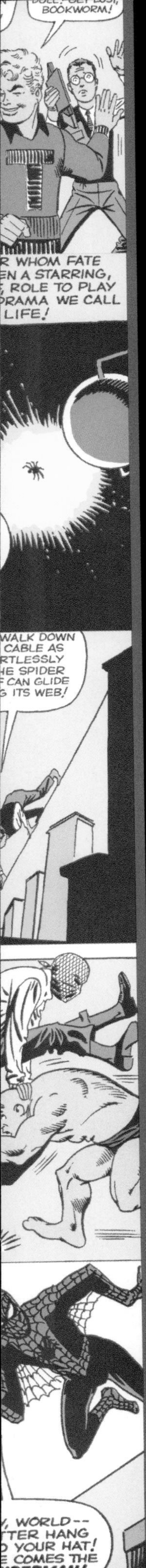
BOOKWORM!

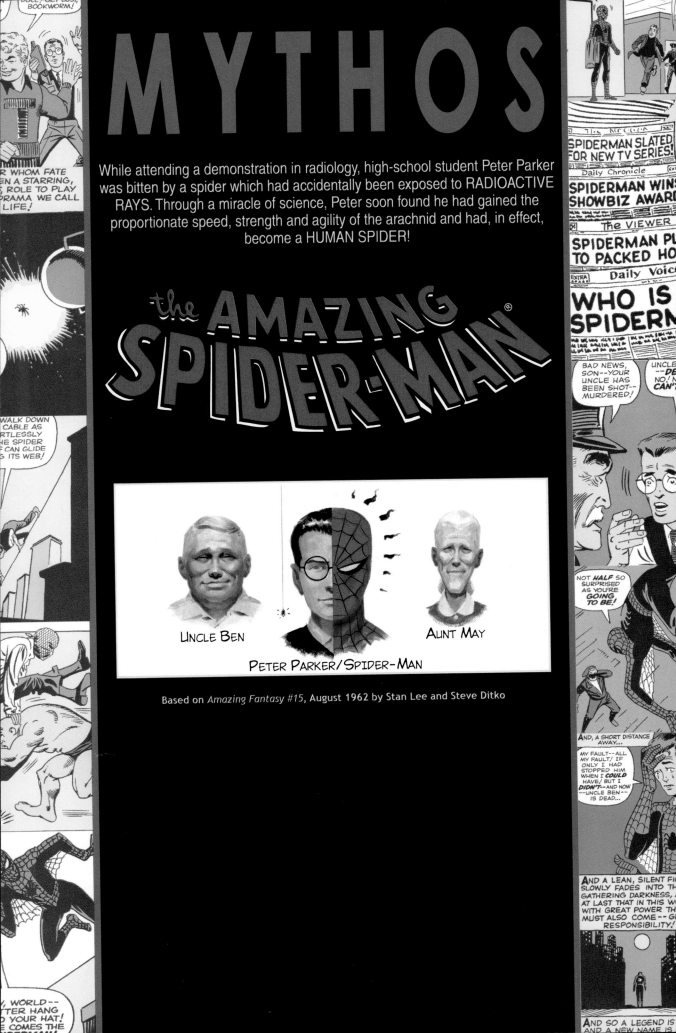

MYTHOS

While attending a demonstration in radiology, high-school student Peter Parker was bitten by a spider which had accidentally been exposed to RADIOACTIVE RAYS. Through a miracle of science, Peter soon found he had gained the proportionate speed, strength and agility of the arachnid and had, in effect, become a HUMAN SPIDER!

the AMAZING SPIDER-MAN®

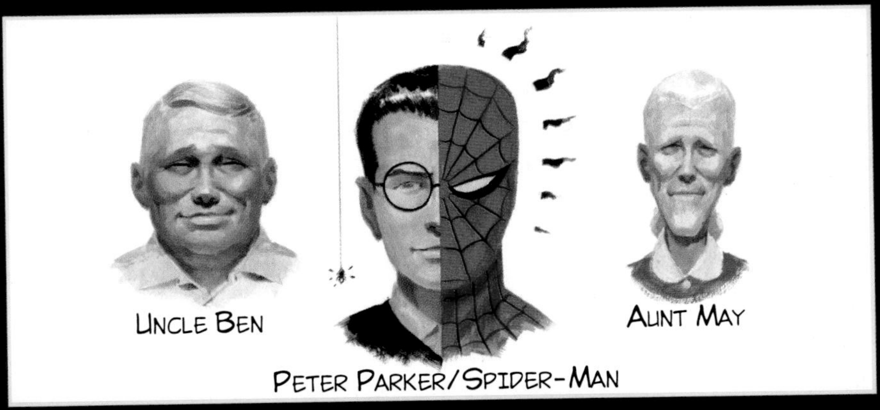
UNCLE BEN
AUNT MAY
PETER PARKER/SPIDER-MAN

Based on *Amazing Fantasy #15*, August 1962 by Stan Lee and Steve Ditko

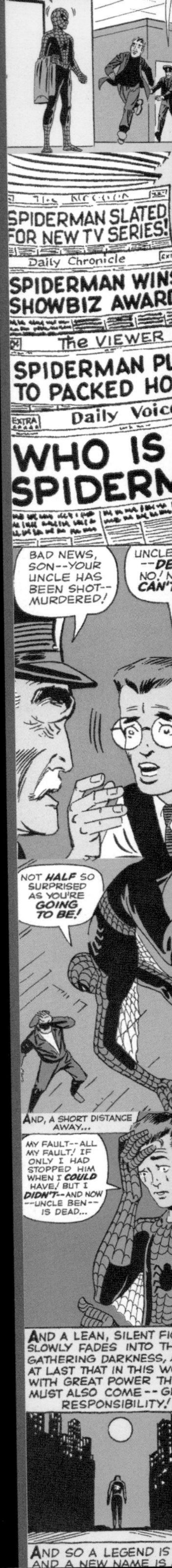
SPIDERMAN SLATED FOR NEW TV SERIES!
Daily Chronicle
The VIEWER
Daily Voice
BAD NEWS, SON--YOUR UNCLE HAS BEEN SHOT--MURDERED!
NOT HALF SO SURPRISED AS YOU'RE GOING TO BE!
AND, A SHORT DISTANCE AWAY...
MY FAULT--ALL MY FAULT! IF ONLY I HAD STOPPED HIM WHEN I COULD HAVE! BUT I DIDN'T--AND NOW --UNCLE BEN-- IS DEAD...

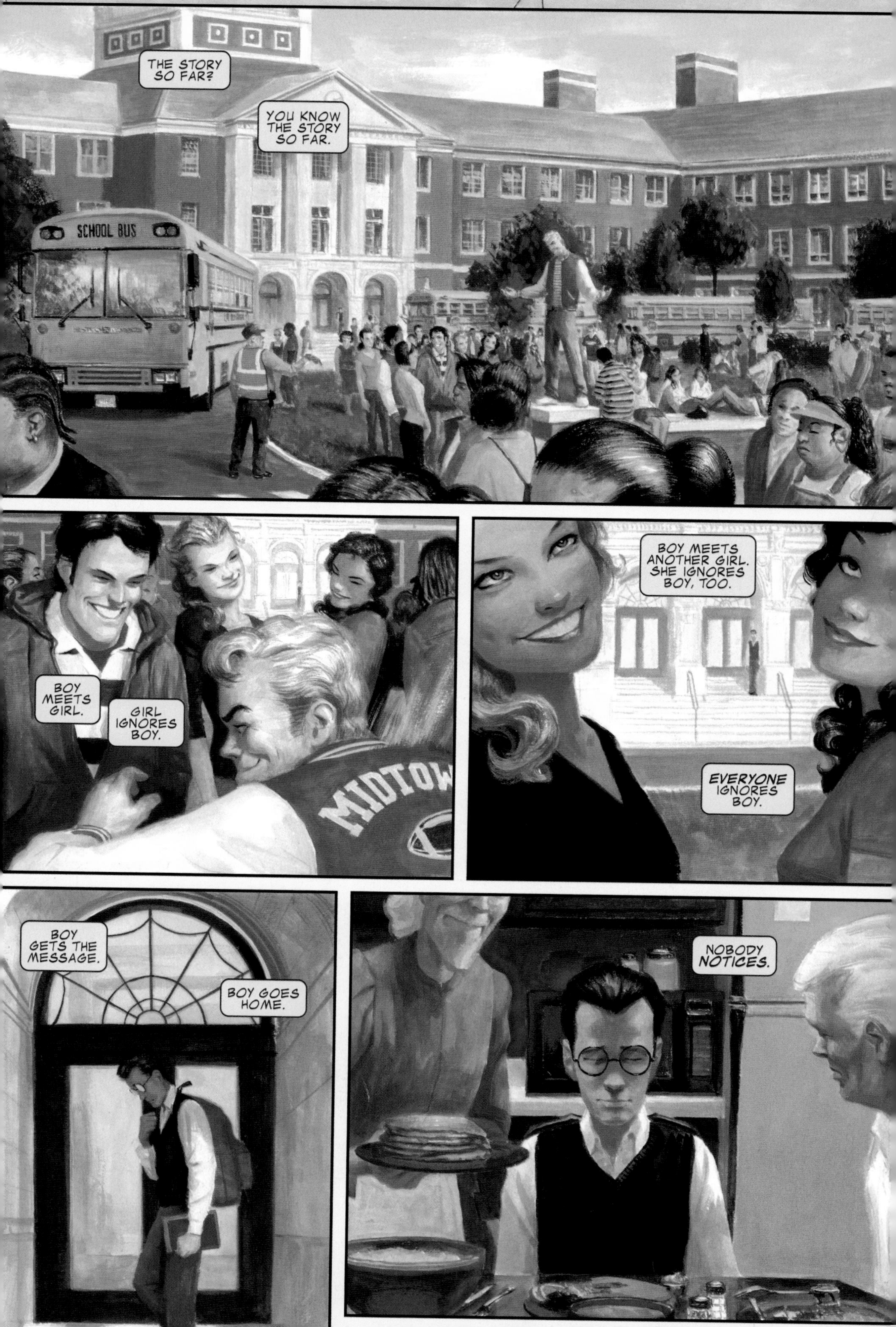
THE STORY SO FAR?
YOU KNOW THE STORY SO FAR.
SCHOOL BUS
BOY MEETS GIRL.
GIRL IGNORES BOY.
MIDTOW
BOY MEETS ANOTHER GIRL. SHE IGNORES BOY, TOO.
EVERYONE IGNORES BOY.
BOY GETS THE MESSAGE.
BOY GOES HOME.
NOBODY NOTICES.

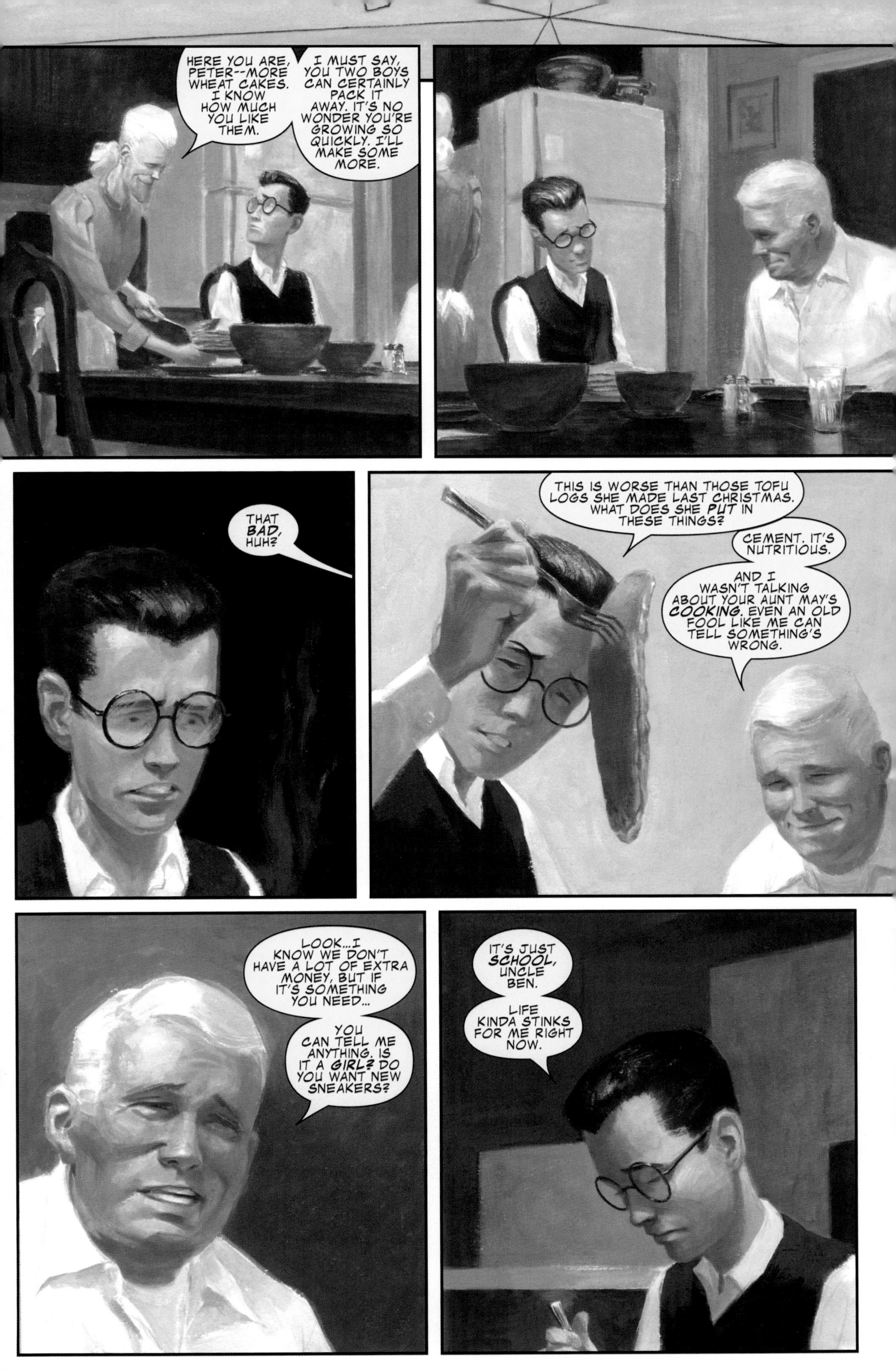
HERE YOU ARE, PETER--MORE WHEAT CAKES. I KNOW HOW MUCH YOU LIKE THEM.
I MUST SAY, YOU TWO BOYS CAN CERTAINLY PACK IT AWAY. IT'S NO WONDER YOU'RE GROWING SO QUICKLY. I'LL MAKE SOME MORE.
THAT *BAD*, HUH?
THIS IS WORSE THAN THOSE TOFU LOGS SHE MADE LAST CHRISTMAS. WHAT DOES SHE *PUT* IN THESE THINGS?
CEMENT. IT'S NUTRITIOUS.
AND I WASN'T TALKING ABOUT YOUR AUNT MAY'S *COOKING*. EVEN AN OLD FOOL LIKE ME CAN TELL SOMETHING'S WRONG.
LOOK...I KNOW WE DON'T HAVE A LOT OF EXTRA MONEY, BUT IF IT'S SOMETHING YOU NEED...
YOU CAN TELL ME ANYTHING. IS IT A *GIRL?* DO YOU WANT NEW SNEAKERS?
IT'S JUST *SCHOOL*, UNCLE BEN.
LIFE KINDA STINKS FOR ME RIGHT NOW.

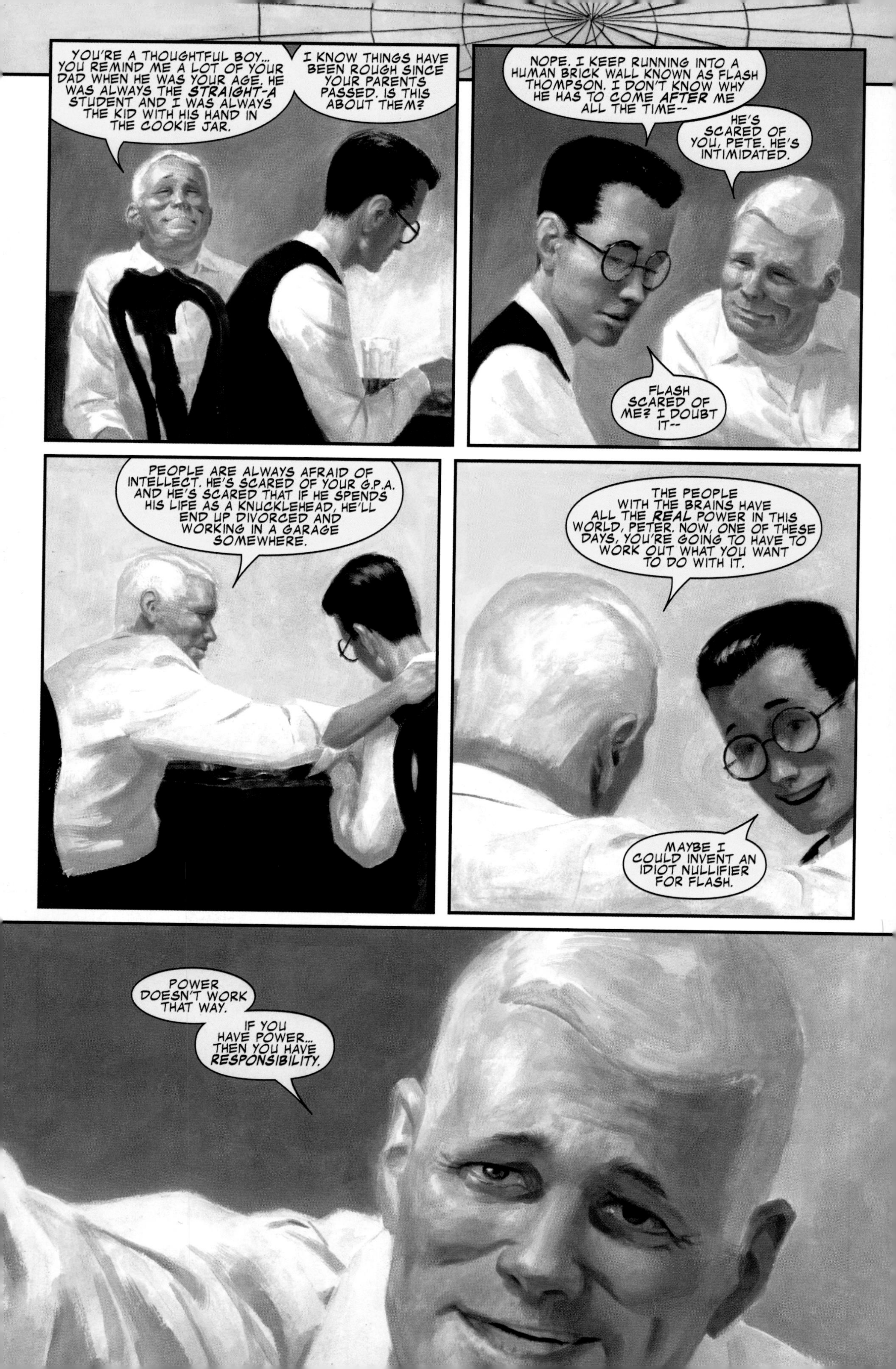
YOU'RE A THOUGHTFUL BOY... YOU REMIND ME A LOT OF YOUR DAD WHEN HE WAS YOUR AGE. HE WAS ALWAYS THE STRAIGHT-A STUDENT AND I WAS ALWAYS THE KID WITH HIS HAND IN THE COOKIE JAR.
I KNOW THINGS HAVE BEEN ROUGH SINCE YOUR PARENTS PASSED. IS THIS ABOUT THEM?
NOPE. I KEEP RUNNING INTO A HUMAN BRICK WALL KNOWN AS FLASH THOMPSON. I DON'T KNOW WHY HE HAS TO COME AFTER ME ALL THE TIME--
HE'S SCARED OF YOU, PETE. HE'S INTIMIDATED.
FLASH SCARED OF ME? I DOUBT IT--
PEOPLE ARE ALWAYS AFRAID OF INTELLECT. HE'S SCARED OF YOUR G.P.A. AND HE'S SCARED THAT IF HE SPENDS HIS LIFE AS A KNUCKLEHEAD, HE'LL END UP DIVORCED AND WORKING IN A GARAGE SOMEWHERE.
THE PEOPLE WITH THE BRAINS HAVE ALL THE REAL POWER IN THIS WORLD, PETER. NOW, ONE OF THESE DAYS, YOU'RE GOING TO HAVE TO WORK OUT WHAT YOU WANT TO DO WITH IT.
MAYBE I COULD INVENT AN IDIOT NULLIFIER FOR FLASH.
POWER DOESN'T WORK THAT WAY.
IF YOU HAVE POWER... THEN YOU HAVE RESPONSIBILITY.

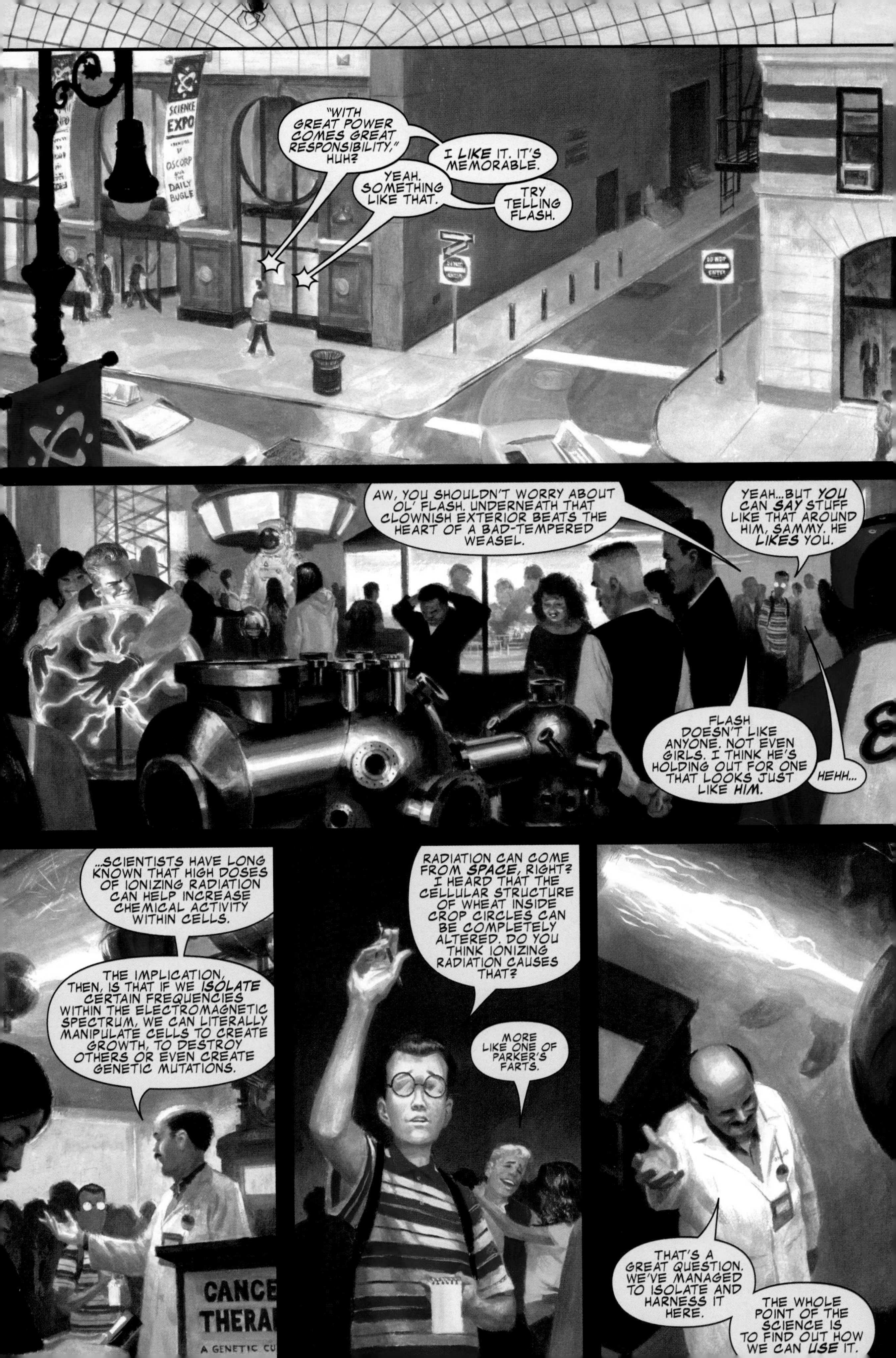
SCIENCE EXPO
OSCORP
DAILY BUGLE
"WITH GREAT POWER COMES GREAT RESPONSIBILITY," HUH?
I LIKE IT. IT'S MEMORABLE.
YEAH. SOMETHING LIKE THAT.
TRY TELLING FLASH.
AW, YOU SHOULDN'T WORRY ABOUT OL' FLASH. UNDERNEATH THAT CLOWNISH EXTERIOR BEATS THE HEART OF A BAD-TEMPERED WEASEL.
YEAH...BUT YOU CAN SAY STUFF LIKE THAT AROUND HIM, SAMMY. HE LIKES YOU.
FLASH DOESN'T LIKE ANYONE. NOT EVEN GIRLS. I THINK HE'S HOLDING OUT FOR ONE THAT LOOKS JUST LIKE HIM.
HEHH...
...SCIENTISTS HAVE LONG KNOWN THAT HIGH DOSES OF IONIZING RADIATION CAN HELP INCREASE CHEMICAL ACTIVITY WITHIN CELLS.
THE IMPLICATION, THEN, IS THAT IF WE ISOLATE CERTAIN FREQUENCIES WITHIN THE ELECTROMAGNETIC SPECTRUM, WE CAN LITERALLY MANIPULATE CELLS TO CREATE GROWTH, TO DESTROY OTHERS OR EVEN CREATE GENETIC MUTATIONS.
CANCE
THERA
A GENETIC CU
RADIATION CAN COME FROM SPACE, RIGHT? I HEARD THAT THE CELLULAR STRUCTURE OF WHEAT INSIDE CROP CIRCLES CAN BE COMPLETELY ALTERED. DO YOU THINK IONIZING RADIATION CAUSES THAT?
MORE LIKE ONE OF PARKER'S FARTS.
THAT'S A GREAT QUESTION. WE'VE MANAGED TO ISOLATE AND HARNESS IT HERE.
THE WHOLE POINT OF THE SCIENCE IS TO FIND OUT HOW WE CAN USE IT.

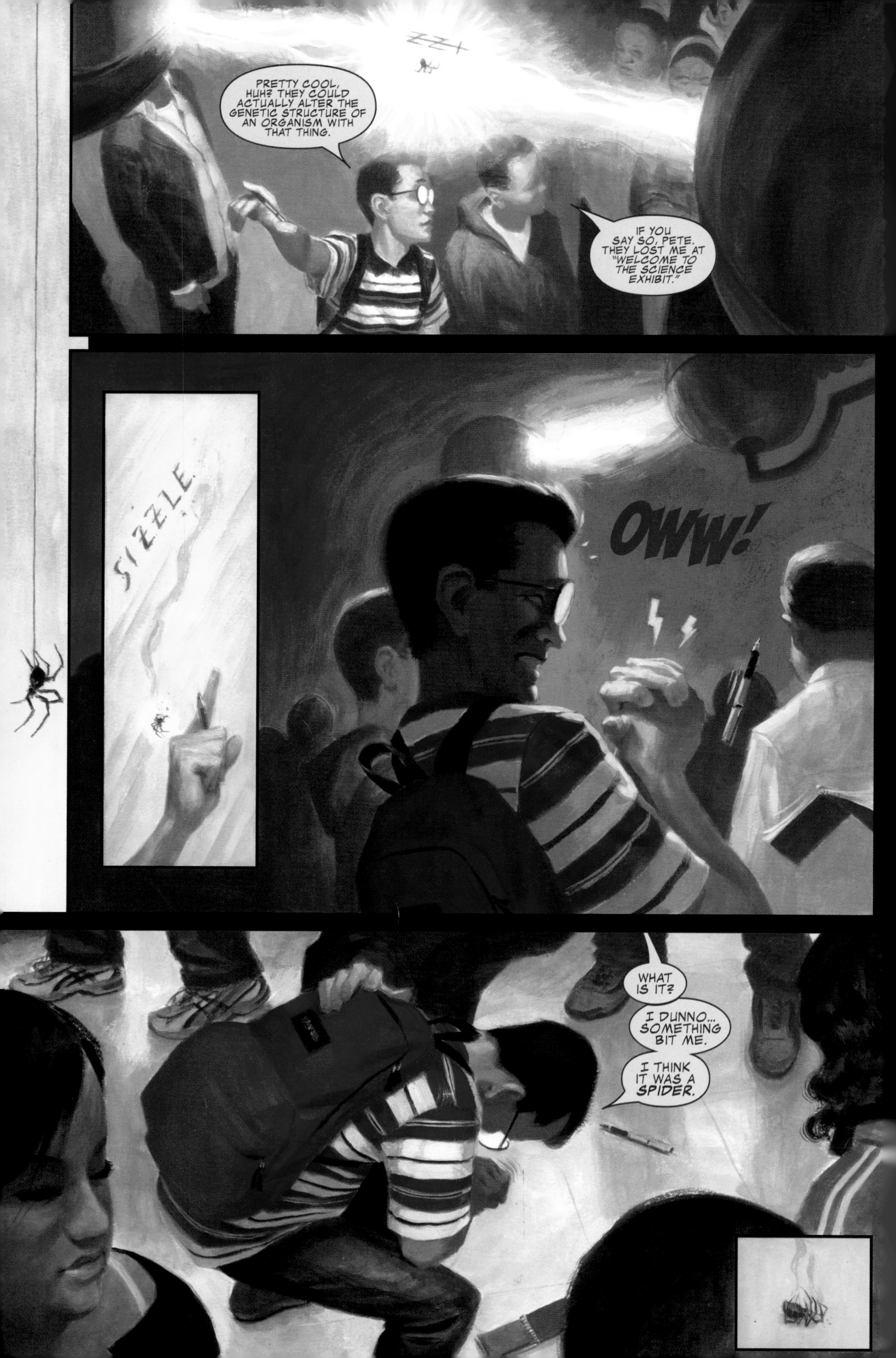
ZZT
PRETTY COOL, HUH? THEY COULD ACTUALLY ALTER THE GENETIC STRUCTURE OF AN ORGANISM WITH THAT THING.
IF YOU SAY SO, PETE. THEY LOST ME AT "WELCOME TO THE SCIENCE EXHIBIT."
SIZZLE
OWW!
WHAT IS IT?
I DUNNO... SOMETHING BIT ME.
I THINK IT WAS A SPIDER.

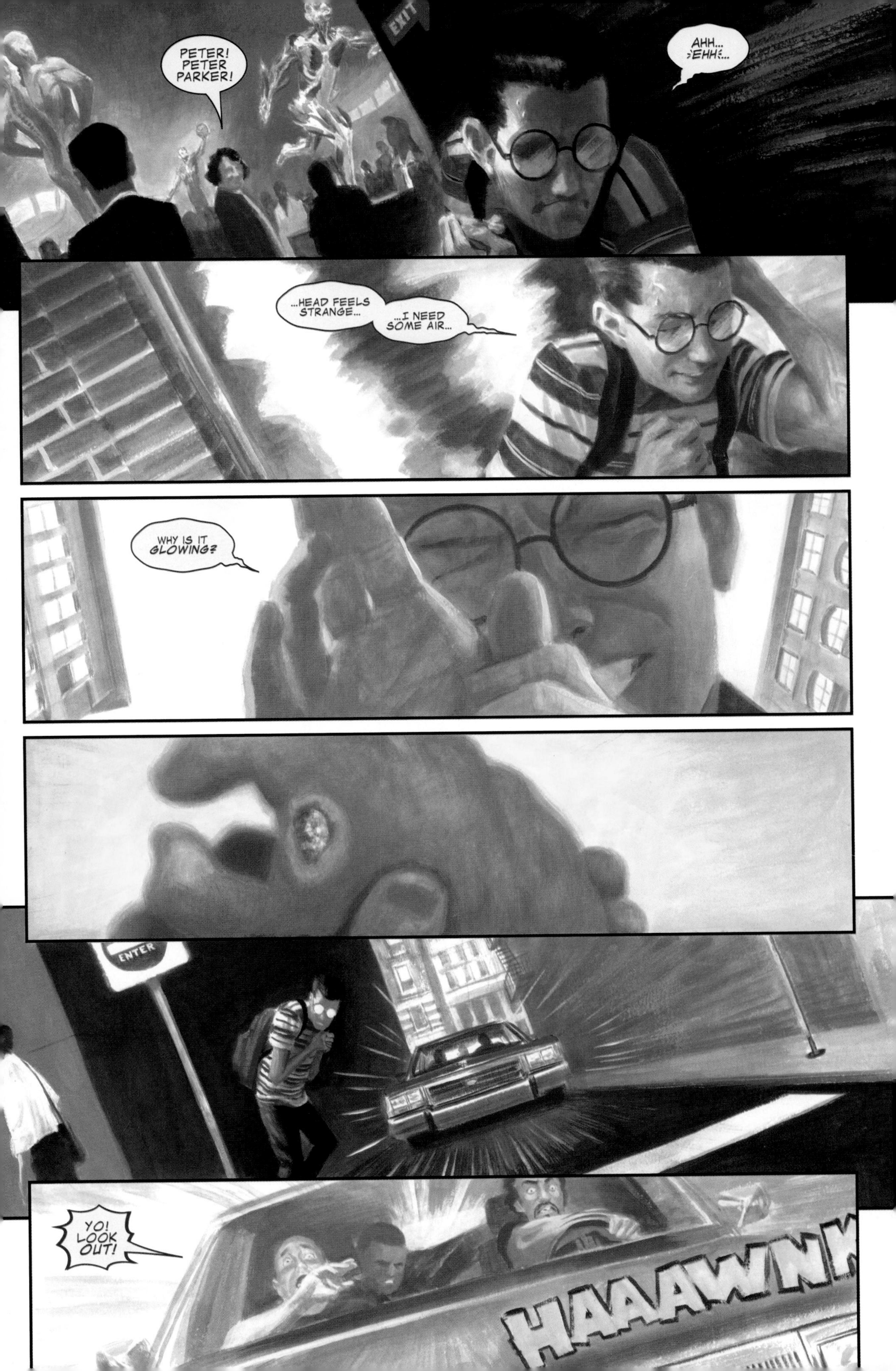
PETER! PETER PARKER!
AHH... EHH...
...HEAD FEELS STRANGE...
...I NEED SOME AIR...
WHY IS IT GLOWING?
ENTER
YO! LOOK OUT!
HAAAWNK

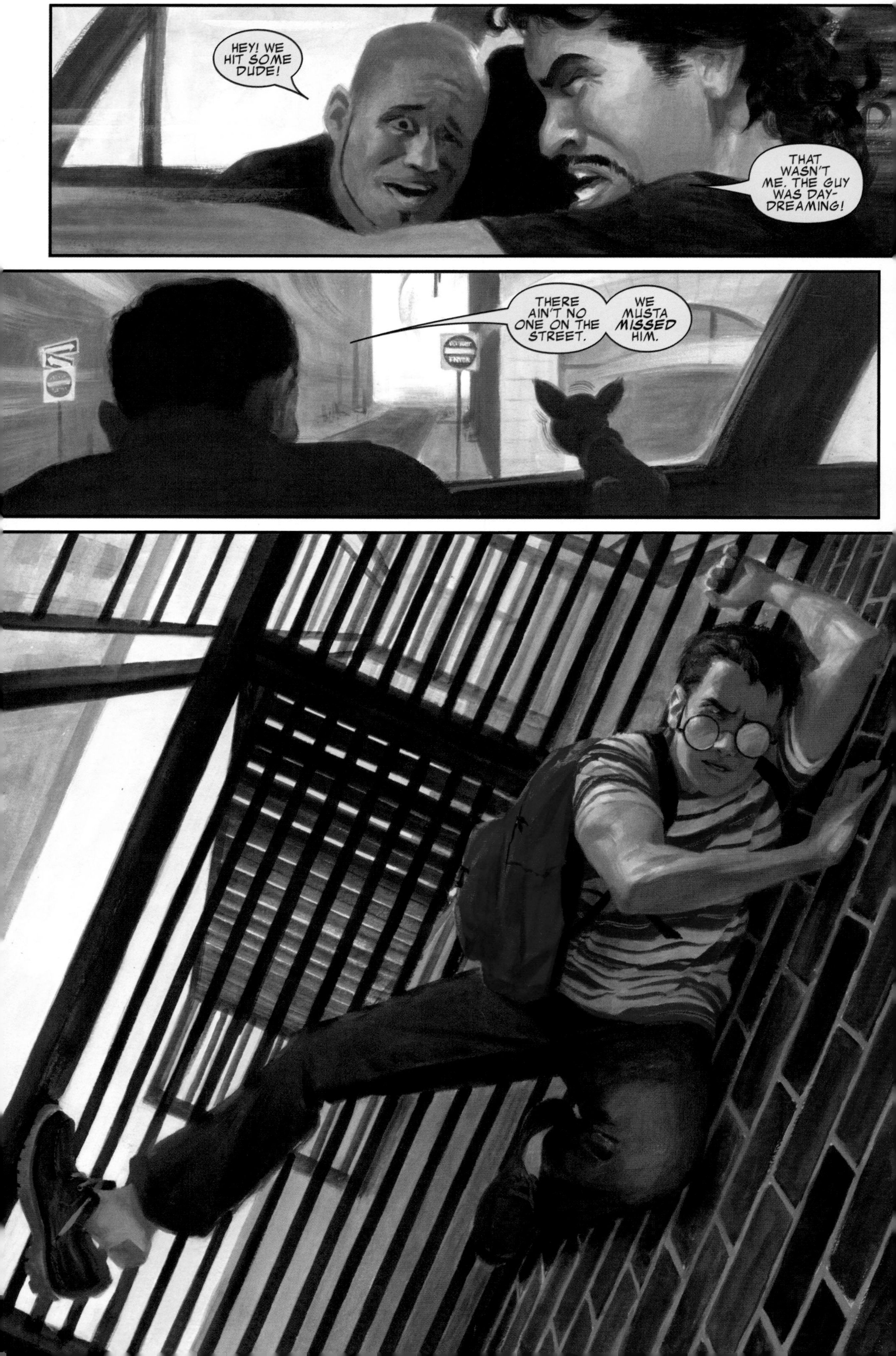
HEY! WE HIT SOME DUDE!
THAT WASN'T ME. THE GUY WAS DAY-DREAMING!
THERE AIN'T NO ONE ON THE STREET.
WE MUSTA *MISSED* HIM.

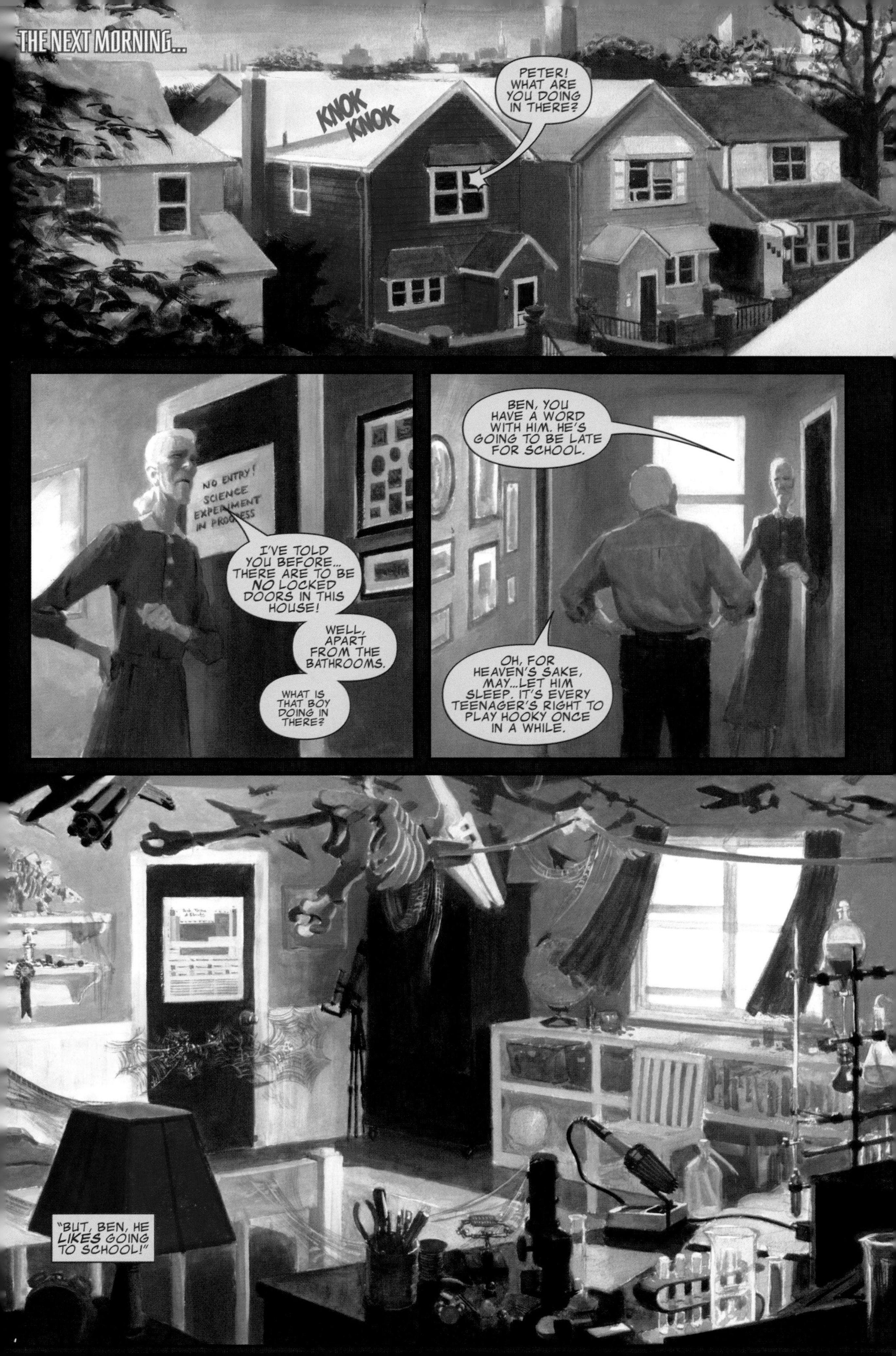
THE NEXT MORNING...
KNOK KNOK
PETER! WHAT ARE YOU DOING IN THERE?
NO ENTRY! SCIENCE EXPERIMENT IN PROGRESS
I'VE TOLD YOU BEFORE... THERE ARE TO BE NO LOCKED DOORS IN THIS HOUSE!
WELL, APART FROM THE BATHROOMS.
WHAT IS THAT BOY DOING IN THERE?
BEN, YOU HAVE A WORD WITH HIM. HE'S GOING TO BE LATE FOR SCHOOL.
OH, FOR HEAVEN'S SAKE, MAY...LET HIM SLEEP. IT'S EVERY TEENAGER'S RIGHT TO PLAY HOOKY ONCE IN A WHILE.
"BUT, BEN, HE LIKES GOING TO SCHOOL!"

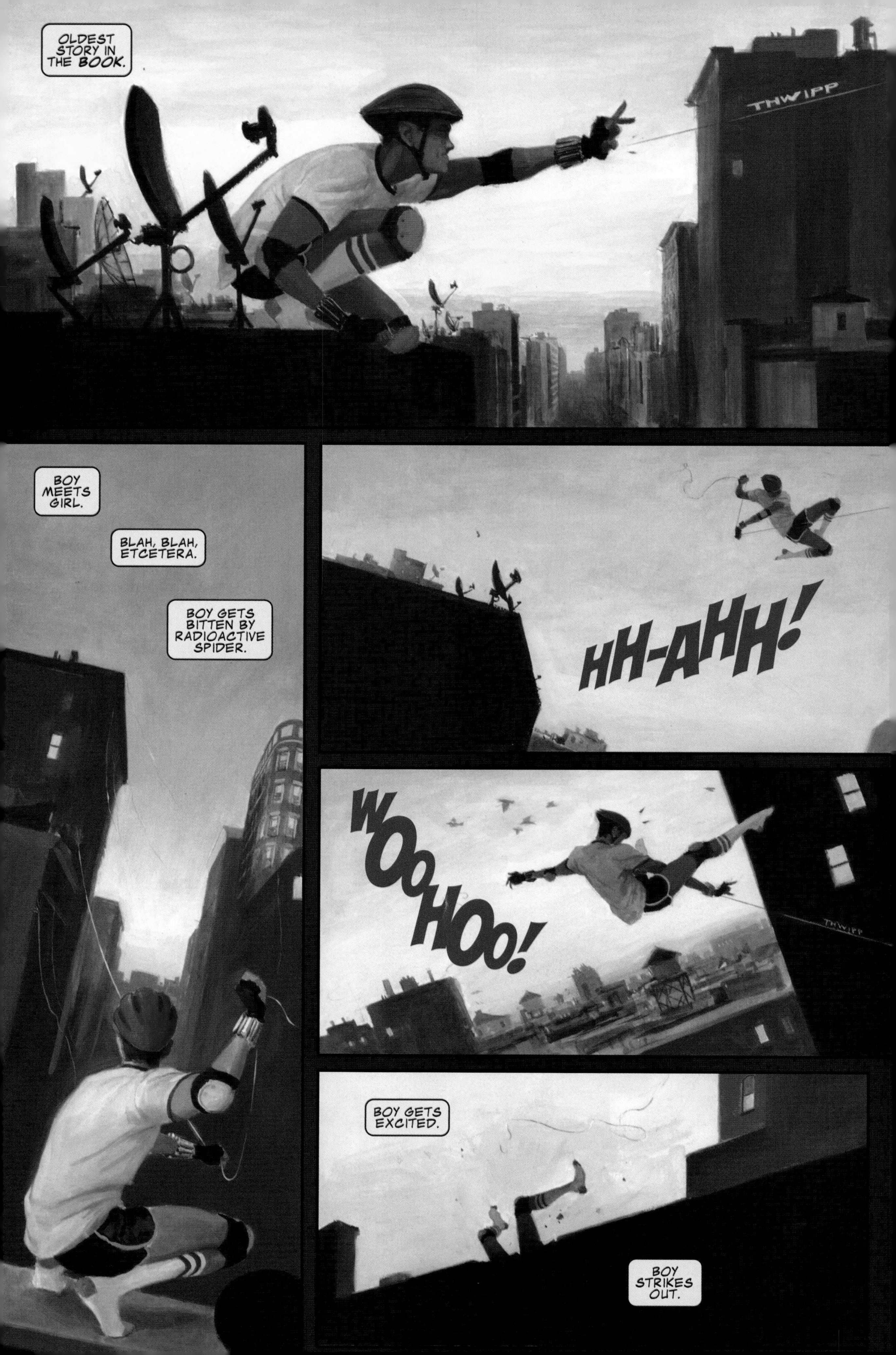
OLDEST STORY IN THE BOOK.
THWIPP
BOY MEETS GIRL.
BLAH, BLAH, ETCETERA.
BOY GETS BITTEN BY RADIOACTIVE SPIDER.
HH-AHH!
WOOHOO!
THWIPP
BOY GETS EXCITED.
BOY STRIKES OUT.

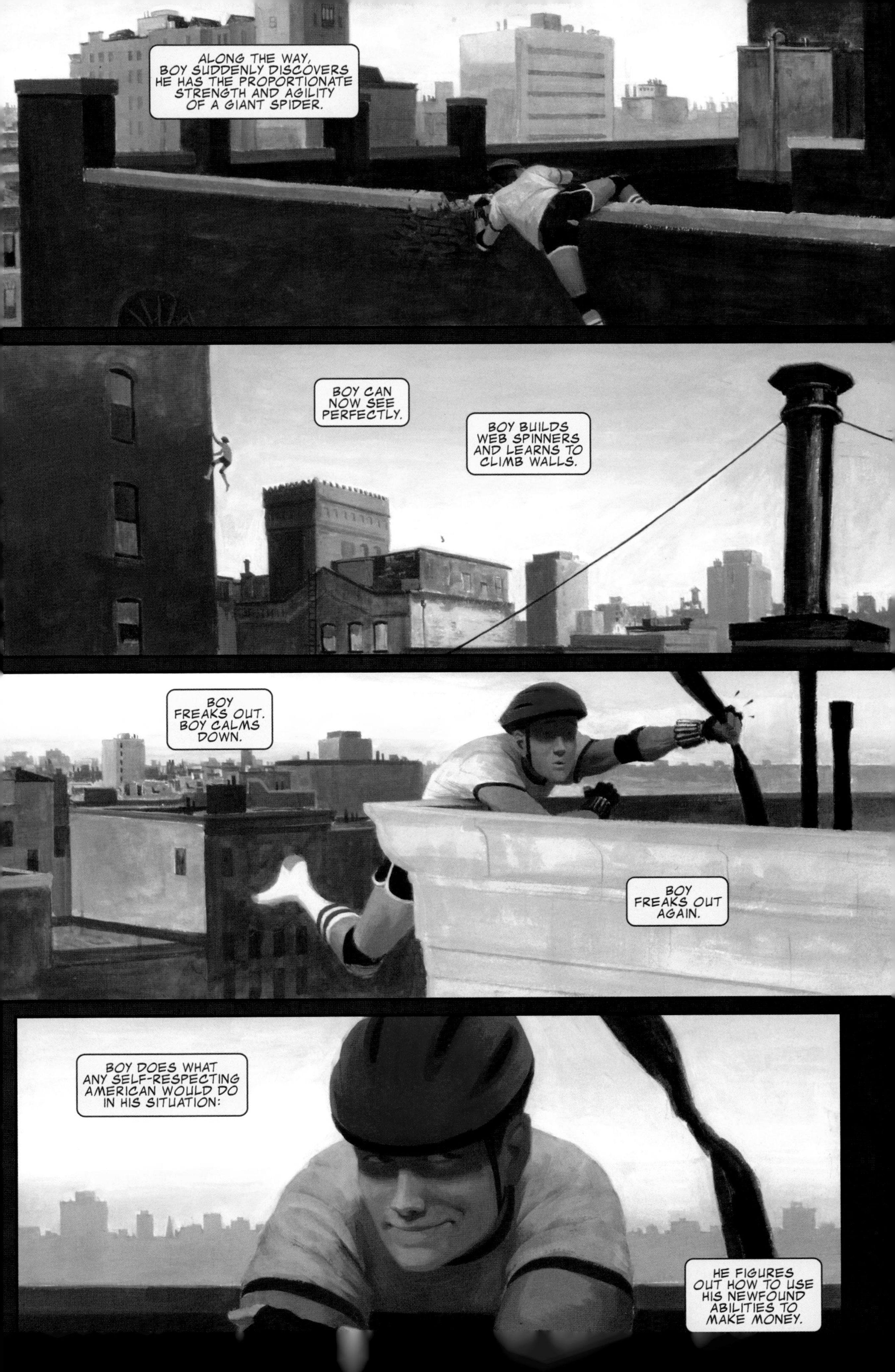
ALONG THE WAY, BOY SUDDENLY DISCOVERS HE HAS THE PROPORTIONATE STRENGTH AND AGILITY OF A GIANT SPIDER.
BOY CAN NOW SEE PERFECTLY.
BOY BUILDS WEB SPINNERS AND LEARNS TO CLIMB WALLS.
BOY FREAKS OUT. BOY CALMS DOWN.
BOY FREAKS OUT AGAIN.
BOY DOES WHAT ANY SELF-RESPECTING AMERICAN WOULD DO IN HIS SITUATION:
HE FIGURES OUT HOW TO USE HIS NEWFOUND ABILITIES TO MAKE MONEY.

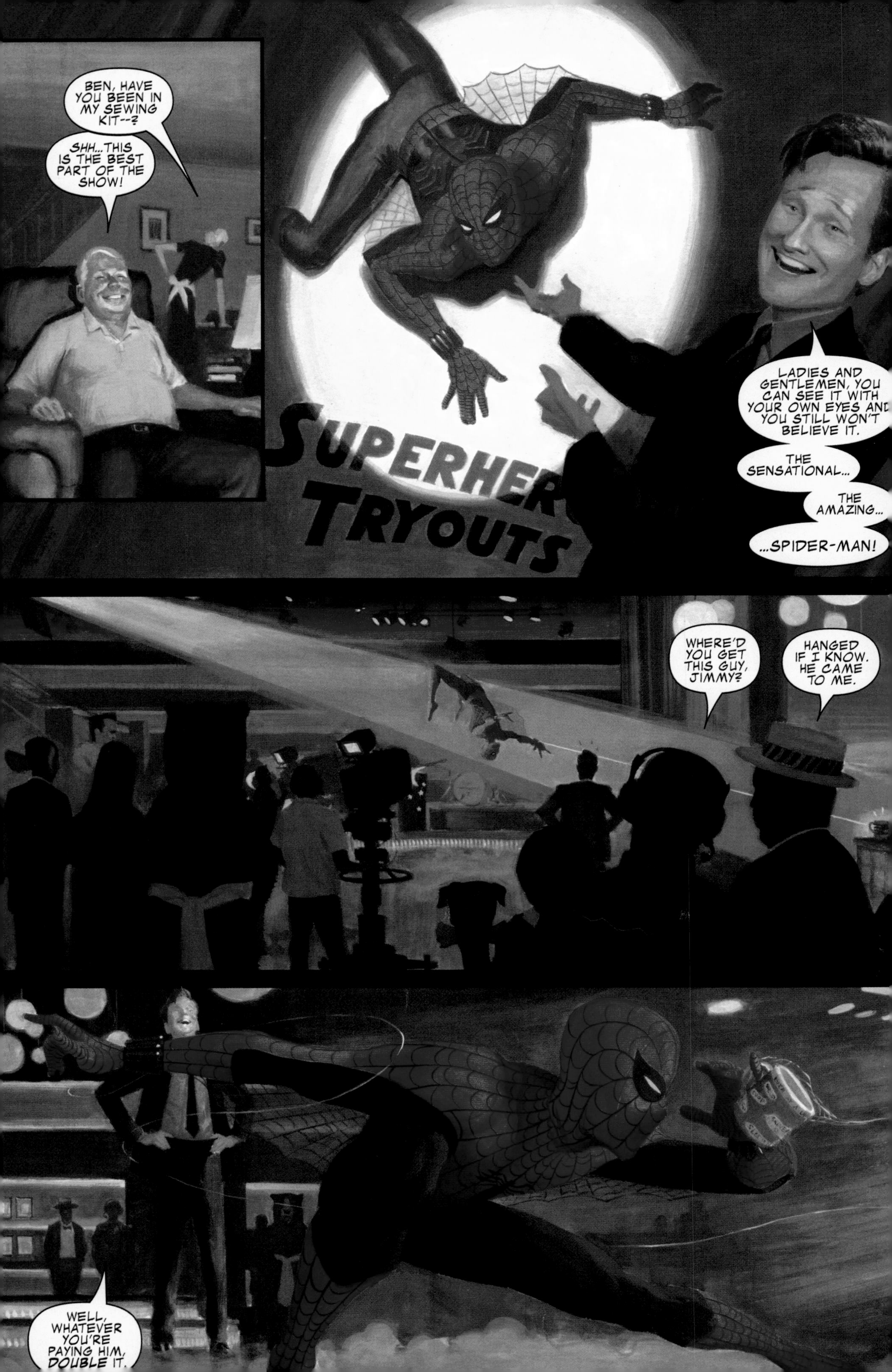
BEN, HAVE YOU BEEN IN MY SEWING KIT--?
SHH...THIS IS THE BEST PART OF THE SHOW!
SUPERHERO TRYOUTS
LADIES AND GENTLEMEN, YOU CAN SEE IT WITH YOUR OWN EYES AND YOU STILL WON'T BELIEVE IT.
THE SENSATIONAL...
THE AMAZING...
...SPIDER-MAN!
WHERE'D YOU GET THIS GUY, JIMMY?
HANGED IF I KNOW. HE CAME TO ME.
WELL, WHATEVER YOU'RE PAYING HIM, DOUBLE IT.

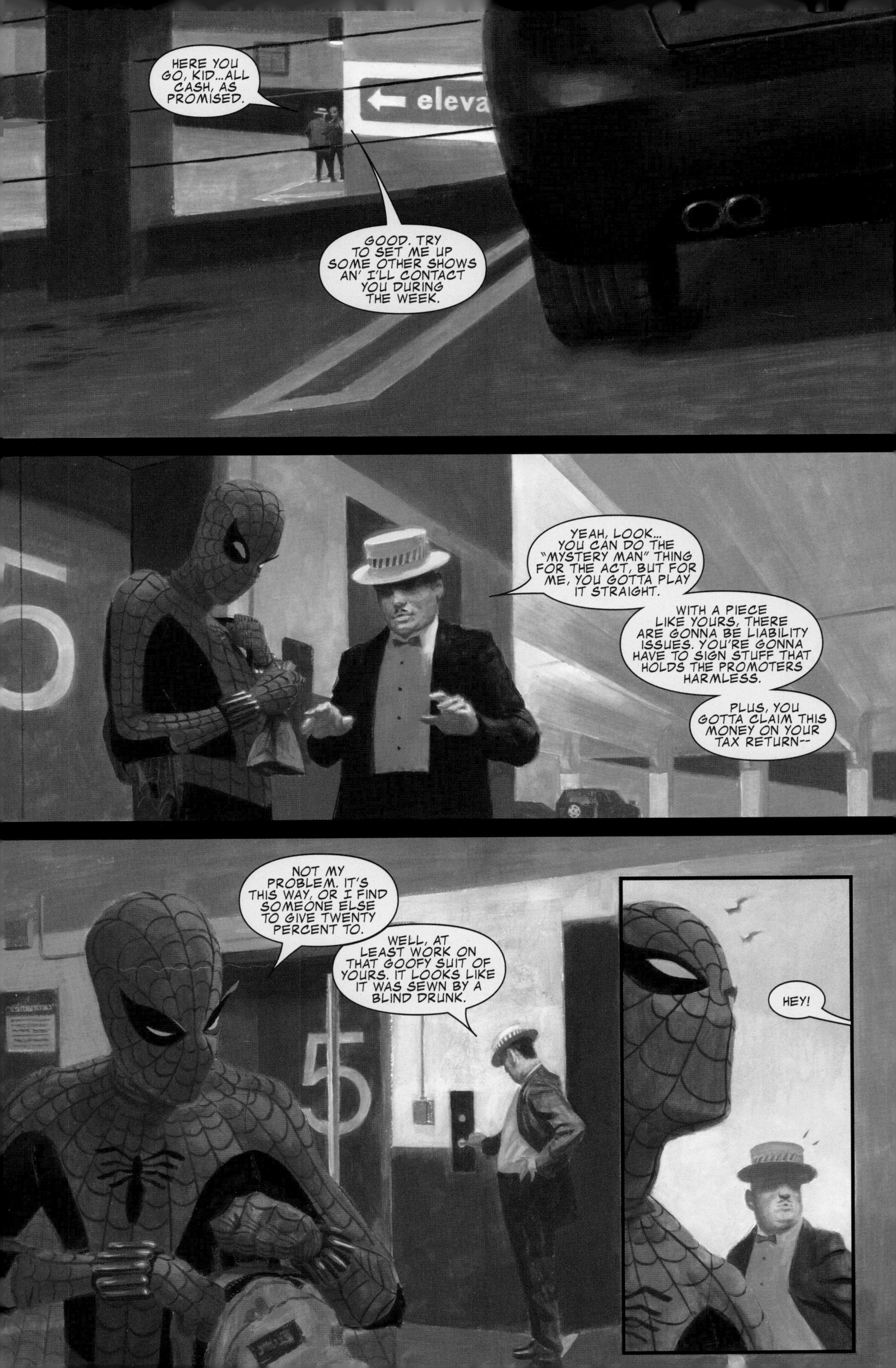
HERE YOU GO, KID...ALL CASH, AS PROMISED.
eleva
GOOD. TRY TO SET ME UP SOME OTHER SHOWS AN' I'LL CONTACT YOU DURING THE WEEK.
YEAH, LOOK... YOU CAN DO THE "MYSTERY MAN" THING FOR THE ACT, BUT FOR ME, YOU GOTTA PLAY IT STRAIGHT.
WITH A PIECE LIKE YOURS, THERE ARE GONNA BE LIABILITY ISSUES. YOU'RE GONNA HAVE TO SIGN STUFF THAT HOLDS THE PROMOTERS HARMLESS.
PLUS, YOU GOTTA CLAIM THIS MONEY ON YOUR TAX RETURN--
NOT MY PROBLEM. IT'S THIS WAY, OR I FIND SOMEONE ELSE TO GIVE TWENTY PERCENT TO.
WELL, AT LEAST WORK ON THAT GOOFY SUIT OF YOURS. IT LOOKS LIKE IT WAS SEWN BY A BLIND DRUNK.
HEY!

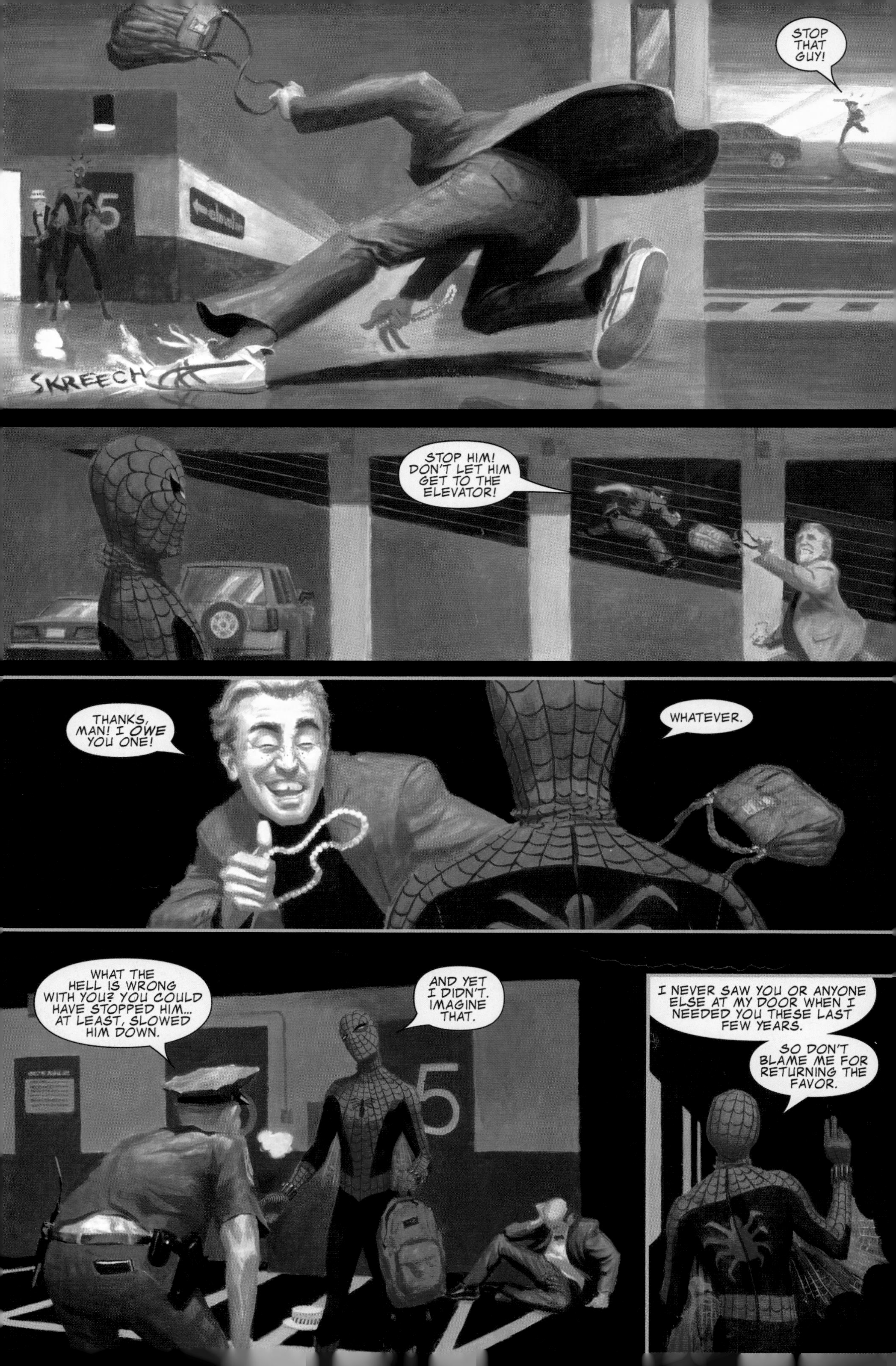
STOP THAT GUY!
SKREECH
STOP HIM! DON'T LET HIM GET TO THE ELEVATOR!
THANKS, MAN! I OWE YOU ONE!
WHATEVER.
WHAT THE HELL IS WRONG WITH YOU? YOU COULD HAVE STOPPED HIM... AT LEAST, SLOWED HIM DOWN.
AND YET I DIDN'T. IMAGINE THAT.
I NEVER SAW YOU OR ANYONE ELSE AT MY DOOR WHEN I NEEDED YOU THESE LAST FEW YEARS.
SO DON'T BLAME ME FOR RETURNING THE FAVOR.

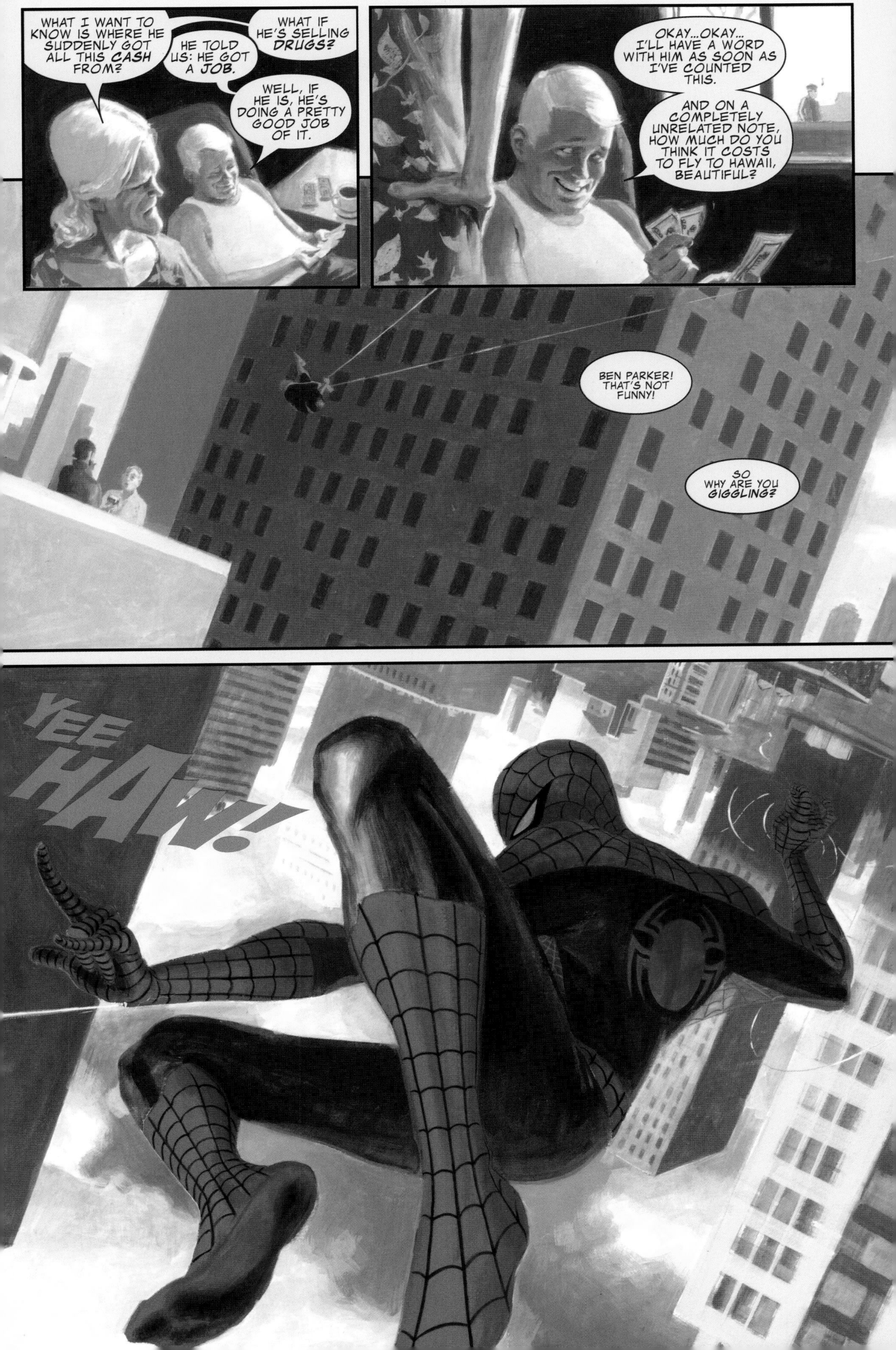
WHAT I WANT TO KNOW IS WHERE HE SUDDENLY GOT ALL THIS CASH FROM?
WHAT IF HE'S SELLING DRUGS?
HE TOLD US: HE GOT A JOB.
WELL, IF HE IS, HE'S DOING A PRETTY GOOD JOB OF IT.
OKAY...OKAY... I'LL HAVE A WORD WITH HIM AS SOON AS I'VE COUNTED THIS.
AND ON A COMPLETELY UNRELATED NOTE, HOW MUCH DO YOU THINK IT COSTS TO FLY TO HAWAII, BEAUTIFUL?
BEN PARKER! THAT'S NOT FUNNY!
SO WHY ARE YOU GIGGLING?
YEE HAW!

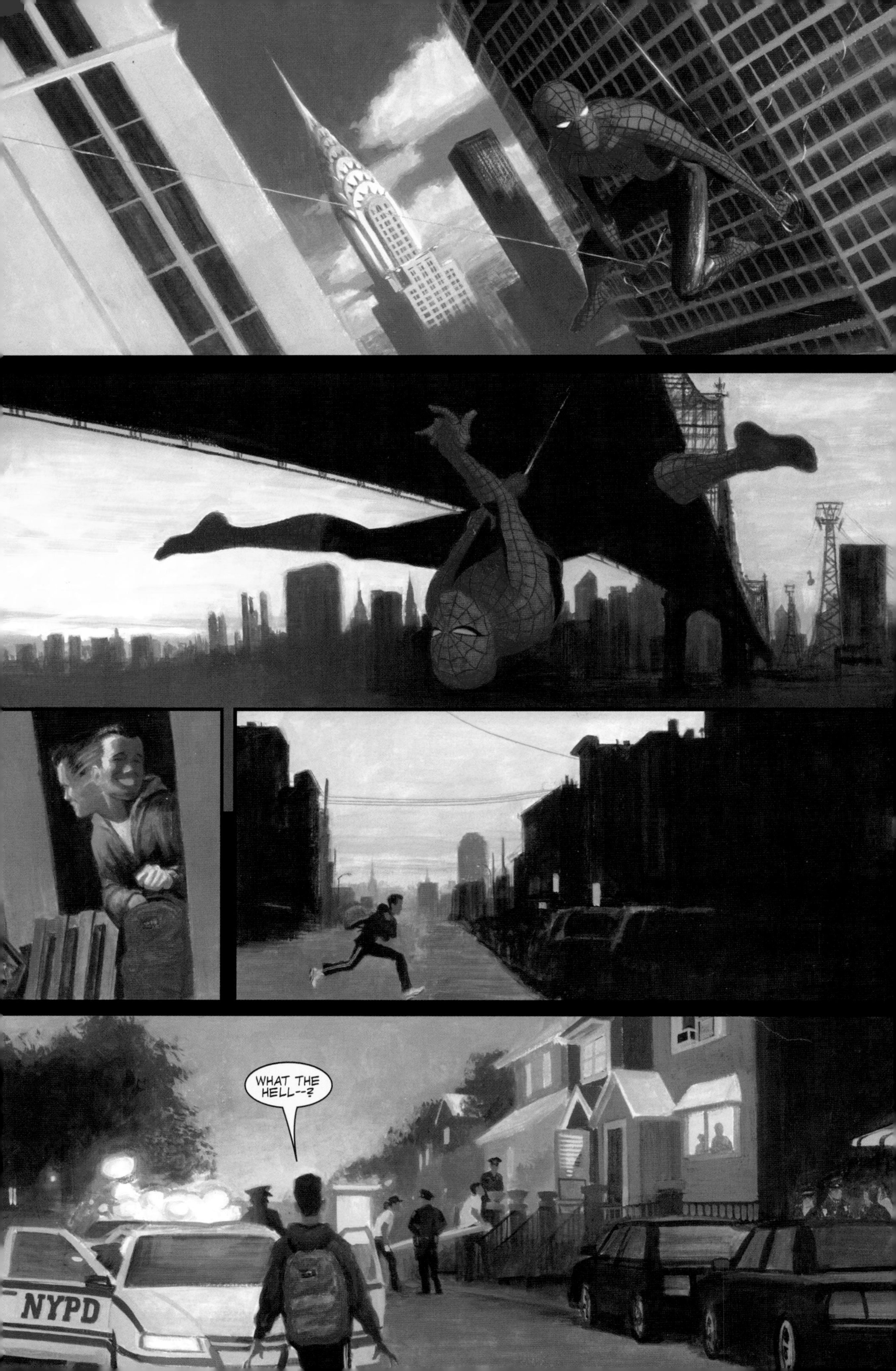
WHAT THE HELL--?
NYPD

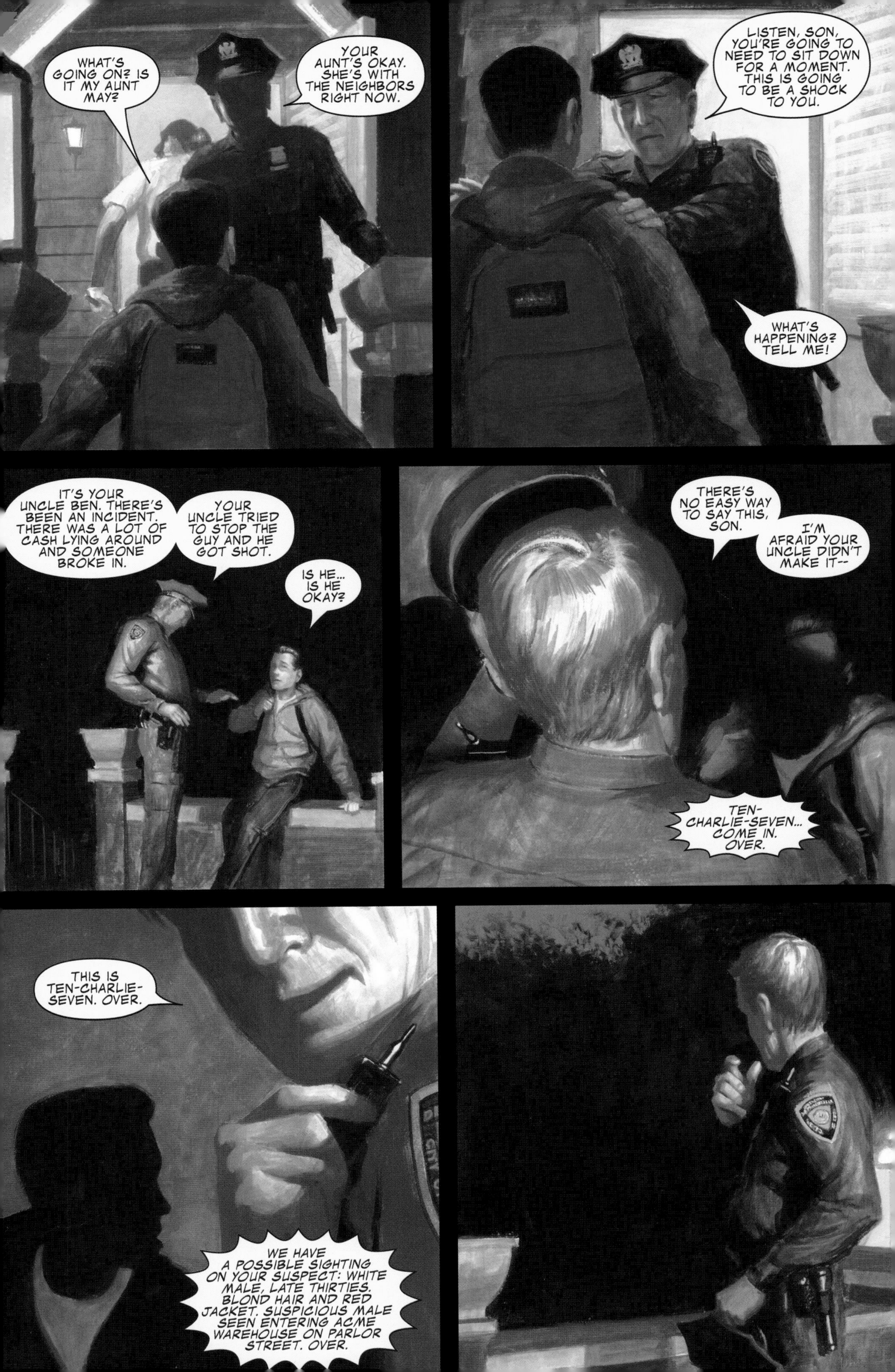
WHAT'S GOING ON? IS IT MY AUNT MAY?
YOUR AUNT'S OKAY. SHE'S WITH THE NEIGHBORS RIGHT NOW.
LISTEN, SON, YOU'RE GOING TO NEED TO SIT DOWN FOR A MOMENT. THIS IS GOING TO BE A SHOCK TO YOU.
WHAT'S HAPPENING? TELL ME!
IT'S YOUR UNCLE BEN. THERE'S BEEN AN INCIDENT. THERE WAS A LOT OF CASH LYING AROUND AND SOMEONE BROKE IN.
YOUR UNCLE TRIED TO STOP THE GUY AND HE GOT SHOT.
IS HE... IS HE OKAY?
THERE'S NO EASY WAY TO SAY THIS, SON.
I'M AFRAID YOUR UNCLE DIDN'T MAKE IT--
TEN-CHARLIE-SEVEN... COME IN. OVER.
THIS IS TEN-CHARLIE-SEVEN. OVER.
WE HAVE A POSSIBLE SIGHTING ON YOUR SUSPECT: WHITE MALE, LATE THIRTIES. BLOND HAIR AND RED JACKET. SUSPICIOUS MALE SEEN ENTERING ACME WAREHOUSE ON PARLOR STREET. OVER.

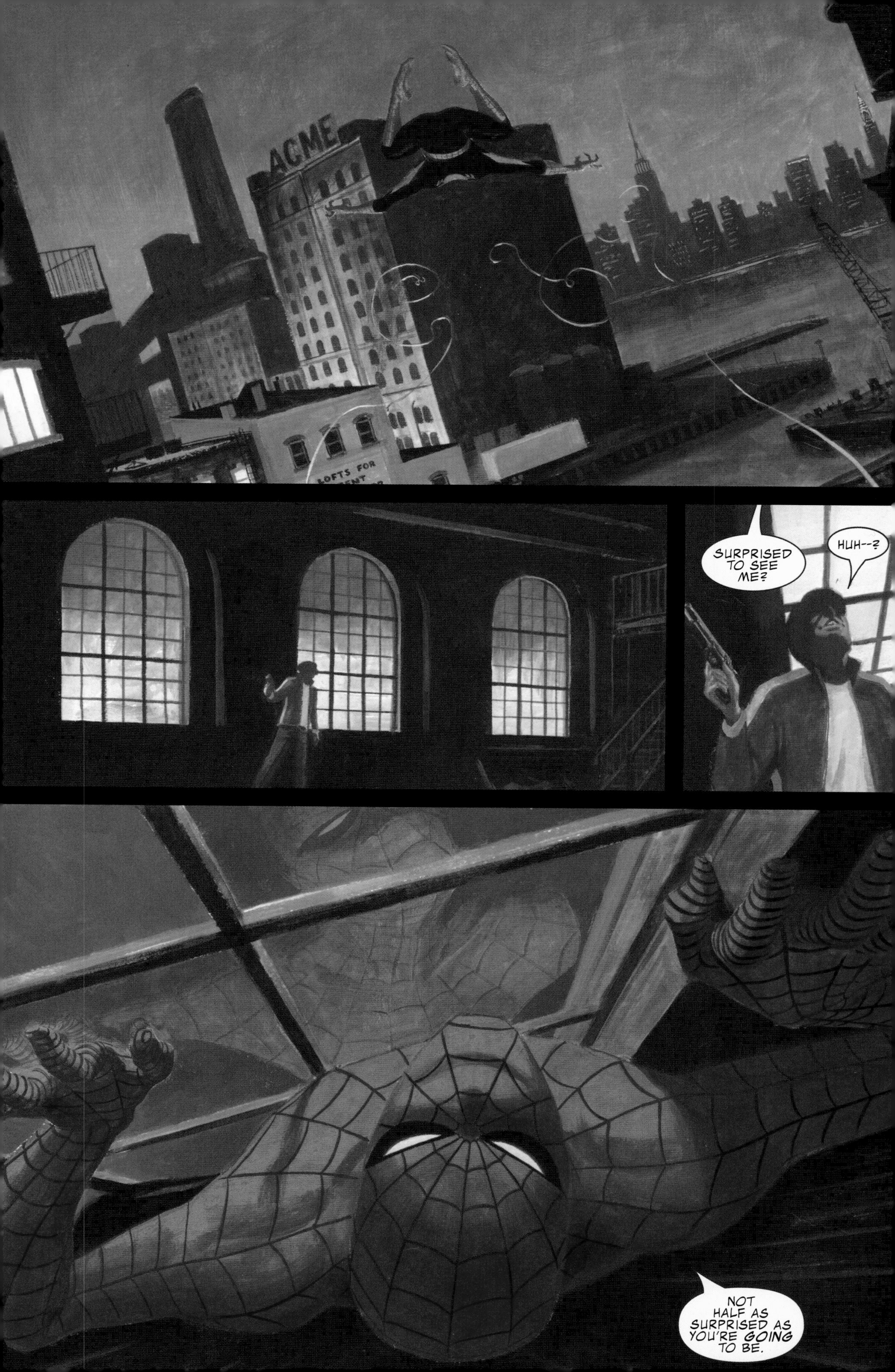
ACME
LOFTS FOR RENT
SURPRISED TO SEE ME?
HUH--?
NOT HALF AS SURPRISED AS YOU'RE GOING TO BE.

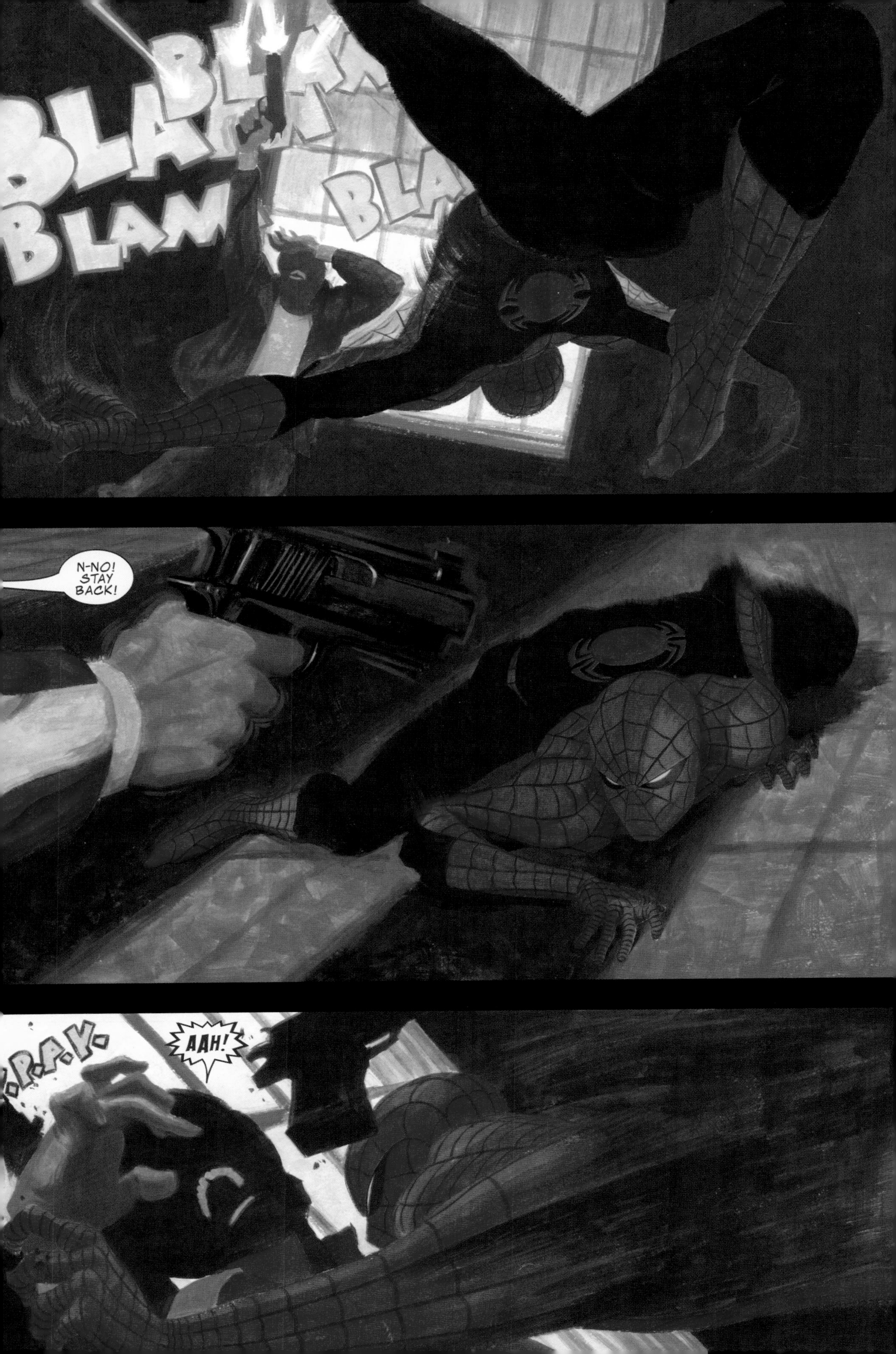
BLAM
BLAM
BLAM
BLAM
N-NO! STAY BACK!
AAH!

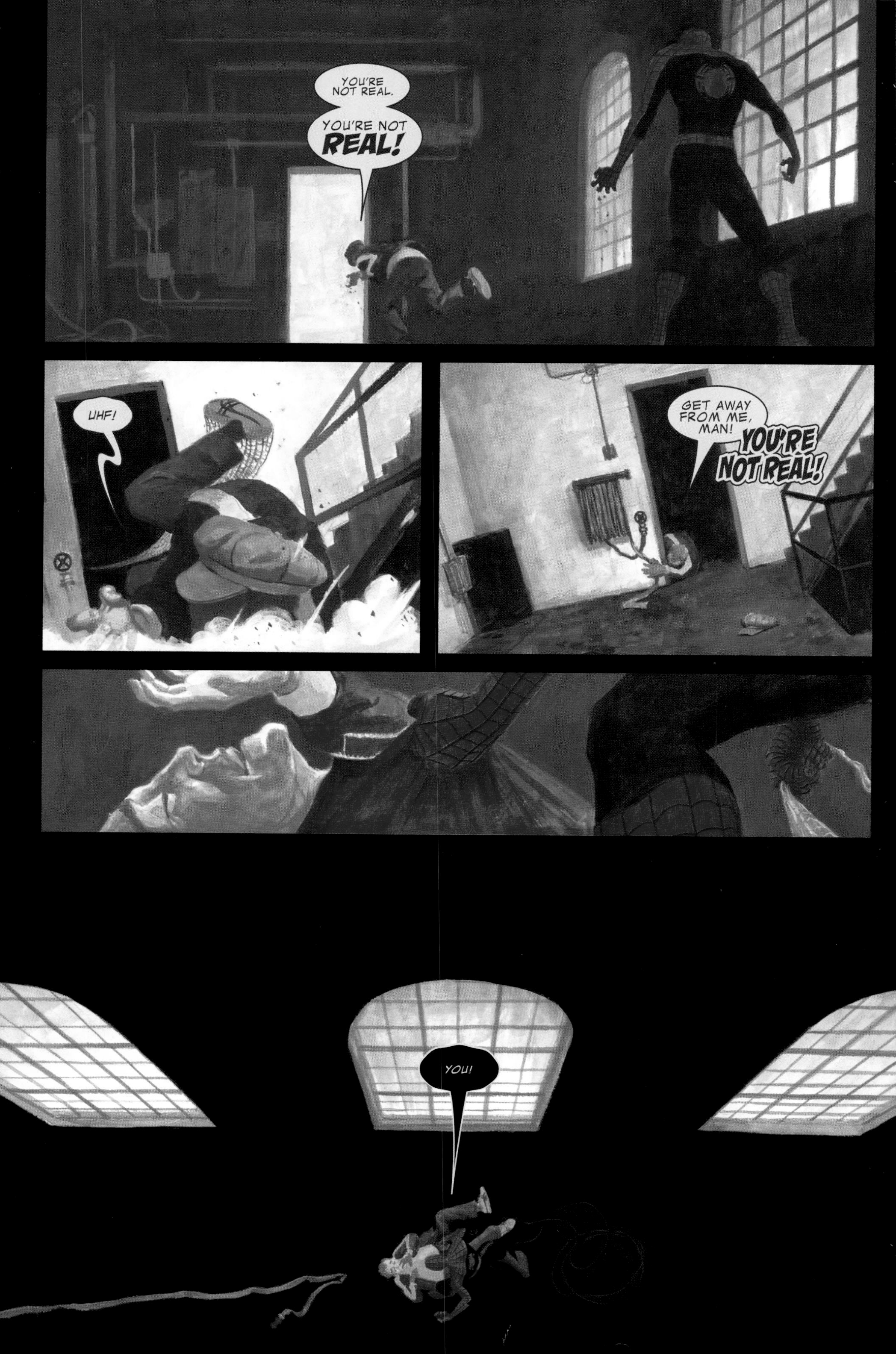
YOU'RE NOT REAL.
YOU'RE NOT REAL!
UHF!
GET AWAY FROM ME, MAN!
YOU'RE NOT REAL!
YOU!

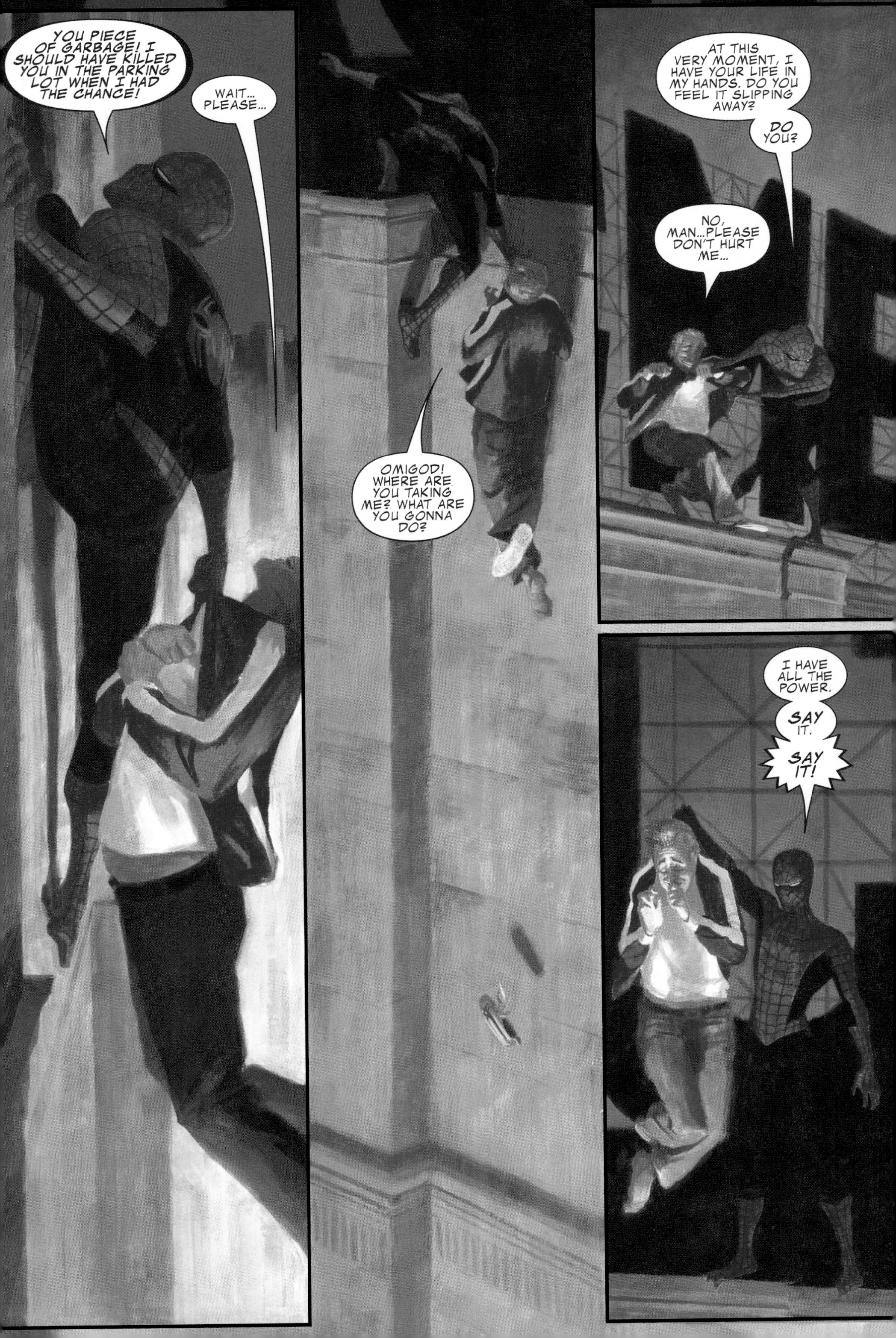
YOU PIECE OF GARBAGE! I SHOULD HAVE KILLED YOU IN THE PARKING LOT WHEN I HAD THE CHANCE!
WAIT... PLEASE...
OMIGOD! WHERE ARE YOU TAKING ME? WHAT ARE YOU GONNA DO?
AT THIS VERY MOMENT, I HAVE YOUR LIFE IN MY HANDS. DO YOU FEEL IT SLIPPING AWAY?
DO YOU?
NO, MAN...PLEASE DON'T HURT ME...
I HAVE ALL THE POWER.
SAY IT.
SAY IT!

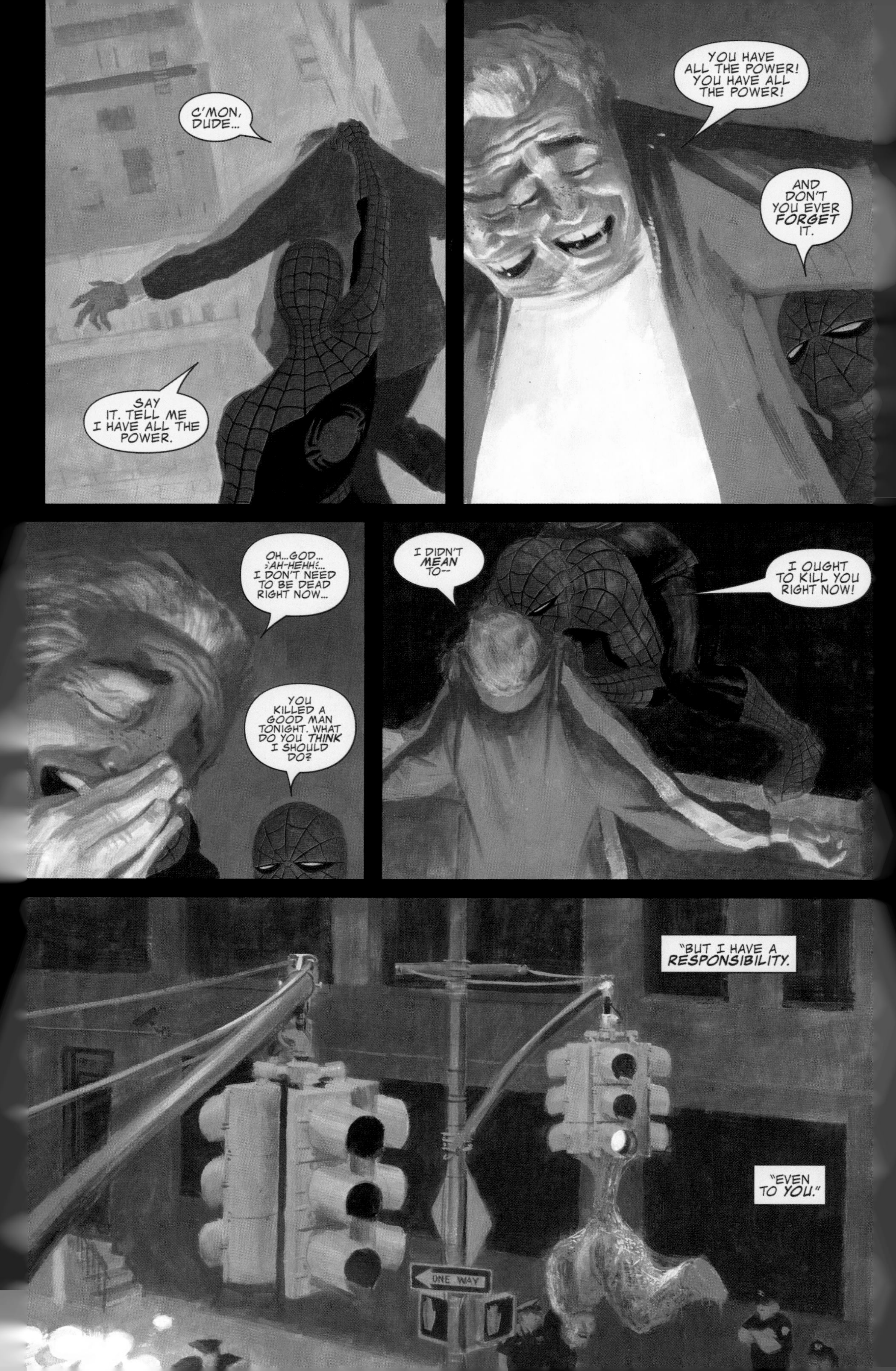
C'MON, DUDE...
SAY IT. TELL ME I HAVE ALL THE POWER.
YOU HAVE ALL THE POWER! YOU HAVE ALL THE POWER!
AND DON'T YOU EVER FORGET IT.
OH...GOD... AH-HEHH... I DON'T NEED TO BE DEAD RIGHT NOW...
YOU KILLED A GOOD MAN TONIGHT. WHAT DO YOU THINK I SHOULD DO?
I DIDN'T MEAN TO--
I OUGHT TO KILL YOU RIGHT NOW!
"BUT I HAVE A RESPONSIBILITY.
"EVEN TO YOU."
ONE WAY

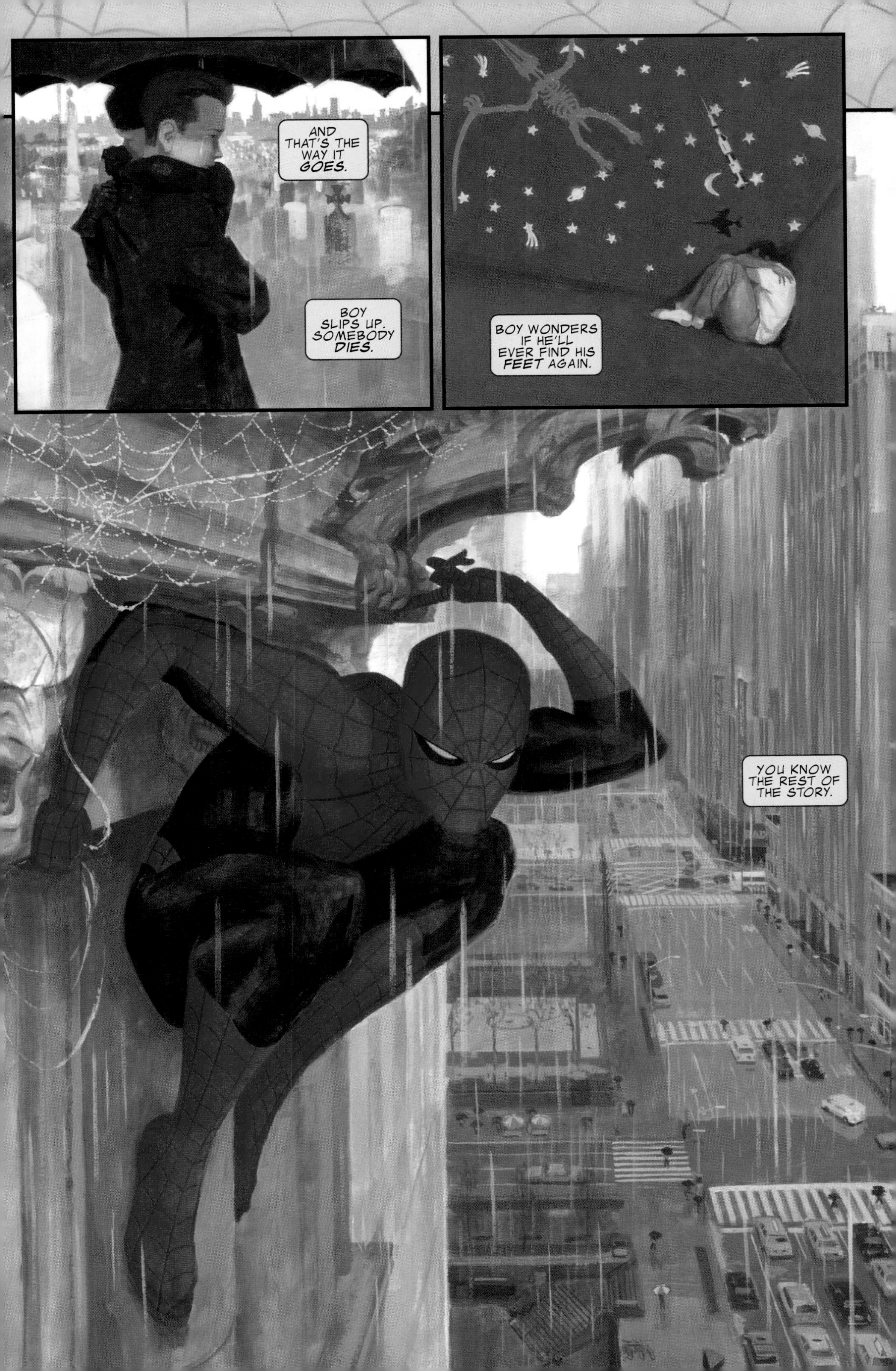
AND THAT'S THE WAY IT GOES.
BOY SLIPS UP. SOMEBODY DIES.
BOY WONDERS IF HE'LL EVER FIND HIS FEET AGAIN.
YOU KNOW THE REST OF THE STORY.

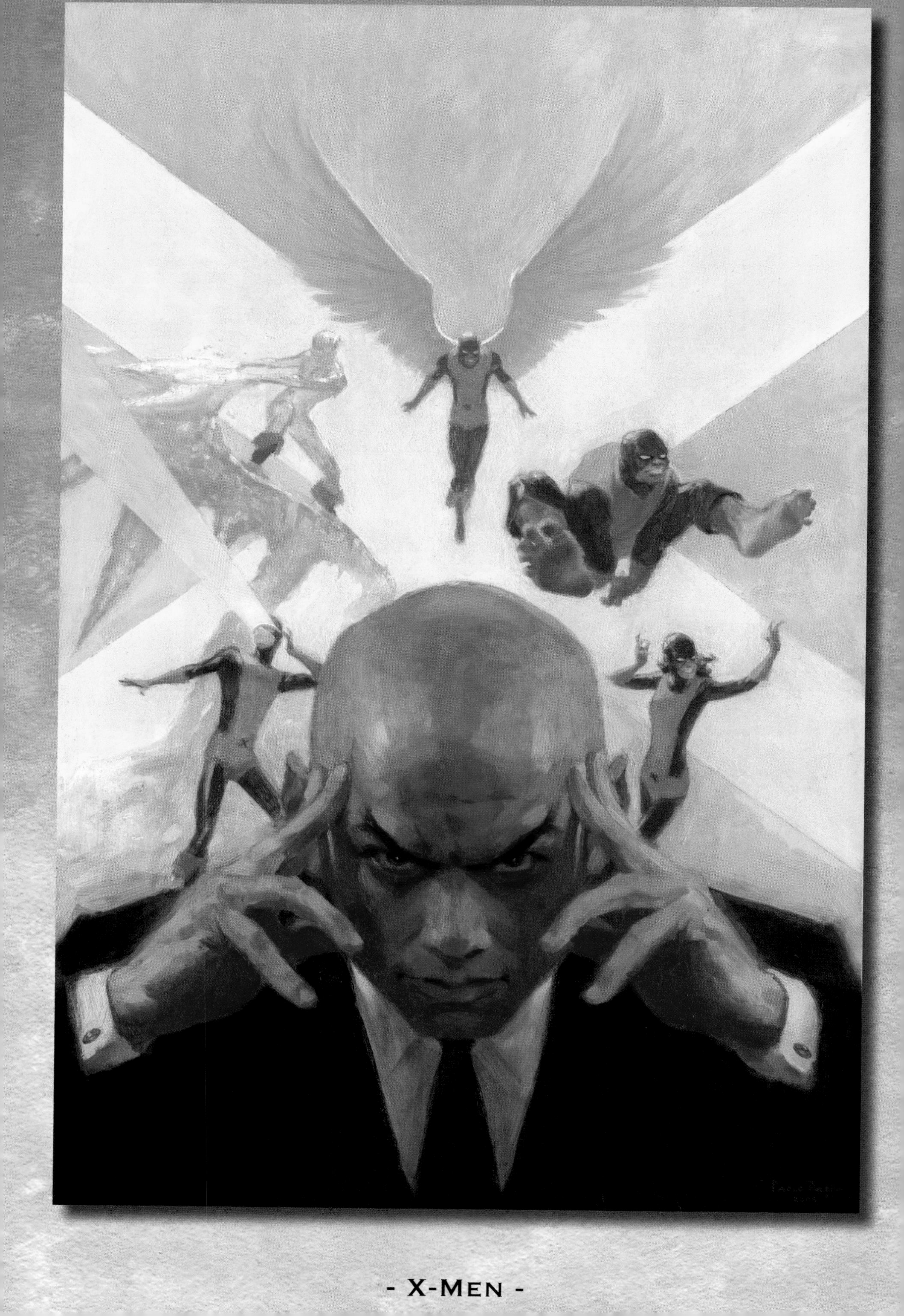

- X-Men -

WE CAN'T STOP HIM! CALL FOR RE-INFORCEMENTS!
KLACK!

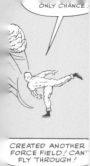

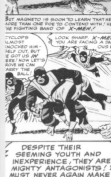

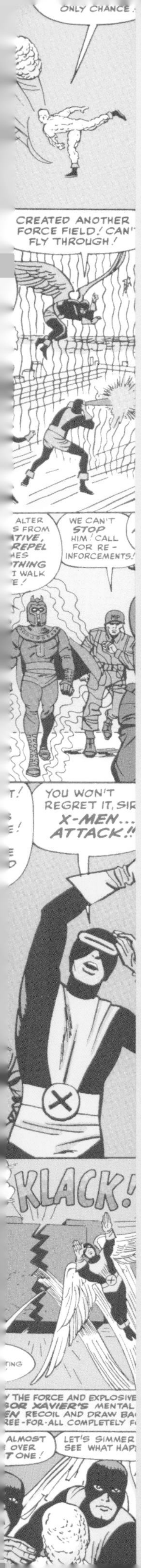

MYTHOS

Cyclops! Marvel Girl! Angel! Beast! Iceman! Children of the atom, students of Charles Xavier, MUTANTS—feared and hated by the world they have sworn to protect. These are the STRANGEST heroes of all—these are...

the X-MEN

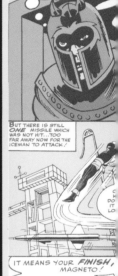

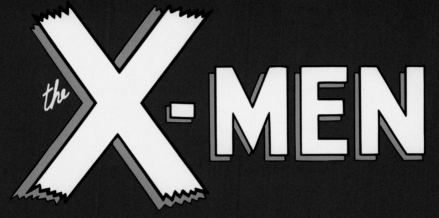

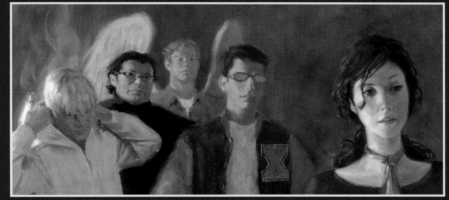

ICEMAN	BEAST	ANGEL	CYCLOPS	MARVEL GIRL
Bobby Drake	Hank McCoy	Warren Worthington III	Scott Summers	Jean Grey

Based on *X-MEN #1, September 1963* by STAN LEE and JACK KIRBY

DESPITE THEIR SEEMING YOUTH AND INEXPERIENCE, THEY ARE MIGHTY ANTAGONISTS! I MUST NEVER AGAIN MAKE THE MISTAKE OF UNDER-ESTIMATING THEM! BUT I SHALL STILL PROVE TO BE THEIR MASTER!
BUT THERE IS STILL ONE MISSILE WHICH WAS NOT HIT...TOO FAR AWAY NOW FOR THE ICEMAN TO ATTACK!
IT MEANS YOUR FINISH, MAGNETO!
CYCLOPS CREATED A TUNNEL FOR US UNDER THE BLAST WITH HIS ENERGY BEAM... SAVING US FROM THE IMPACT! AND NOW..
YOU'RE THE OLDEST, BEAST, SO YOU'RE FIRST!

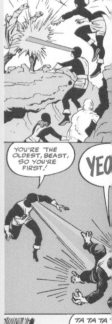

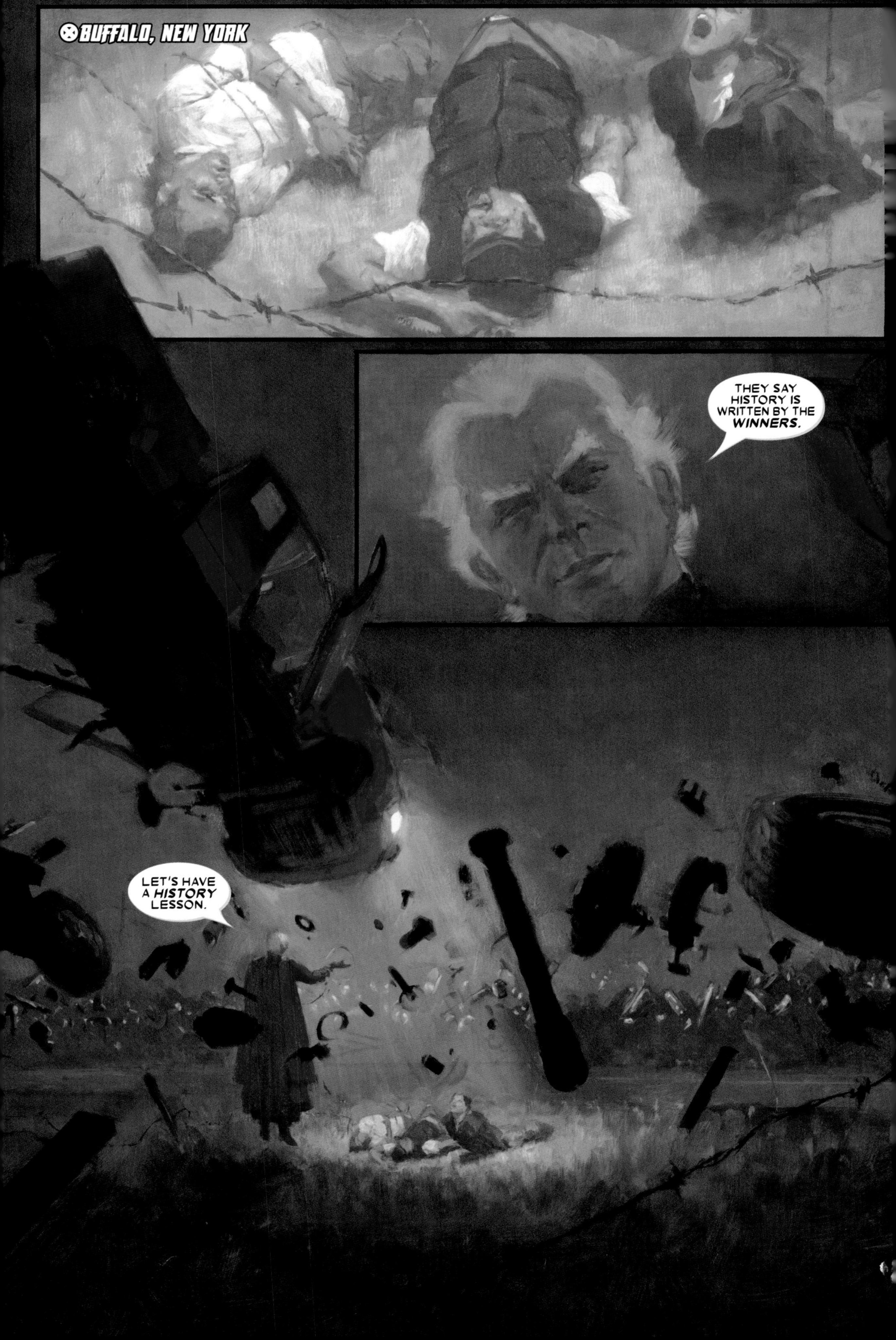
BUFFALO, NEW YORK
THEY SAY HISTORY IS WRITTEN BY THE WINNERS.
LET'S HAVE A HISTORY LESSON.

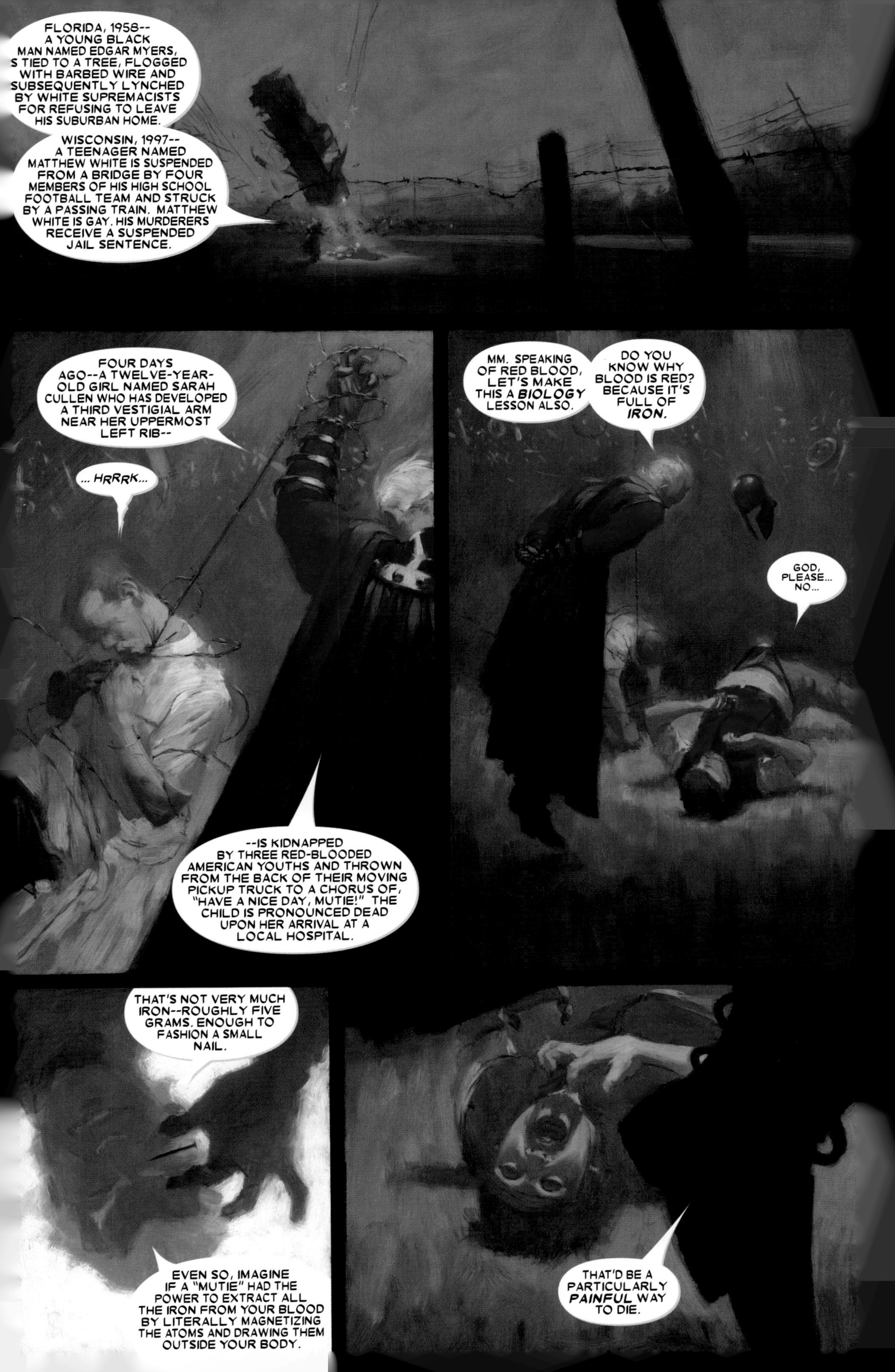
FLORIDA, 1958-- A YOUNG BLACK MAN NAMED EDGAR MYERS, S TIED TO A TREE, FLOGGED WITH BARBED WIRE AND SUBSEQUENTLY LYNCHED BY WHITE SUPREMACISTS FOR REFUSING TO LEAVE HIS SUBURBAN HOME.
WISCONSIN, 1997-- A TEENAGER NAMED MATTHEW WHITE IS SUSPENDED FROM A BRIDGE BY FOUR MEMBERS OF HIS HIGH SCHOOL FOOTBALL TEAM AND STRUCK BY A PASSING TRAIN. MATTHEW WHITE IS GAY. HIS MURDERERS RECEIVE A SUSPENDED JAIL SENTENCE.
FOUR DAYS AGO--A TWELVE-YEAR-OLD GIRL NAMED SARAH CULLEN WHO HAS DEVELOPED A THIRD VESTIGIAL ARM NEAR HER UPPERMOST LEFT RIB--
...HRRRK...
--IS KIDNAPPED BY THREE RED-BLOODED AMERICAN YOUTHS AND THROWN FROM THE BACK OF THEIR MOVING PICKUP TRUCK TO A CHORUS OF, "HAVE A NICE DAY, MUTIE!" THE CHILD IS PRONOUNCED DEAD UPON HER ARRIVAL AT A LOCAL HOSPITAL.
MM. SPEAKING OF RED BLOOD, LET'S MAKE THIS A *BIOLOGY* LESSON ALSO.
DO YOU KNOW WHY BLOOD IS RED? BECAUSE IT'S FULL OF *IRON.*
GOD, PLEASE... NO...
THAT'S NOT VERY MUCH IRON--ROUGHLY FIVE GRAMS. ENOUGH TO FASHION A SMALL NAIL.
EVEN SO, IMAGINE IF A "MUTIE" HAD THE POWER TO EXTRACT ALL THE IRON FROM YOUR BLOOD BY LITERALLY MAGNETIZING THE ATOMS AND DRAWING THEM OUTSIDE YOUR BODY.
THAT'D BE A PARTICULARLY *PAINFUL* WAY TO DIE.

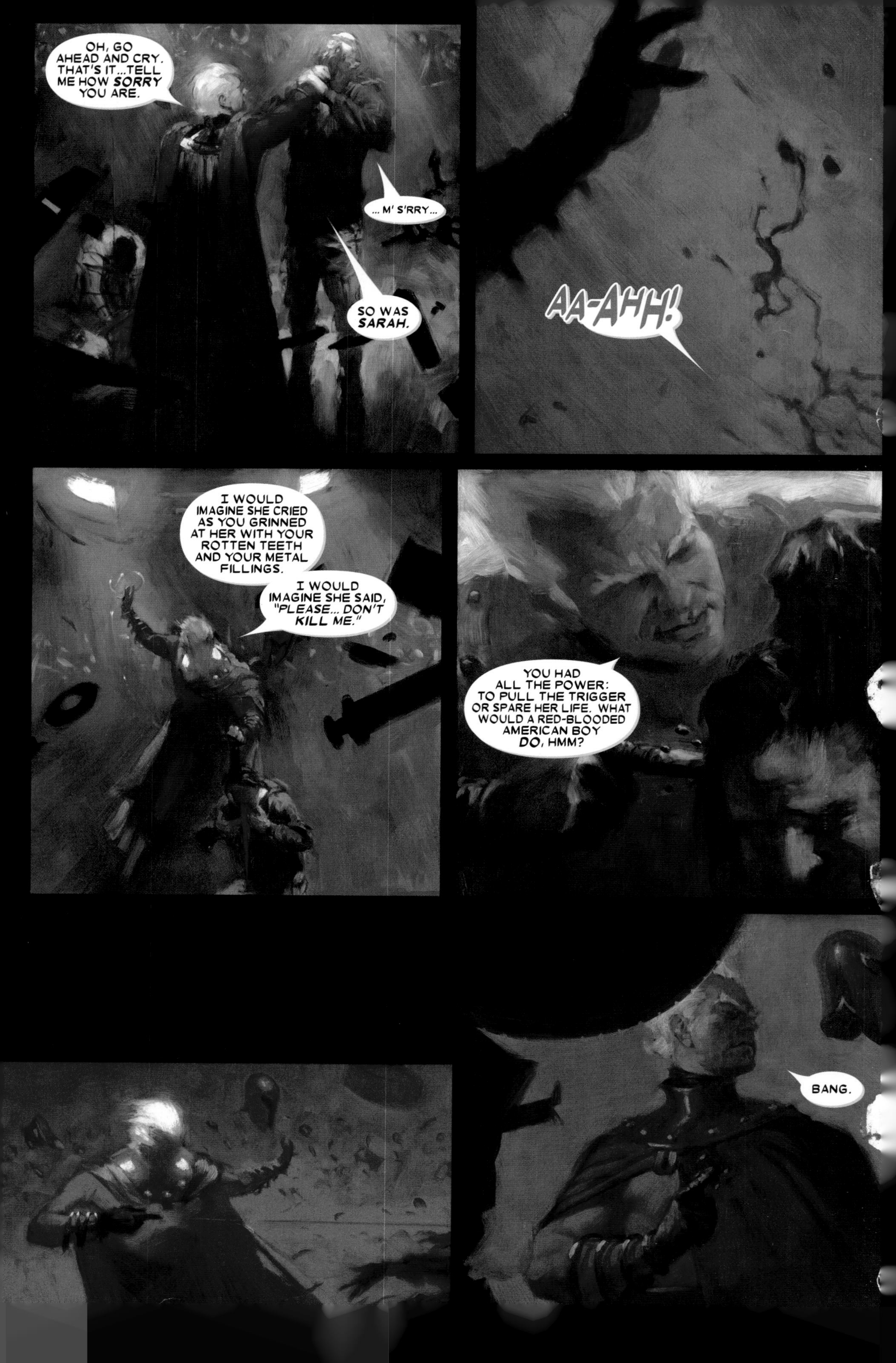
OH, GO AHEAD AND CRY. THAT'S IT...TELL ME HOW SORRY YOU ARE.
... M' S'RRY...
SO WAS SARAH.
AA-AHH!
I WOULD IMAGINE SHE CRIED AS YOU GRINNED AT HER WITH YOUR ROTTEN TEETH AND YOUR METAL FILLINGS.
I WOULD IMAGINE SHE SAID, "PLEASE... DON'T KILL ME."
YOU HAD ALL THE POWER: TO PULL THE TRIGGER OR SPARE HER LIFE. WHAT WOULD A RED-BLOODED AMERICAN BOY DO, HMM?
BANG.

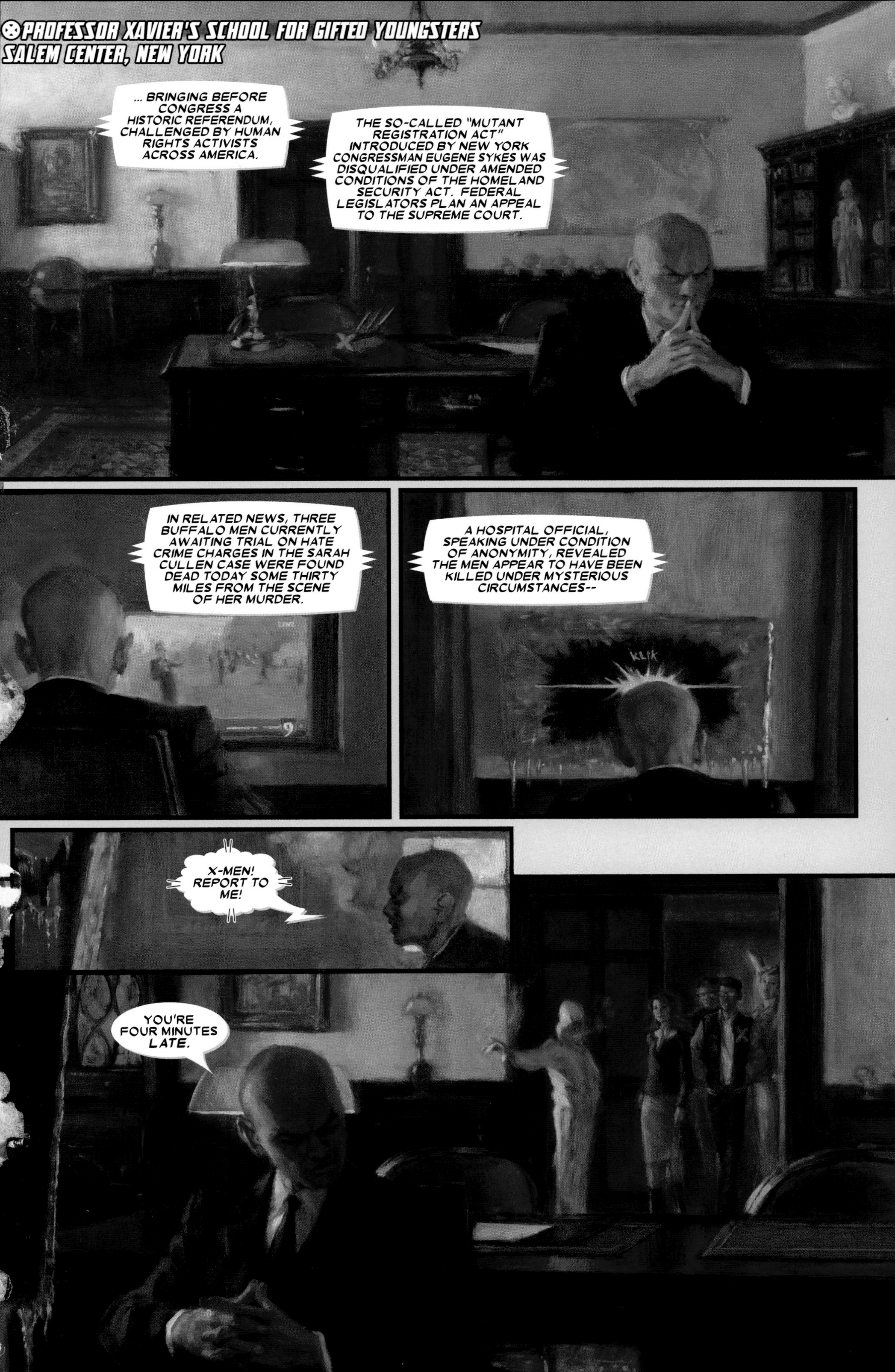
PROFESSOR XAVIER'S SCHOOL FOR GIFTED YOUNGSTERS
SALEM CENTER, NEW YORK
... BRINGING BEFORE CONGRESS A HISTORIC REFERENDUM, CHALLENGED BY HUMAN RIGHTS ACTIVISTS ACROSS AMERICA.
THE SO-CALLED "MUTANT REGISTRATION ACT" INTRODUCED BY NEW YORK CONGRESSMAN EUGENE SYKES WAS DISQUALIFIED UNDER AMENDED CONDITIONS OF THE HOMELAND SECURITY ACT. FEDERAL LEGISLATORS PLAN AN APPEAL TO THE SUPREME COURT.
IN RELATED NEWS, THREE BUFFALO MEN CURRENTLY AWAITING TRIAL ON HATE CRIME CHARGES IN THE SARAH CULLEN CASE WERE FOUND DEAD TODAY SOME THIRTY MILES FROM THE SCENE OF HER MURDER.
A HOSPITAL OFFICIAL, SPEAKING UNDER CONDITION OF ANONYMITY, REVEALED THE MEN APPEAR TO HAVE BEEN KILLED UNDER MYSTERIOUS CIRCUMSTANCES--
KLIK
X-MEN! REPORT TO ME!
YOU'RE FOUR MINUTES LATE.

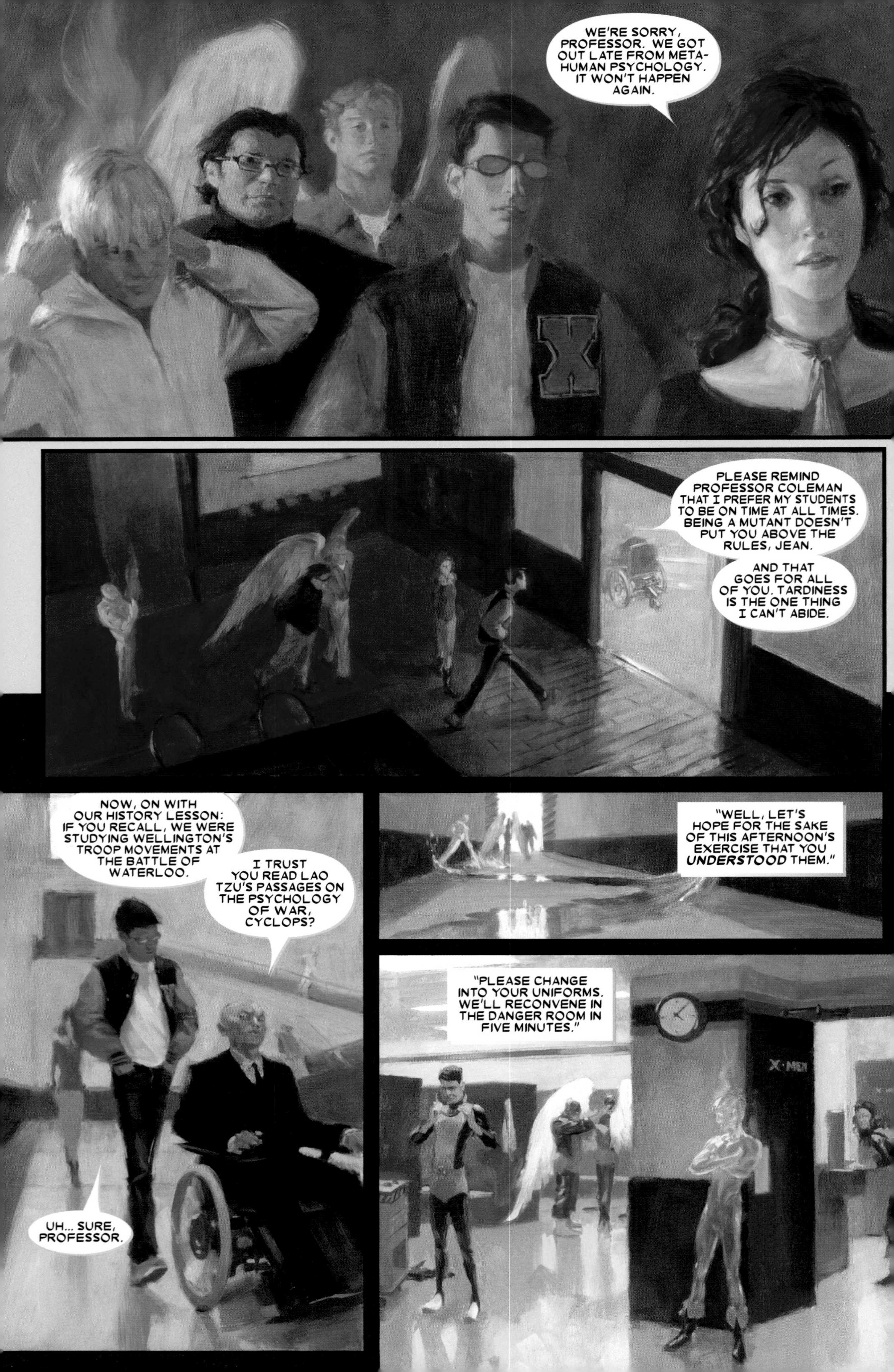

WE'RE SORRY, PROFESSOR. WE GOT OUT LATE FROM META-HUMAN PSYCHOLOGY. IT WON'T HAPPEN AGAIN.
PLEASE REMIND PROFESSOR COLEMAN THAT I PREFER MY STUDENTS TO BE ON TIME AT ALL TIMES. BEING A MUTANT DOESN'T PUT YOU ABOVE THE RULES, JEAN.
AND THAT GOES FOR ALL OF YOU. TARDINESS IS THE ONE THING I CAN'T ABIDE.
NOW, ON WITH OUR HISTORY LESSON: IF YOU RECALL, WE WERE STUDYING WELLINGTON'S TROOP MOVEMENTS AT THE BATTLE OF WATERLOO.
I TRUST YOU READ LAO TZU'S PASSAGES ON THE PSYCHOLOGY OF WAR, CYCLOPS?
UH... SURE, PROFESSOR.
"WELL, LET'S HOPE FOR THE SAKE OF THIS AFTERNOON'S EXERCISE THAT YOU *UNDERSTOOD* THEM."
"PLEASE CHANGE INTO YOUR UNIFORMS. WE'LL RECONVENE IN THE DANGER ROOM IN FIVE MINUTES."
X-MEN

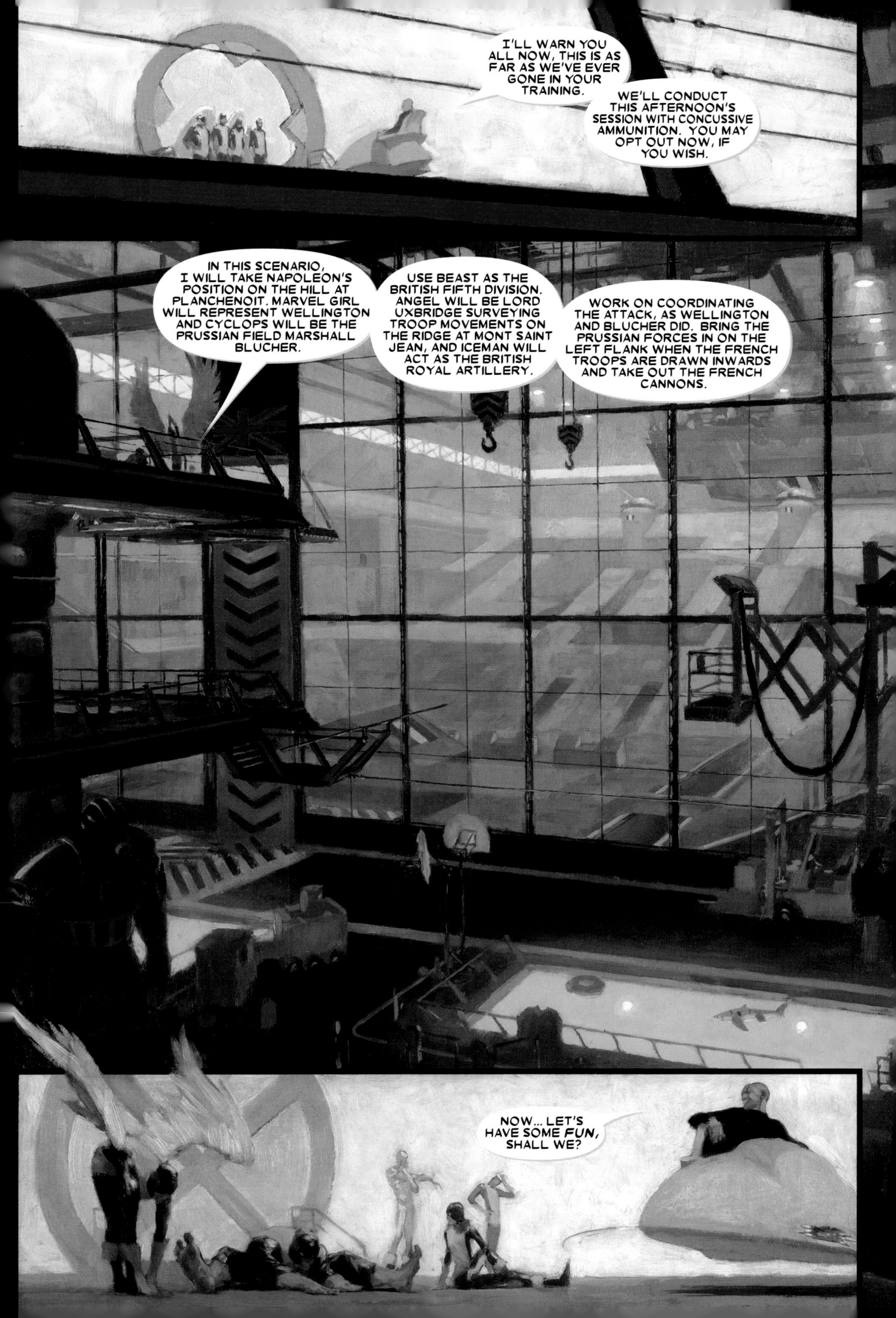
I'LL WARN YOU ALL NOW, THIS IS AS FAR AS WE'VE EVER GONE IN YOUR TRAINING.
WE'LL CONDUCT THIS AFTERNOON'S SESSION WITH CONCUSSIVE AMMUNITION. YOU MAY OPT OUT NOW, IF YOU WISH.
IN THIS SCENARIO, I WILL TAKE NAPOLEON'S POSITION ON THE HILL AT PLANCHENOIT. MARVEL GIRL WILL REPRESENT WELLINGTON AND CYCLOPS WILL BE THE PRUSSIAN FIELD MARSHALL BLUCHER.
USE BEAST AS THE BRITISH FIFTH DIVISION. ANGEL WILL BE LORD UXBRIDGE SURVEYING TROOP MOVEMENTS ON THE RIDGE AT MONT SAINT JEAN, AND ICEMAN WILL ACT AS THE BRITISH ROYAL ARTILLERY.
WORK ON COORDINATING THE ATTACK, AS WELLINGTON AND BLUCHER DID. BRING THE PRUSSIAN FORCES IN ON THE LEFT FLANK WHEN THE FRENCH TROOPS ARE DRAWN INWARDS AND TAKE OUT THE FRENCH CANNONS.
NOW... LET'S HAVE SOME *FUN*, SHALL WE?

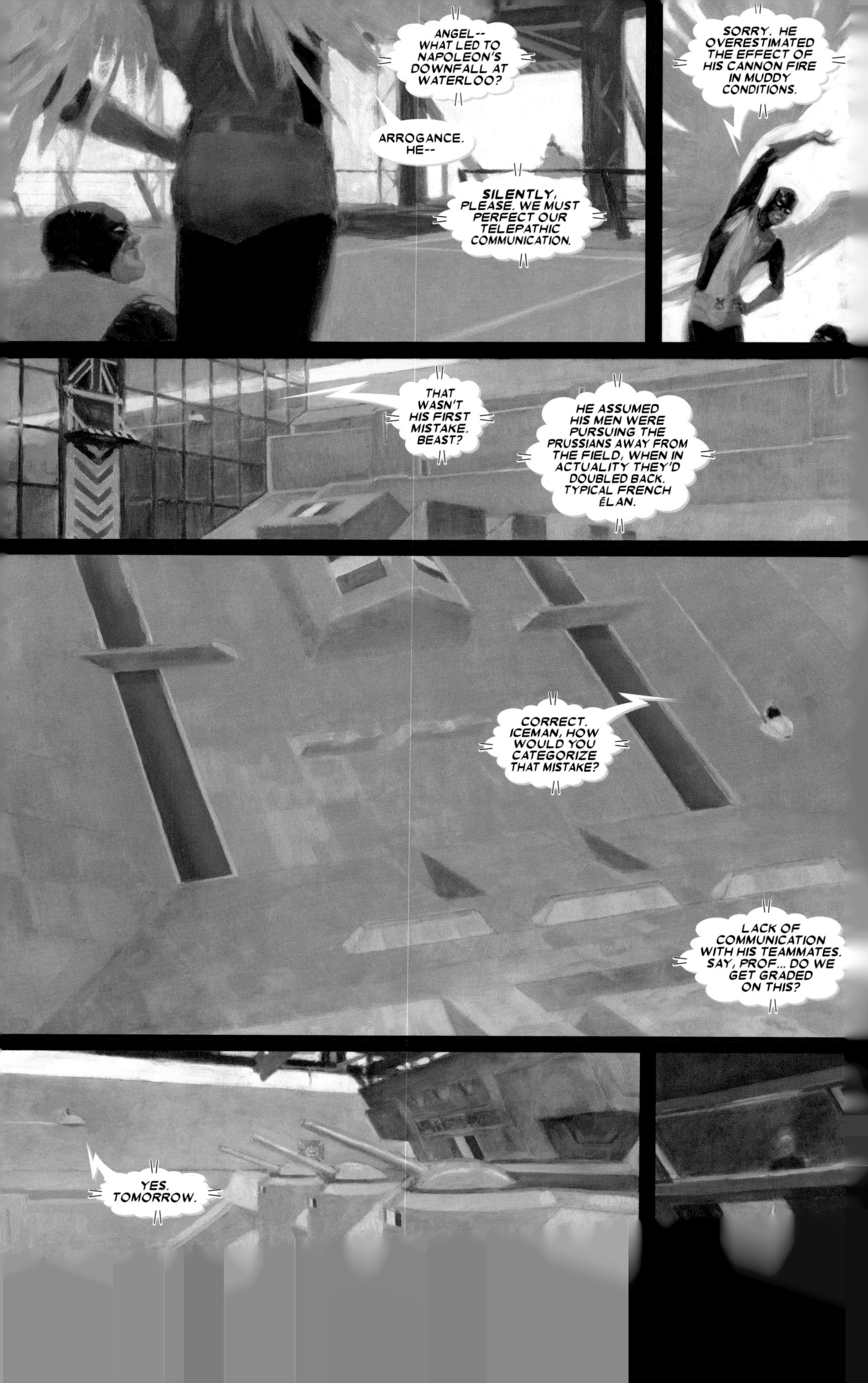
ANGEL-- WHAT LED TO NAPOLEON'S DOWNFALL AT WATERLOO?
ARROGANCE. HE--
SILENTLY, PLEASE. WE MUST PERFECT OUR TELEPATHIC COMMUNICATION.
SORRY. HE OVERESTIMATED THE EFFECT OF HIS CANNON FIRE IN MUDDY CONDITIONS.
THAT WASN'T HIS FIRST MISTAKE. BEAST?
HE ASSUMED HIS MEN WERE PURSUING THE PRUSSIANS AWAY FROM THE FIELD, WHEN IN ACTUALITY THEY'D DOUBLED BACK. TYPICAL FRENCH ÉLAN.
CORRECT. ICEMAN, HOW WOULD YOU CATEGORIZE THAT MISTAKE?
LACK OF COMMUNICATION WITH HIS TEAMMATES. SAY, PROF... DO WE GET GRADED ON THIS?
YES. TOMORROW.

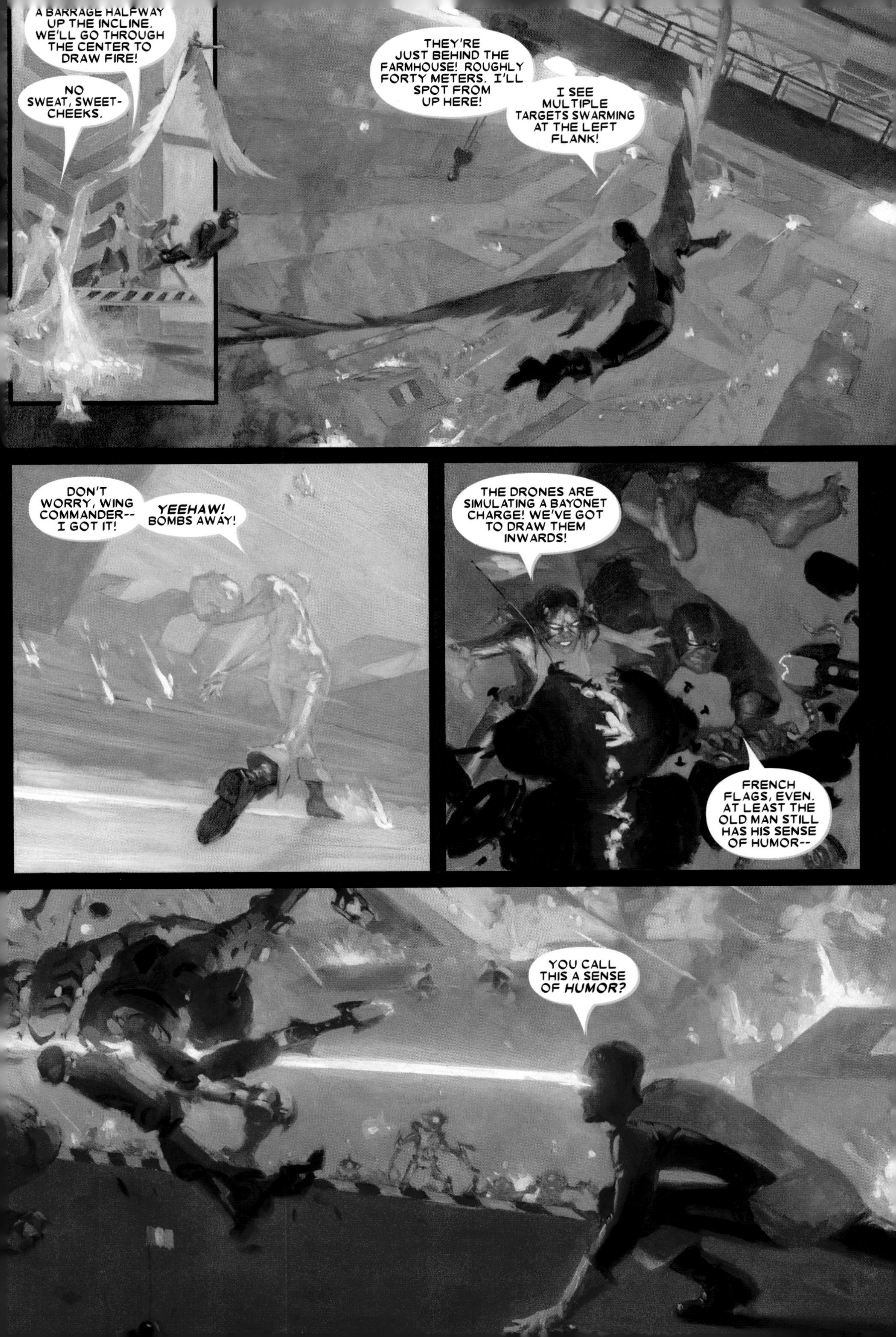
A BARRAGE HALFWAY UP THE INCLINE. WE'LL GO THROUGH THE CENTER TO DRAW FIRE!
NO SWEAT, SWEET-CHEEKS.
THEY'RE JUST BEHIND THE FARMHOUSE! ROUGHLY FORTY METERS. I'LL SPOT FROM UP HERE!
I SEE MULTIPLE TARGETS SWARMING AT THE LEFT FLANK!
DON'T WORRY, WING COMMANDER-- I GOT IT!
YEEHAW! BOMBS AWAY!
THE DRONES ARE SIMULATING A BAYONET CHARGE! WE'VE GOT TO DRAW THEM INWARDS!
FRENCH FLAGS, EVEN. AT LEAST THE OLD MAN STILL HAS HIS SENSE OF HUMOR--
YOU CALL THIS A SENSE OF *HUMOR?*

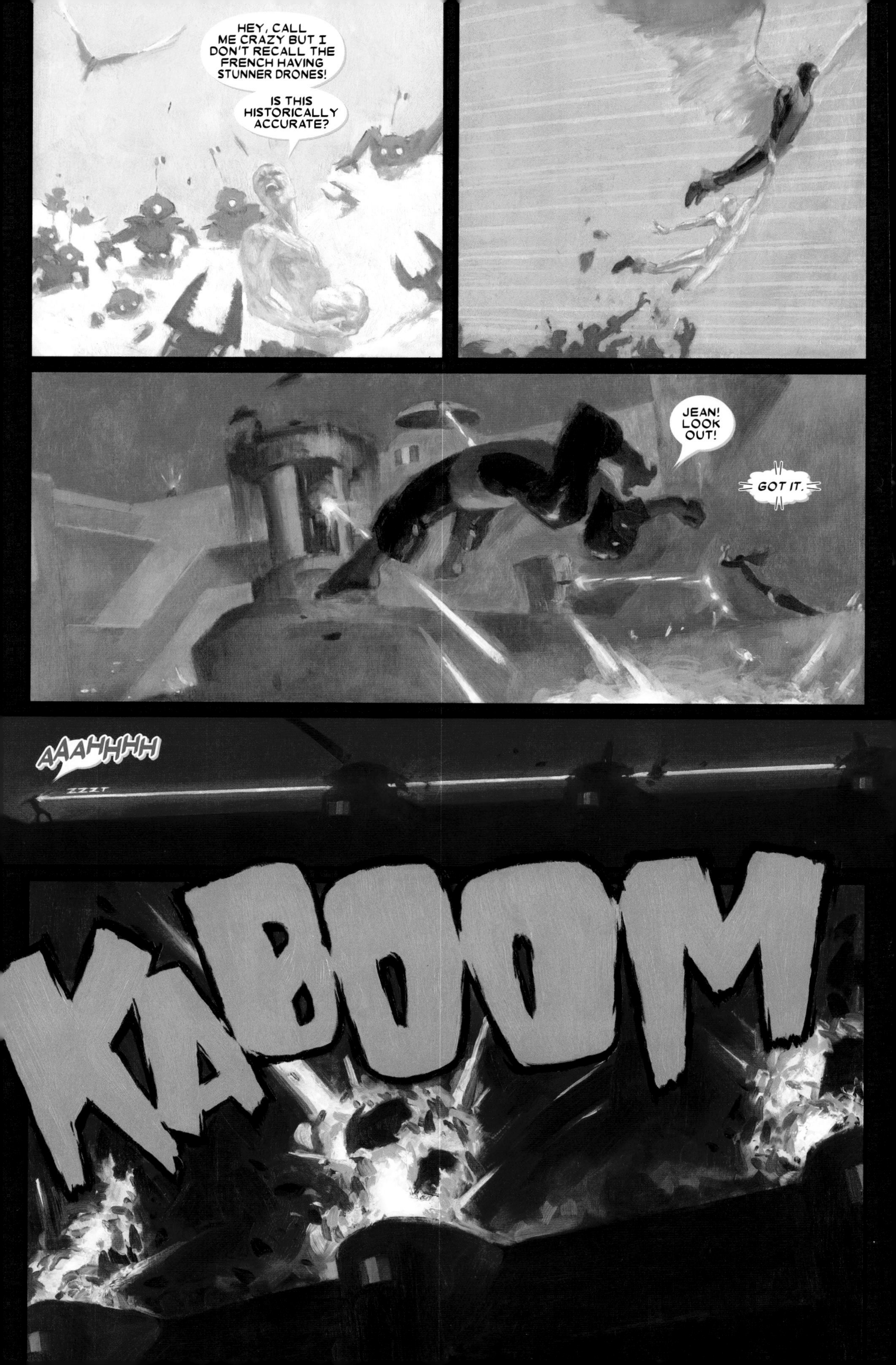
HEY, CALL ME CRAZY BUT I DON'T RECALL THE FRENCH HAVING STUNNER DRONES!
IS THIS HISTORICALLY ACCURATE?
JEAN! LOOK OUT!
GOT IT.
AAAHHHH
ZZZT
KABOOM!

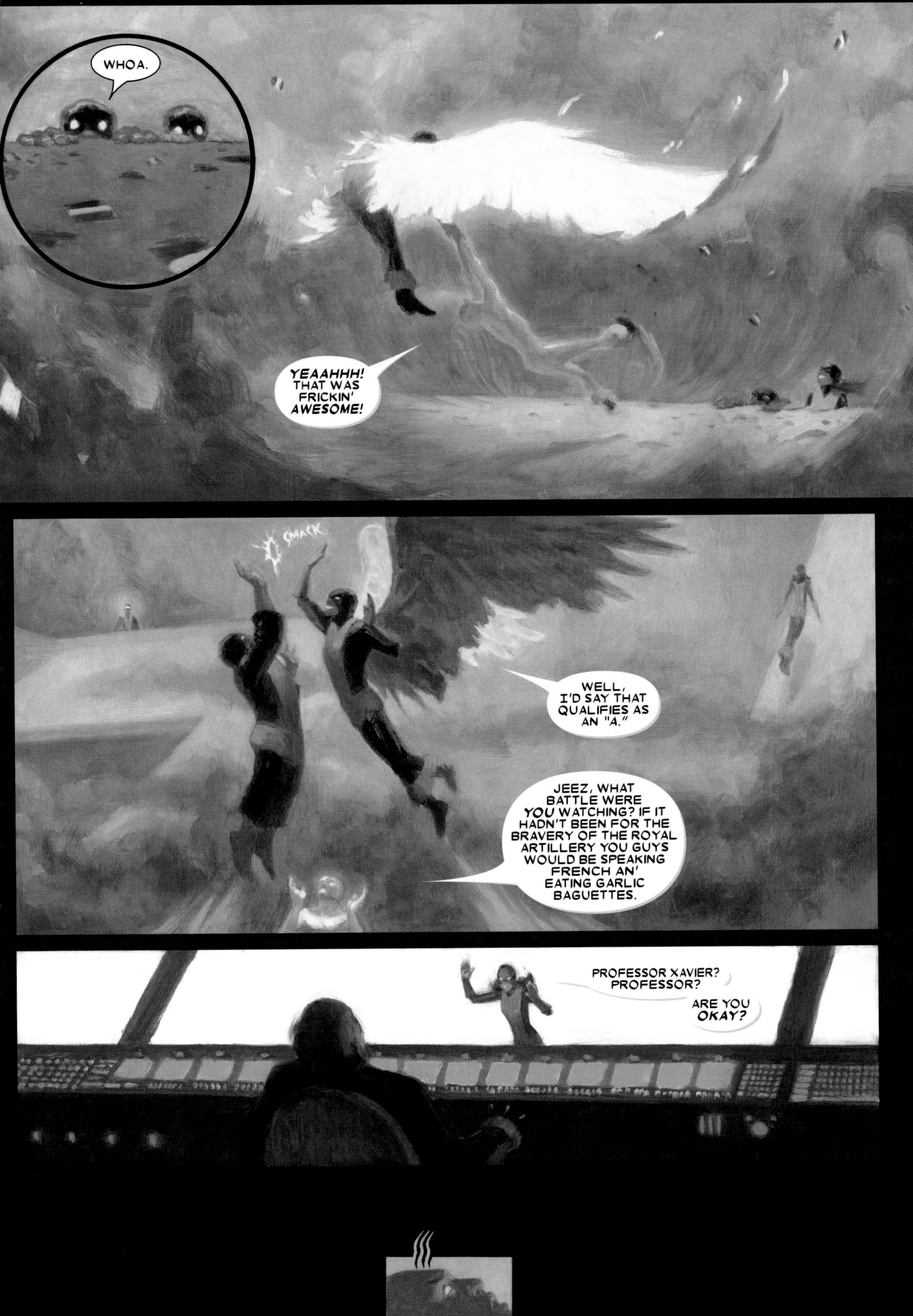
WHOA.
YEAAHHH! THAT WAS FRICKIN' AWESOME!
SMACK
WELL, I'D SAY THAT QUALIFIES AS AN "A."
JEEZ, WHAT BATTLE WERE YOU WATCHING? IF IT HADN'T BEEN FOR THE BRAVERY OF THE ROYAL ARTILLERY YOU GUYS WOULD BE SPEAKING FRENCH AN' EATING GARLIC BAGUETTES.
PROFESSOR XAVIER? PROFESSOR?
ARE YOU OKAY?

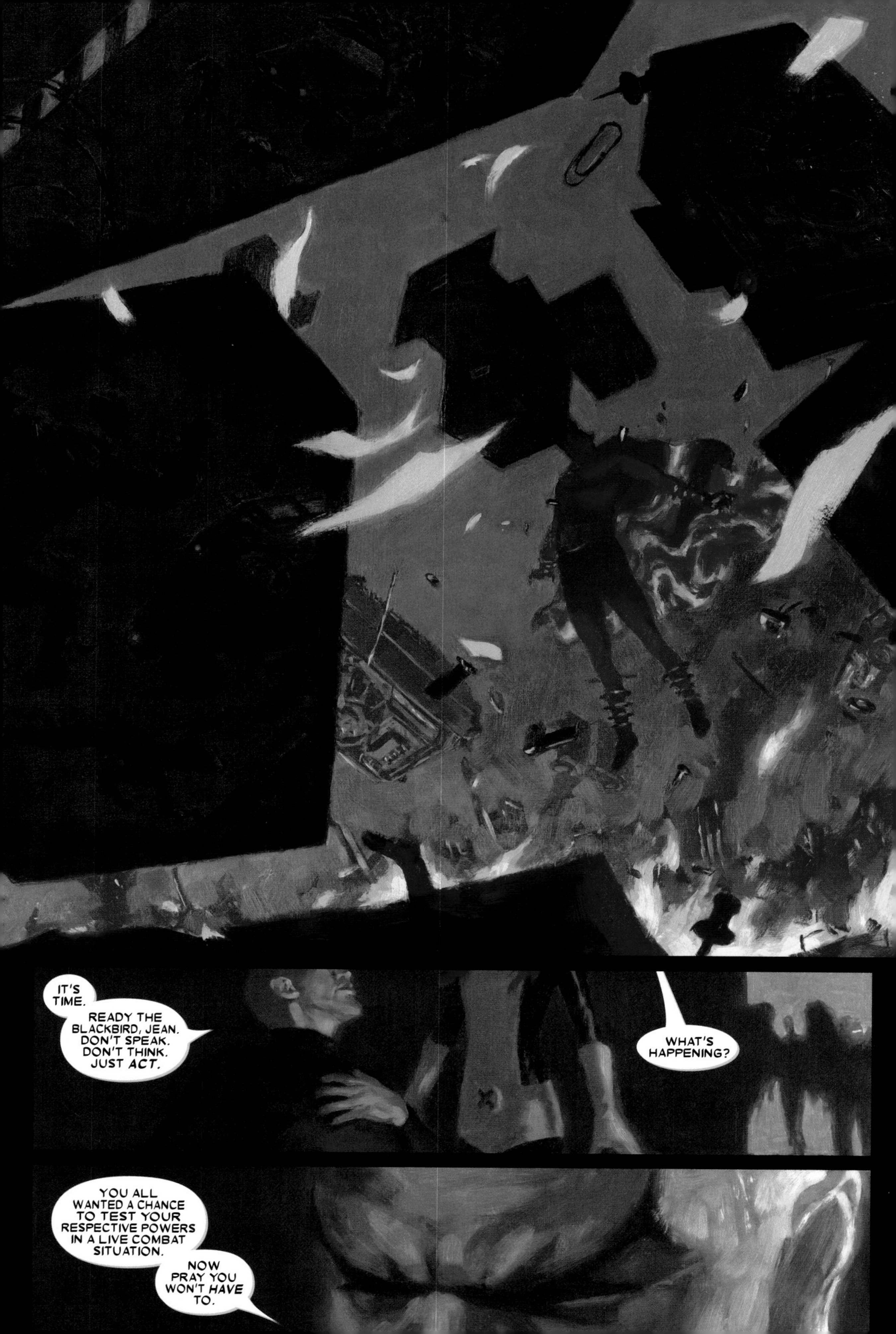
IT'S TIME.
READY THE BLACKBIRD, JEAN. DON'T SPEAK. DON'T THINK. JUST *ACT.*
WHAT'S HAPPENING?
YOU ALL WANTED A CHANCE TO TEST YOUR RESPECTIVE POWERS IN A LIVE COMBAT SITUATION.
NOW PRAY YOU WON'T *HAVE* TO.

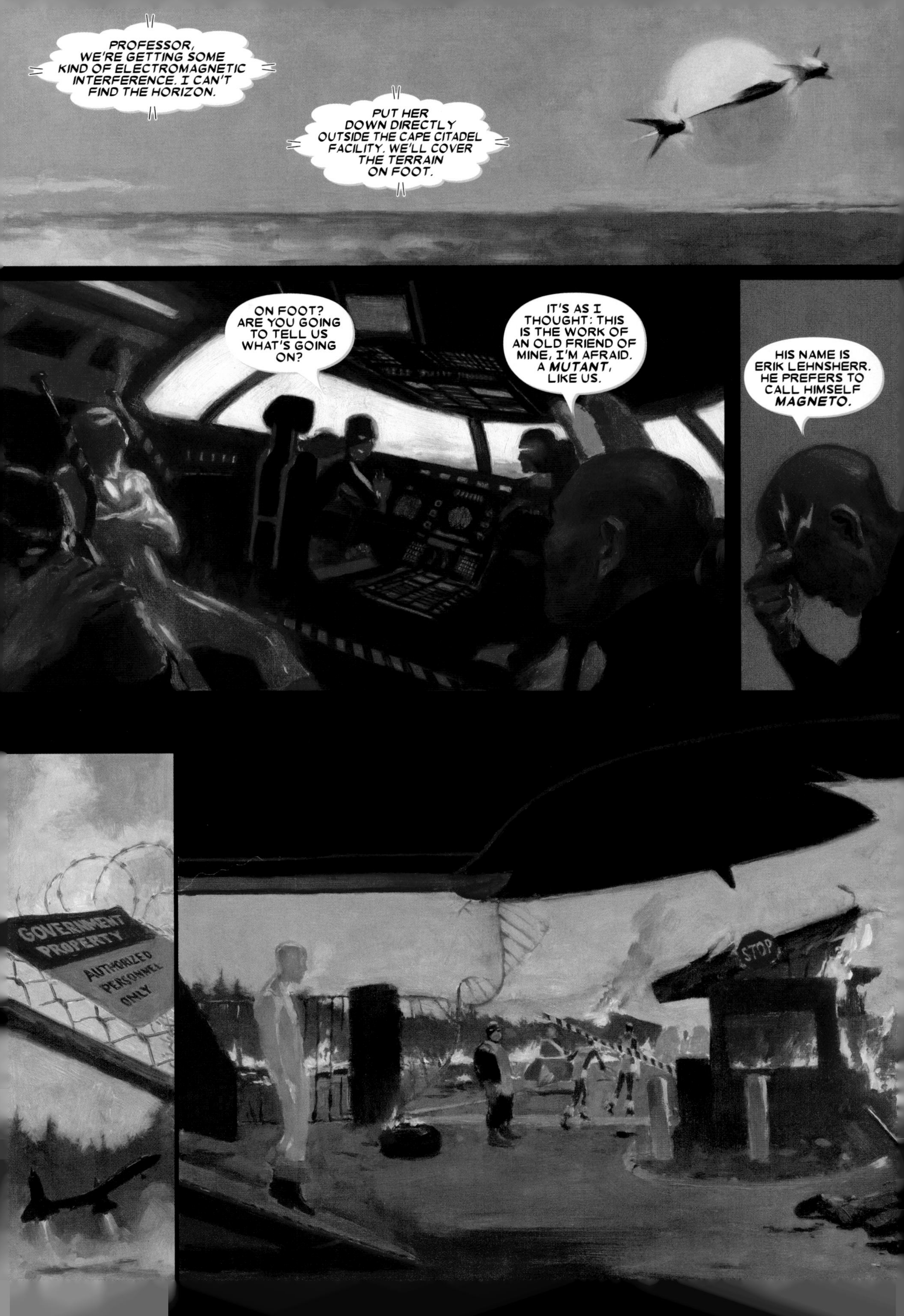
PROFESSOR, WE'RE GETTING SOME KIND OF ELECTROMAGNETIC INTERFERENCE. I CAN'T FIND THE HORIZON.
PUT HER DOWN DIRECTLY OUTSIDE THE CAPE CITADEL FACILITY. WE'LL COVER THE TERRAIN ON FOOT.
ON FOOT? ARE YOU GOING TO TELL US WHAT'S GOING ON?
IT'S AS I THOUGHT: THIS IS THE WORK OF AN OLD FRIEND OF MINE, I'M AFRAID. A *MUTANT*, LIKE US.
HIS NAME IS ERIK LEHNSHERR. HE PREFERS TO CALL HIMSELF *MAGNETO*.
GOVERNMENT PROPERTY
AUTHORIZED PERSONNEL ONLY
STOP

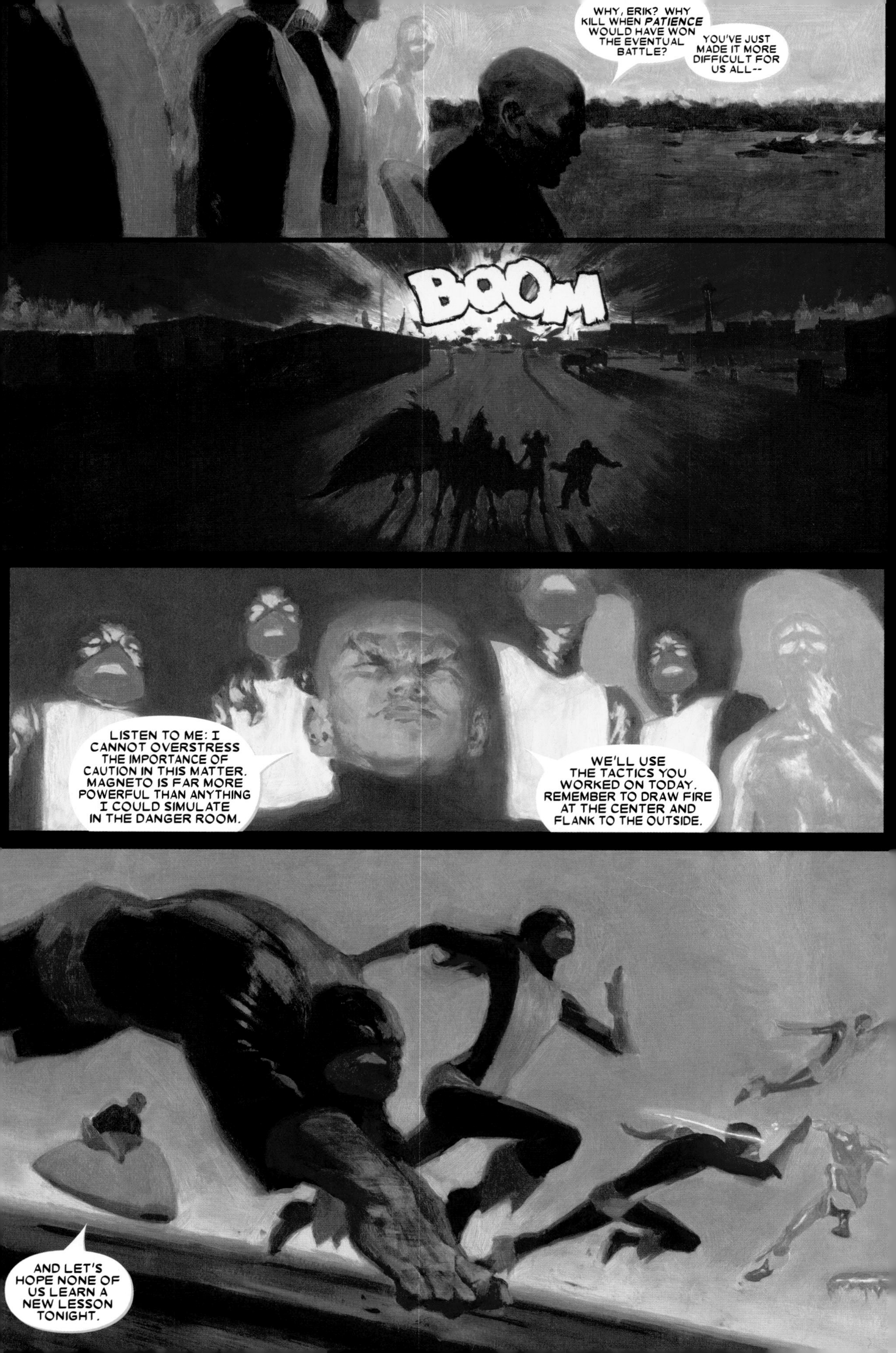
WHY, ERIK? WHY KILL WHEN PATIENCE WOULD HAVE WON THE EVENTUAL BATTLE?
YOU'VE JUST MADE IT MORE DIFFICULT FOR US ALL--
BOOM
LISTEN TO ME: I CANNOT OVERSTRESS THE IMPORTANCE OF CAUTION IN THIS MATTER. MAGNETO IS FAR MORE POWERFUL THAN ANYTHING I COULD SIMULATE IN THE DANGER ROOM.
WE'LL USE THE TACTICS YOU WORKED ON TODAY. REMEMBER TO DRAW FIRE AT THE CENTER AND FLANK TO THE OUTSIDE.
AND LET'S HOPE NONE OF US LEARN A NEW LESSON TONIGHT.

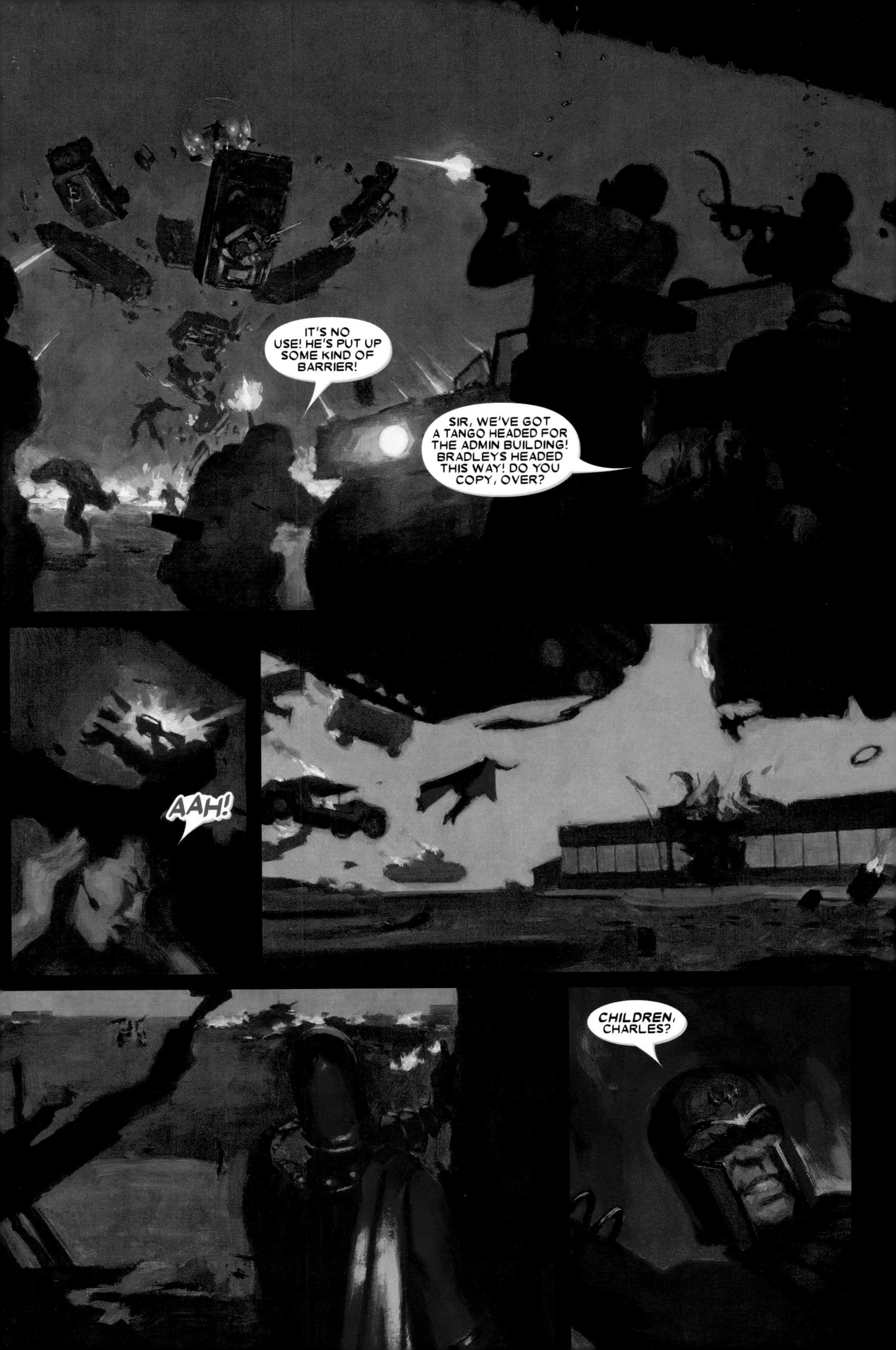
IT'S NO USE! HE'S PUT UP SOME KIND OF BARRIER!
SIR, WE'VE GOT A TANGO HEADED FOR THE ADMIN BUILDING! BRADLEYS HEADED THIS WAY! DO YOU COPY, OVER?
AAH!
CHILDREN, CHARLES?

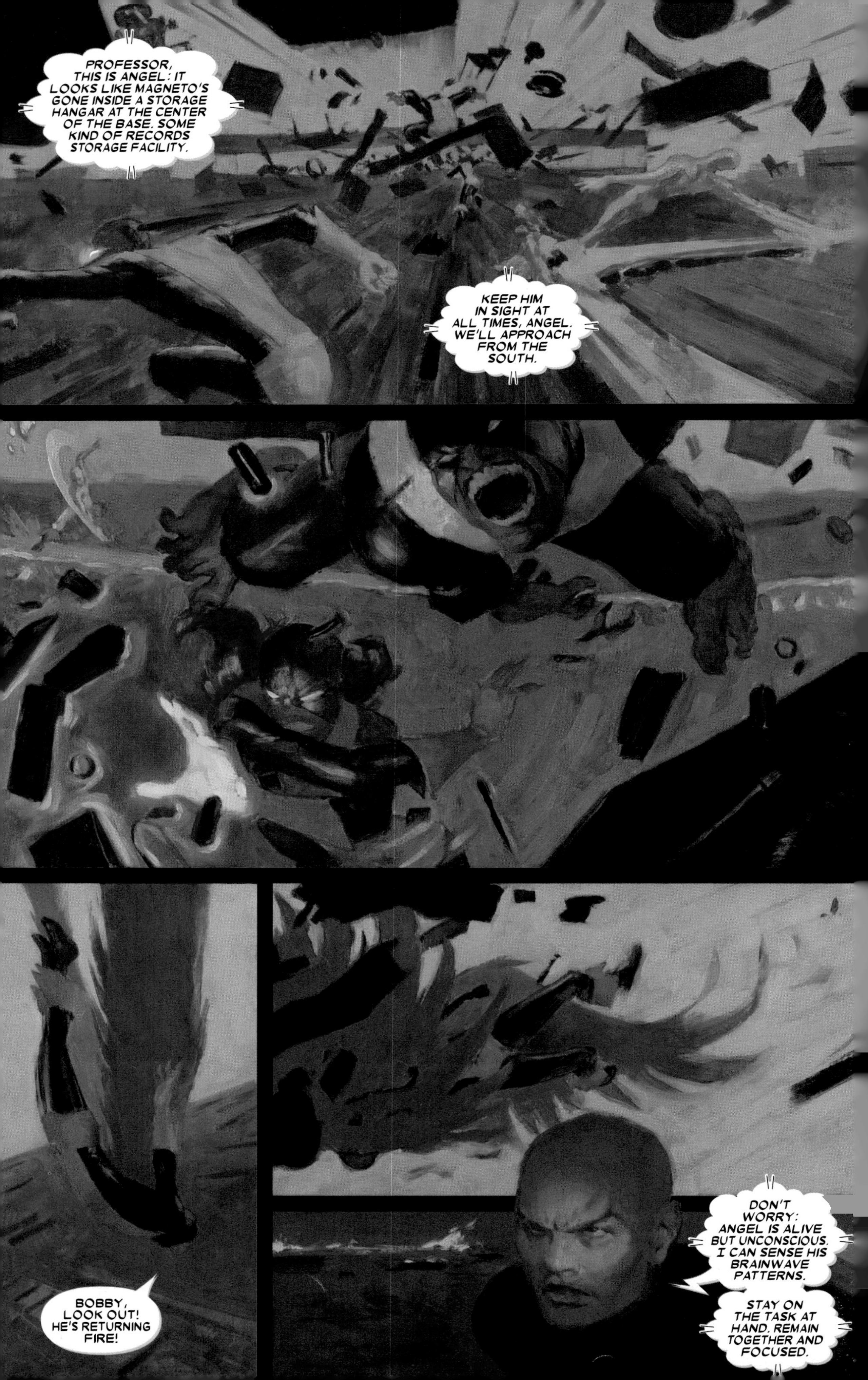
PROFESSOR, THIS IS ANGEL: IT LOOKS LIKE MAGNETO'S GONE INSIDE A STORAGE HANGAR AT THE CENTER OF THE BASE. SOME KIND OF RECORDS STORAGE FACILITY.
KEEP HIM IN SIGHT AT ALL TIMES, ANGEL. WE'LL APPROACH FROM THE SOUTH.
BOBBY, LOOK OUT! HE'S RETURNING FIRE!
DON'T WORRY: ANGEL IS ALIVE BUT UNCONSCIOUS. I CAN SENSE HIS BRAINWAVE PATTERNS.
STAY ON THE TASK AT HAND. REMAIN TOGETHER AND FOCUSED.

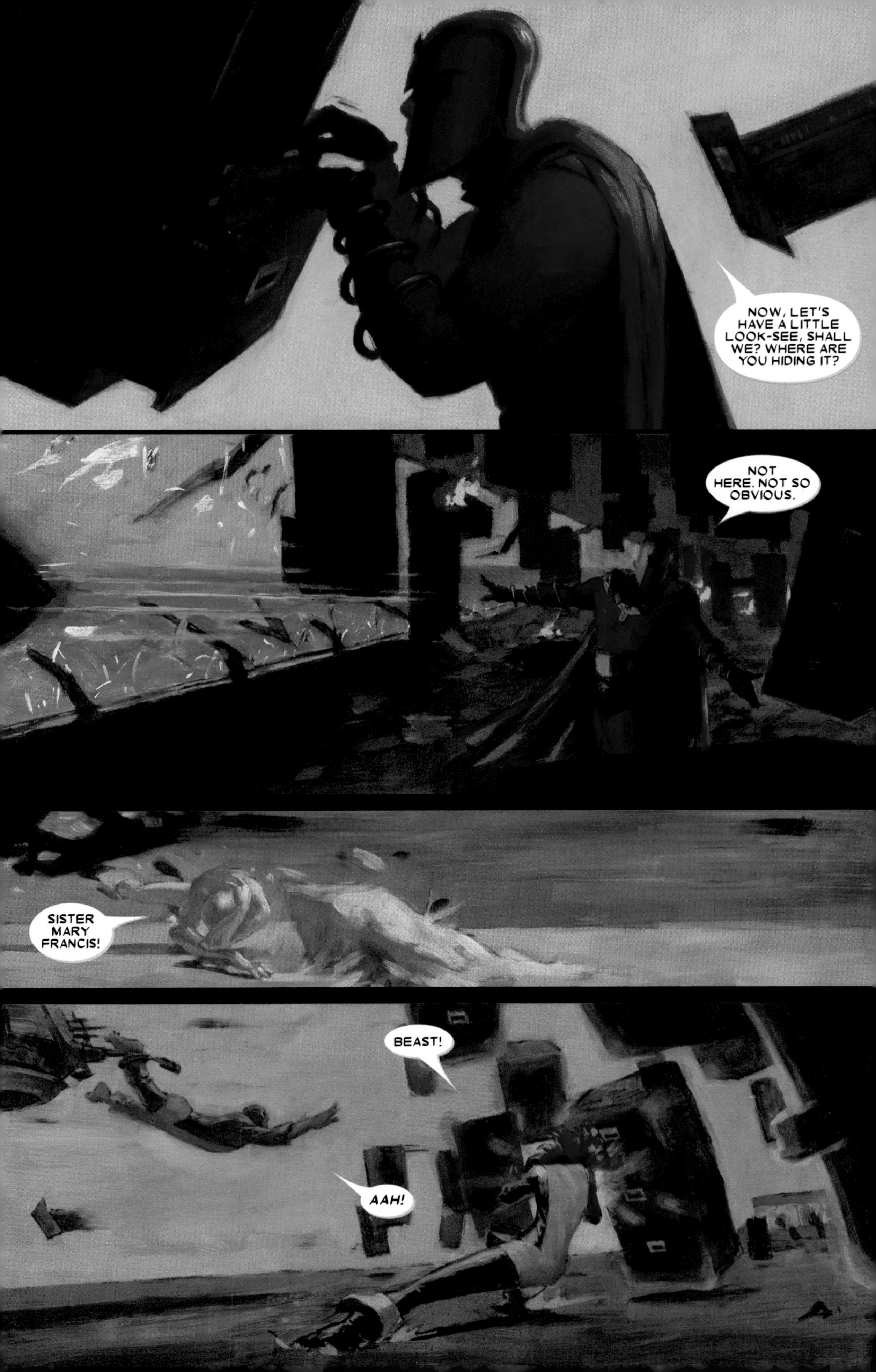
NOW, LET'S HAVE A LITTLE LOOK-SEE, SHALL WE? WHERE ARE YOU HIDING IT?
NOT HERE. NOT SO OBVIOUS.
SISTER MARY FRANCIS!
BEAST!
AAH!

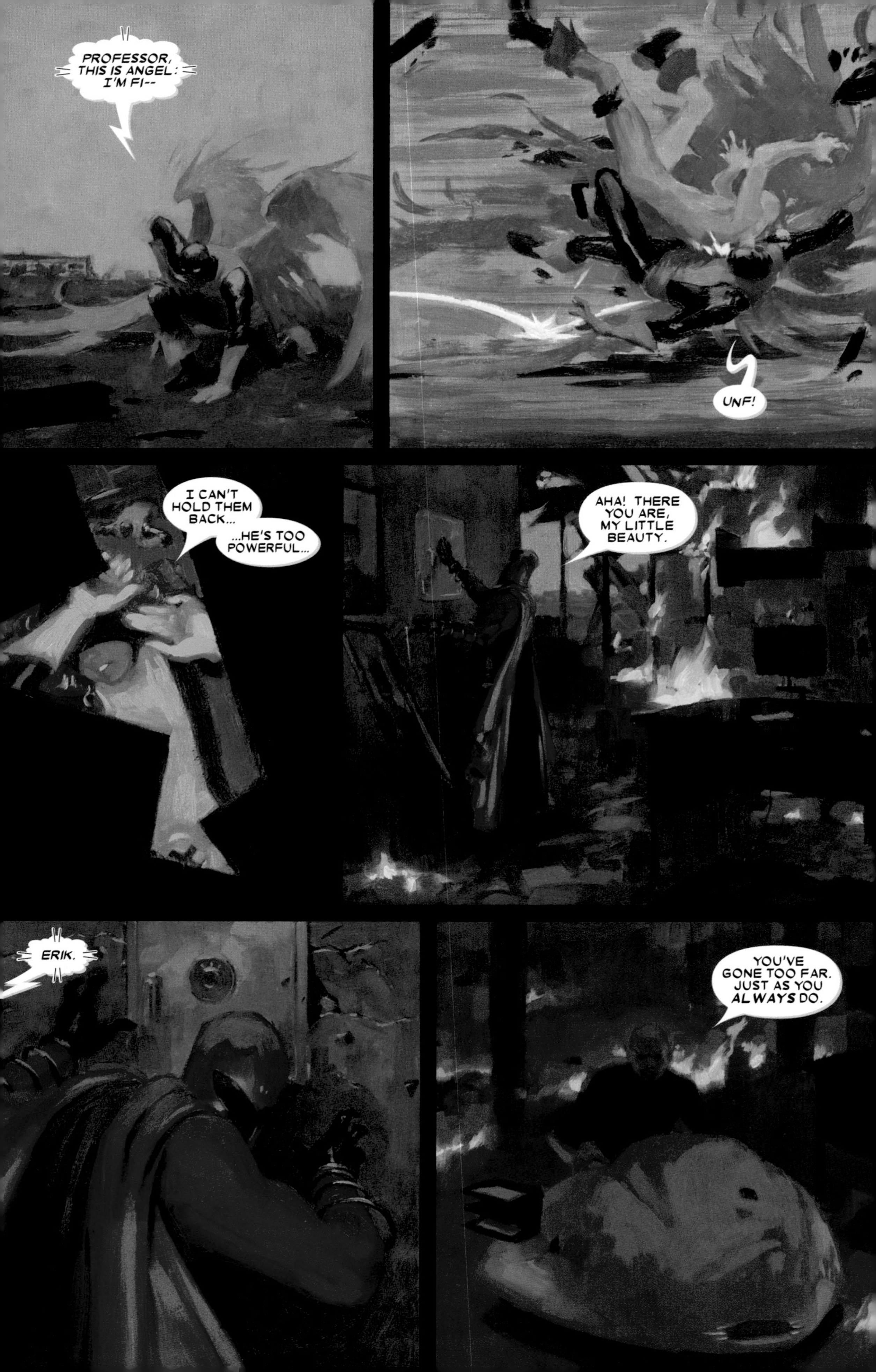
PROFESSOR, THIS IS ANGEL: I'M FI--
UNF!
I CAN'T HOLD THEM BACK...
...HE'S TOO POWERFUL...
AHA! THERE YOU ARE, MY LITTLE BEAUTY.
ERIK.
YOU'VE GONE TOO FAR. JUST AS YOU ALWAYS DO.

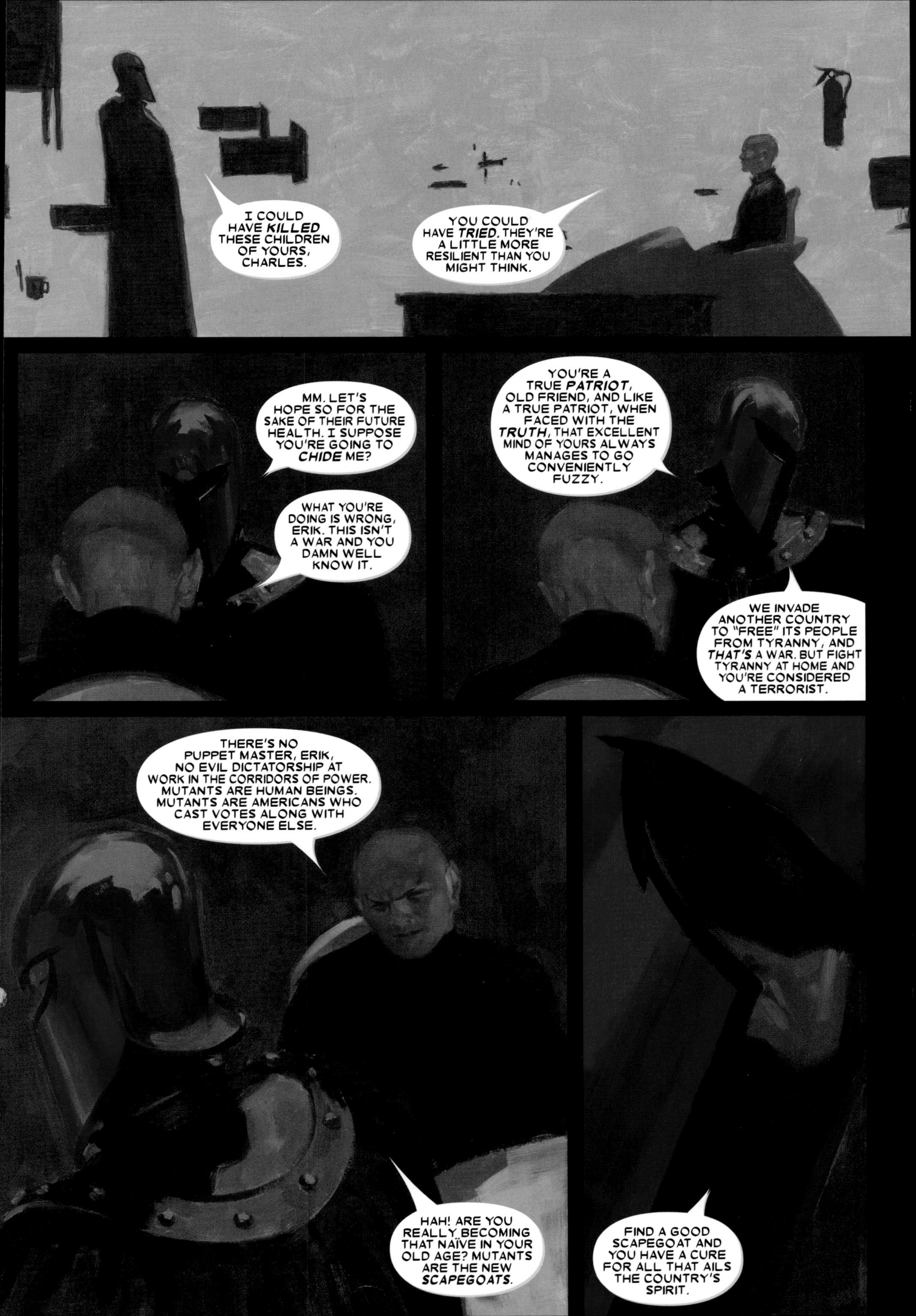
I COULD HAVE KILLED THESE CHILDREN OF YOURS, CHARLES.
YOU COULD HAVE TRIED. THEY'RE A LITTLE MORE RESILIENT THAN YOU MIGHT THINK.
MM. LET'S HOPE SO FOR THE SAKE OF THEIR FUTURE HEALTH. I SUPPOSE YOU'RE GOING TO CHIDE ME?
WHAT YOU'RE DOING IS WRONG, ERIK. THIS ISN'T A WAR AND YOU DAMN WELL KNOW IT.
YOU'RE A TRUE PATRIOT, OLD FRIEND, AND LIKE A TRUE PATRIOT, WHEN FACED WITH THE TRUTH, THAT EXCELLENT MIND OF YOURS ALWAYS MANAGES TO GO CONVENIENTLY FUZZY.
WE INVADE ANOTHER COUNTRY TO "FREE" ITS PEOPLE FROM TYRANNY, AND THAT'S A WAR. BUT FIGHT TYRANNY AT HOME AND YOU'RE CONSIDERED A TERRORIST.
THERE'S NO PUPPET MASTER, ERIK, NO EVIL DICTATORSHIP AT WORK IN THE CORRIDORS OF POWER. MUTANTS ARE HUMAN BEINGS. MUTANTS ARE AMERICANS WHO CAST VOTES ALONG WITH EVERYONE ELSE.
HAH! ARE YOU REALLY BECOMING THAT NAÏVE IN YOUR OLD AGE? MUTANTS ARE THE NEW SCAPEGOATS.
FIND A GOOD SCAPEGOAT AND YOU HAVE A CURE FOR ALL THAT AILS THE COUNTRY'S SPIRIT.

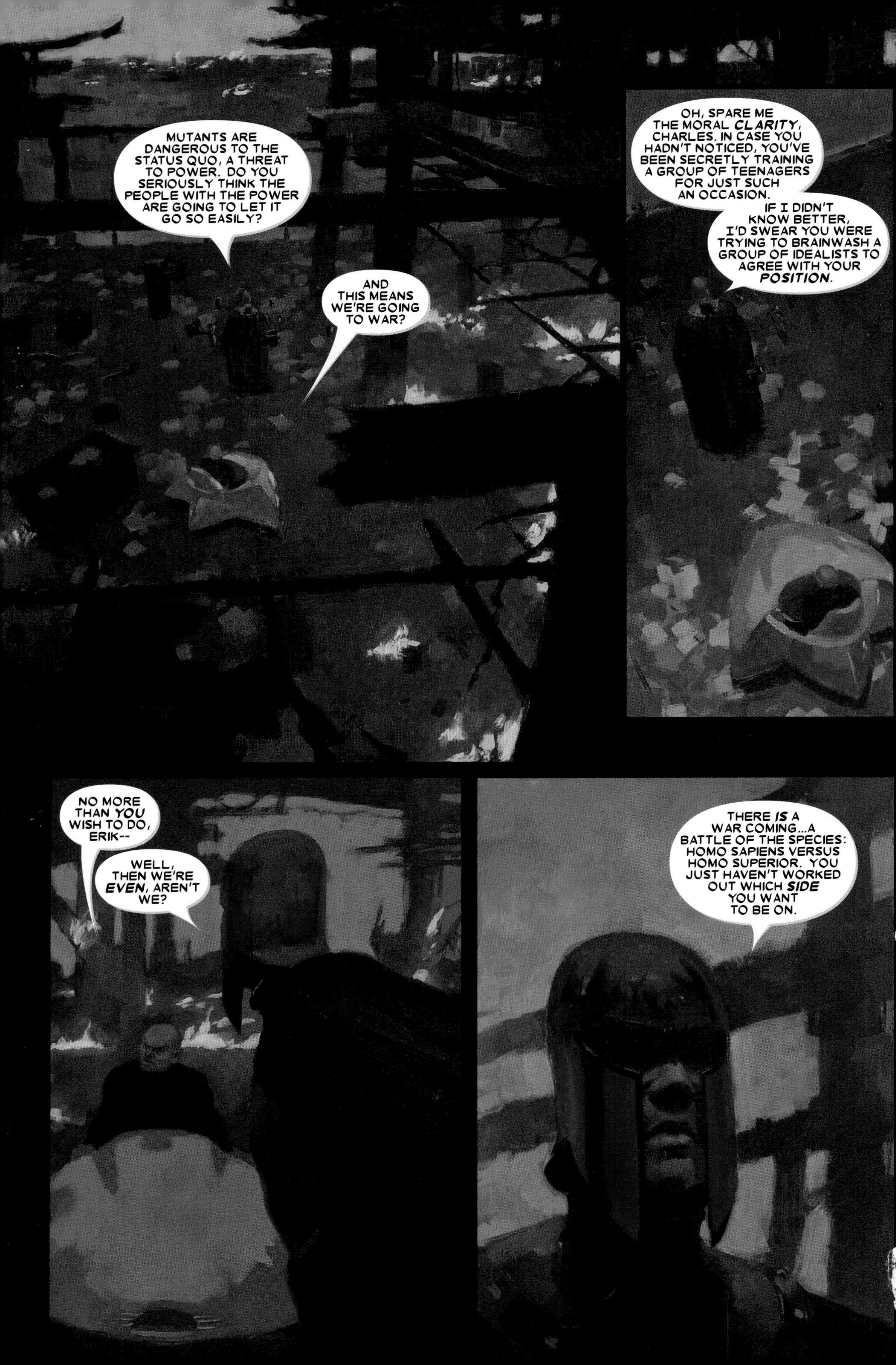
MUTANTS ARE DANGEROUS TO THE STATUS QUO, A THREAT TO POWER. DO YOU SERIOUSLY THINK THE PEOPLE WITH THE POWER ARE GOING TO LET IT GO SO EASILY?
AND THIS MEANS WE'RE GOING TO WAR?
OH, SPARE ME THE MORAL *CLARITY*, CHARLES. IN CASE YOU HADN'T NOTICED, YOU'VE BEEN SECRETLY TRAINING A GROUP OF TEENAGERS FOR JUST SUCH AN OCCASION.
IF I DIDN'T KNOW BETTER, I'D SWEAR YOU WERE TRYING TO BRAINWASH A GROUP OF IDEALISTS TO AGREE WITH YOUR *POSITION*.
NO MORE THAN *YOU* WISH TO DO, ERIK--
WELL, THEN WE'RE *EVEN*, AREN'T WE?
THERE *IS* A WAR COMING...A BATTLE OF THE SPECIES: HOMO SAPIENS VERSUS HOMO SUPERIOR. YOU JUST HAVEN'T WORKED OUT WHICH *SIDE* YOU WANT TO BE ON.

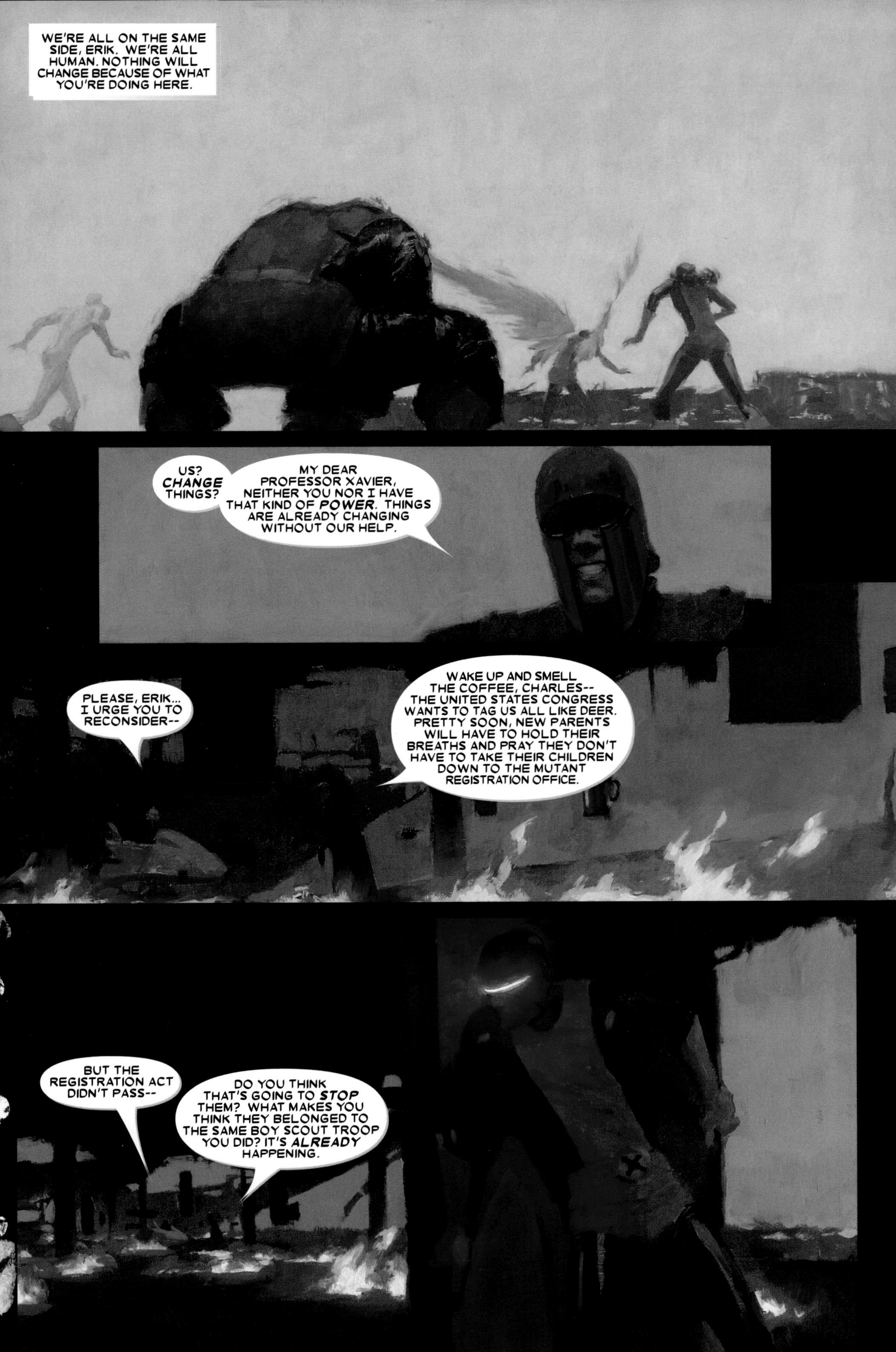
WE'RE ALL ON THE SAME SIDE, ERIK. WE'RE ALL HUMAN. NOTHING WILL CHANGE BECAUSE OF WHAT YOU'RE DOING HERE.
US? CHANGE THINGS?
MY DEAR PROFESSOR XAVIER, NEITHER YOU NOR I HAVE THAT KIND OF POWER. THINGS ARE ALREADY CHANGING WITHOUT OUR HELP.
PLEASE, ERIK... I URGE YOU TO RECONSIDER--
WAKE UP AND SMELL THE COFFEE, CHARLES-- THE UNITED STATES CONGRESS WANTS TO TAG US ALL LIKE DEER. PRETTY SOON, NEW PARENTS WILL HAVE TO HOLD THEIR BREATHS AND PRAY THEY DON'T HAVE TO TAKE THEIR CHILDREN DOWN TO THE MUTANT REGISTRATION OFFICE.
BUT THE REGISTRATION ACT DIDN'T PASS--
DO YOU THINK THAT'S GOING TO STOP THEM? WHAT MAKES YOU THINK THEY BELONGED TO THE SAME BOY SCOUT TROOP YOU DID? IT'S ALREADY HAPPENING.

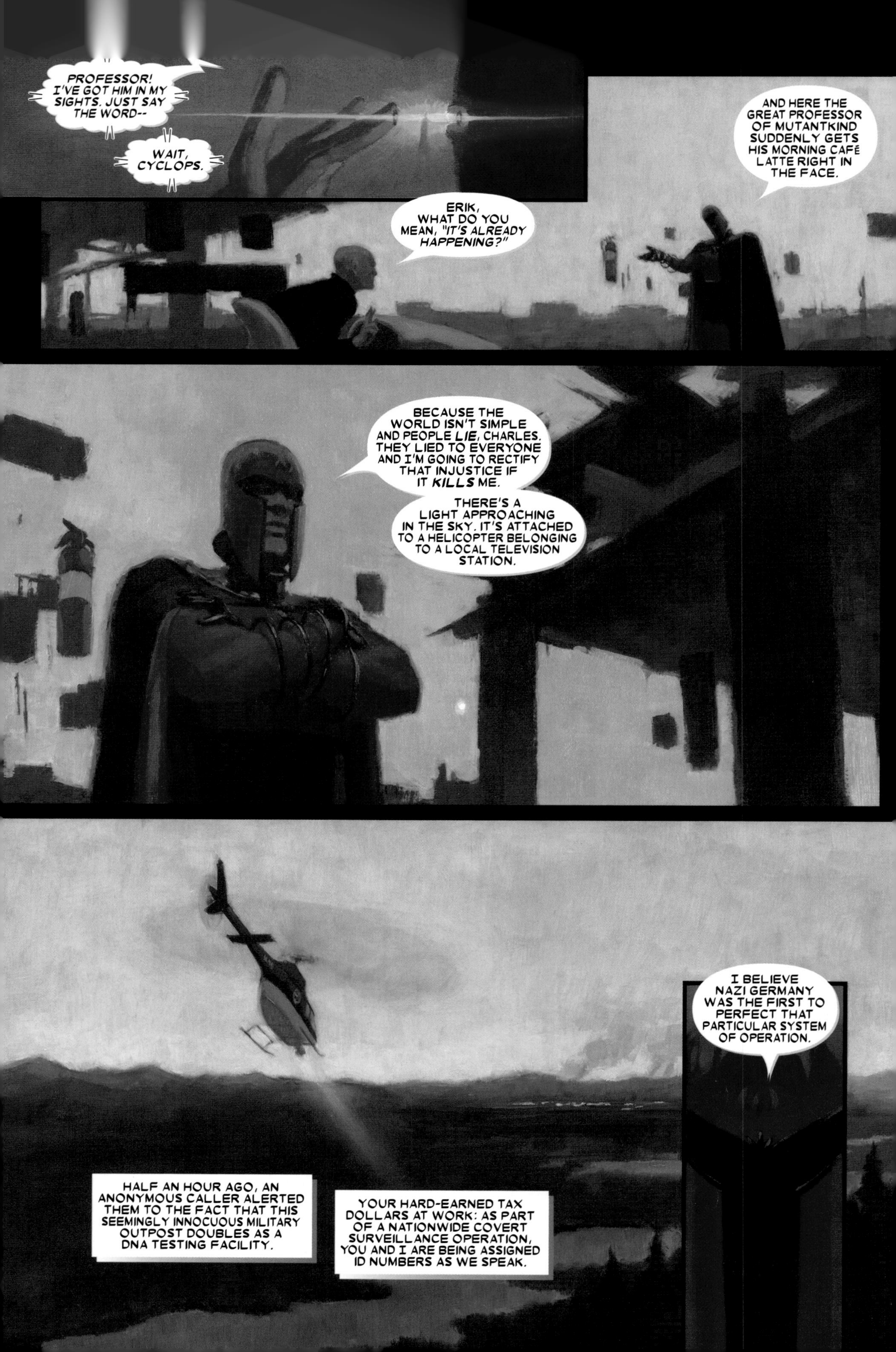
PROFESSOR! I'VE GOT HIM IN MY SIGHTS. JUST SAY THE WORD--
WAIT, CYCLOPS.
AND HERE THE GREAT PROFESSOR OF MUTANTKIND SUDDENLY GETS HIS MORNING CAFÉ LATTE RIGHT IN THE FACE.
ERIK, WHAT DO YOU MEAN, "IT'S ALREADY HAPPENING?"
BECAUSE THE WORLD ISN'T SIMPLE AND PEOPLE LIE, CHARLES. THEY LIED TO EVERYONE AND I'M GOING TO RECTIFY THAT INJUSTICE IF IT KILLS ME.
THERE'S A LIGHT APPROACHING IN THE SKY. IT'S ATTACHED TO A HELICOPTER BELONGING TO A LOCAL TELEVISION STATION.
HALF AN HOUR AGO, AN ANONYMOUS CALLER ALERTED THEM TO THE FACT THAT THIS SEEMINGLY INNOCUOUS MILITARY OUTPOST DOUBLES AS A DNA TESTING FACILITY.
YOUR HARD-EARNED TAX DOLLARS AT WORK: AS PART OF A NATIONWIDE COVERT SURVEILLANCE OPERATION, YOU AND I ARE BEING ASSIGNED ID NUMBERS AS WE SPEAK.
I BELIEVE NAZI GERMANY WAS THE FIRST TO PERFECT THAT PARTICULAR SYSTEM OF OPERATION.

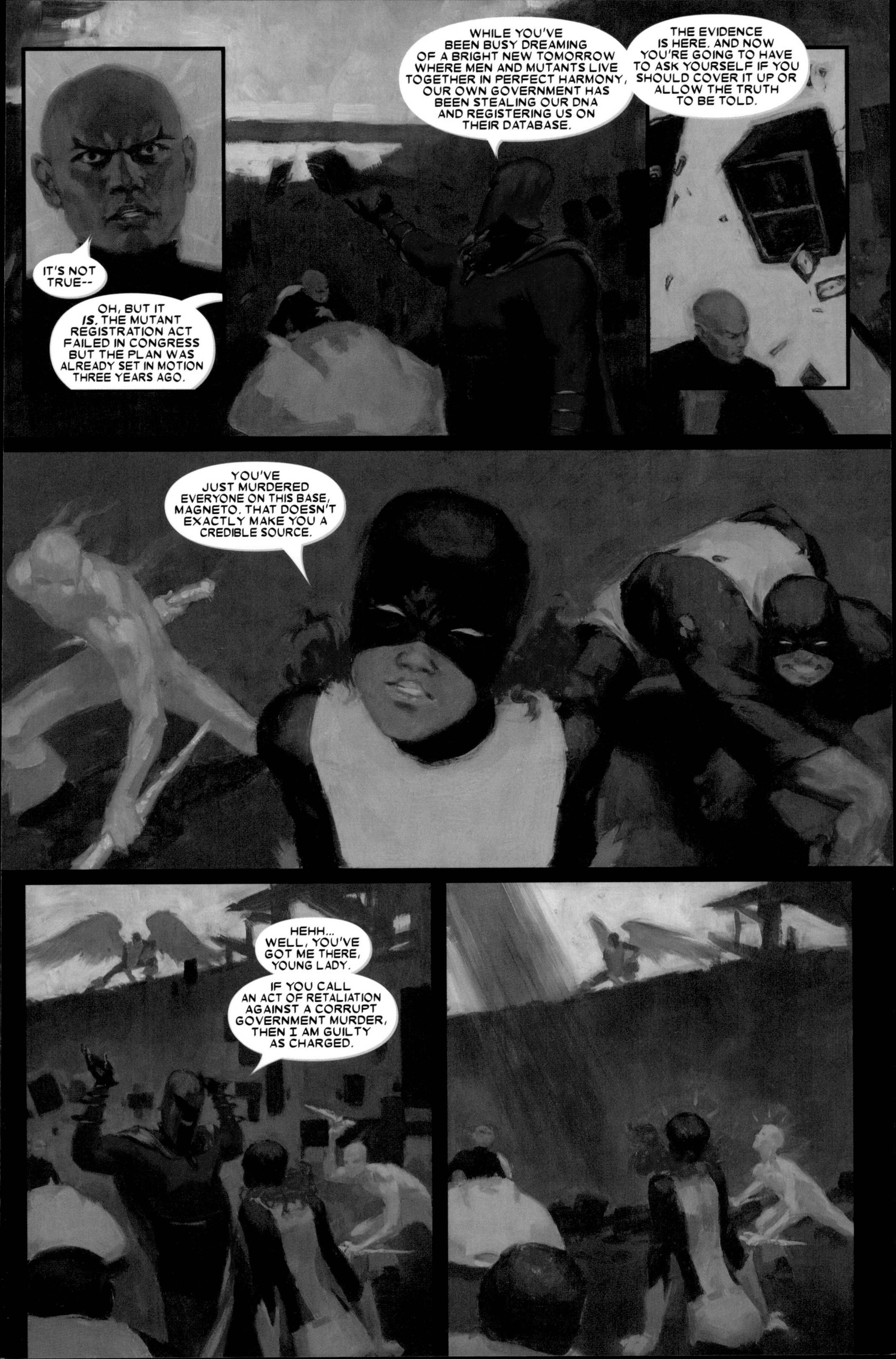
IT'S NOT TRUE--
OH, BUT IT IS. THE MUTANT REGISTRATION ACT FAILED IN CONGRESS BUT THE PLAN WAS ALREADY SET IN MOTION THREE YEARS AGO.
WHILE YOU'VE BEEN BUSY DREAMING OF A BRIGHT NEW TOMORROW WHERE MEN AND MUTANTS LIVE TOGETHER IN PERFECT HARMONY, OUR OWN GOVERNMENT HAS BEEN STEALING OUR DNA AND REGISTERING US ON THEIR DATABASE.
THE EVIDENCE IS HERE. AND NOW YOU'RE GOING TO HAVE TO ASK YOURSELF IF YOU SHOULD COVER IT UP OR ALLOW THE TRUTH TO BE TOLD.
YOU'VE JUST MURDERED EVERYONE ON THIS BASE, MAGNETO. THAT DOESN'T EXACTLY MAKE YOU A CREDIBLE SOURCE.
HEHH... WELL, YOU'VE GOT ME THERE, YOUNG LADY.
IF YOU CALL AN ACT OF RETALIATION AGAINST A CORRUPT GOVERNMENT MURDER, THEN I AM GUILTY AS CHARGED.

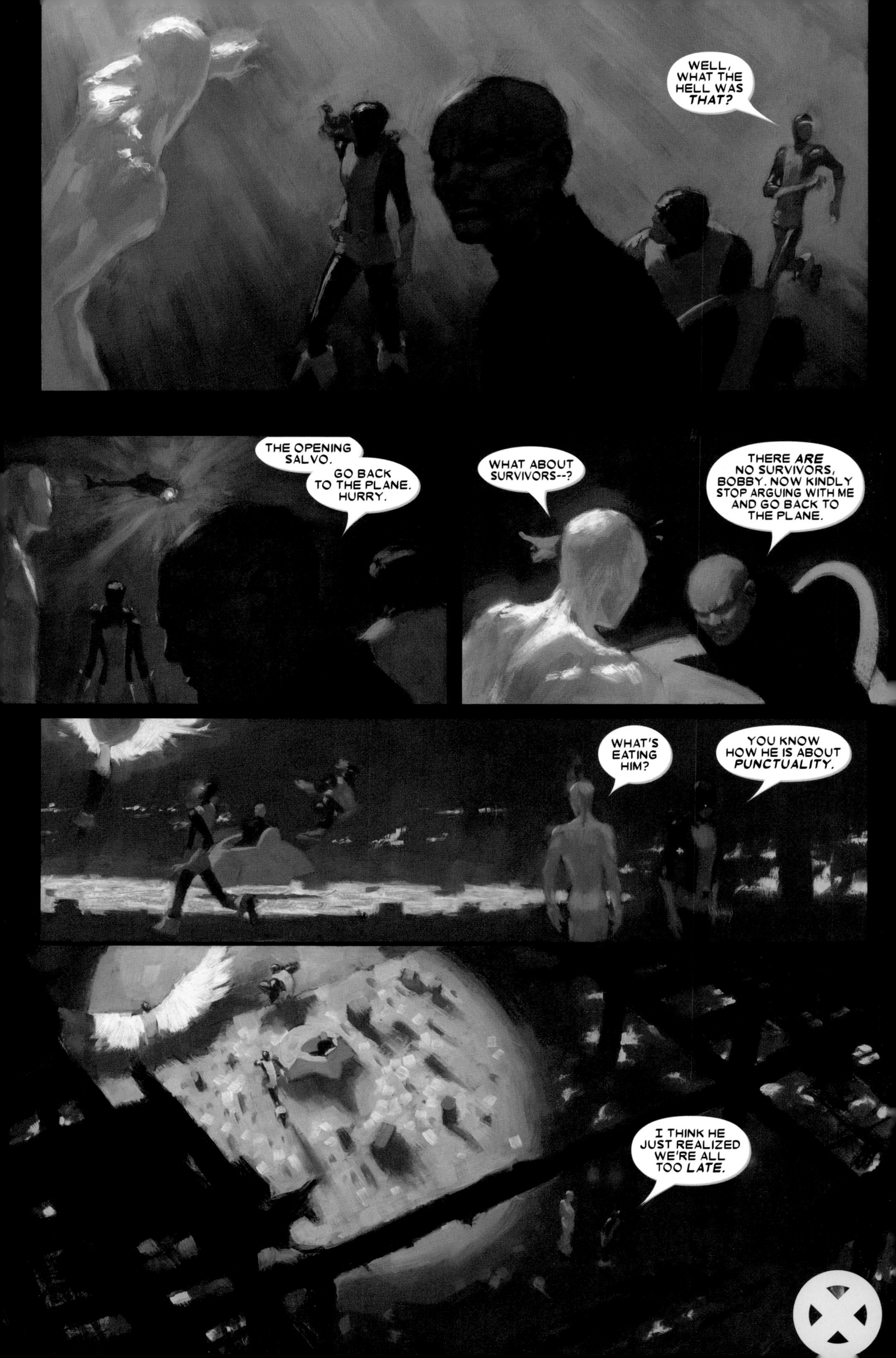
WELL, WHAT THE HELL WAS *THAT?*
THE OPENING SALVO. GO BACK TO THE PLANE. HURRY.
WHAT ABOUT SURVIVORS--?
THERE *ARE* NO SURVIVORS, BOBBY. NOW KINDLY STOP ARGUING WITH ME AND GO BACK TO THE PLANE.
WHAT'S EATING HIM?
YOU KNOW HOW HE IS ABOUT *PUNCTUALITY.*
I THINK HE JUST REALIZED WE'RE ALL TOO *LATE.*

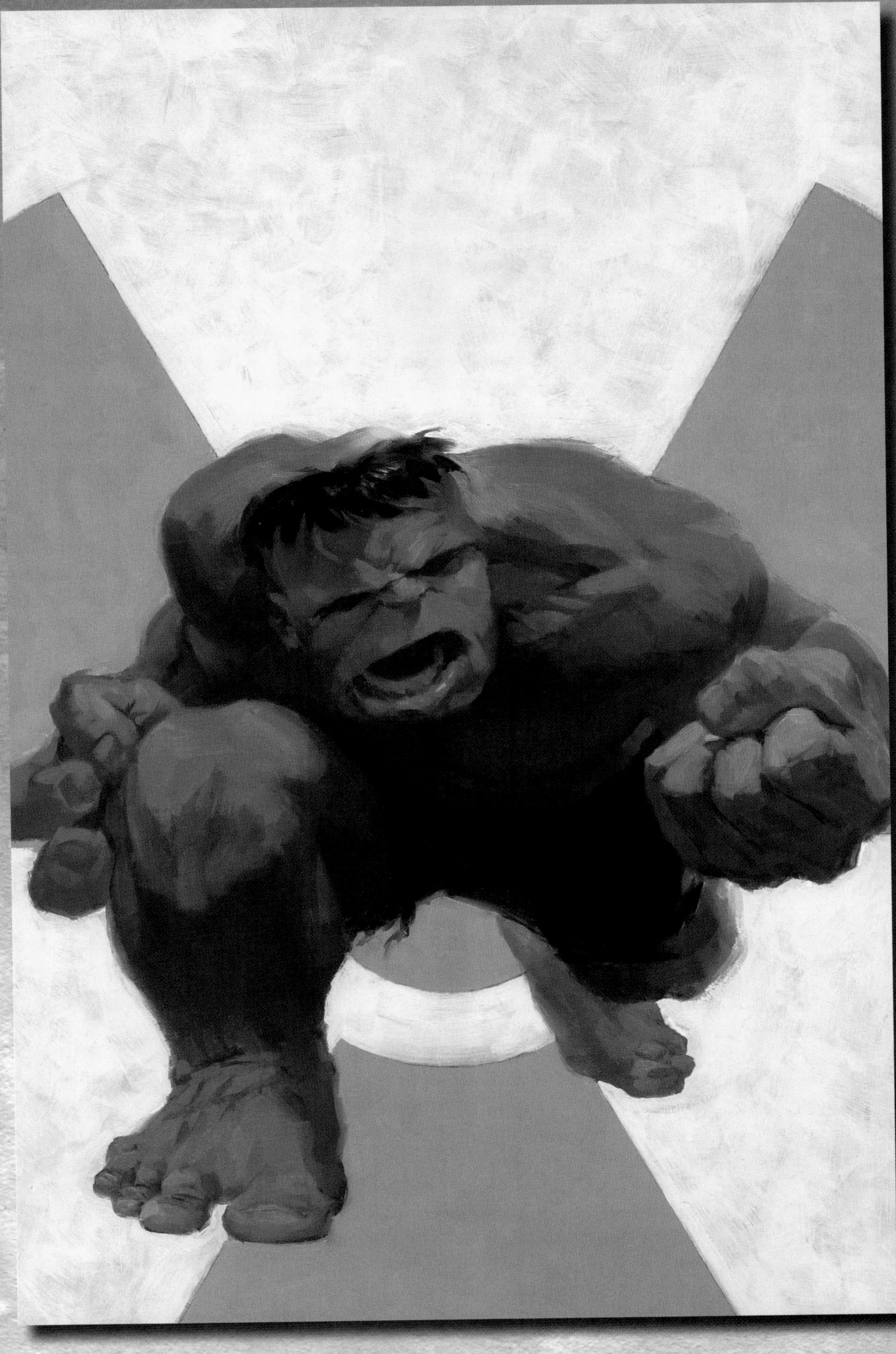

- Hulk -

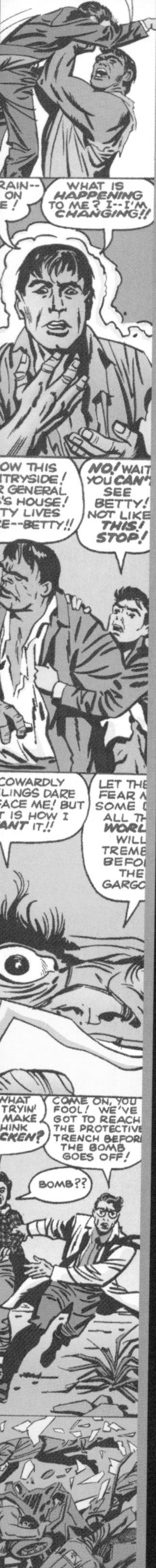
WHAT IS HAPPENING TO ME? I--I'M CHANGING!!
BOMB??

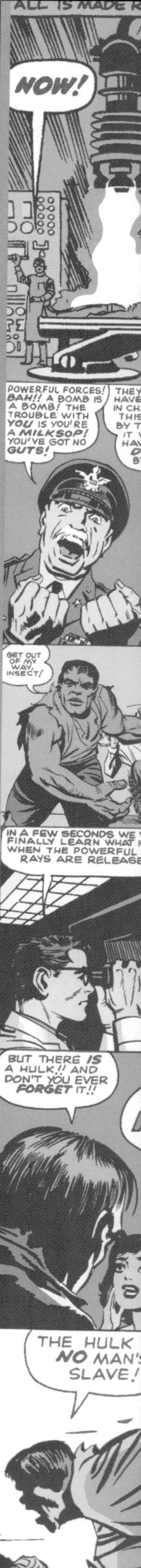
NOW!
POWERFUL FORCES! BAH!! A BOMB IS A BOMB! THE TROUBLE WITH YOU IS YOU'RE A MILKSOP! YOU'VE GOT NO GUTS!
GET OUT OF MY WAY, INSECT!
BUT THERE IS A HULK!! AND DON'T YOU EVER FORGET IT!!

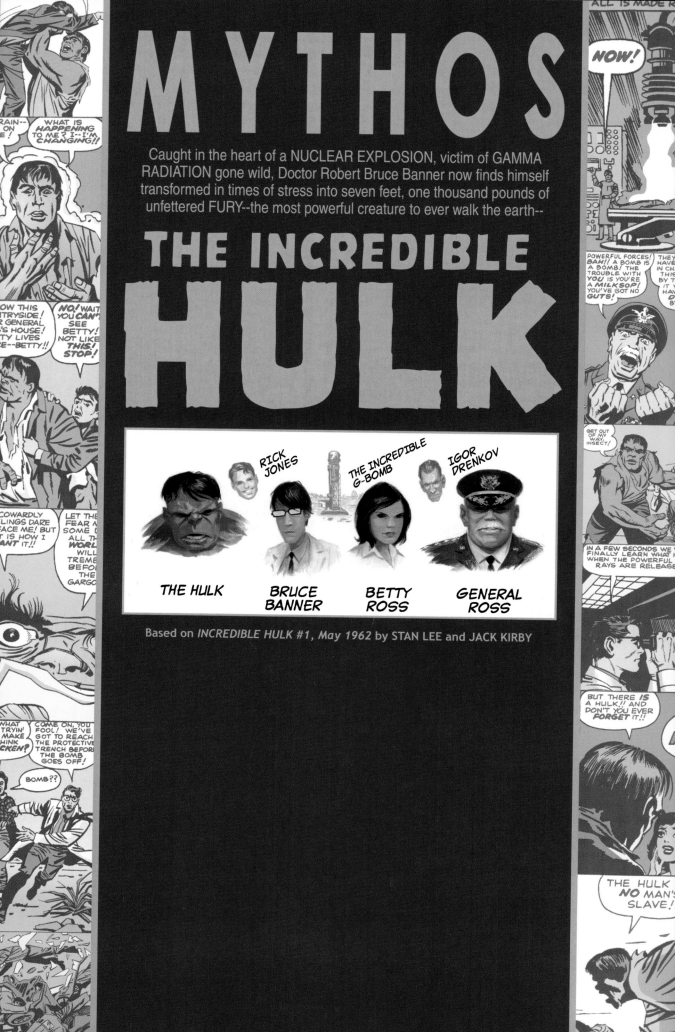

MYTHOS

Caught in the heart of a NUCLEAR EXPLOSION, victim of GAMMA RADIATION gone wild, Doctor Robert Bruce Banner now finds himself transformed in times of stress into seven feet, one thousand pounds of unfettered FURY--the most powerful creature to ever walk the earth--

THE INCREDIBLE HULK

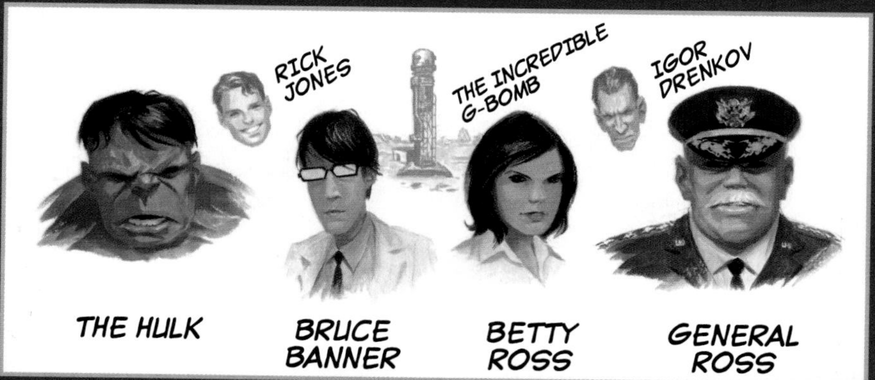
RICK JONES
THE INCREDIBLE G-BOMB
IGOR DRENKOV
THE HULK
BRUCE BANNER
BETTY ROSS
GENERAL ROSS

Based on *INCREDIBLE HULK #1, May 1962* by STAN LEE and JACK KIRBY

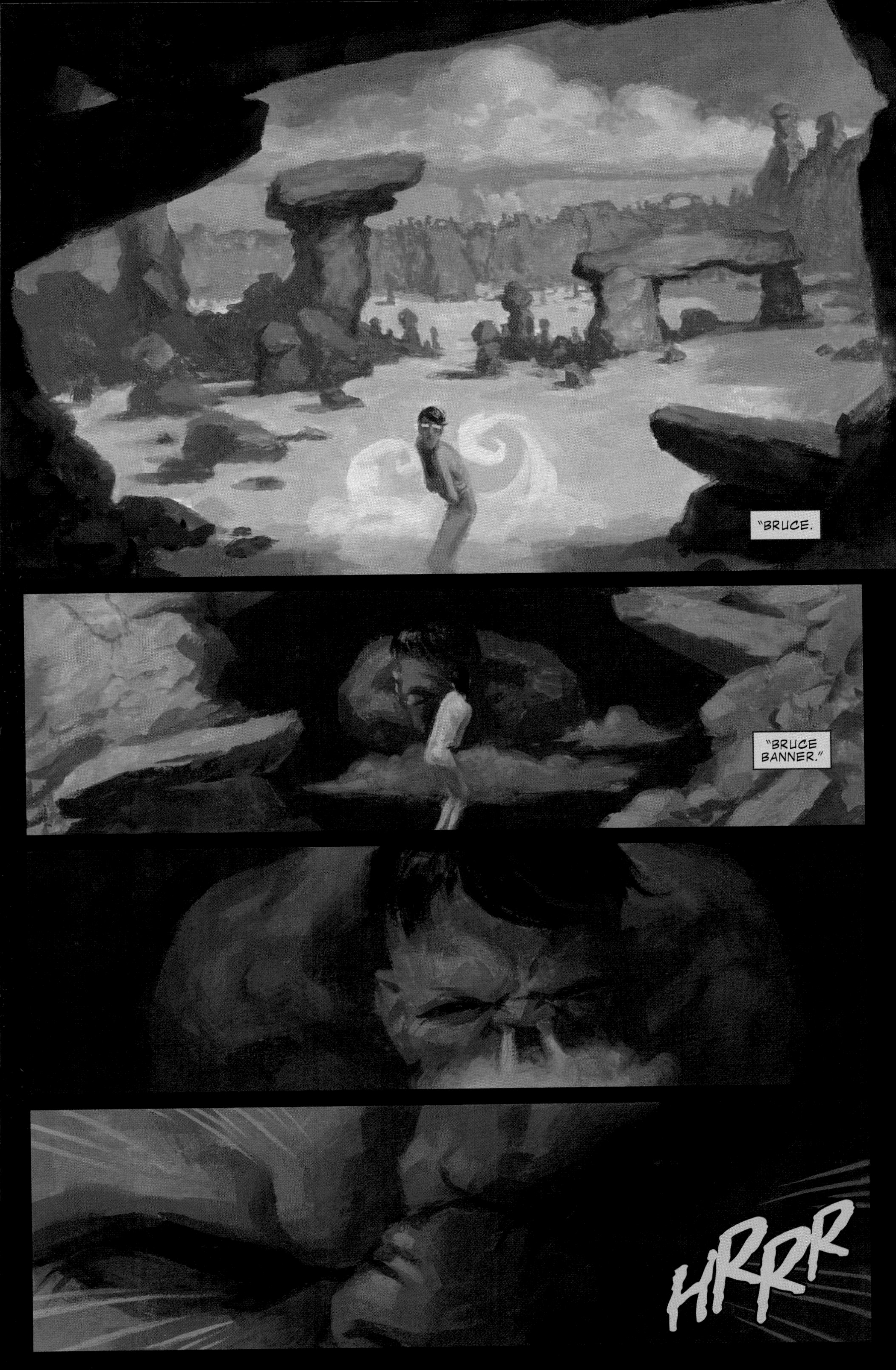
"BRUCE.
"BRUCE BANNER."
HRRR

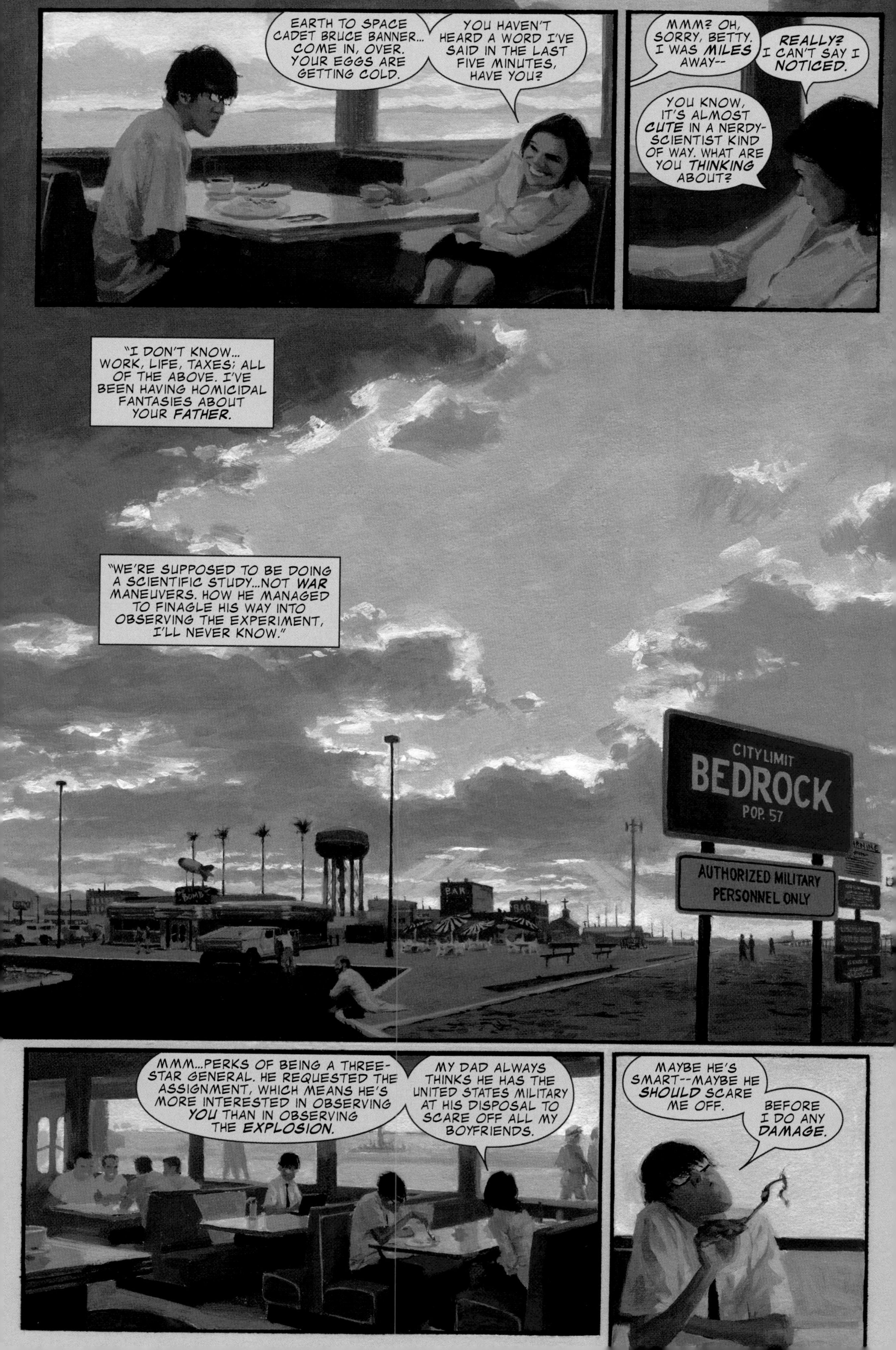

EARTH TO SPACE CADET BRUCE BANNER... COME IN, OVER. YOUR EGGS ARE GETTING COLD.
YOU HAVEN'T HEARD A WORD I'VE SAID IN THE LAST FIVE MINUTES, HAVE YOU?
MMM? OH, SORRY, BETTY. I WAS MILES AWAY--
REALLY? I CAN'T SAY I NOTICED.
YOU KNOW, IT'S ALMOST CUTE IN A NERDY-SCIENTIST KIND OF WAY. WHAT ARE YOU THINKING ABOUT?
"I DON'T KNOW... WORK, LIFE, TAXES; ALL OF THE ABOVE. I'VE BEEN HAVING HOMICIDAL FANTASIES ABOUT YOUR FATHER.
"WE'RE SUPPOSED TO BE DOING A SCIENTIFIC STUDY...NOT WAR MANEUVERS. HOW HE MANAGED TO FINAGLE HIS WAY INTO OBSERVING THE EXPERIMENT, I'LL NEVER KNOW."
CITY LIMIT
BEDROCK
POP. 57
AUTHORIZED MILITARY PERSONNEL ONLY
BAR
BAR
MMM...PERKS OF BEING A THREE-STAR GENERAL. HE REQUESTED THE ASSIGNMENT, WHICH MEANS HE'S MORE INTERESTED IN OBSERVING YOU THAN IN OBSERVING THE EXPLOSION.
MY DAD ALWAYS THINKS HE HAS THE UNITED STATES MILITARY AT HIS DISPOSAL TO SCARE OFF ALL MY BOYFRIENDS.
MAYBE HE'S SMART--MAYBE HE SHOULD SCARE ME OFF.
BEFORE I DO ANY DAMAGE.

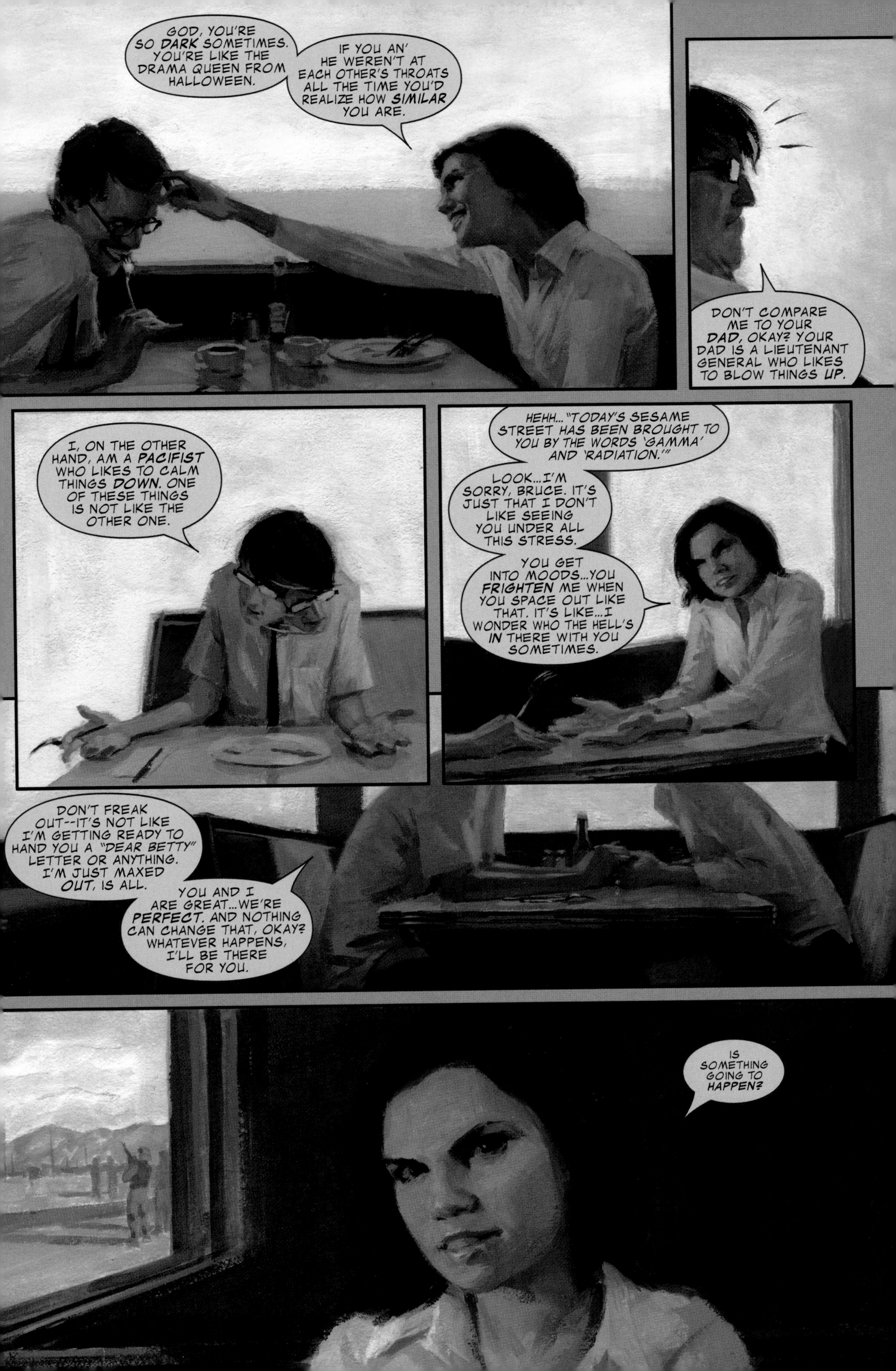
GOD, YOU'RE SO DARK SOMETIMES. YOU'RE LIKE THE DRAMA QUEEN FROM HALLOWEEN.
IF YOU AN' HE WEREN'T AT EACH OTHER'S THROATS ALL THE TIME YOU'D REALIZE HOW SIMILAR YOU ARE.
DON'T COMPARE ME TO YOUR DAD, OKAY? YOUR DAD IS A LIEUTENANT GENERAL WHO LIKES TO BLOW THINGS UP.
I, ON THE OTHER HAND, AM A PACIFIST WHO LIKES TO CALM THINGS DOWN. ONE OF THESE THINGS IS NOT LIKE THE OTHER ONE.
HEHH... "TODAY'S SESAME STREET HAS BEEN BROUGHT TO YOU BY THE WORDS 'GAMMA' AND 'RADIATION.'"
LOOK...I'M SORRY, BRUCE. IT'S JUST THAT I DON'T LIKE SEEING YOU UNDER ALL THIS STRESS.
YOU GET INTO MOODS...YOU FRIGHTEN ME WHEN YOU SPACE OUT LIKE THAT. IT'S LIKE...I WONDER WHO THE HELL'S IN THERE WITH YOU SOMETIMES.
DON'T FREAK OUT--IT'S NOT LIKE I'M GETTING READY TO HAND YOU A "DEAR BETTY" LETTER OR ANYTHING. I'M JUST MAXED OUT, IS ALL.
YOU AND I ARE GREAT...WE'RE PERFECT. AND NOTHING CAN CHANGE THAT, OKAY? WHATEVER HAPPENS, I'LL BE THERE FOR YOU.
IS SOMETHING GOING TO HAPPEN?

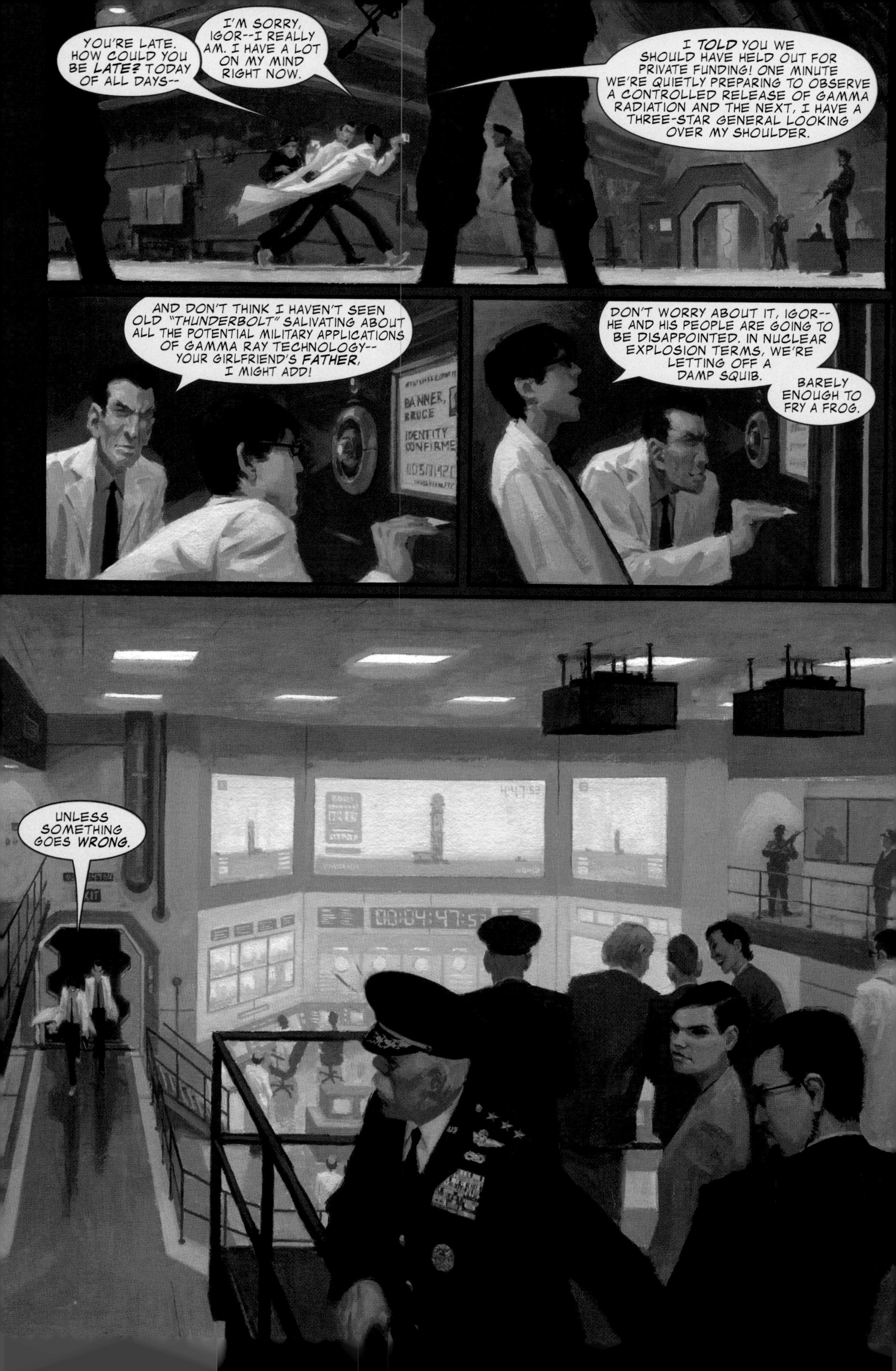
YOU'RE LATE. HOW COULD YOU BE LATE? TODAY OF ALL DAYS--
I'M SORRY, IGOR--I REALLY AM. I HAVE A LOT ON MY MIND RIGHT NOW.
I TOLD YOU WE SHOULD HAVE HELD OUT FOR PRIVATE FUNDING! ONE MINUTE WE'RE QUIETLY PREPARING TO OBSERVE A CONTROLLED RELEASE OF GAMMA RADIATION AND THE NEXT, I HAVE A THREE-STAR GENERAL LOOKING OVER MY SHOULDER.
AND DON'T THINK I HAVEN'T SEEN OLD "THUNDERBOLT" SALIVATING ABOUT ALL THE POTENTIAL MILITARY APPLICATIONS OF GAMMA RAY TECHNOLOGY-- YOUR GIRLFRIEND'S FATHER, I MIGHT ADD!
BANNER, BRUCE
IDENTITY CONFIRMED
DON'T WORRY ABOUT IT, IGOR-- HE AND HIS PEOPLE ARE GOING TO BE DISAPPOINTED. IN NUCLEAR EXPLOSION TERMS, WE'RE LETTING OFF A DAMP SQUIB.
BARELY ENOUGH TO FRY A FROG.
UNLESS SOMETHING GOES WRONG.
EXIT

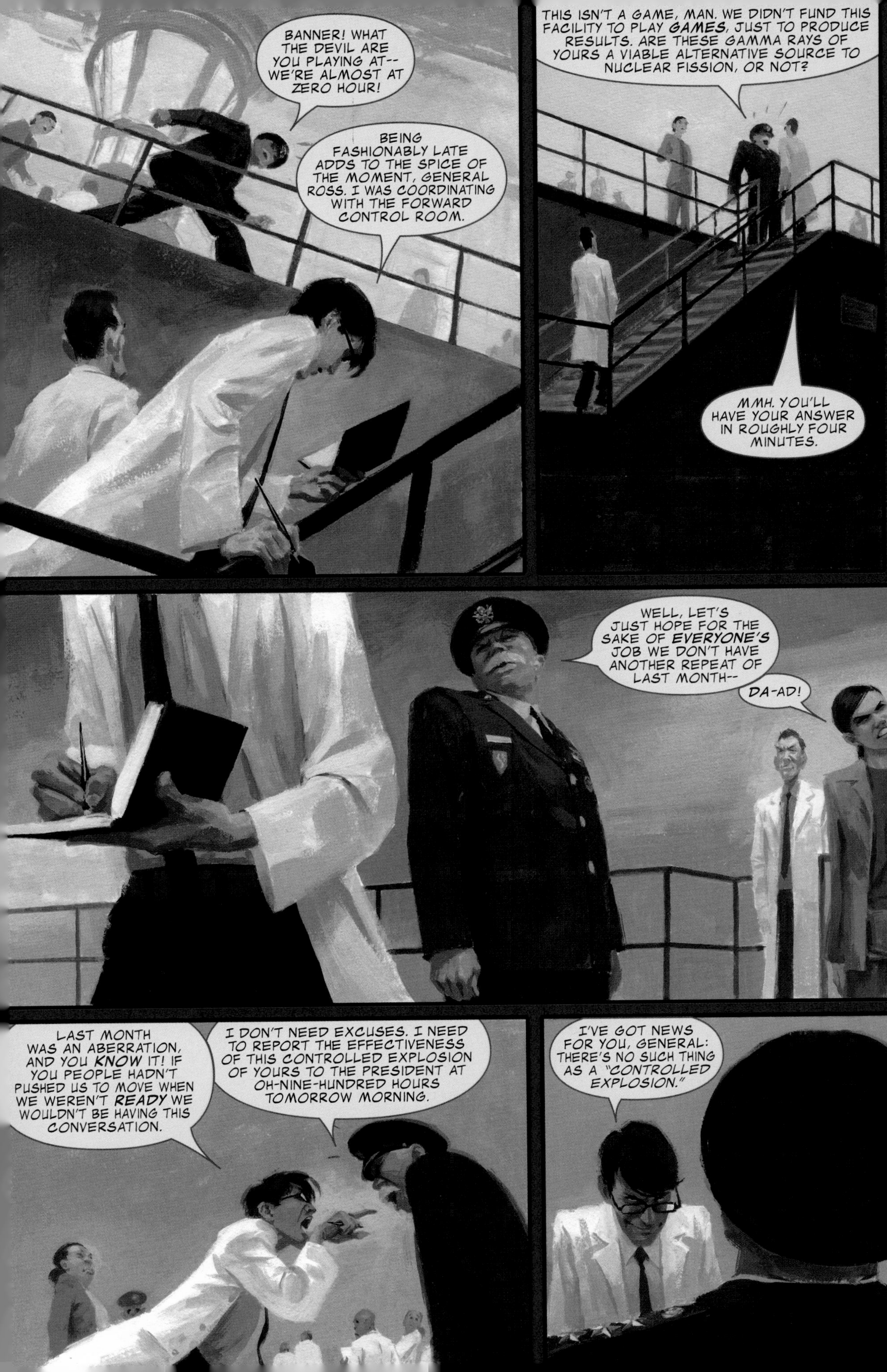
BANNER! WHAT THE DEVIL ARE YOU PLAYING AT-- WE'RE ALMOST AT ZERO HOUR!
BEING FASHIONABLY LATE ADDS TO THE SPICE OF THE MOMENT, GENERAL ROSS. I WAS COORDINATING WITH THE FORWARD CONTROL ROOM.
THIS ISN'T A GAME, MAN. WE DIDN'T FUND THIS FACILITY TO PLAY GAMES, JUST TO PRODUCE RESULTS. ARE THESE GAMMA RAYS OF YOURS A VIABLE ALTERNATIVE SOURCE TO NUCLEAR FISSION, OR NOT?
MMH. YOU'LL HAVE YOUR ANSWER IN ROUGHLY FOUR MINUTES.
WELL, LET'S JUST HOPE FOR THE SAKE OF EVERYONE'S JOB WE DON'T HAVE ANOTHER REPEAT OF LAST MONTH--
DA-AD!
LAST MONTH WAS AN ABERRATION, AND YOU KNOW IT! IF YOU PEOPLE HADN'T PUSHED US TO MOVE WHEN WE WEREN'T READY WE WOULDN'T BE HAVING THIS CONVERSATION.
I DON'T NEED EXCUSES. I NEED TO REPORT THE EFFECTIVENESS OF THIS CONTROLLED EXPLOSION OF YOURS TO THE PRESIDENT AT OH-NINE-HUNDRED HOURS TOMORROW MORNING.
I'VE GOT NEWS FOR YOU, GENERAL: THERE'S NO SUCH THING AS A "CONTROLLED EXPLOSION."

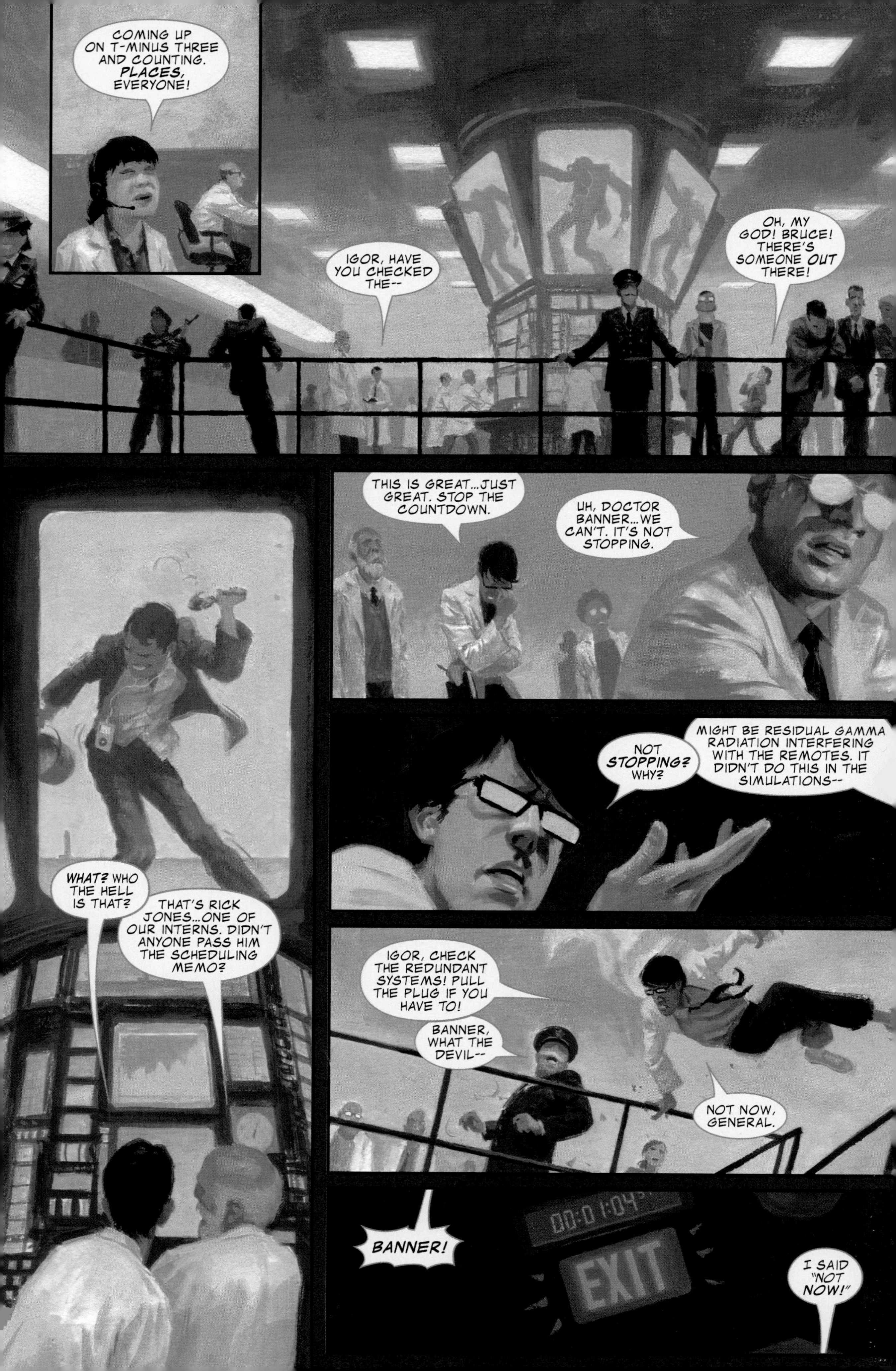
COMING UP ON T-MINUS THREE AND COUNTING. PLACES, EVERYONE!
IGOR, HAVE YOU CHECKED THE--
OH, MY GOD! BRUCE! THERE'S SOMEONE OUT THERE!
WHAT? WHO THE HELL IS THAT?
THAT'S RICK JONES...ONE OF OUR INTERNS. DIDN'T ANYONE PASS HIM THE SCHEDULING MEMO?
THIS IS GREAT...JUST GREAT. STOP THE COUNTDOWN.
UH, DOCTOR BANNER...WE CAN'T. IT'S NOT STOPPING.
NOT STOPPING? WHY?
MIGHT BE RESIDUAL GAMMA RADIATION INTERFERING WITH THE REMOTES. IT DIDN'T DO THIS IN THE SIMULATIONS--
IGOR, CHECK THE REDUNDANT SYSTEMS! PULL THE PLUG IF YOU HAVE TO!
BANNER, WHAT THE DEVIL--
NOT NOW, GENERAL.
BANNER!
EXIT
I SAID "NOT NOW!"

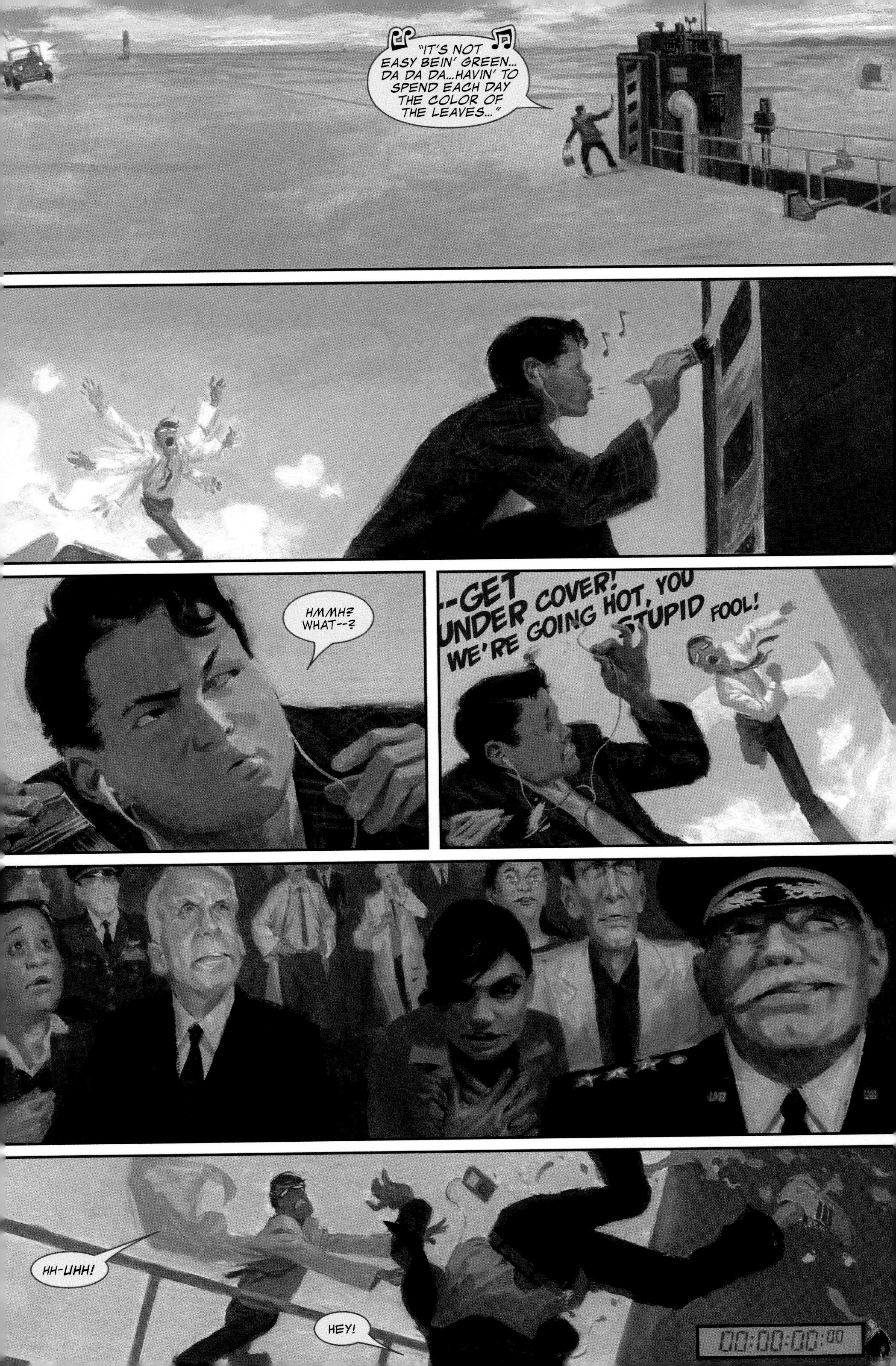
"IT'S NOT EASY BEIN' GREEN... DA DA DA...HAVIN' TO SPEND EACH DAY THE COLOR OF THE LEAVES..."
HMMH? WHAT--?
--GET UNDER COVER! WE'RE GOING HOT, YOU STUPID FOOL!
HH-UHH!
HEY!
00:00:00:00

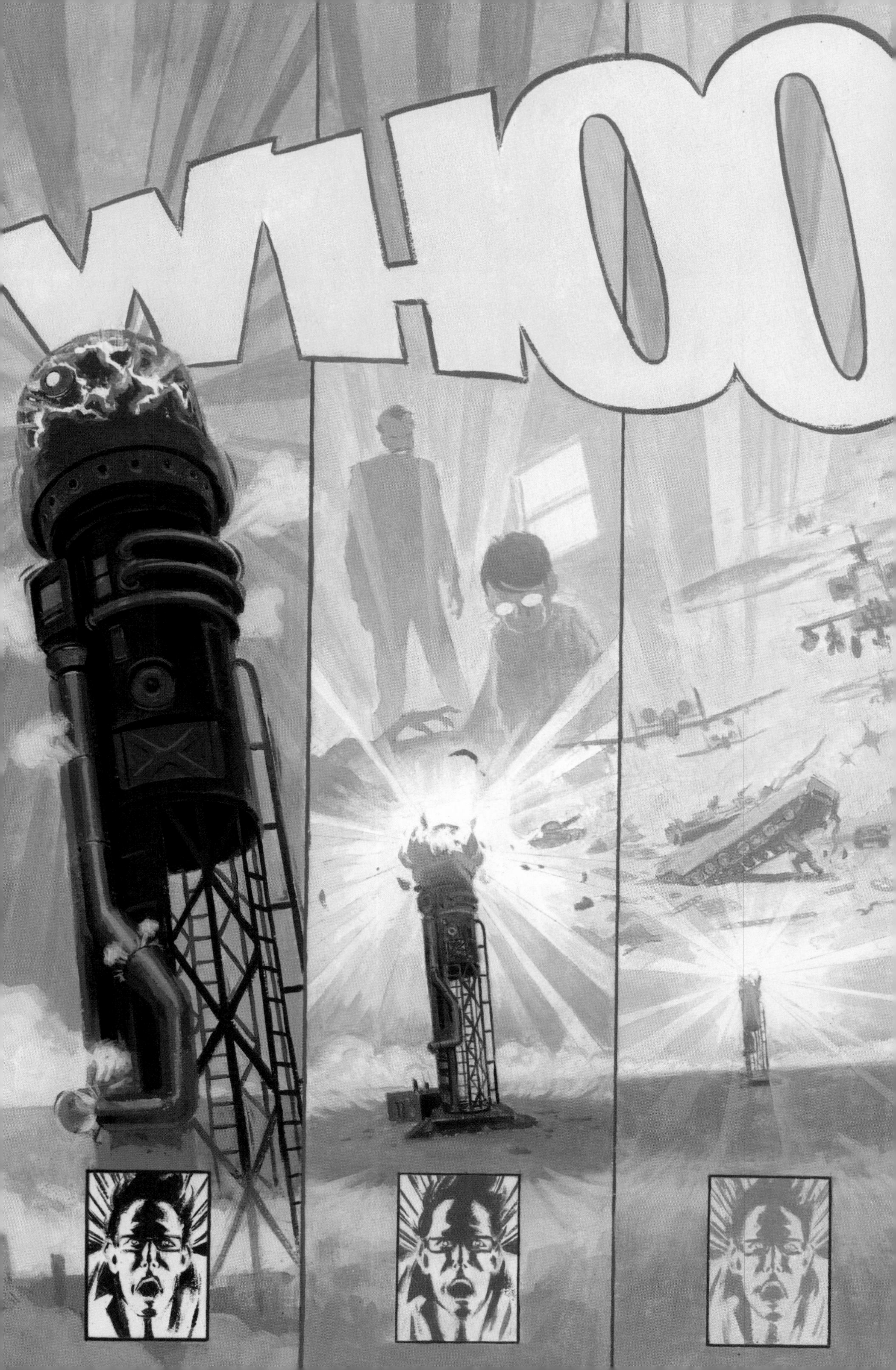
WHOO

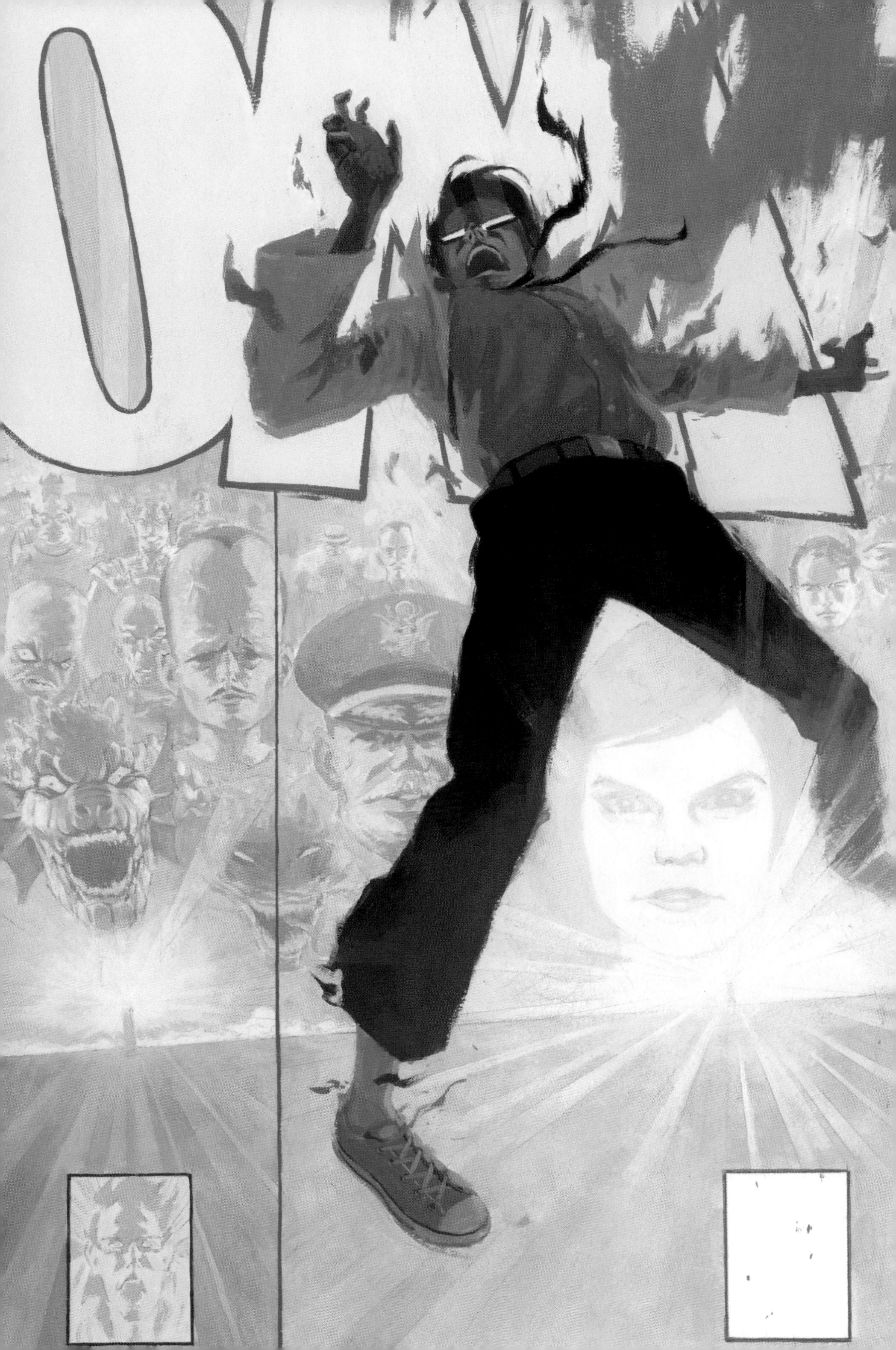

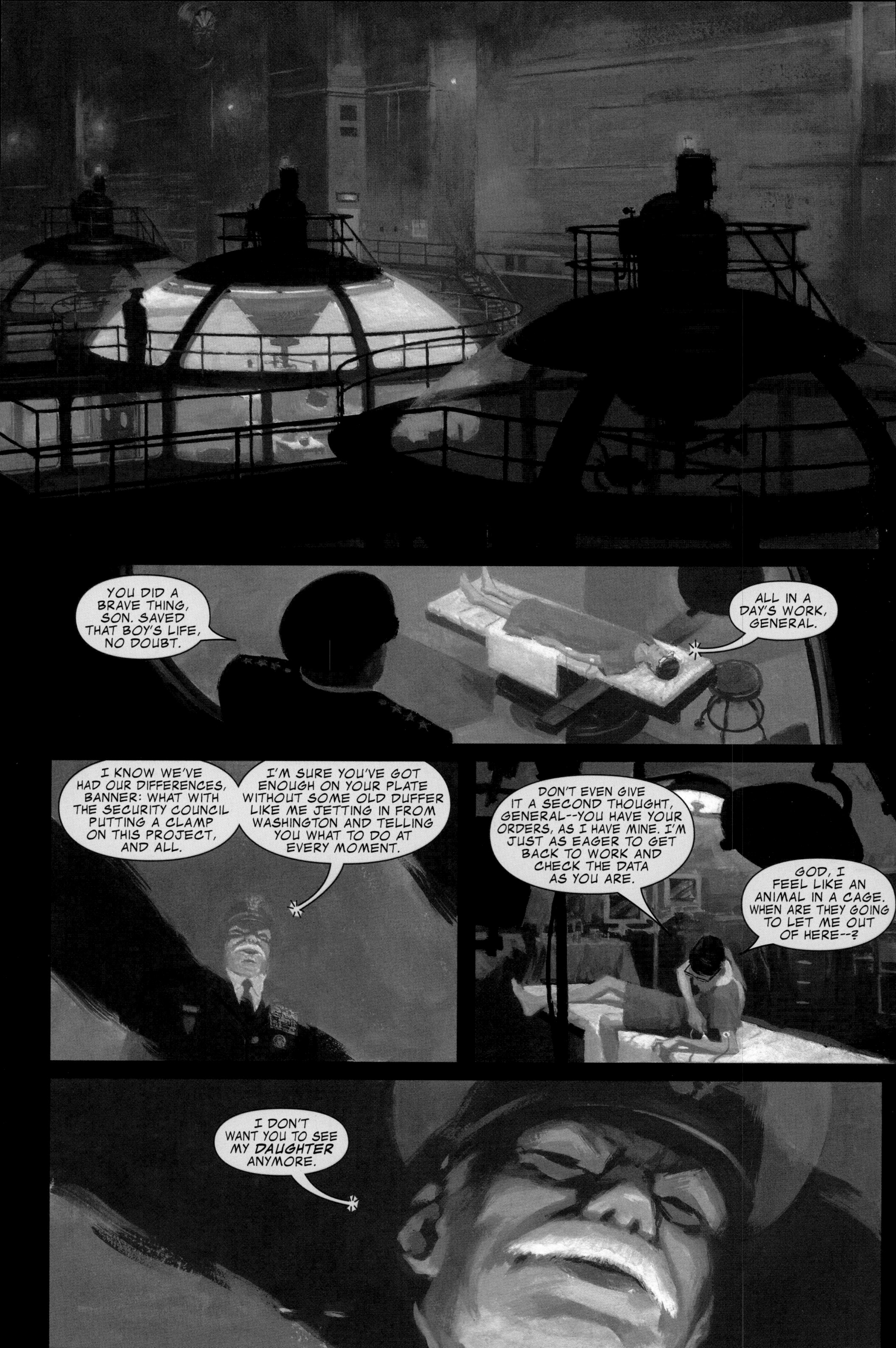
YOU DID A BRAVE THING, SON. SAVED THAT BOY'S LIFE, NO DOUBT.
ALL IN A DAY'S WORK, GENERAL.
I KNOW WE'VE HAD OUR DIFFERENCES, BANNER: WHAT WITH THE SECURITY COUNCIL PUTTING A CLAMP ON THIS PROJECT, AND ALL.
I'M SURE YOU'VE GOT ENOUGH ON YOUR PLATE WITHOUT SOME OLD DUFFER LIKE ME JETTING IN FROM WASHINGTON AND TELLING YOU WHAT TO DO AT EVERY MOMENT.
DON'T EVEN GIVE IT A SECOND THOUGHT, GENERAL--YOU HAVE YOUR ORDERS, AS I HAVE MINE. I'M JUST AS EAGER TO GET BACK TO WORK AND CHECK THE DATA AS YOU ARE.
GOD, I FEEL LIKE AN ANIMAL IN A CAGE. WHEN ARE THEY GOING TO LET ME OUT OF HERE--?
I DON'T WANT YOU TO SEE MY *DAUGHTER* ANYMORE.

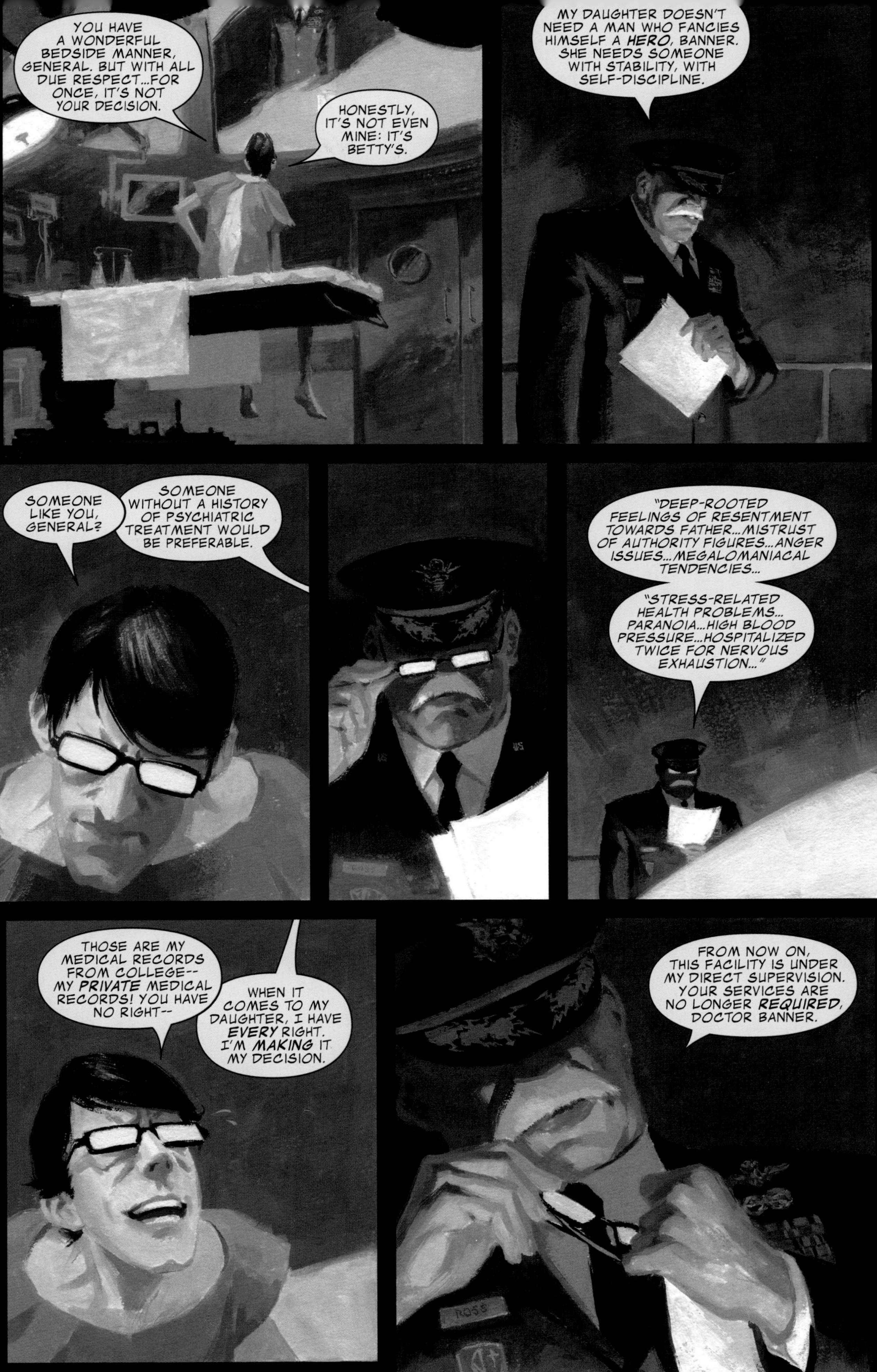
YOU HAVE A WONDERFUL BEDSIDE MANNER, GENERAL. BUT WITH ALL DUE RESPECT...FOR ONCE, IT'S NOT YOUR DECISION.
HONESTLY, IT'S NOT EVEN MINE: IT'S BETTY'S.
MY DAUGHTER DOESN'T NEED A MAN WHO FANCIES HIMSELF A *HERO*, BANNER. SHE NEEDS SOMEONE WITH STABILITY, WITH SELF-DISCIPLINE.
SOMEONE LIKE YOU, GENERAL?
SOMEONE WITHOUT A HISTORY OF PSYCHIATRIC TREATMENT WOULD BE PREFERABLE.
"DEEP-ROOTED FEELINGS OF RESENTMENT TOWARDS FATHER...MISTRUST OF AUTHORITY FIGURES...ANGER ISSUES...MEGALOMANIACAL TENDENCIES...
"STRESS-RELATED HEALTH PROBLEMS... PARANOIA...HIGH BLOOD PRESSURE...HOSPITALIZED TWICE FOR NERVOUS EXHAUSTION..."
THOSE ARE MY MEDICAL RECORDS FROM COLLEGE-- MY *PRIVATE* MEDICAL RECORDS! YOU HAVE NO RIGHT--
WHEN IT COMES TO MY DAUGHTER, I HAVE *EVERY* RIGHT. I'M *MAKING* IT MY DECISION.
FROM NOW ON, THIS FACILITY IS UNDER MY DIRECT SUPERVISION. YOUR SERVICES ARE NO LONGER *REQUIRED*, DOCTOR BANNER.
ROSS

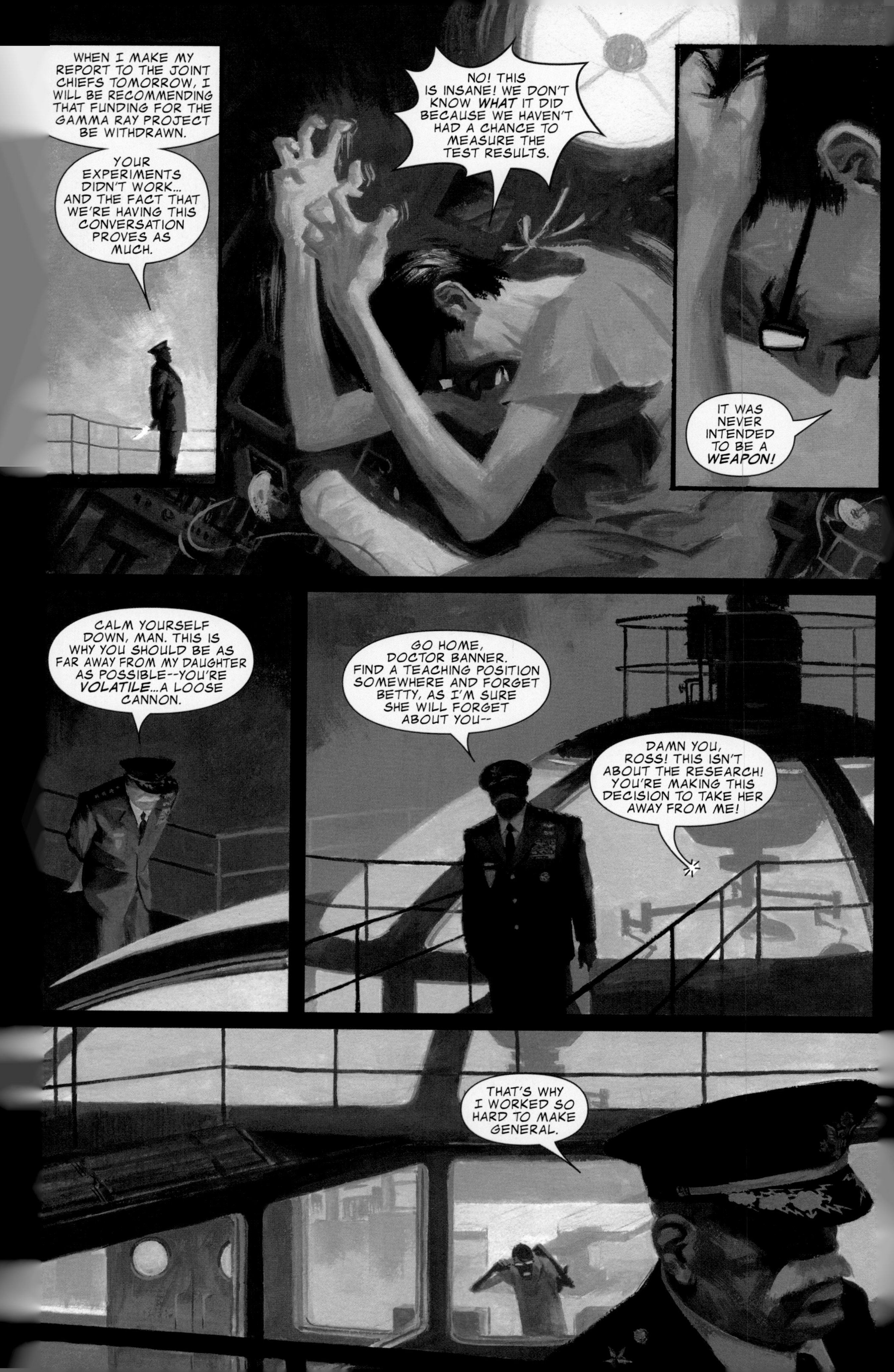
WHEN I MAKE MY REPORT TO THE JOINT CHIEFS TOMORROW, I WILL BE RECOMMENDING THAT FUNDING FOR THE GAMMA RAY PROJECT BE WITHDRAWN.
YOUR EXPERIMENTS DIDN'T WORK... AND THE FACT THAT WE'RE HAVING THIS CONVERSATION PROVES AS MUCH.
NO! THIS IS INSANE! WE DON'T KNOW *WHAT* IT DID BECAUSE WE HAVEN'T HAD A CHANCE TO MEASURE THE TEST RESULTS.
IT WAS NEVER INTENDED TO BE A *WEAPON!*
CALM YOURSELF DOWN, MAN. THIS IS WHY YOU SHOULD BE AS FAR AWAY FROM MY DAUGHTER AS POSSIBLE--YOU'RE *VOLATILE*...A LOOSE CANNON.
GO HOME, DOCTOR BANNER. FIND A TEACHING POSITION SOMEWHERE AND FORGET BETTY, AS I'M SURE SHE WILL FORGET ABOUT YOU--
DAMN YOU, ROSS! THIS ISN'T ABOUT THE RESEARCH! YOU'RE MAKING THIS DECISION TO TAKE HER AWAY FROM ME!
THAT'S WHY I WORKED SO HARD TO MAKE GENERAL.

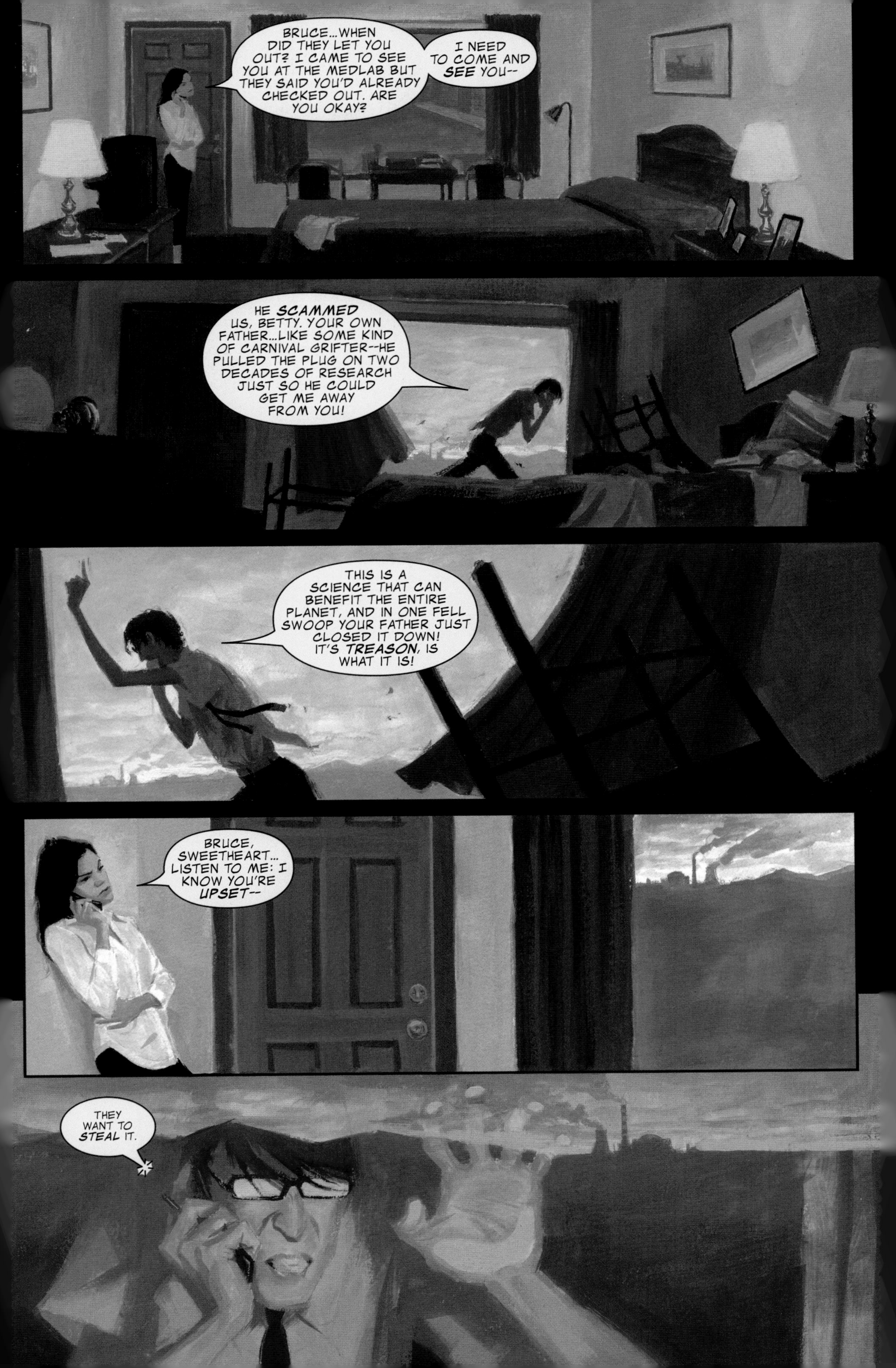
BRUCE...WHEN DID THEY LET YOU OUT? I CAME TO SEE YOU AT THE MEDLAB BUT THEY SAID YOU'D ALREADY CHECKED OUT. ARE YOU OKAY?
I NEED TO COME AND SEE YOU--
HE SCAMMED US, BETTY. YOUR OWN FATHER...LIKE SOME KIND OF CARNIVAL GRIFTER--HE PULLED THE PLUG ON TWO DECADES OF RESEARCH JUST SO HE COULD GET ME AWAY FROM YOU!
THIS IS A SCIENCE THAT CAN BENEFIT THE ENTIRE PLANET, AND IN ONE FELL SWOOP YOUR FATHER JUST CLOSED IT DOWN! IT'S TREASON, IS WHAT IT IS!
BRUCE, SWEETHEART... LISTEN TO ME: I KNOW YOU'RE UPSET--
THEY WANT TO STEAL IT.

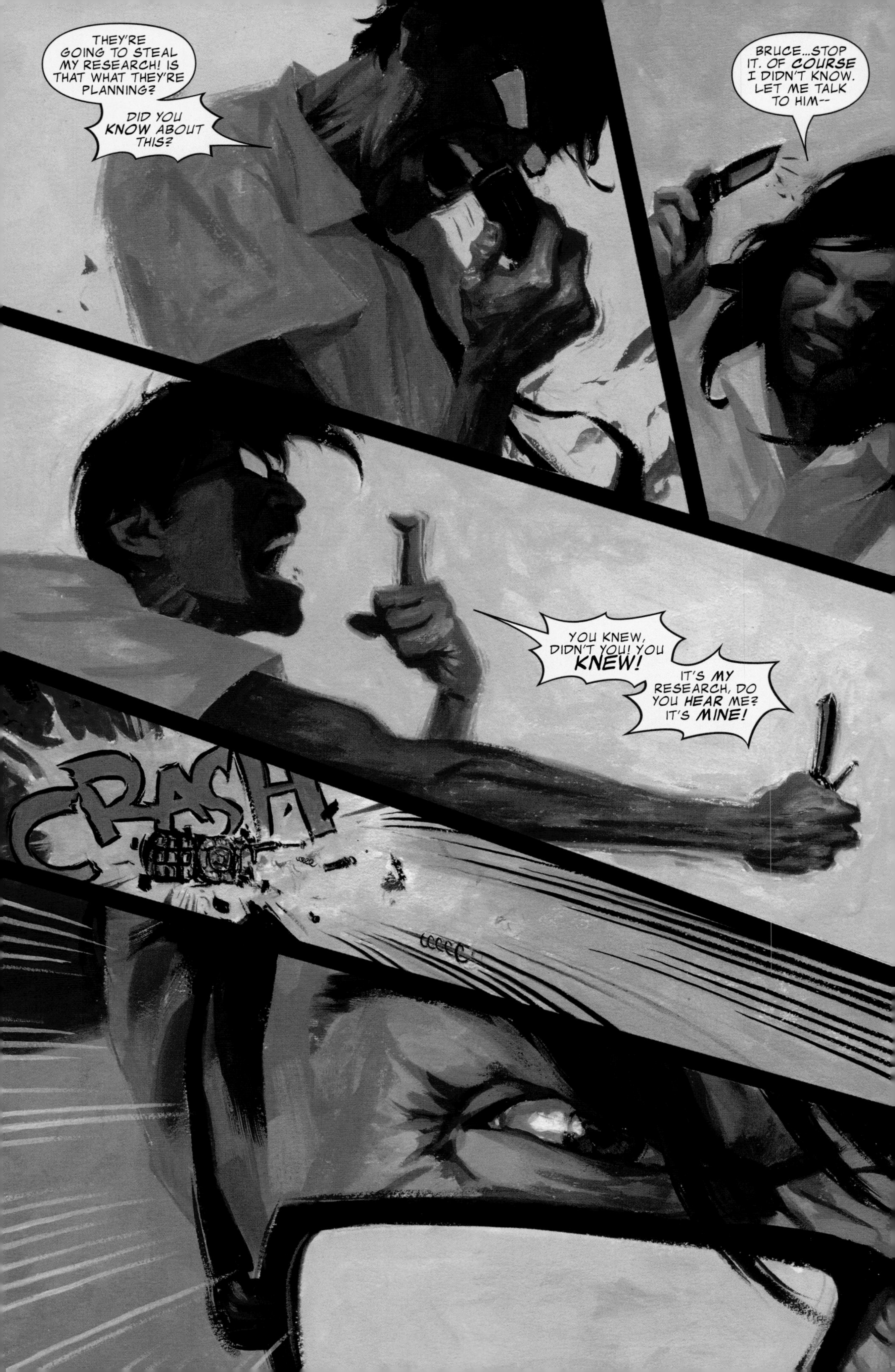
THEY'RE GOING TO STEAL MY RESEARCH! IS THAT WHAT THEY'RE PLANNING?
DID YOU KNOW ABOUT THIS?
BRUCE...STOP IT. OF COURSE I DIDN'T KNOW. LET ME TALK TO HIM--
YOU KNEW, DIDN'T YOU! YOU KNEW!
IT'S MY RESEARCH, DO YOU HEAR ME? IT'S MINE!
CRASH

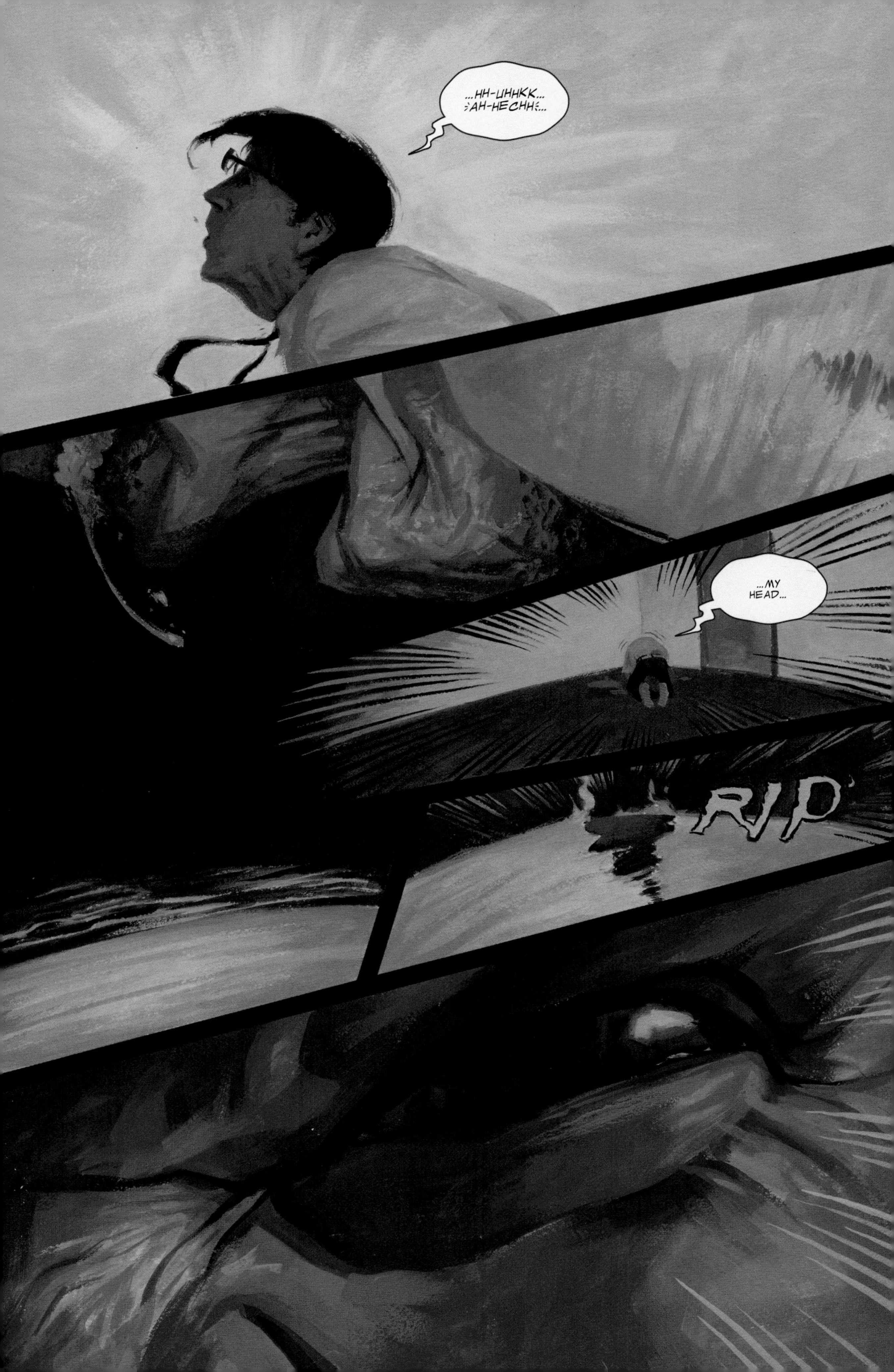
...HH-UHHKK...
AH-HECHH...
...MY HEAD...
RIP

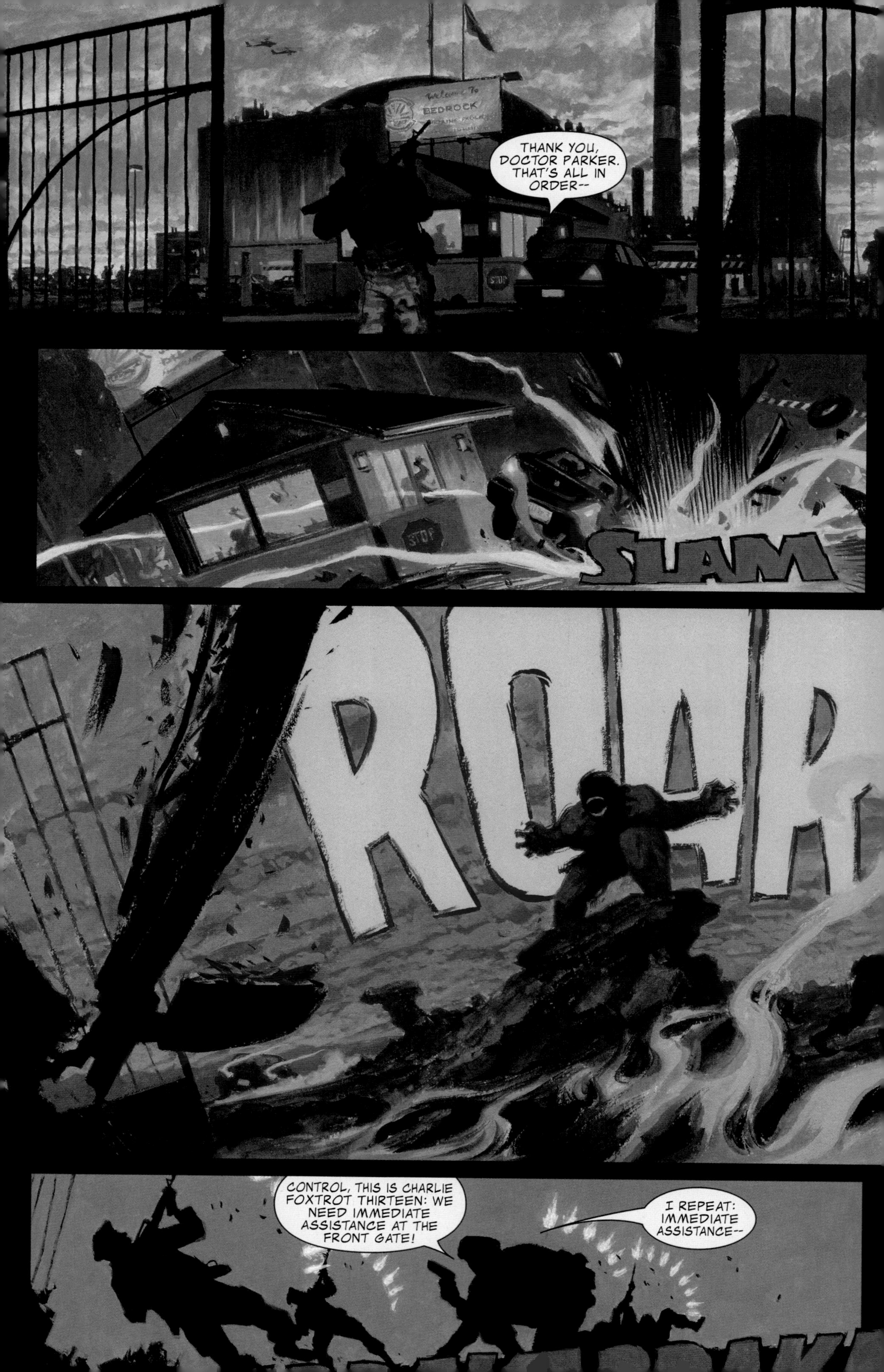
BEDROCK
THANK YOU, DOCTOR PARKER. THAT'S ALL IN ORDER--
STOP
SLAM
ROAR
CONTROL, THIS IS CHARLIE FOXTROT THIRTEEN: WE NEED IMMEDIATE ASSISTANCE AT THE FRONT GATE!
I REPEAT: IMMEDIATE ASSISTANCE--

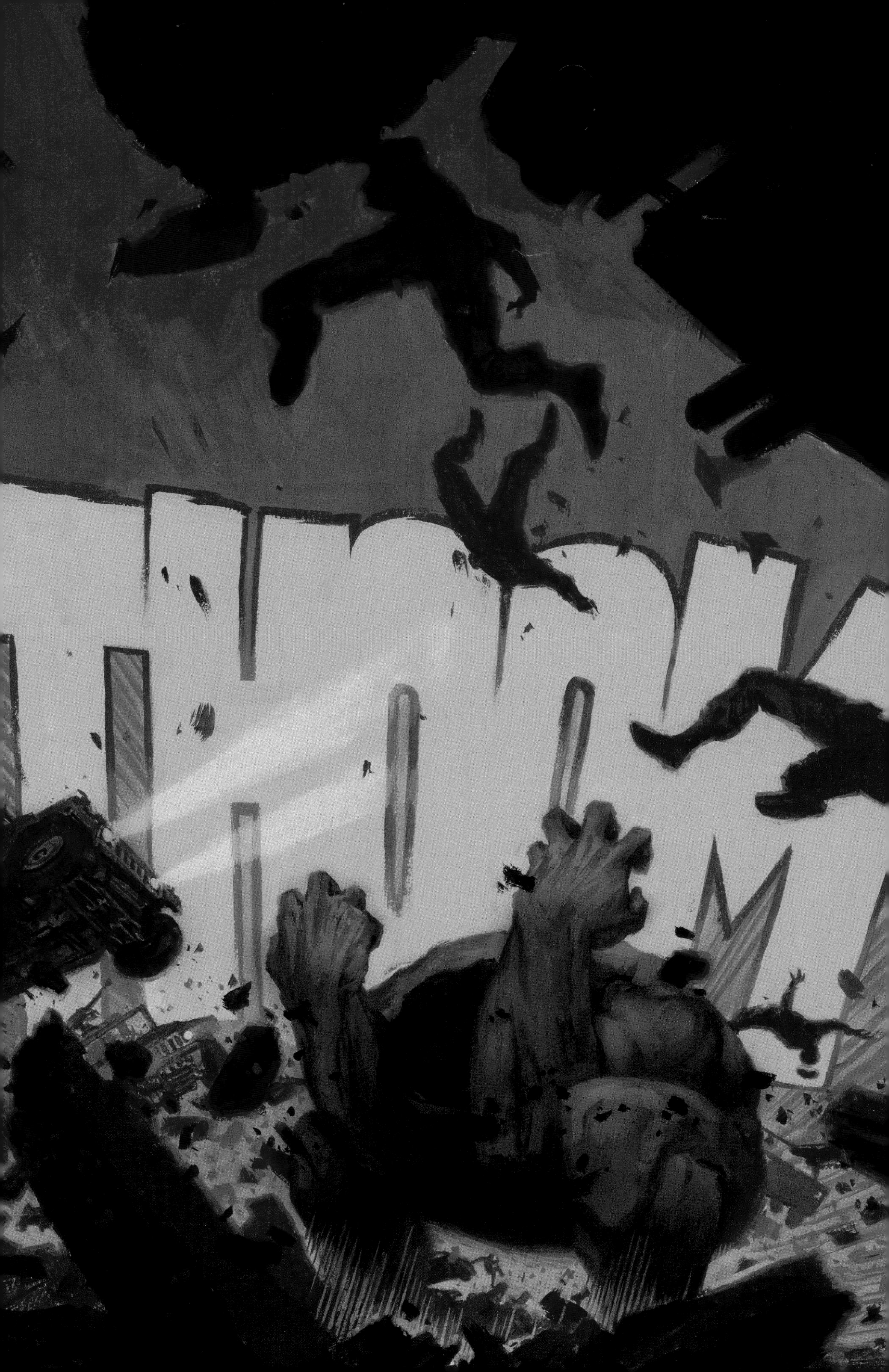

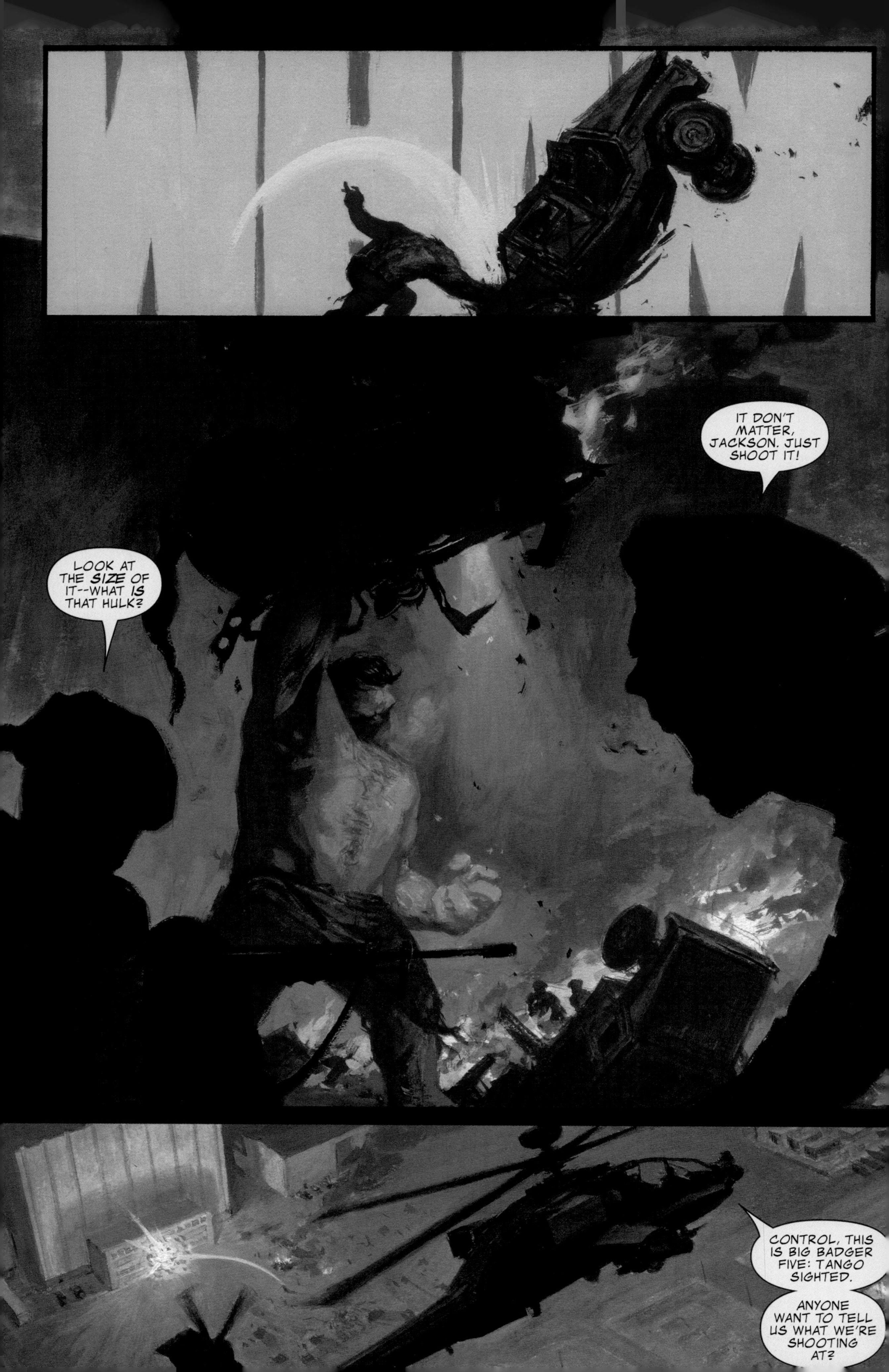
IT DON'T MATTER, JACKSON. JUST SHOOT IT!
LOOK AT THE SIZE OF IT--WHAT IS THAT HULK?
CONTROL, THIS IS BIG BADGER FIVE: TANGO SIGHTED.
ANYONE WANT TO TELL US WHAT WE'RE SHOOTING AT?

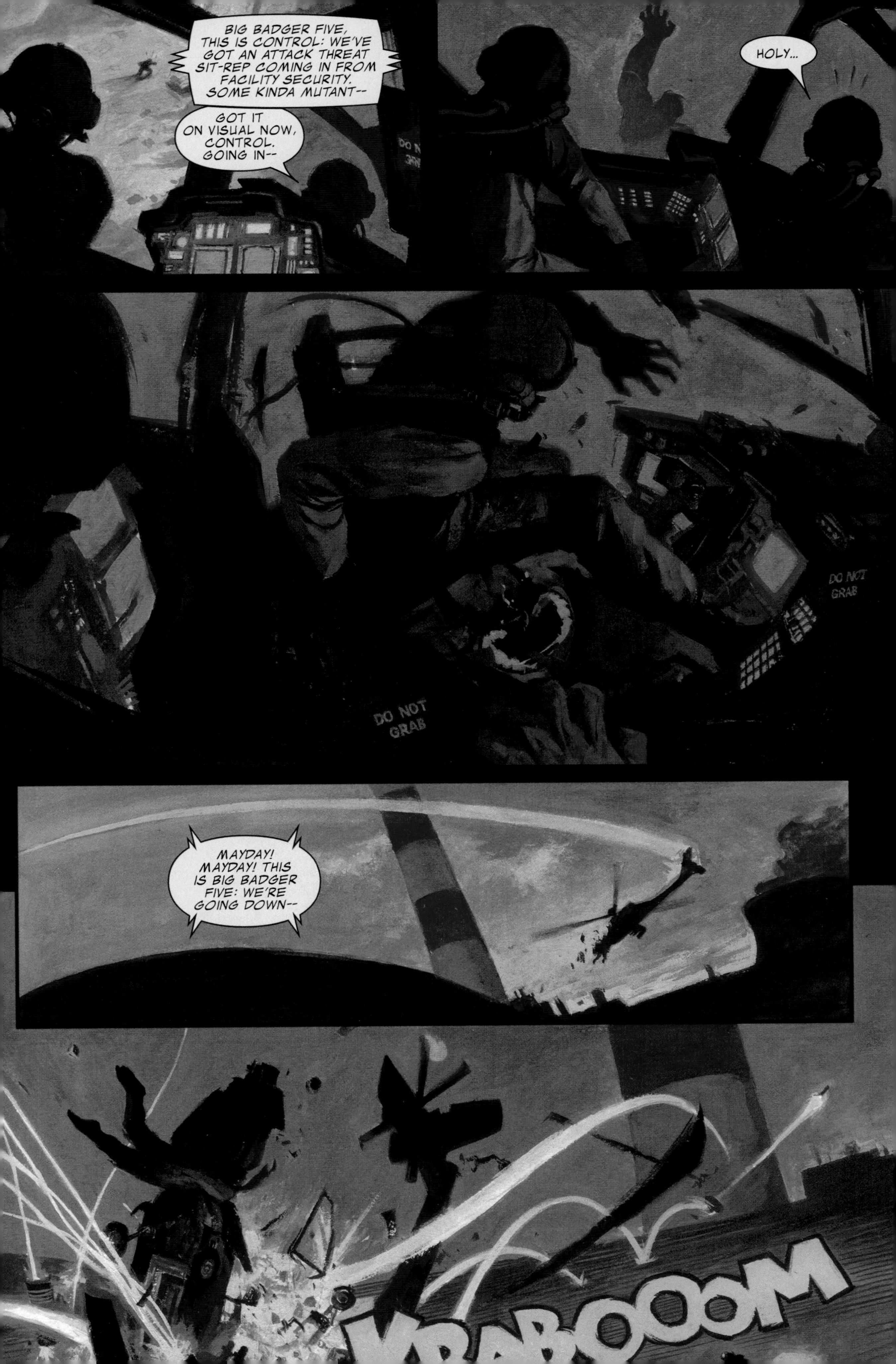
BIG BADGER FIVE, THIS IS CONTROL: WE'VE GOT AN ATTACK THREAT SIT-REP COMING IN FROM FACILITY SECURITY. SOME KINDA MUTANT--
GOT IT ON VISUAL NOW, CONTROL. GOING IN--
HOLY...
DO NOT GRAB
DO NOT GRAB
MAYDAY! MAYDAY! THIS IS BIG BADGER FIVE: WE'RE GOING DOWN--
KRABOOOM

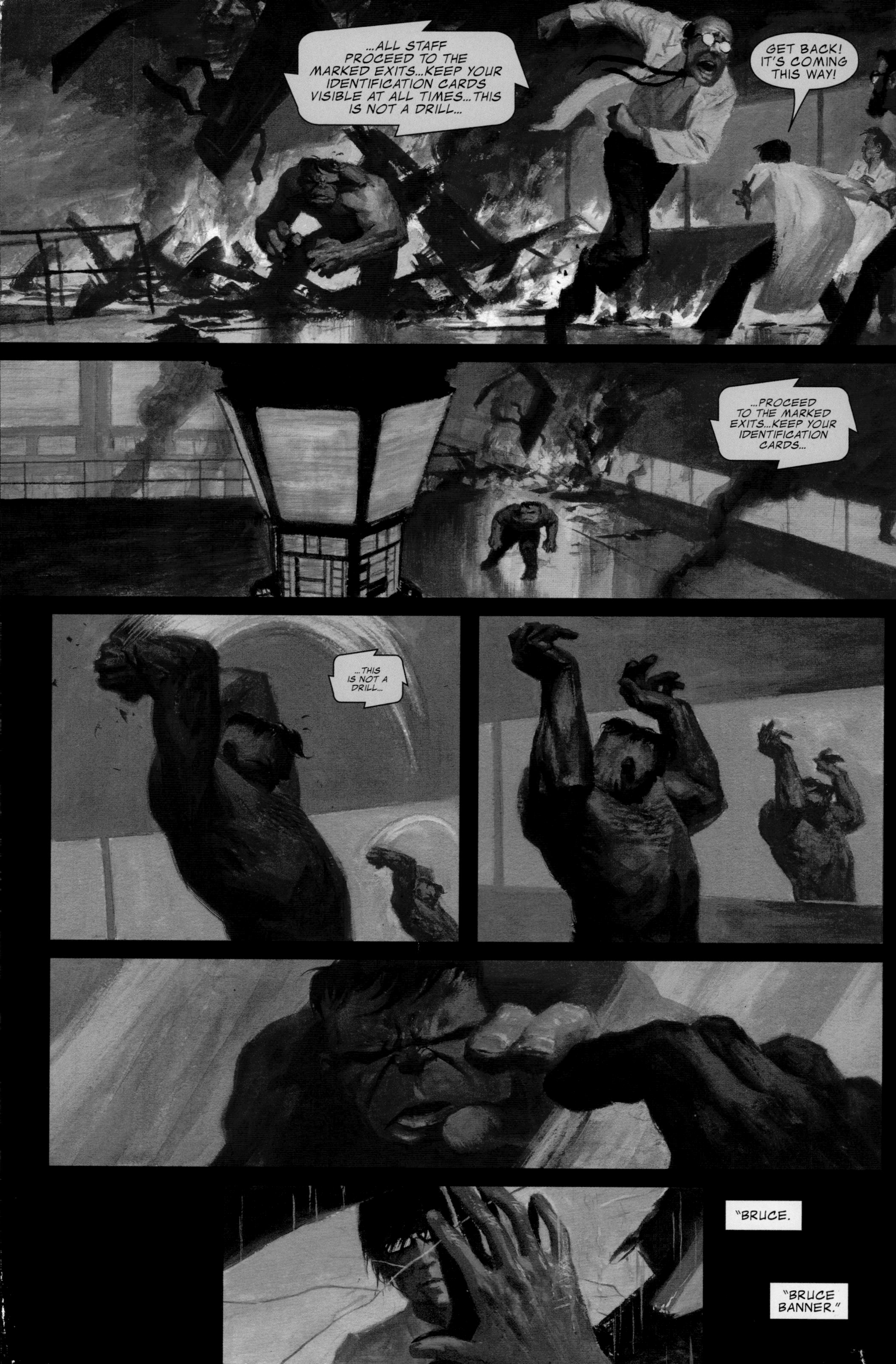
...ALL STAFF PROCEED TO THE MARKED EXITS...KEEP YOUR IDENTIFICATION CARDS VISIBLE AT ALL TIMES...THIS IS NOT A DRILL...
GET BACK! IT'S COMING THIS WAY!
...PROCEED TO THE MARKED EXITS...KEEP YOUR IDENTIFICATION CARDS...
...THIS IS NOT A DRILL...
"BRUCE.
"BRUCE BANNER."

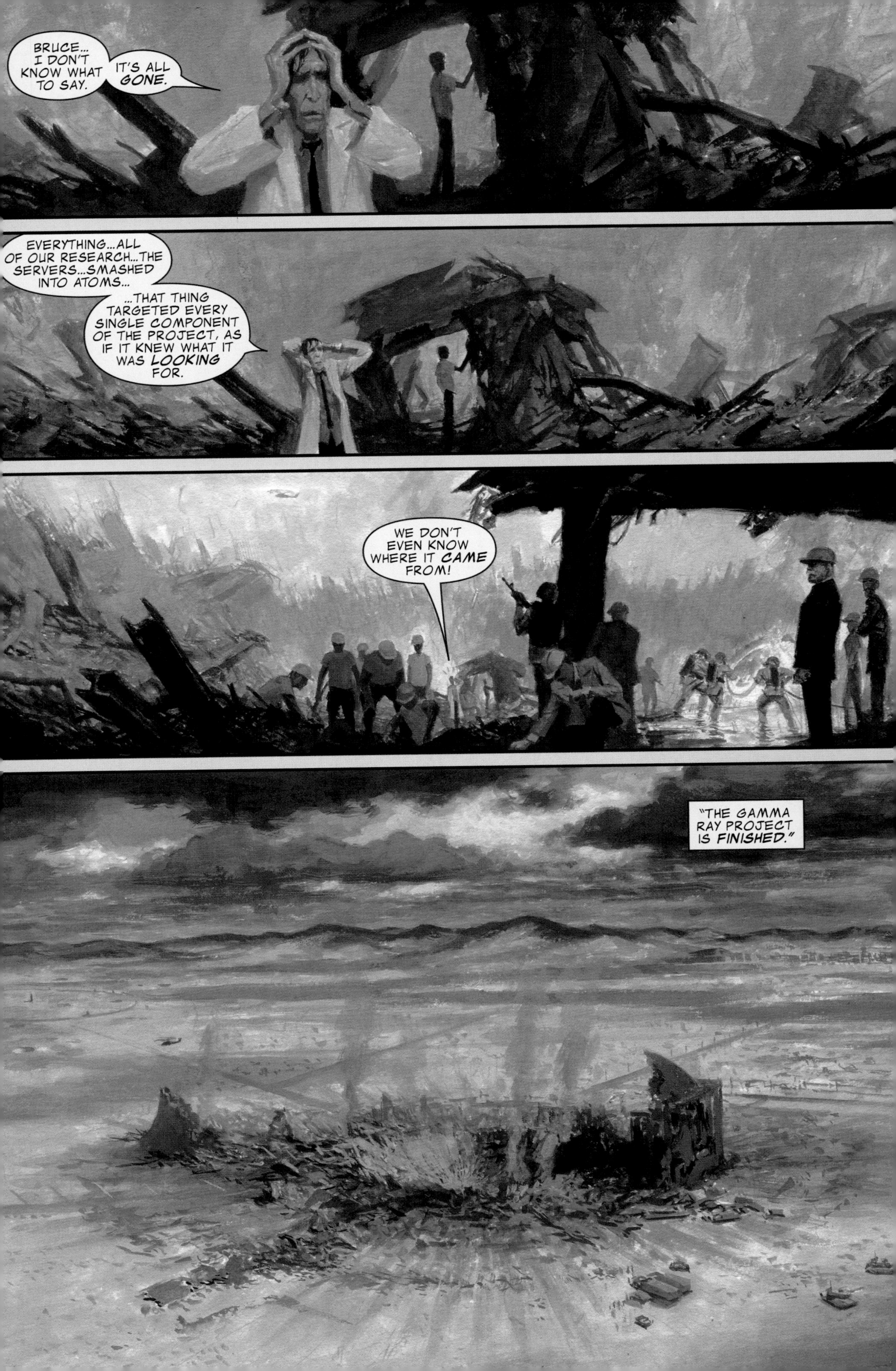
BRUCE... I DON'T KNOW WHAT TO SAY.
IT'S ALL GONE.
EVERYTHING...ALL OF OUR RESEARCH...THE SERVERS...SMASHED INTO ATOMS...
...THAT THING TARGETED EVERY SINGLE COMPONENT OF THE PROJECT, AS IF IT KNEW WHAT IT WAS LOOKING FOR.
WE DON'T EVEN KNOW WHERE IT CAME FROM!
"THE GAMMA RAY PROJECT IS FINISHED."

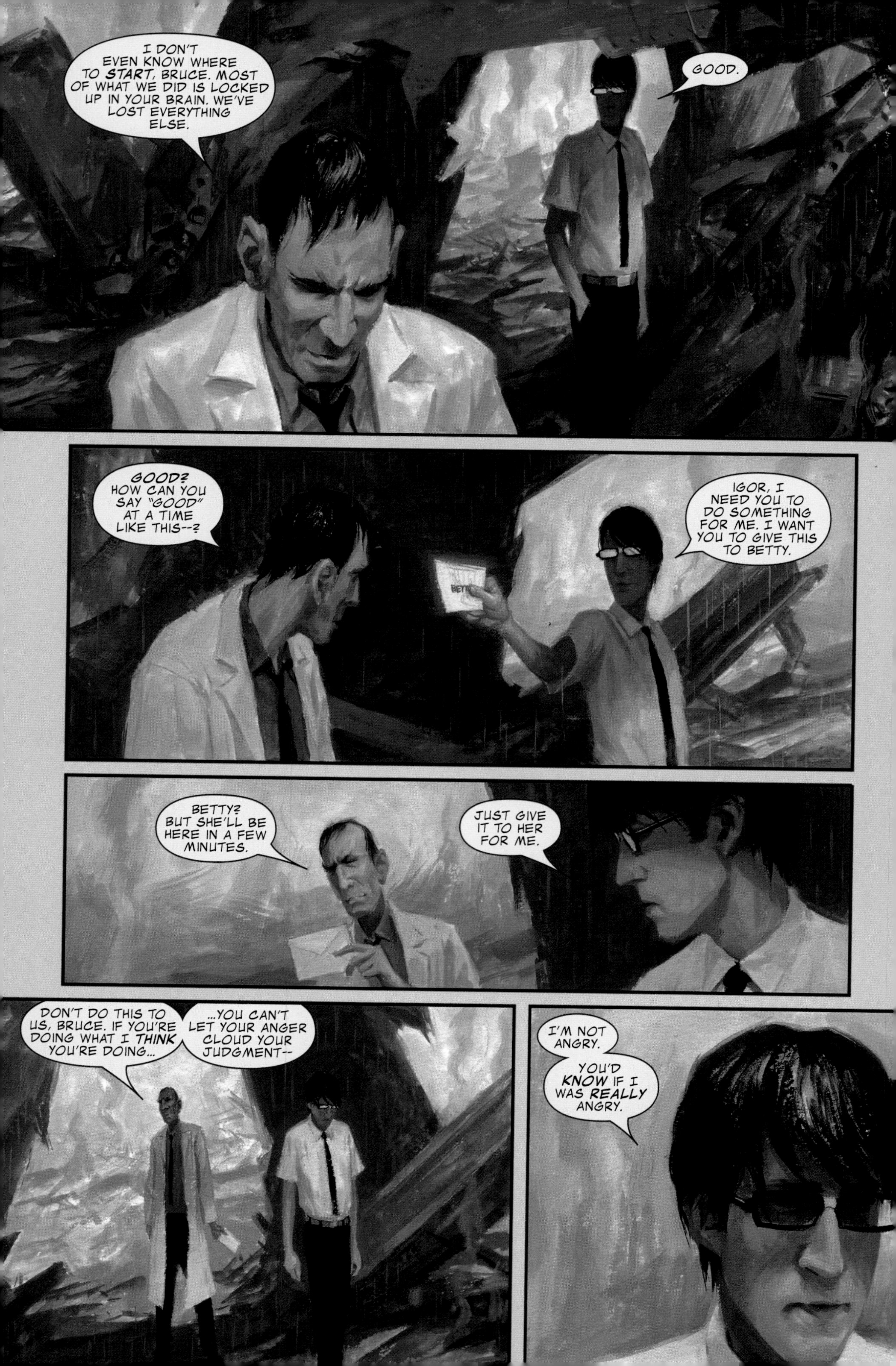

I DON'T EVEN KNOW WHERE TO START, BRUCE. MOST OF WHAT WE DID IS LOCKED UP IN YOUR BRAIN. WE'VE LOST EVERYTHING ELSE.
GOOD.
GOOD? HOW CAN YOU SAY "GOOD" AT A TIME LIKE THIS--?
IGOR, I NEED YOU TO DO SOMETHING FOR ME. I WANT YOU TO GIVE THIS TO BETTY.
BETTY? BUT SHE'LL BE HERE IN A FEW MINUTES.
JUST GIVE IT TO HER FOR ME.
DON'T DO THIS TO US, BRUCE. IF YOU'RE DOING WHAT I THINK YOU'RE DOING...
...YOU CAN'T LET YOUR ANGER CLOUD YOUR JUDGMENT--
I'M NOT ANGRY.
YOU'D KNOW IF I WAS REALLY ANGRY.

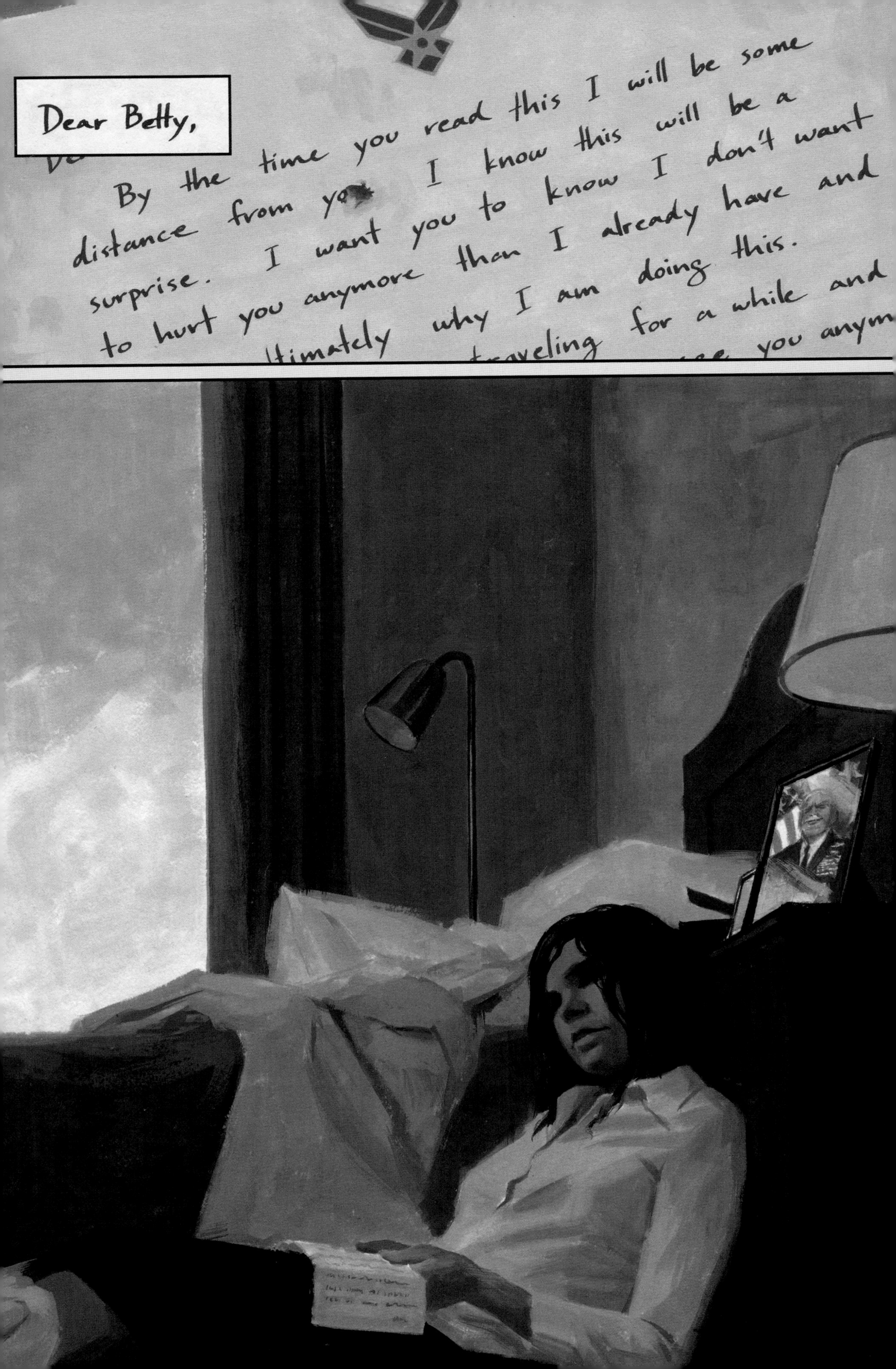
Dear Betty,
By the time you read this I will be some
distance from yo I know this will be a
surprise. I want you to know I don't want
to hurt you anymore than I already have and
ltimately why I am doing this.
traveling for a while and
you anym

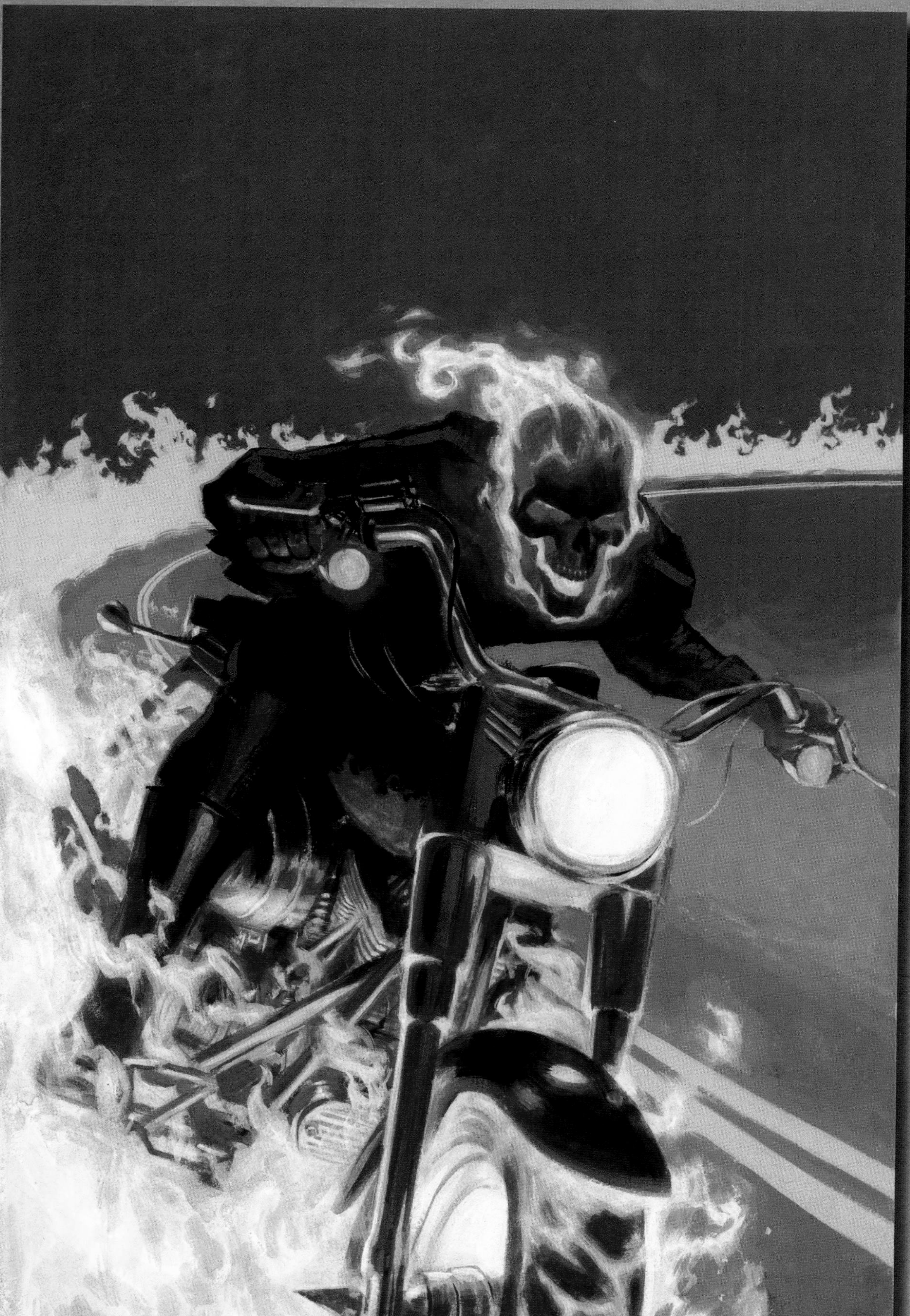

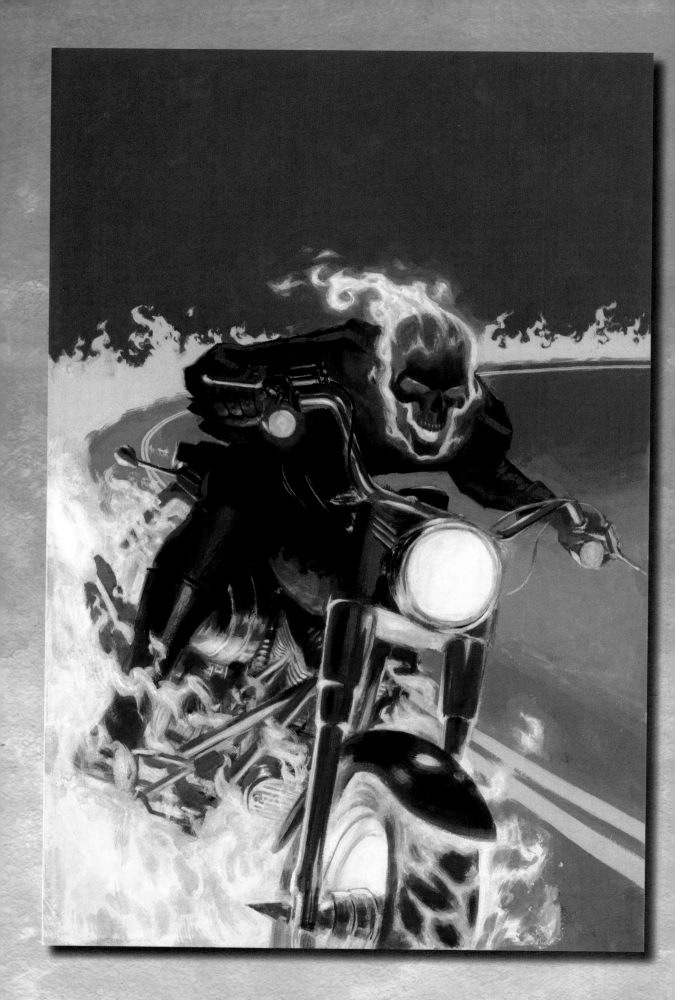

- Ghost Rider -

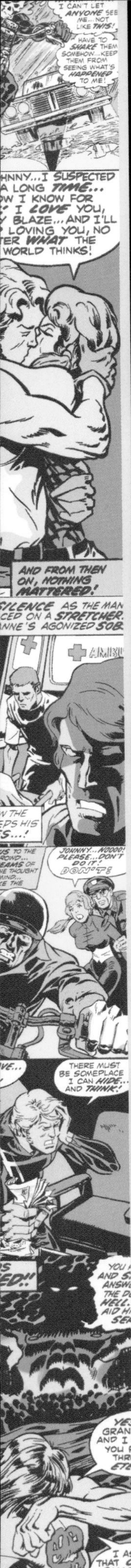

I CAN'T LET ANYONE SEE ME... NOT LIKE THIS!
HAVE TO SHAKE THEM SOMEHOW... KEEP THEM FROM SEEING WHAT'S HAPPENED TO ME!
AND FROM THEN ON, NOTHING MATTERED!
JOHNNY... NOOOO! PLEASE... DON'T DO IT!
THERE MUST BE SOMEPLACE I CAN HIDE... AND THINK!

MYTHOS

The Saga of Johnny Blaze: To save his adoptive father's life, a young cyclist sold his soul to the Devil. But Satan deceived him, and now each night brings an awful transformation. His face bursts into a flaming skull, his strength grows, and his soul is as one with the fiery regions of Hell. The mortal Johnny Blaze becomes...

GHOST RIDER

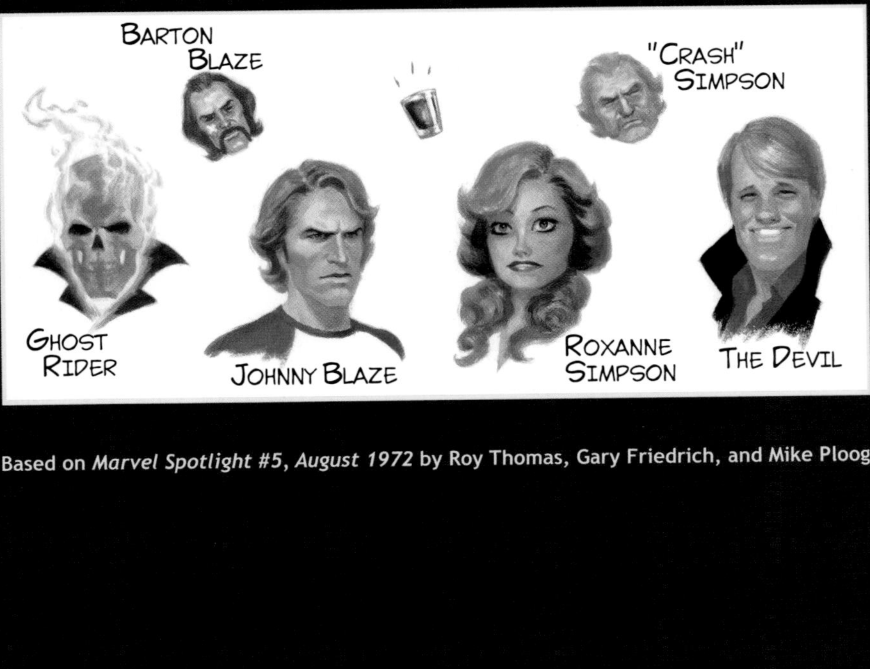

BARTON BLAZE
"CRASH" SIMPSON
GHOST RIDER
JOHNNY BLAZE
ROXANNE SIMPSON
THE DEVIL

Based on *Marvel Spotlight #5, August 1972* by Roy Thomas, Gary Friedrich, and Mike Ploog

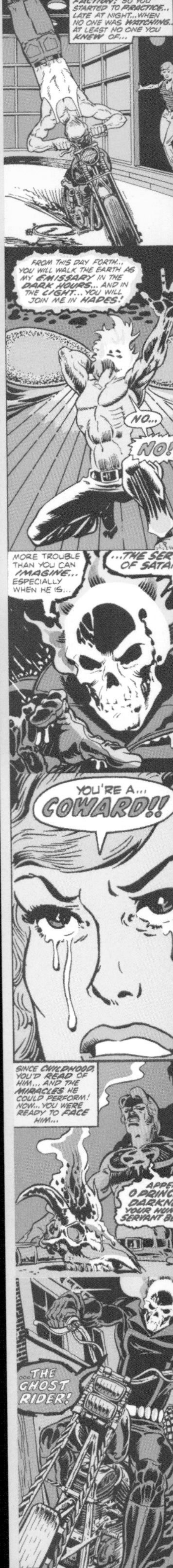

FROM THIS DAY FORTH... YOU WILL WALK THE EARTH AS MY EMISSARY IN THE DARK HOURS... AND IN THE LIGHT... YOU WILL JOIN ME IN HADES!
NO...
NO!
MORE TROUBLE THAN YOU CAN IMAGINE... ESPECIALLY WHEN HE IS...
YOU'RE A... COWARD!!
SINCE CHILDHOOD, YOU'D READ OF HIM... AND THE MIRACLES HE COULD PERFORM! NOW... YOU WERE READY TO FACE HIM...
...THE GHOST RIDER!

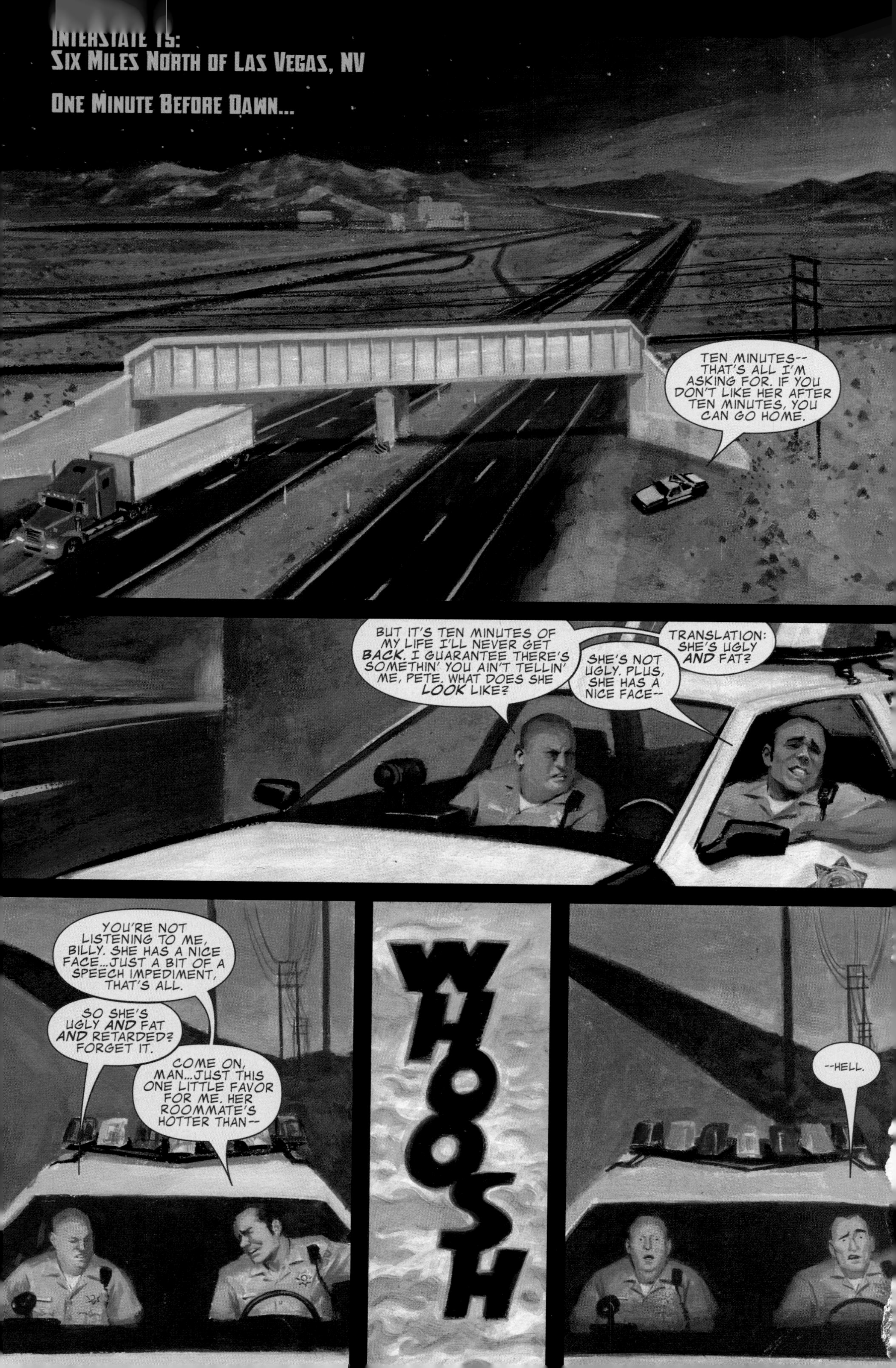
INTERSTATE 15:
SIX MILES NORTH OF LAS VEGAS, NV
ONE MINUTE BEFORE DAWN...
TEN MINUTES-- THAT'S ALL I'M ASKING FOR. IF YOU DON'T LIKE HER AFTER TEN MINUTES, YOU CAN GO HOME.
BUT IT'S TEN MINUTES OF MY LIFE I'LL NEVER GET BACK. I GUARANTEE THERE'S SOMETHIN' YOU AIN'T TELLIN' ME, PETE. WHAT DOES SHE LOOK LIKE?
SHE'S NOT UGLY. PLUS, SHE HAS A NICE FACE--
TRANSLATION: SHE'S UGLY AND FAT?
YOU'RE NOT LISTENING TO ME, BILLY. SHE HAS A NICE FACE...JUST A BIT OF A SPEECH IMPEDIMENT, THAT'S ALL.
SO SHE'S UGLY AND FAT AND RETARDED? FORGET IT.
COME ON, MAN...JUST THIS ONE LITTLE FAVOR FOR ME. HER ROOMMATE'S HOTTER THAN--
WHOOSH
--HELL.

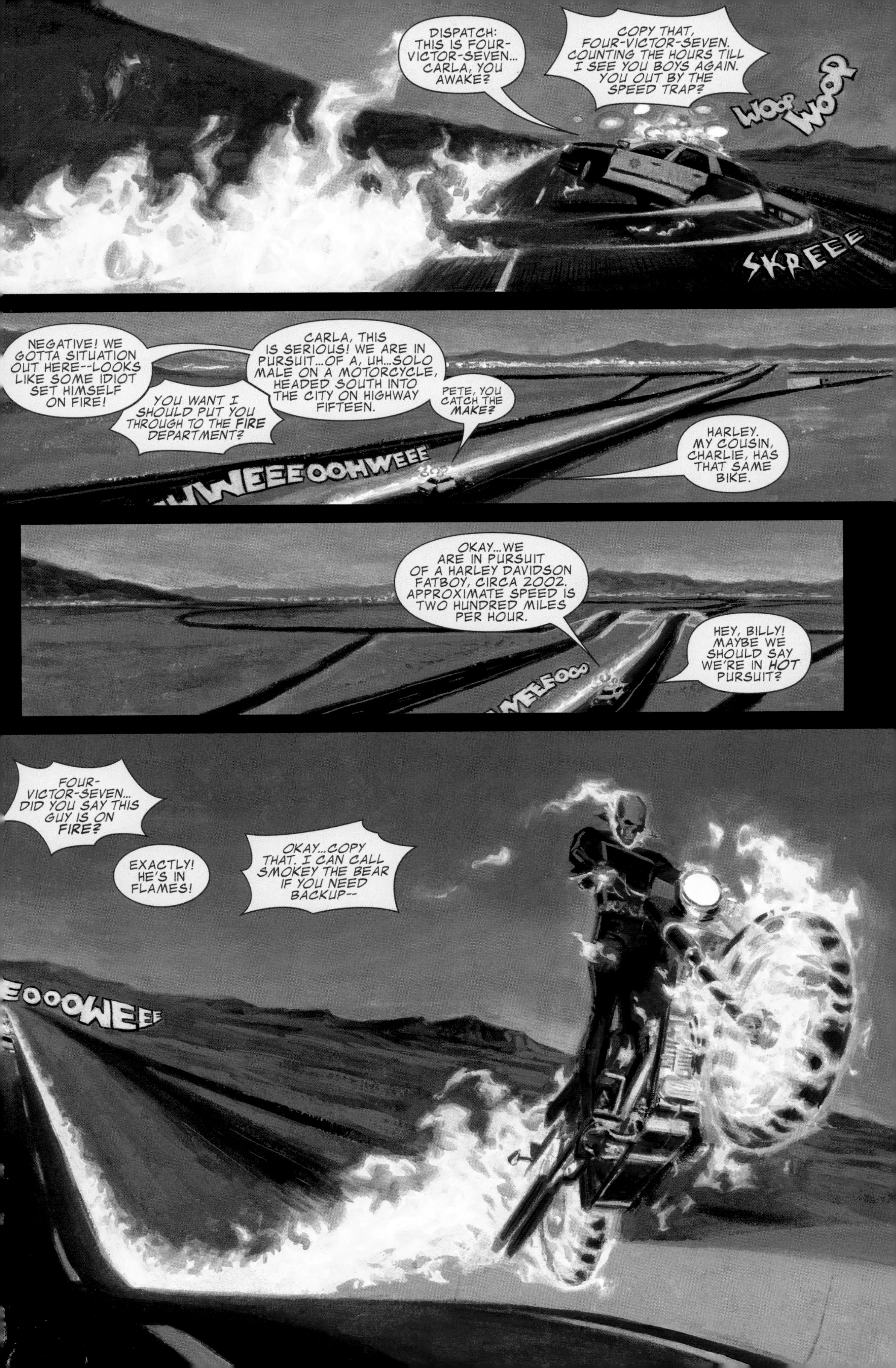
DISPATCH: THIS IS FOUR-VICTOR-SEVEN... CARLA, YOU AWAKE?
COPY THAT, FOUR-VICTOR-SEVEN. COUNTING THE HOURS TILL I SEE YOU BOYS AGAIN. YOU OUT BY THE SPEED TRAP?
WOOP WOOP
SKREEE
NEGATIVE! WE GOTTA SITUATION OUT HERE--LOOKS LIKE SOME IDIOT SET HIMSELF ON FIRE!
YOU WANT I SHOULD PUT YOU THROUGH TO THE FIRE DEPARTMENT?
CARLA, THIS IS SERIOUS! WE ARE IN PURSUIT...OF A, UH...SOLO MALE ON A MOTORCYCLE, HEADED SOUTH INTO THE CITY ON HIGHWAY FIFTEEN.
PETE, YOU CATCH THE MAKE?
HARLEY. MY COUSIN, CHARLIE, HAS THAT SAME BIKE.
HWEEEOOHWEEE
OKAY...WE ARE IN PURSUIT OF A HARLEY DAVIDSON FATBOY, CIRCA 2002. APPROXIMATE SPEED IS TWO HUNDRED MILES PER HOUR.
HEY, BILLY! MAYBE WE SHOULD SAY WE'RE IN HOT PURSUIT?
WEEEOOO
FOUR-VICTOR-SEVEN... DID YOU SAY THIS GUY IS ON FIRE?
EXACTLY! HE'S IN FLAMES!
OKAY...COPY THAT. I CAN CALL SMOKEY THE BEAR IF YOU NEED BACKUP--
EOOOWEEE

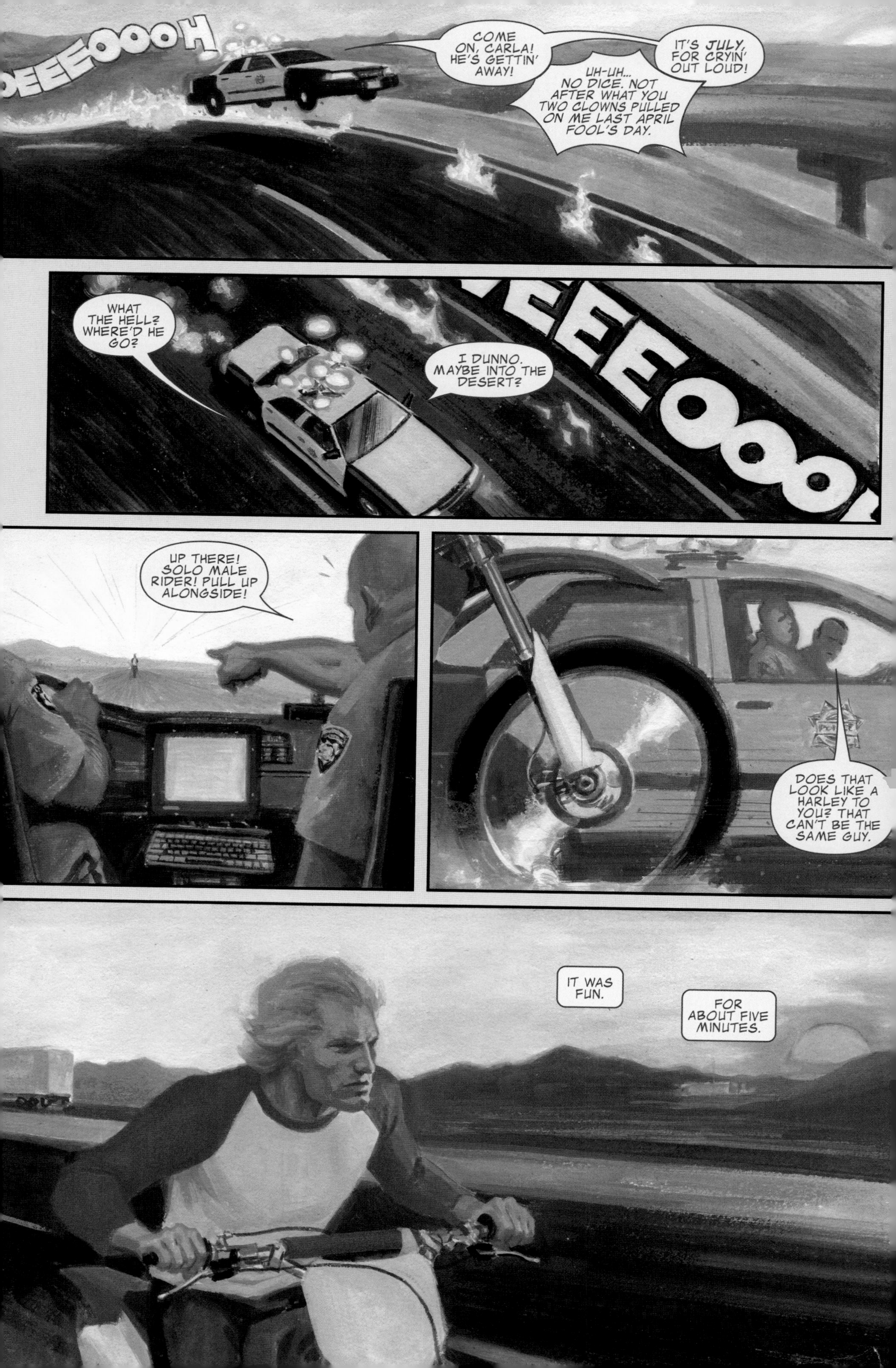
EEEEOOOOH
COME ON, CARLA! HE'S GETTIN' AWAY!
IT'S JULY, FOR CRYIN' OUT LOUD!
UH-UH... NO DICE. NOT AFTER WHAT YOU TWO CLOWNS PULLED ON ME LAST APRIL FOOL'S DAY.
EEEOOOO
WHAT THE HELL? WHERE'D HE GO?
I DUNNO. MAYBE INTO THE DESERT?
UP THERE! SOLO MALE RIDER! PULL UP ALONGSIDE!
DOES THAT LOOK LIKE A HARLEY TO YOU? THAT CAN'T BE THE SAME GUY.
IT WAS FUN.
FOR ABOUT FIVE MINUTES.

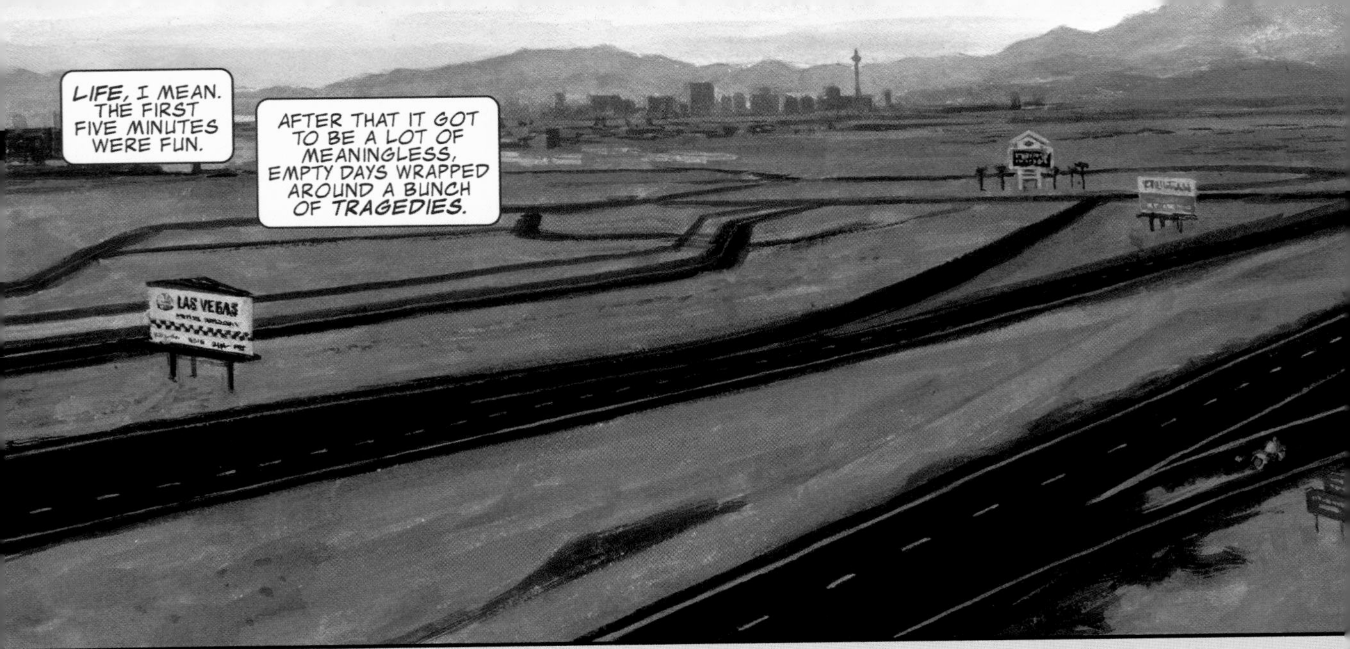

LIFE, I MEAN. THE FIRST FIVE MINUTES WERE FUN.
AFTER THAT IT GOT TO BE A LOT OF MEANINGLESS, EMPTY DAYS WRAPPED AROUND A BUNCH OF TRAGEDIES.
LAS VEGAS

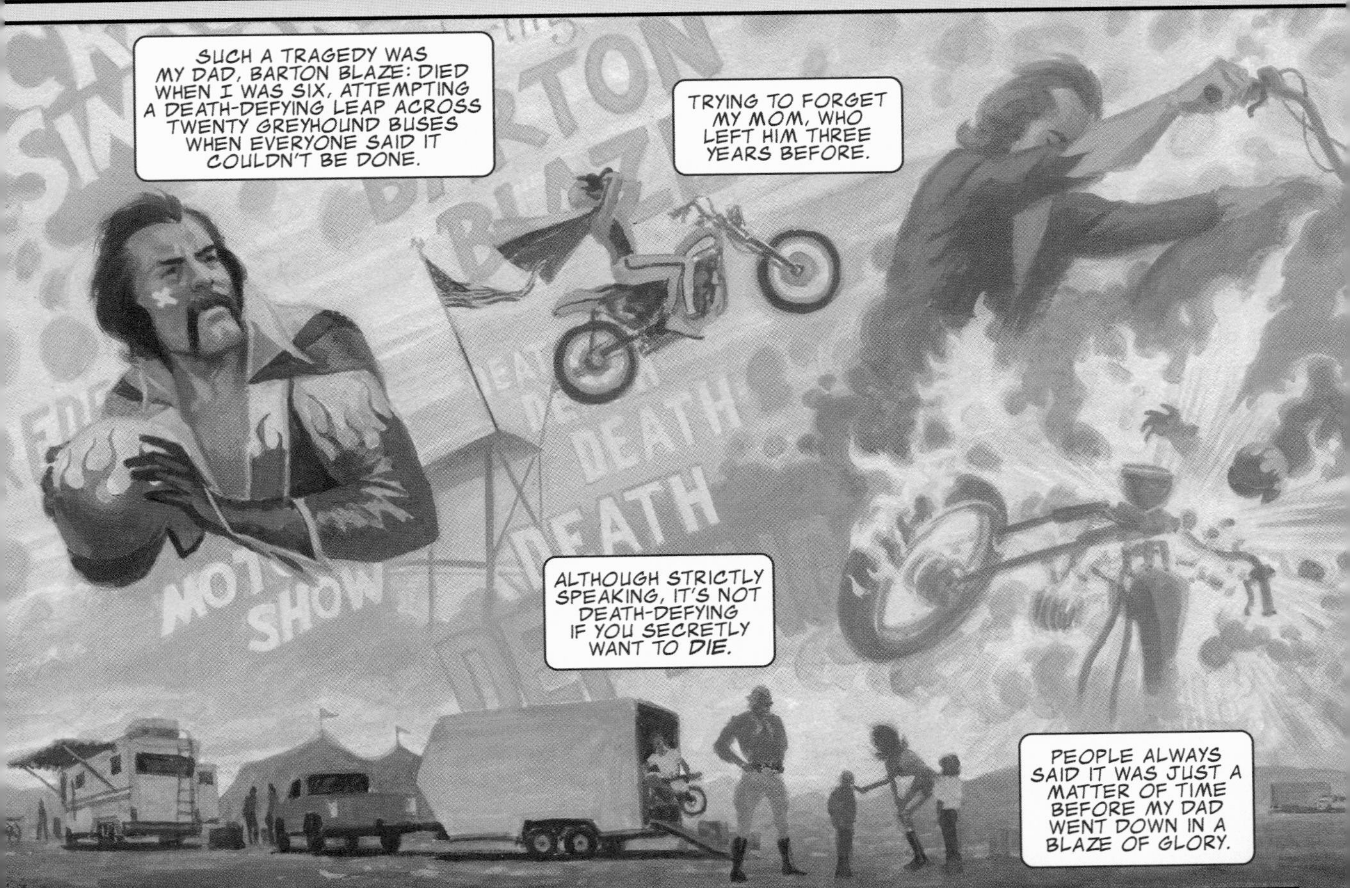

SUCH A TRAGEDY WAS MY DAD, BARTON BLAZE: DIED WHEN I WAS SIX, ATTEMPTING A DEATH-DEFYING LEAP ACROSS TWENTY GREYHOUND BUSES WHEN EVERYONE SAID IT COULDN'T BE DONE.
TRYING TO FORGET MY MOM, WHO LEFT HIM THREE YEARS BEFORE.
DEATH
DEATH
SHOW
ALTHOUGH STRICTLY SPEAKING, IT'S NOT DEATH-DEFYING IF YOU SECRETLY WANT TO DIE.
PEOPLE ALWAYS SAID IT WAS JUST A MATTER OF TIME BEFORE MY DAD WENT DOWN IN A BLAZE OF GLORY.

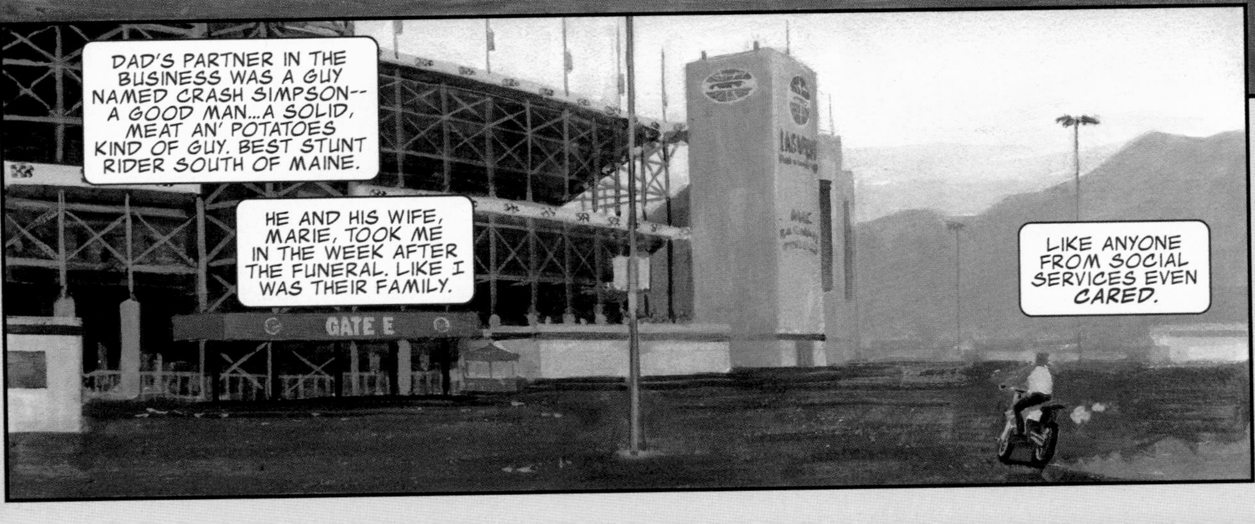

DAD'S PARTNER IN THE BUSINESS WAS A GUY NAMED CRASH SIMPSON--A GOOD MAN...A SOLID, MEAT AN' POTATOES KIND OF GUY. BEST STUNT RIDER SOUTH OF MAINE.
HE AND HIS WIFE, MARIE, TOOK ME IN THE WEEK AFTER THE FUNERAL. LIKE I WAS THEIR FAMILY.
GATE E
LIKE ANYONE FROM SOCIAL SERVICES EVEN CARED.

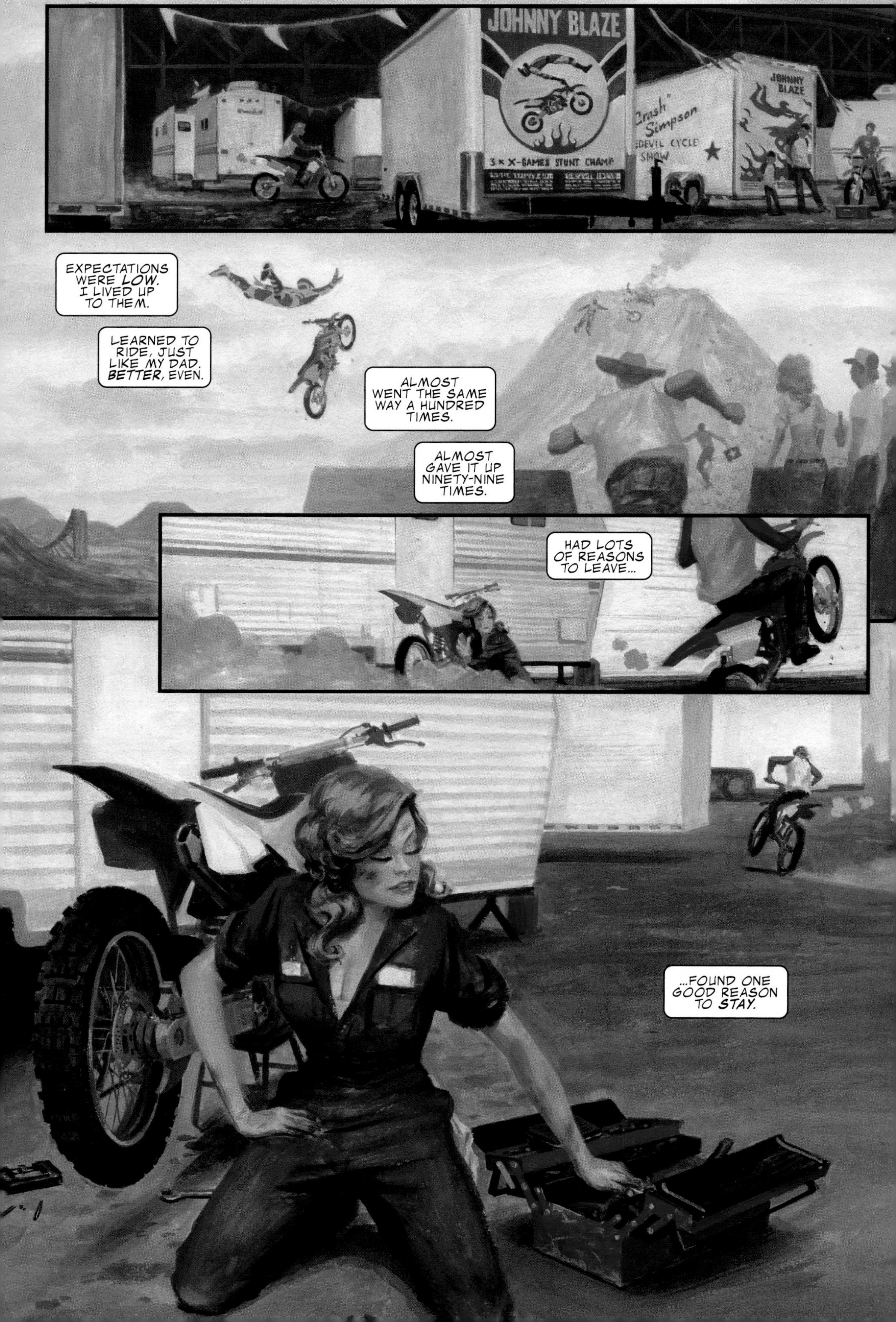
JOHNNY BLAZE
3 × X-GAMES STUNT CHAMP
JOHNNY BLAZE
"Crash" Simpson
SHOW
EXPECTATIONS WERE LOW. I LIVED UP TO THEM.
LEARNED TO RIDE, JUST LIKE MY DAD. BETTER, EVEN.
ALMOST WENT THE SAME WAY A HUNDRED TIMES.
ALMOST GAVE IT UP NINETY-NINE TIMES.
HAD LOTS OF REASONS TO LEAVE...
...FOUND ONE GOOD REASON TO STAY.

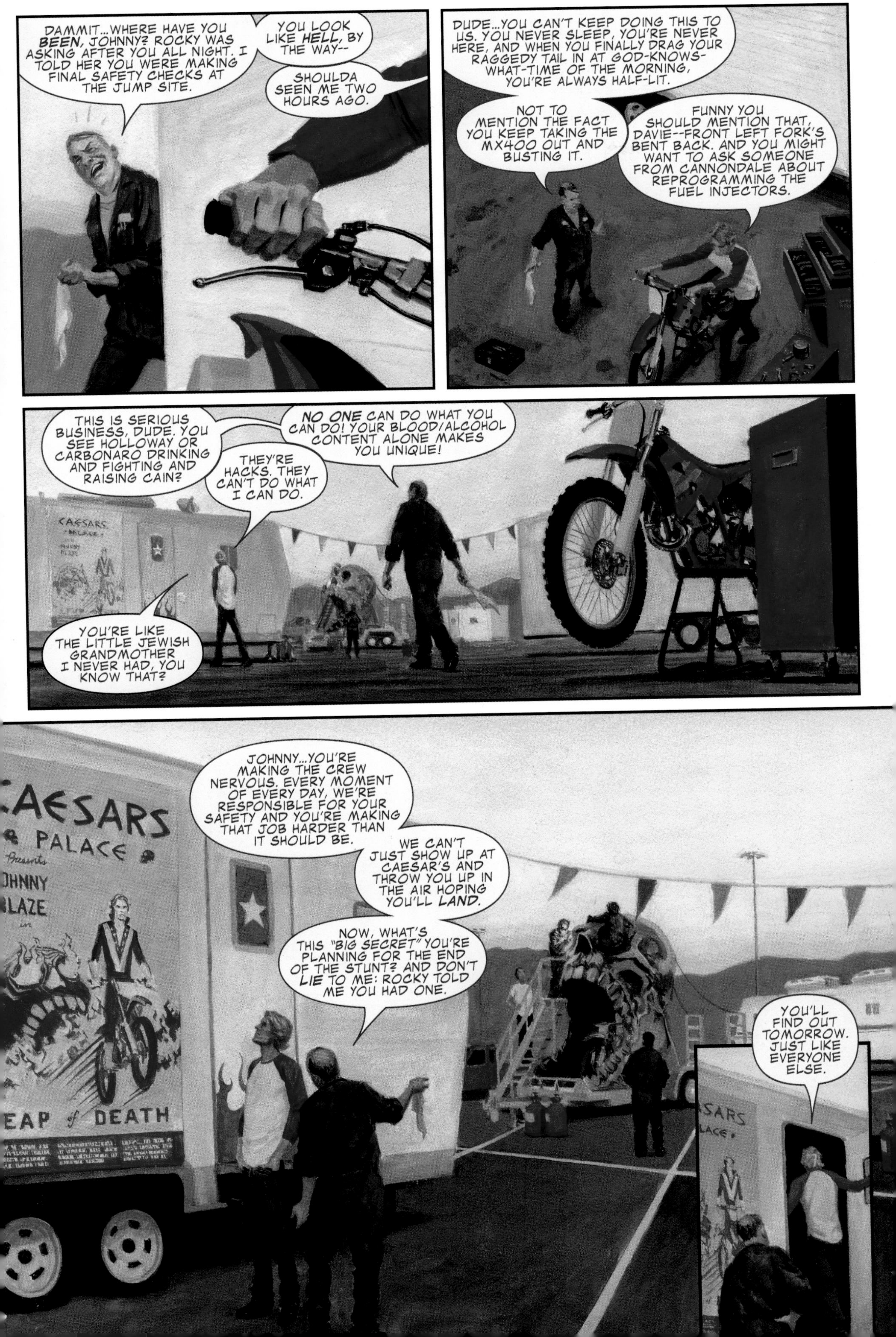
DAMMIT...WHERE HAVE YOU BEEN, JOHNNY? ROCKY WAS ASKING AFTER YOU ALL NIGHT. I TOLD HER YOU WERE MAKING FINAL SAFETY CHECKS AT THE JUMP SITE.
YOU LOOK LIKE HELL, BY THE WAY--
SHOULDA SEEN ME TWO HOURS AGO.
DUDE...YOU CAN'T KEEP DOING THIS TO US. YOU NEVER SLEEP, YOU'RE NEVER HERE, AND WHEN YOU FINALLY DRAG YOUR RAGGEDY TAIL IN AT GOD-KNOWS-WHAT-TIME OF THE MORNING, YOU'RE ALWAYS HALF-LIT.
NOT TO MENTION THE FACT YOU KEEP TAKING THE MX400 OUT AND BUSTING IT.
FUNNY YOU SHOULD MENTION THAT, DAVIE--FRONT LEFT FORK'S BENT BACK. AND YOU MIGHT WANT TO ASK SOMEONE FROM CANNONDALE ABOUT REPROGRAMMING THE FUEL INJECTORS.
THIS IS SERIOUS BUSINESS, DUDE. YOU SEE HOLLOWAY OR CARBONARO DRINKING AND FIGHTING AND RAISING CAIN?
THEY'RE HACKS. THEY CAN'T DO WHAT I CAN DO.
NO ONE CAN DO WHAT YOU CAN DO! YOUR BLOOD/ALCOHOL CONTENT ALONE MAKES YOU UNIQUE!
YOU'RE LIKE THE LITTLE JEWISH GRANDMOTHER I NEVER HAD, YOU KNOW THAT?
AESARS
PALACE
Presents
OHNNY
LAZE
in
EAP of DEATH
JOHNNY...YOU'RE MAKING THE CREW NERVOUS. EVERY MOMENT OF EVERY DAY, WE'RE RESPONSIBLE FOR YOUR SAFETY AND YOU'RE MAKING THAT JOB HARDER THAN IT SHOULD BE.
WE CAN'T JUST SHOW UP AT CAESAR'S AND THROW YOU UP IN THE AIR HOPING YOU'LL LAND.
NOW, WHAT'S THIS "BIG SECRET" YOU'RE PLANNING FOR THE END OF THE STUNT? AND DON'T LIE TO ME: ROCKY TOLD ME YOU HAD ONE.
YOU'LL FIND OUT TOMORROW. JUST LIKE EVERYONE ELSE.

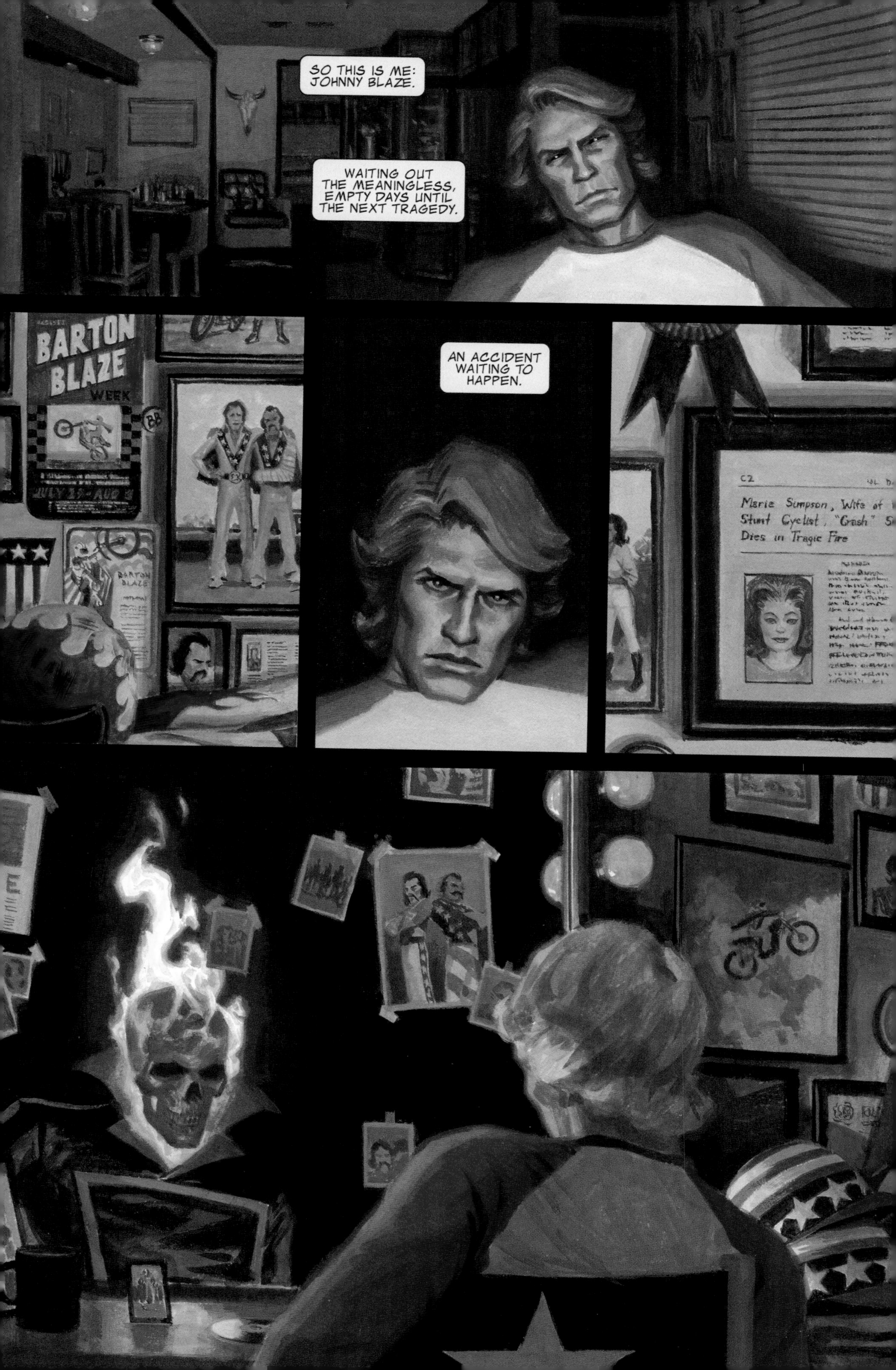
SO THIS IS ME: JOHNNY BLAZE.
WAITING OUT THE MEANINGLESS, EMPTY DAYS UNTIL THE NEXT TRAGEDY.
BARTON BLAZE
WEEK
AN ACCIDENT WAITING TO HAPPEN.
C2
Marie Simpson, Wife of
Stunt Cyclist, "Crash"
Dies in Tragic Fire

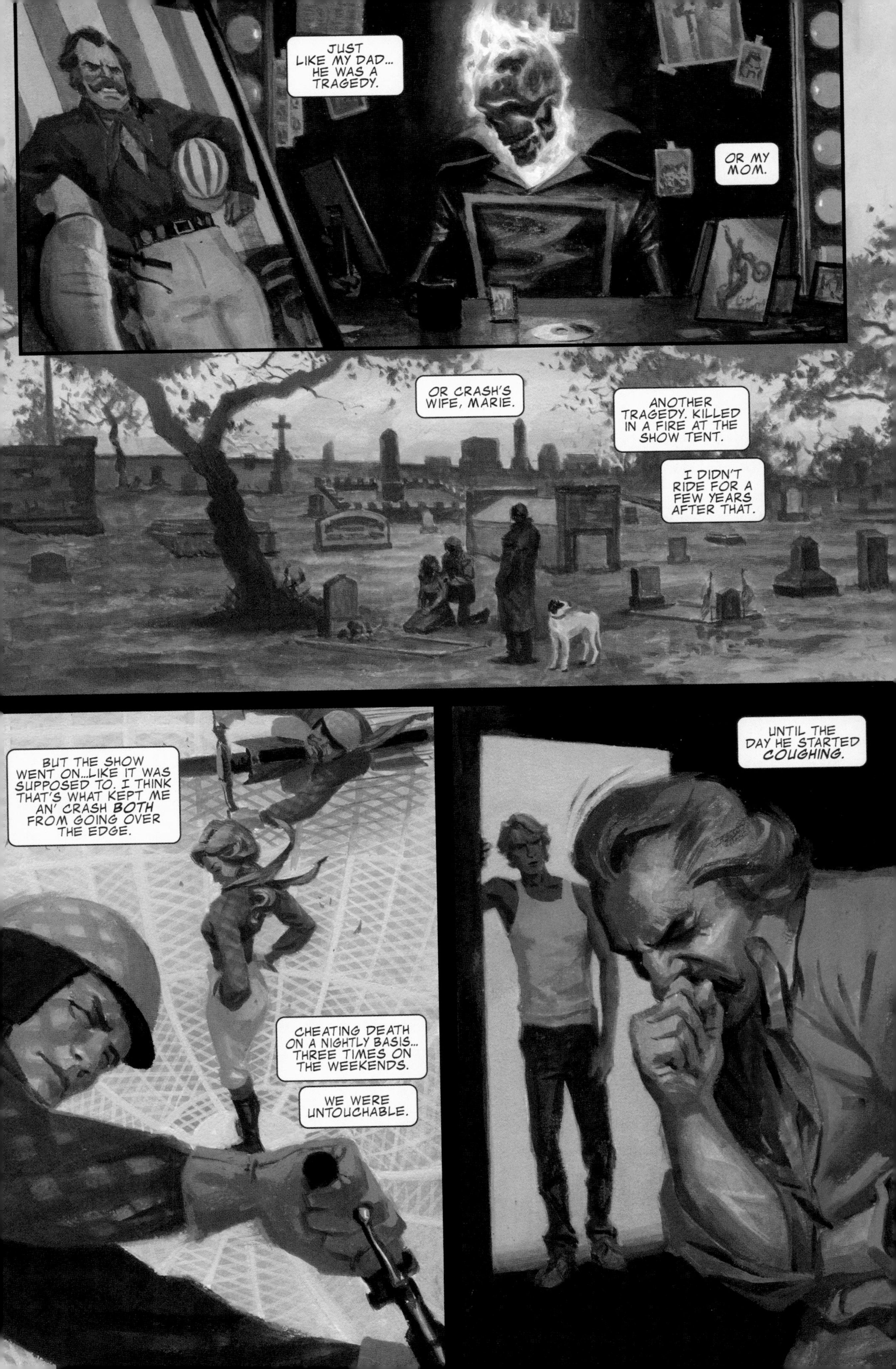
JUST LIKE MY DAD... HE WAS A TRAGEDY.
OR MY MOM.
OR CRASH'S WIFE, MARIE.
ANOTHER TRAGEDY. KILLED IN A FIRE AT THE SHOW TENT.
I DIDN'T RIDE FOR A FEW YEARS AFTER THAT.
BUT THE SHOW WENT ON...LIKE IT WAS SUPPOSED TO. I THINK THAT'S WHAT KEPT ME AN' CRASH BOTH FROM GOING OVER THE EDGE.
CHEATING DEATH ON A NIGHTLY BASIS... THREE TIMES ON THE WEEKENDS.
WE WERE UNTOUCHABLE.
UNTIL THE DAY HE STARTED COUGHING.

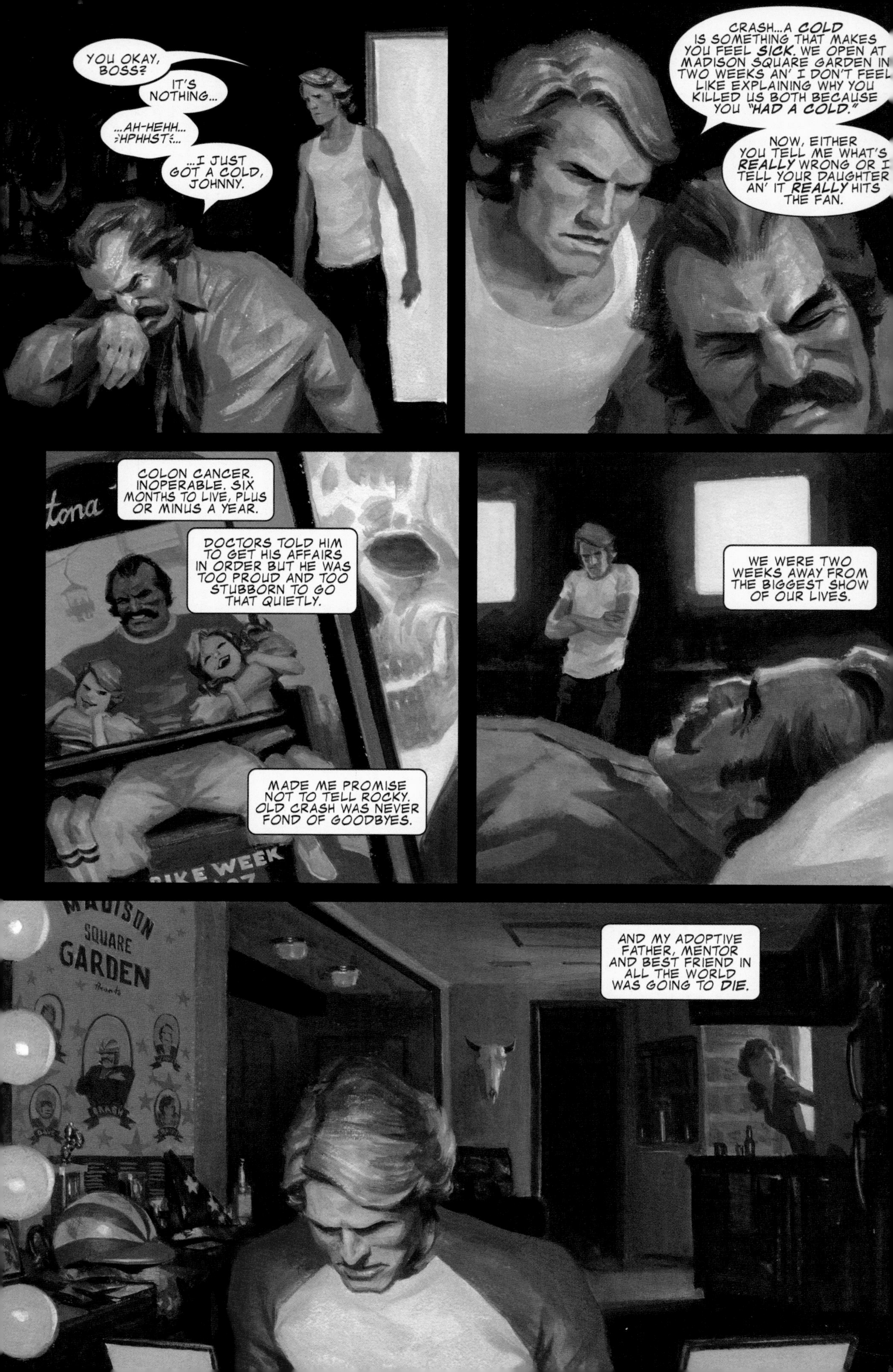

YOU OKAY, BOSS?
IT'S NOTHING...
...AH-HEHH... HPHHST...
...I JUST GOT A COLD, JOHNNY.
CRASH...A COLD IS SOMETHING THAT MAKES YOU FEEL SICK. WE OPEN AT MADISON SQUARE GARDEN IN TWO WEEKS AN' I DON'T FEEL LIKE EXPLAINING WHY YOU KILLED US BOTH BECAUSE YOU "HAD A COLD."
NOW, EITHER YOU TELL ME WHAT'S REALLY WRONG OR I TELL YOUR DAUGHTER AN' IT REALLY HITS THE FAN.
COLON CANCER. INOPERABLE. SIX MONTHS TO LIVE, PLUS OR MINUS A YEAR.
DOCTORS TOLD HIM TO GET HIS AFFAIRS IN ORDER BUT HE WAS TOO PROUD AND TOO STUBBORN TO GO THAT QUIETLY.
tona
MADE ME PROMISE NOT TO TELL ROCKY. OLD CRASH WAS NEVER FOND OF GOODBYES.
BIKE WEEK
WE WERE TWO WEEKS AWAY FROM THE BIGGEST SHOW OF OUR LIVES.
MADISON SQUARE GARDEN
AND MY ADOPTIVE FATHER, MENTOR AND BEST FRIEND IN ALL THE WORLD WAS GOING TO DIE.

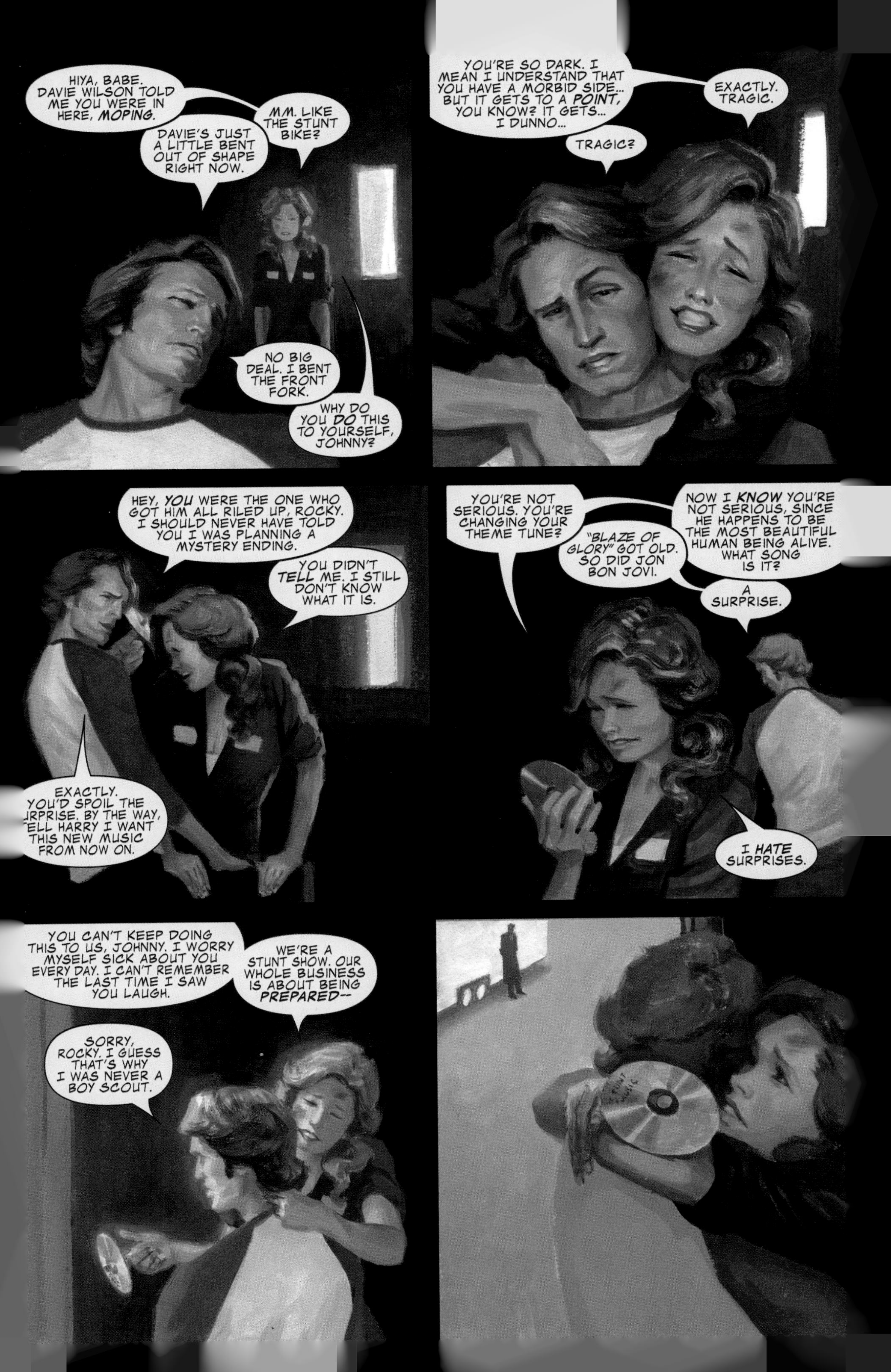
HIYA, BABE. DAVIE WILSON TOLD ME YOU WERE IN HERE, MOPING.
MM. LIKE THE STUNT BIKE?
DAVIE'S JUST A LITTLE BENT OUT OF SHAPE RIGHT NOW.
NO BIG DEAL. I BENT THE FRONT FORK.
WHY DO YOU DO THIS TO YOURSELF, JOHNNY?
YOU'RE SO DARK. I MEAN I UNDERSTAND THAT YOU HAVE A MORBID SIDE... BUT IT GETS TO A POINT, YOU KNOW? IT GETS... I DUNNO...
TRAGIC?
EXACTLY. TRAGIC.
HEY, YOU WERE THE ONE WHO GOT HIM ALL RILED UP, ROCKY. I SHOULD NEVER HAVE TOLD YOU I WAS PLANNING A MYSTERY ENDING.
YOU DIDN'T TELL ME. I STILL DON'T KNOW WHAT IT IS.
EXACTLY. YOU'D SPOIL THE URPRISE. BY THE WAY, TELL HARRY I WANT THIS NEW MUSIC FROM NOW ON.
YOU'RE NOT SERIOUS. YOU'RE CHANGING YOUR THEME TUNE?
"BLAZE OF GLORY" GOT OLD. SO DID JON BON JOVI.
NOW I KNOW YOU'RE NOT SERIOUS, SINCE HE HAPPENS TO BE THE MOST BEAUTIFUL HUMAN BEING ALIVE. WHAT SONG IS IT?
A SURPRISE.
I HATE SURPRISES.
YOU CAN'T KEEP DOING THIS TO US, JOHNNY. I WORRY MYSELF SICK ABOUT YOU EVERY DAY. I CAN'T REMEMBER THE LAST TIME I SAW YOU LAUGH.
WE'RE A STUNT SHOW. OUR WHOLE BUSINESS IS ABOUT BEING PREPARED--
SORRY, ROCKY. I GUESS THAT'S WHY I WAS NEVER A BOY SCOUT.

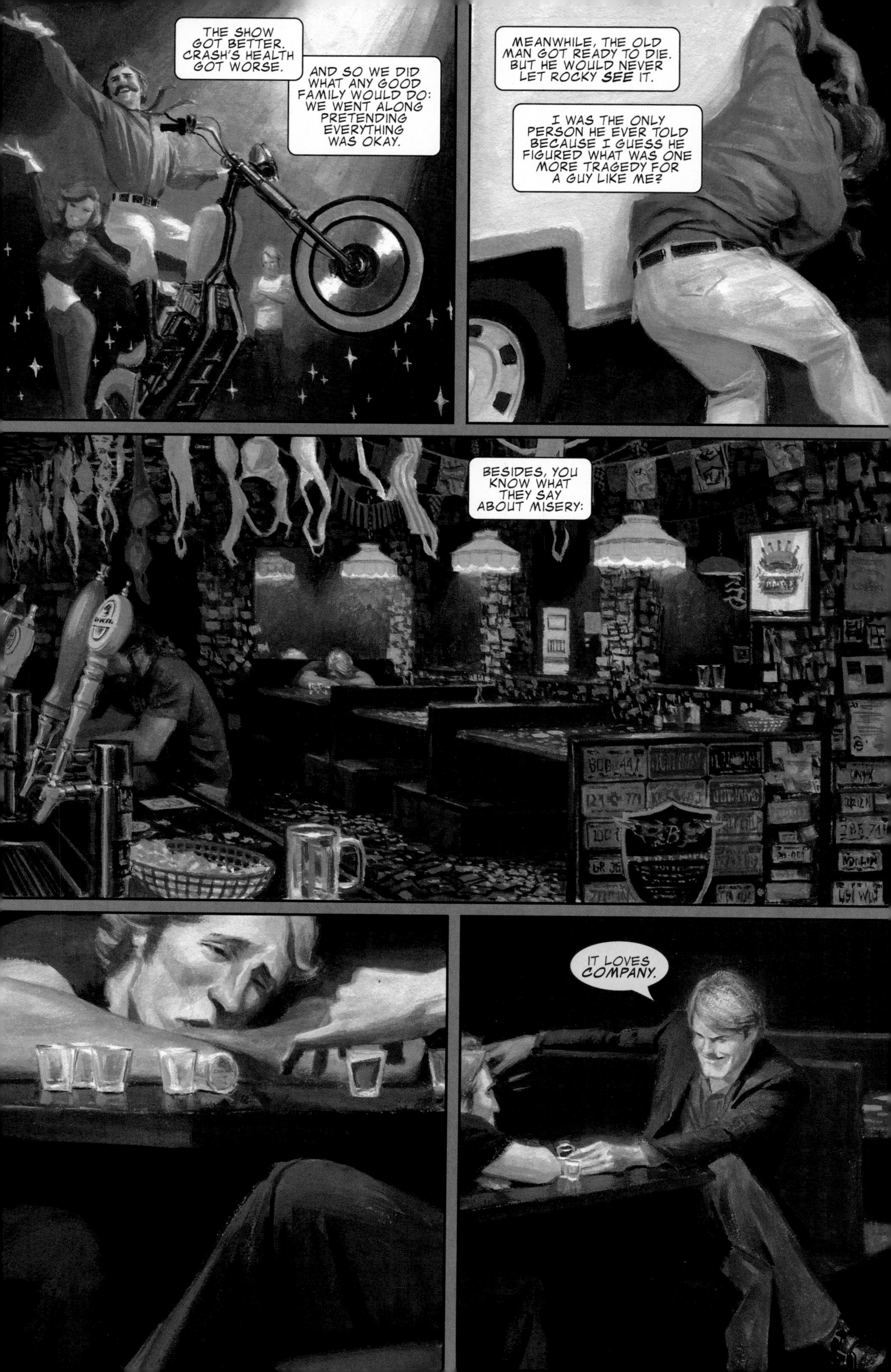

THE SHOW GOT BETTER. CRASH'S HEALTH GOT WORSE.
AND SO WE DID WHAT ANY GOOD FAMILY WOULD DO: WE WENT ALONG PRETENDING EVERYTHING WAS OKAY.
MEANWHILE, THE OLD MAN GOT READY TO DIE. BUT HE WOULD NEVER LET ROCKY SEE IT.
I WAS THE ONLY PERSON HE EVER TOLD BECAUSE I GUESS HE FIGURED WHAT WAS ONE MORE TRAGEDY FOR A GUY LIKE ME?
BESIDES, YOU KNOW WHAT THEY SAY ABOUT MISERY:
IT LOVES COMPANY.

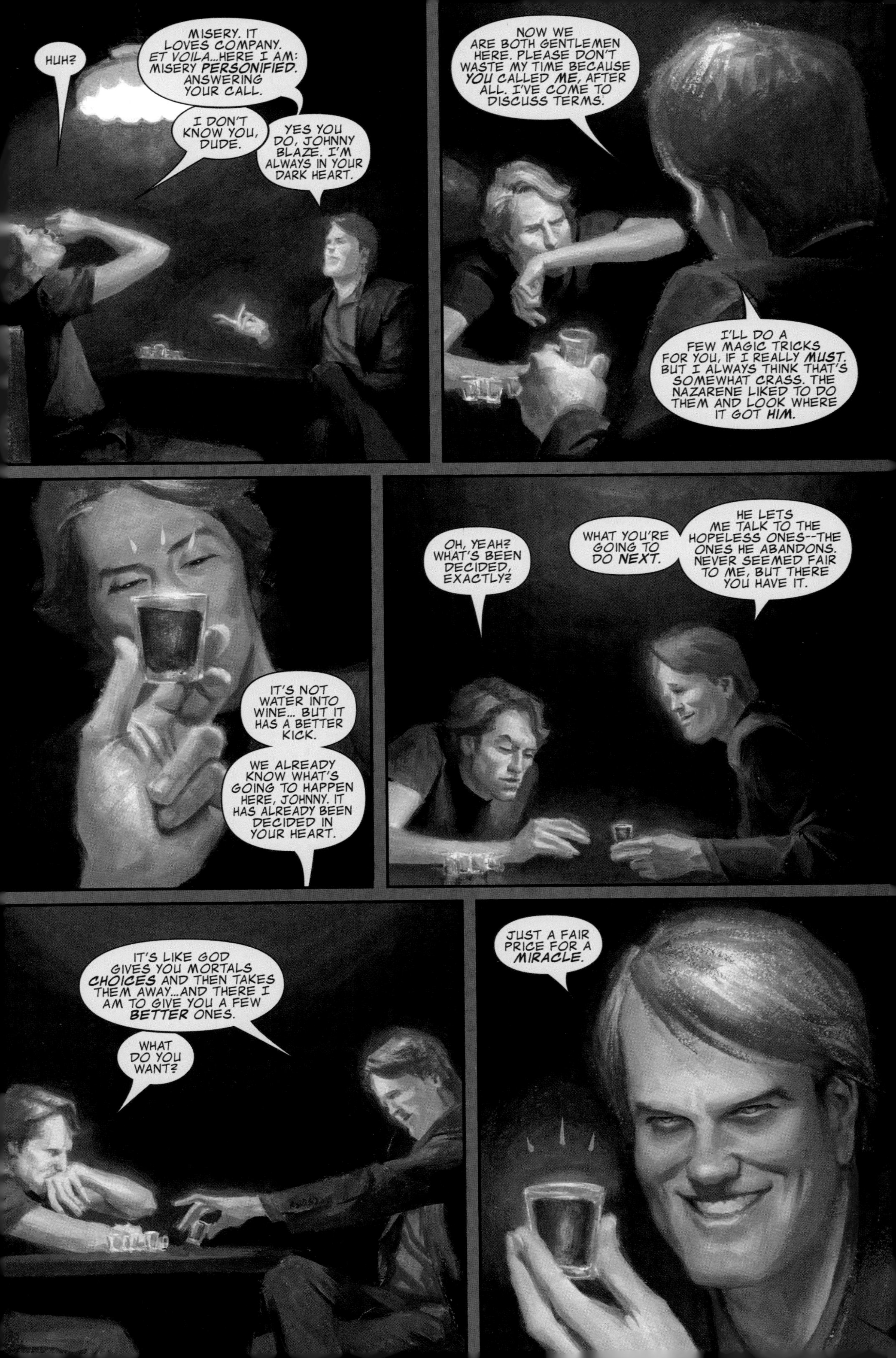
HUH?
MISERY. IT LOVES COMPANY. ET VOILA...HERE I AM: MISERY PERSONIFIED. ANSWERING YOUR CALL.
I DON'T KNOW YOU, DUDE.
YES YOU DO, JOHNNY BLAZE. I'M ALWAYS IN YOUR DARK HEART.
NOW WE ARE BOTH GENTLEMEN HERE. PLEASE DON'T WASTE MY TIME BECAUSE YOU CALLED ME, AFTER ALL. I'VE COME TO DISCUSS TERMS.
I'LL DO A FEW MAGIC TRICKS FOR YOU, IF I REALLY MUST. BUT I ALWAYS THINK THAT'S SOMEWHAT CRASS. THE NAZARENE LIKED TO DO THEM AND LOOK WHERE IT GOT HIM.
IT'S NOT WATER INTO WINE... BUT IT HAS A BETTER KICK.
WE ALREADY KNOW WHAT'S GOING TO HAPPEN HERE, JOHNNY. IT HAS ALREADY BEEN DECIDED IN YOUR HEART.
OH, YEAH? WHAT'S BEEN DECIDED, EXACTLY?
WHAT YOU'RE GOING TO DO NEXT.
HE LETS ME TALK TO THE HOPELESS ONES--THE ONES HE ABANDONS. NEVER SEEMED FAIR TO ME, BUT THERE YOU HAVE IT.
IT'S LIKE GOD GIVES YOU MORTALS CHOICES AND THEN TAKES THEM AWAY...AND THERE I AM TO GIVE YOU A FEW BETTER ONES.
WHAT DO YOU WANT?
JUST A FAIR PRICE FOR A MIRACLE.

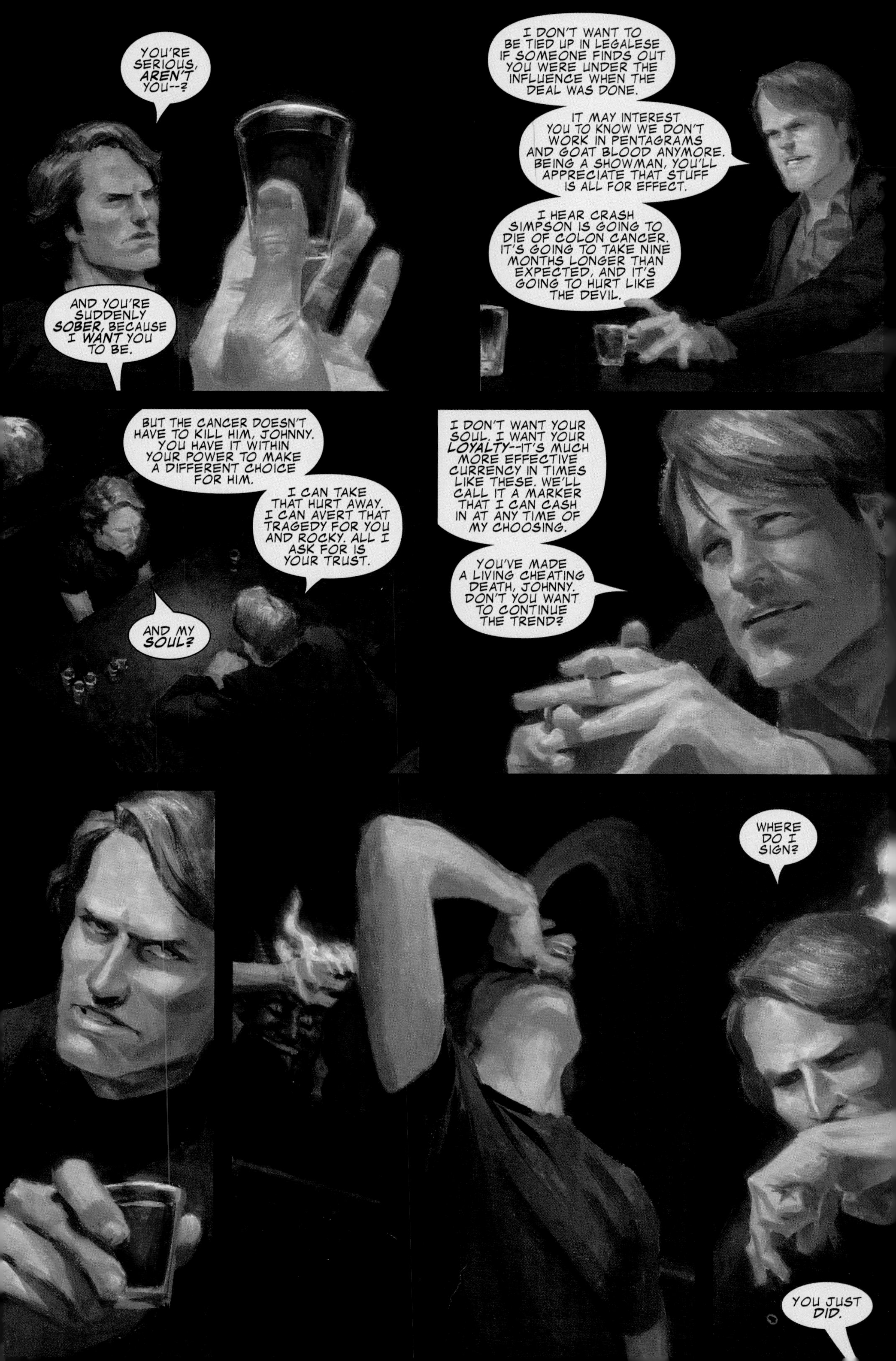
YOU'RE SERIOUS, AREN'T YOU--?
AND YOU'RE SUDDENLY SOBER, BECAUSE I WANT YOU TO BE.
I DON'T WANT TO BE TIED UP IN LEGALESE IF SOMEONE FINDS OUT YOU WERE UNDER THE INFLUENCE WHEN THE DEAL WAS DONE.
IT MAY INTEREST YOU TO KNOW WE DON'T WORK IN PENTAGRAMS AND GOAT BLOOD ANYMORE. BEING A SHOWMAN, YOU'LL APPRECIATE THAT STUFF IS ALL FOR EFFECT.
I HEAR CRASH SIMPSON IS GOING TO DIE OF COLON CANCER. IT'S GOING TO TAKE NINE MONTHS LONGER THAN EXPECTED, AND IT'S GOING TO HURT LIKE THE DEVIL.
BUT THE CANCER DOESN'T HAVE TO KILL HIM, JOHNNY. YOU HAVE IT WITHIN YOUR POWER TO MAKE A DIFFERENT CHOICE FOR HIM.
I CAN TAKE THAT HURT AWAY. I CAN AVERT THAT TRAGEDY FOR YOU AND ROCKY. ALL I ASK FOR IS YOUR TRUST.
AND MY SOUL?
I DON'T WANT YOUR SOUL. I WANT YOUR LOYALTY--IT'S MUCH MORE EFFECTIVE CURRENCY IN TIMES LIKE THESE. WE'LL CALL IT A MARKER THAT I CAN CASH IN AT ANY TIME OF MY CHOOSING.
YOU'VE MADE A LIVING CHEATING DEATH, JOHNNY. DON'T YOU WANT TO CONTINUE THE TREND?
WHERE DO I SIGN?
YOU JUST DID.

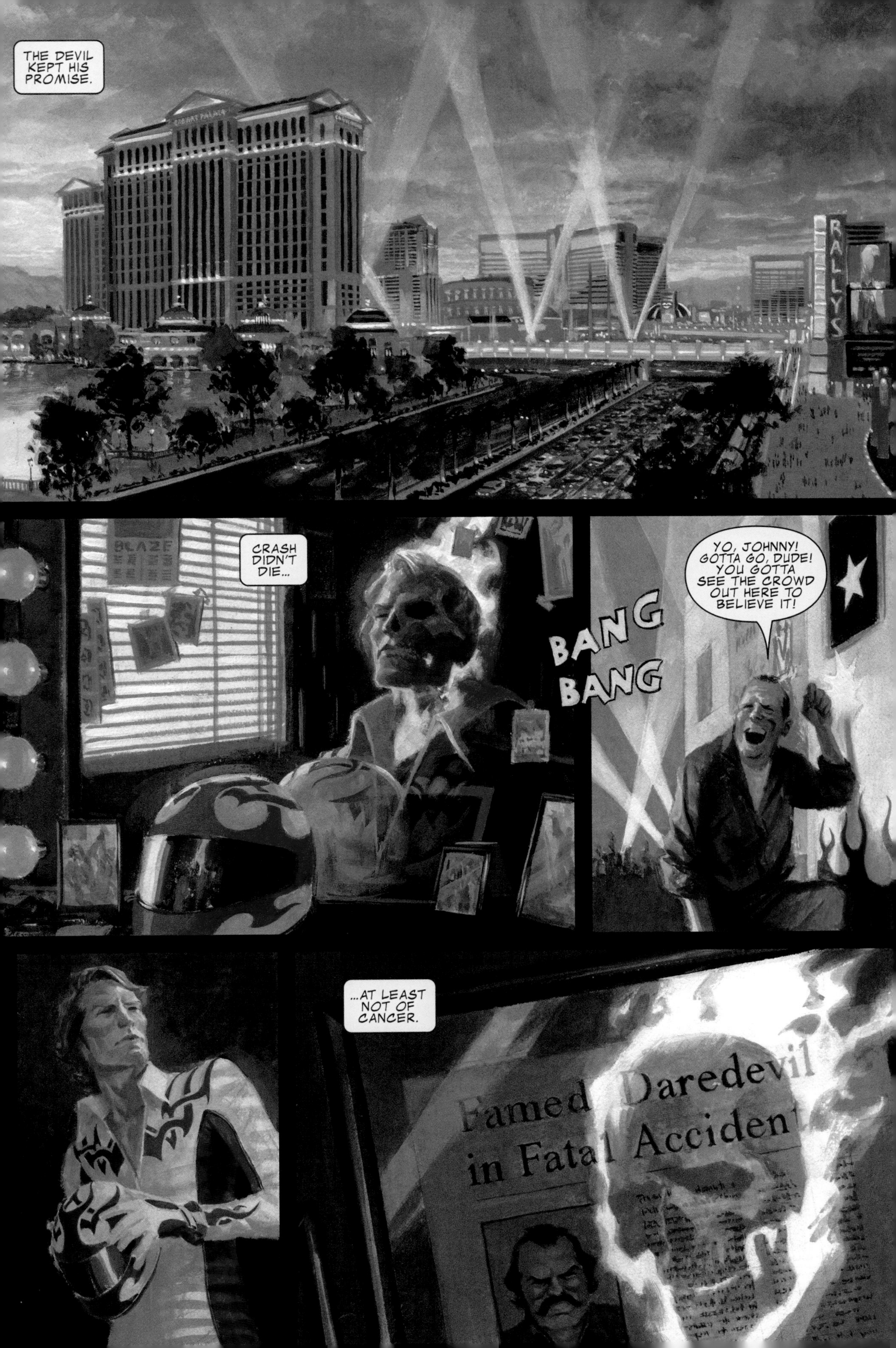
THE DEVIL KEPT HIS PROMISE.
RALLYS
CRASH DIDN'T DIE...
BLAZE
BANG BANG
YO, JOHNNY! GOTTA GO, DUDE! YOU GOTTA SEE THE CROWD OUT HERE TO BELIEVE IT!
...AT LEAST NOT OF CANCER.
Famed Daredevil in Fatal Accident

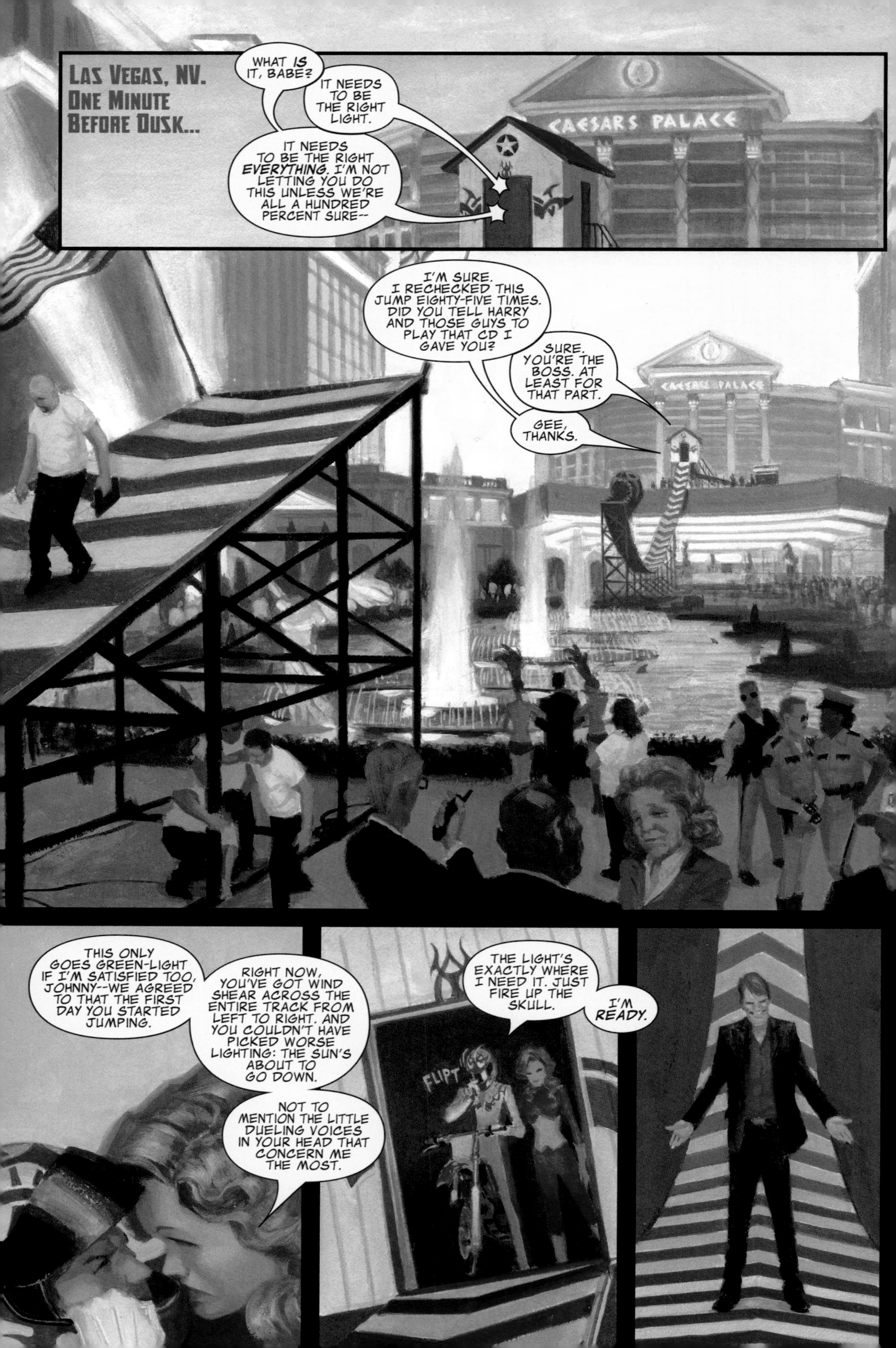
LAS VEGAS, NV. ONE MINUTE BEFORE DUSK...
WHAT IS IT, BABE?
IT NEEDS TO BE THE RIGHT LIGHT.
IT NEEDS TO BE THE RIGHT EVERYTHING. I'M NOT LETTING YOU DO THIS UNLESS WE'RE ALL A HUNDRED PERCENT SURE--
CAESARS PALACE
I'M SURE. I RECHECKED THIS JUMP EIGHTY-FIVE TIMES. DID YOU TELL HARRY AND THOSE GUYS TO PLAY THAT CD I GAVE YOU?
SURE. YOU'RE THE BOSS. AT LEAST FOR THAT PART.
GEE, THANKS.
CAESARS PALACE
THIS ONLY GOES GREEN-LIGHT IF I'M SATISFIED TOO, JOHNNY--WE AGREED TO THAT THE FIRST DAY YOU STARTED JUMPING.
RIGHT NOW, YOU'VE GOT WIND SHEAR ACROSS THE ENTIRE TRACK FROM LEFT TO RIGHT. AND YOU COULDN'T HAVE PICKED WORSE LIGHTING: THE SUN'S ABOUT TO GO DOWN.
NOT TO MENTION THE LITTLE DUELING VOICES IN YOUR HEAD THAT CONCERN ME THE MOST.
THE LIGHT'S EXACTLY WHERE I NEED IT. JUST FIRE UP THE SKULL.
FLIPT
I'M READY.

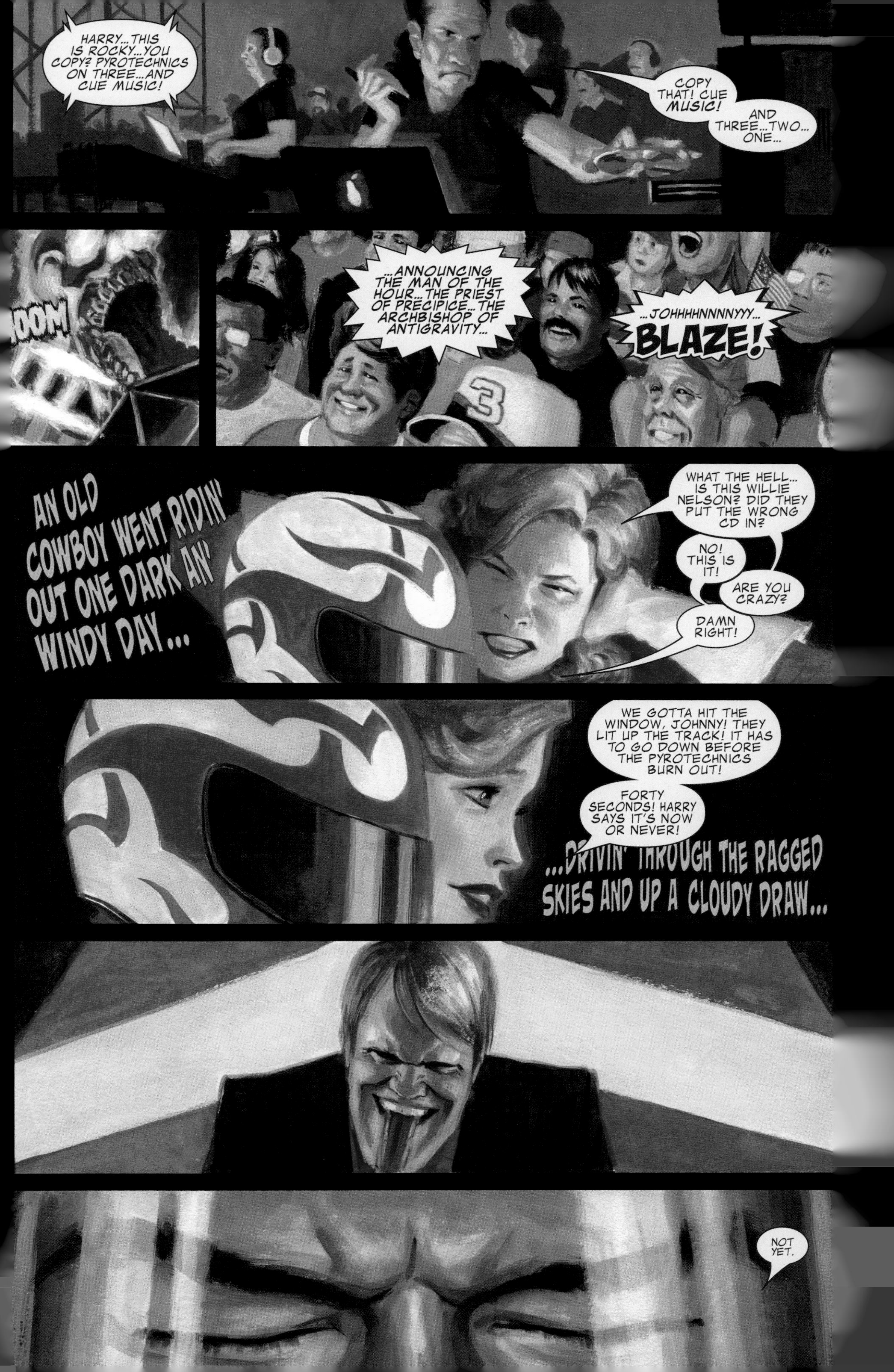
HARRY... THIS IS ROCKY... YOU COPY? PYROTECHNICS ON THREE... AND CUE MUSIC!
COPY THAT! CUE MUSIC!
AND THREE... TWO... ONE...
...ANNOUNCING THE MAN OF THE HOUR... THE PRIEST OF PRECIPICE... THE ARCHBISHOP OF ANTIGRAVITY...
...JOHHHHNNNNYYY... BLAZE!
AN OLD COWBOY WENT RIDIN' OUT ONE DARK AN' WINDY DAY...
WHAT THE HELL... IS THIS WILLIE NELSON? DID THEY PUT THE WRONG CD IN?
NO! THIS IS IT!
ARE YOU CRAZY?
DAMN RIGHT!
WE GOTTA HIT THE WINDOW, JOHNNY! THEY LIT UP THE TRACK! IT HAS TO GO DOWN BEFORE THE PYROTECHNICS BURN OUT!
FORTY SECONDS! HARRY SAYS IT'S NOW OR NEVER!
...DRIVIN' THROUGH THE RAGGED SKIES AND UP A CLOUDY DRAW...
NOT YET.

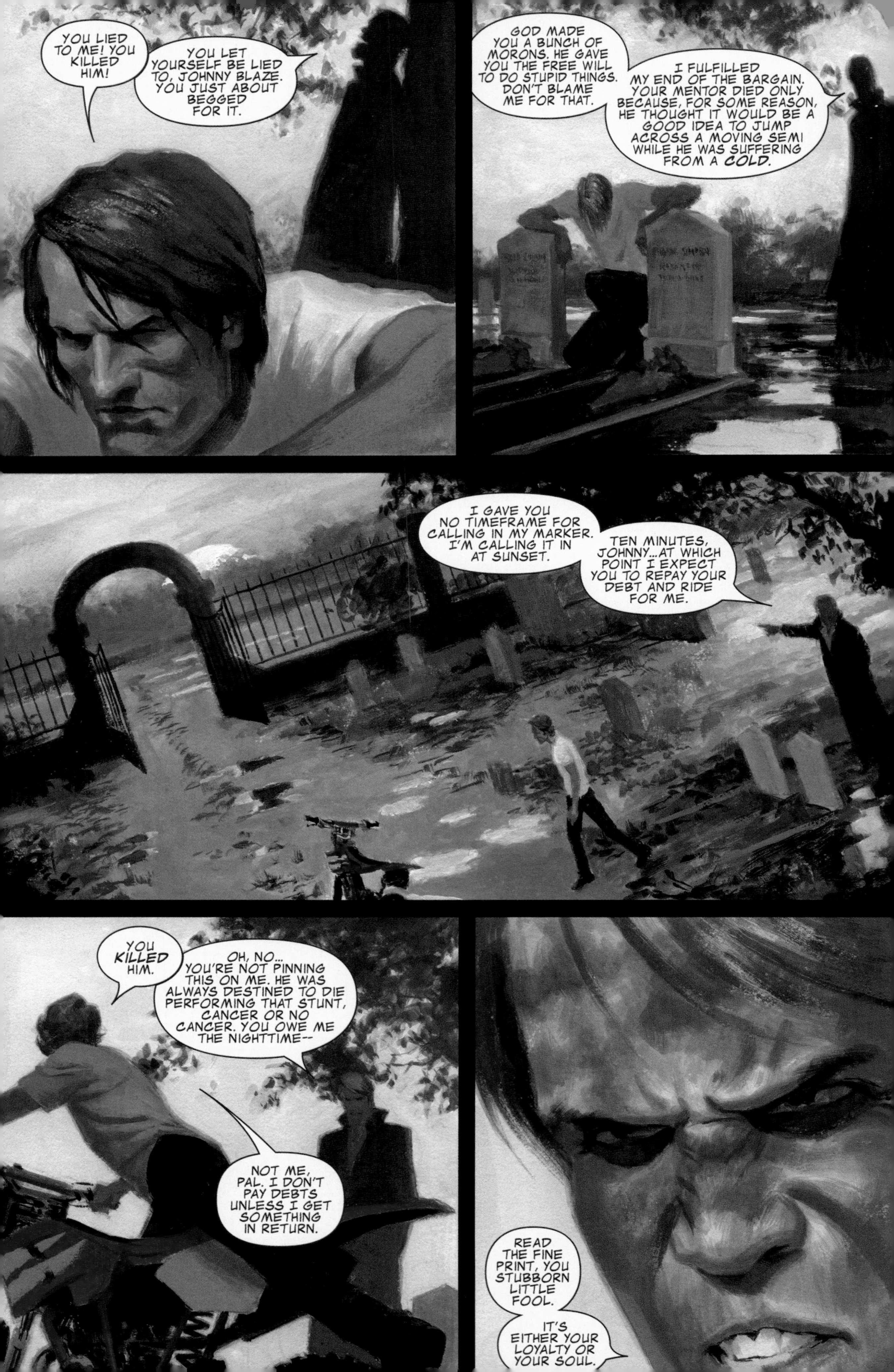
YOU LIED TO ME! YOU KILLED HIM!
YOU LET YOURSELF BE LIED TO, JOHNNY BLAZE. YOU JUST ABOUT BEGGED FOR IT.
GOD MADE YOU A BUNCH OF MORONS. HE GAVE YOU THE FREE WILL TO DO STUPID THINGS. DON'T BLAME ME FOR THAT.
I FULFILLED MY END OF THE BARGAIN. YOUR MENTOR DIED ONLY BECAUSE, FOR SOME REASON, HE THOUGHT IT WOULD BE A GOOD IDEA TO JUMP ACROSS A MOVING SEMI WHILE HE WAS SUFFERING FROM A COLD.
I GAVE YOU NO TIMEFRAME FOR CALLING IN MY MARKER. I'M CALLING IT IN AT SUNSET.
TEN MINUTES, JOHNNY...AT WHICH POINT I EXPECT YOU TO REPAY YOUR DEBT AND RIDE FOR ME.
YOU KILLED HIM.
OH, NO... YOU'RE NOT PINNING THIS ON ME. HE WAS ALWAYS DESTINED TO DIE PERFORMING THAT STUNT, CANCER OR NO CANCER. YOU OWE ME THE NIGHTTIME--
NOT ME, PAL. I DON'T PAY DEBTS UNLESS I GET SOMETHING IN RETURN.
READ THE FINE PRINT, YOU STUBBORN LITTLE FOOL.
IT'S EITHER YOUR LOYALTY OR YOUR SOUL.

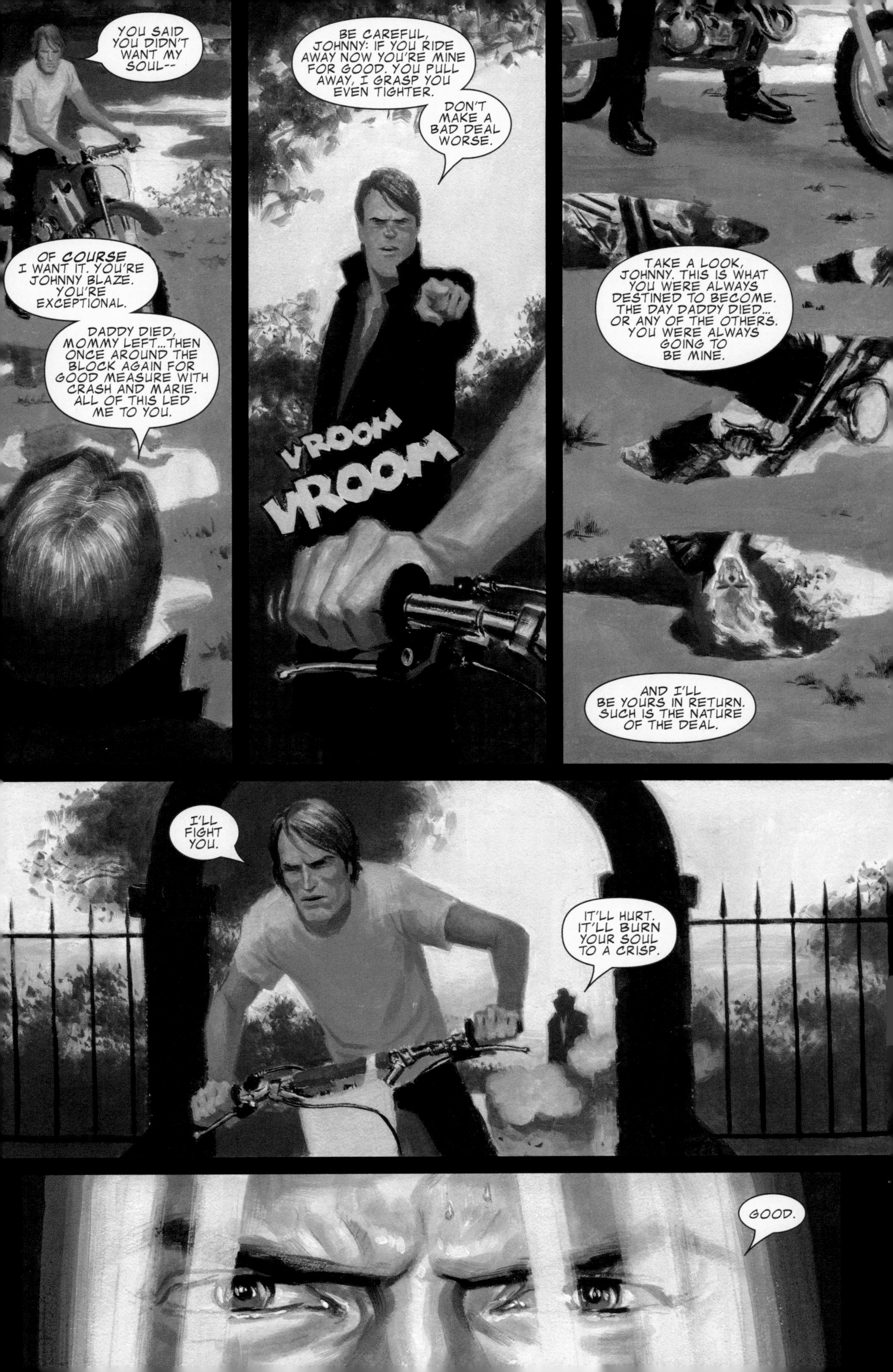

YOU SAID YOU DIDN'T WANT MY SOUL--
OF COURSE I WANT IT. YOU'RE JOHNNY BLAZE. YOU'RE EXCEPTIONAL.
DADDY DIED, MOMMY LEFT...THEN ONCE AROUND THE BLOCK AGAIN FOR GOOD MEASURE WITH CRASH AND MARIE. ALL OF THIS LED ME TO YOU.
BE CAREFUL, JOHNNY: IF YOU RIDE AWAY NOW YOU'RE MINE FOR GOOD. YOU PULL AWAY, I GRASP YOU EVEN TIGHTER.
DON'T MAKE A BAD DEAL WORSE.
VROOM
VROOM
TAKE A LOOK, JOHNNY. THIS IS WHAT YOU WERE ALWAYS DESTINED TO BECOME. THE DAY DADDY DIED... OR ANY OF THE OTHERS. YOU WERE ALWAYS GOING TO BE MINE.
AND I'LL BE YOURS IN RETURN. SUCH IS THE NATURE OF THE DEAL.
I'LL FIGHT YOU.
IT'LL HURT. IT'LL BURN YOUR SOUL TO A CRISP.
GOOD.

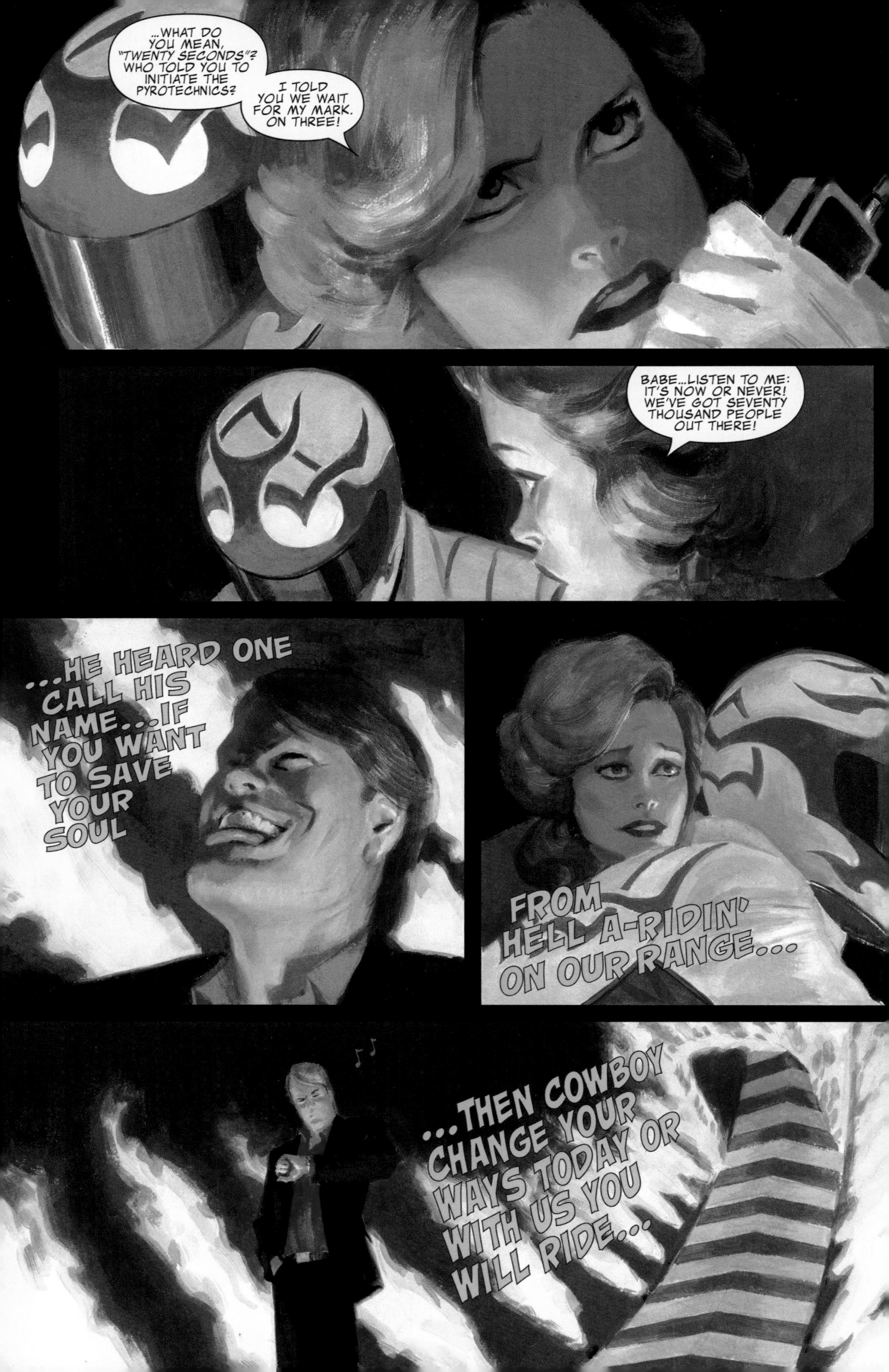
...WHAT DO YOU MEAN, "TWENTY SECONDS"? WHO TOLD YOU TO INITIATE THE PYROTECHNICS?
I TOLD YOU WE WAIT FOR MY MARK. ON THREE!
BABE...LISTEN TO ME: IT'S NOW OR NEVER! WE'VE GOT SEVENTY THOUSAND PEOPLE OUT THERE!
...HE HEARD ONE CALL HIS NAME...IF YOU WANT TO SAVE YOUR SOUL
FROM HELL A-RIDIN' ON OUR RANGE...
...THEN COWBOY CHANGE YOUR WAYS TODAY OR WITH US YOU WILL RIDE...

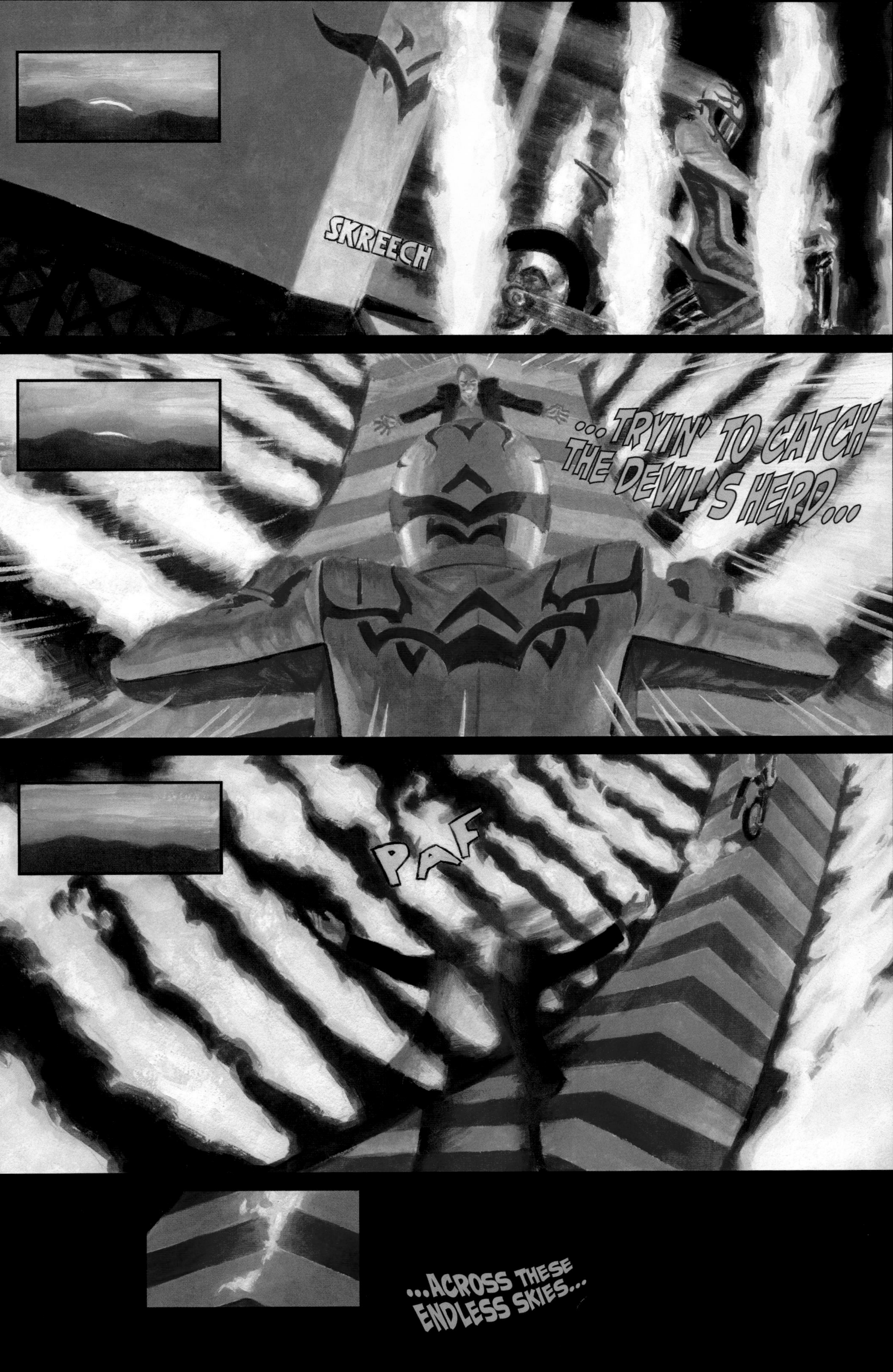
SKREECH
...TRYIN' TO CATCH THE DEVIL'S HERD...
PAF
...ACROSS THESE ENDLESS SKIES...

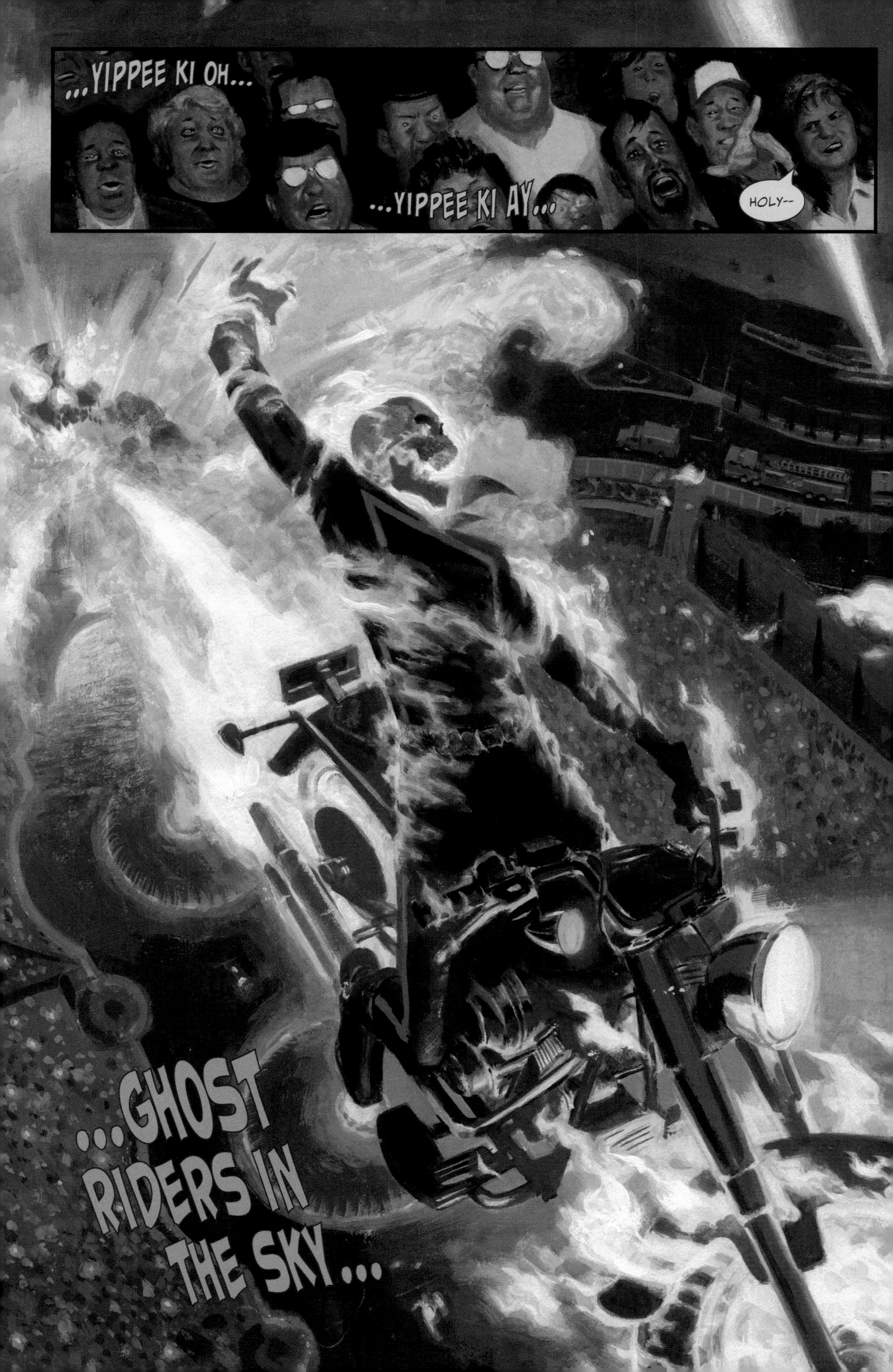
...YIPPEE KI OH...
...YIPPEE KI AY...
HOLY--
...GHOST RIDERS IN THE SKY...

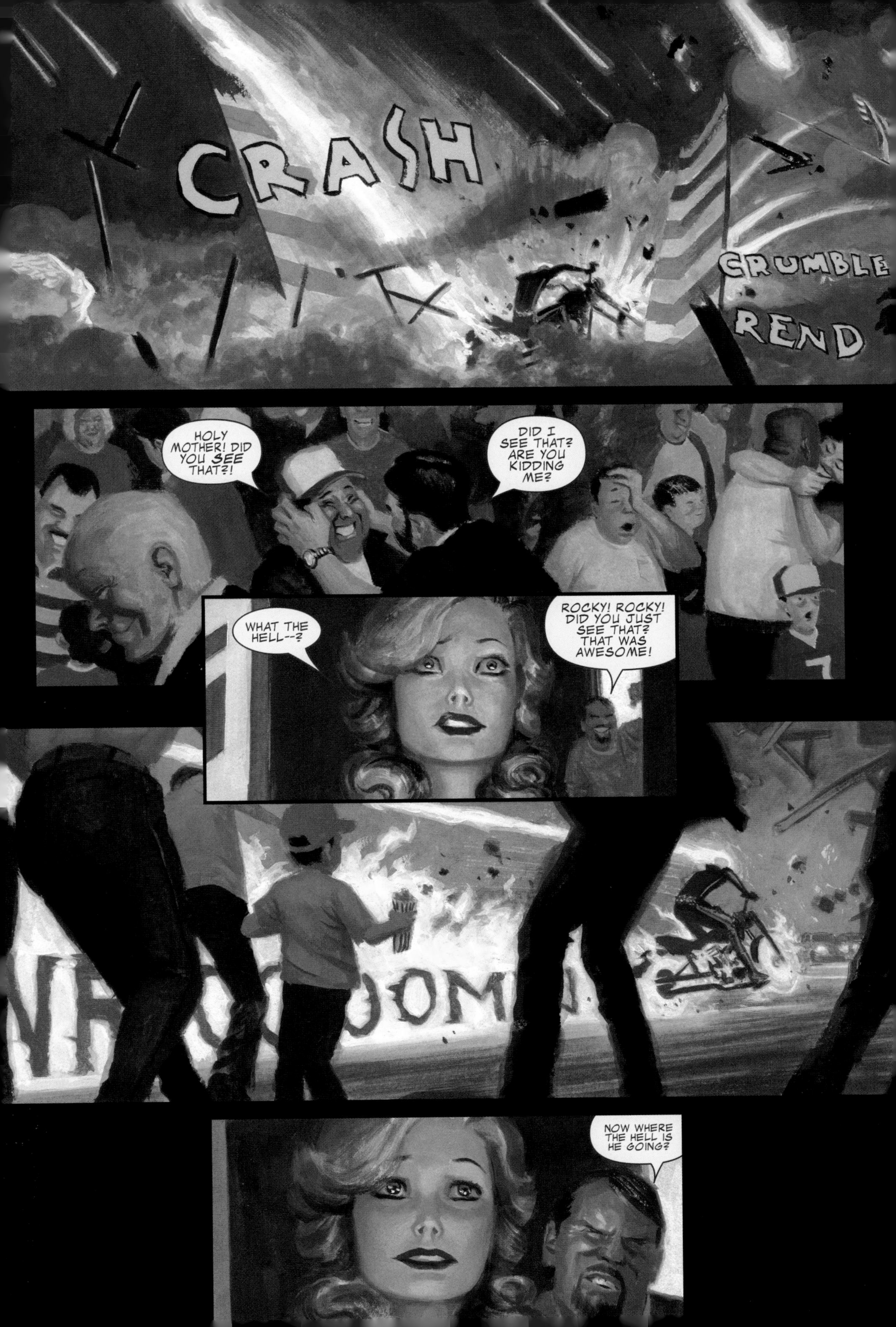
CRASH
CRUMBLE
REND
HOLY MOTHER! DID YOU SEE THAT?!
DID I SEE THAT? ARE YOU KIDDING ME?
WHAT THE HELL--?
ROCKY! ROCKY! DID YOU JUST SEE THAT? THAT WAS AWESOME!
NOW WHERE THE HELL IS HE GOING?

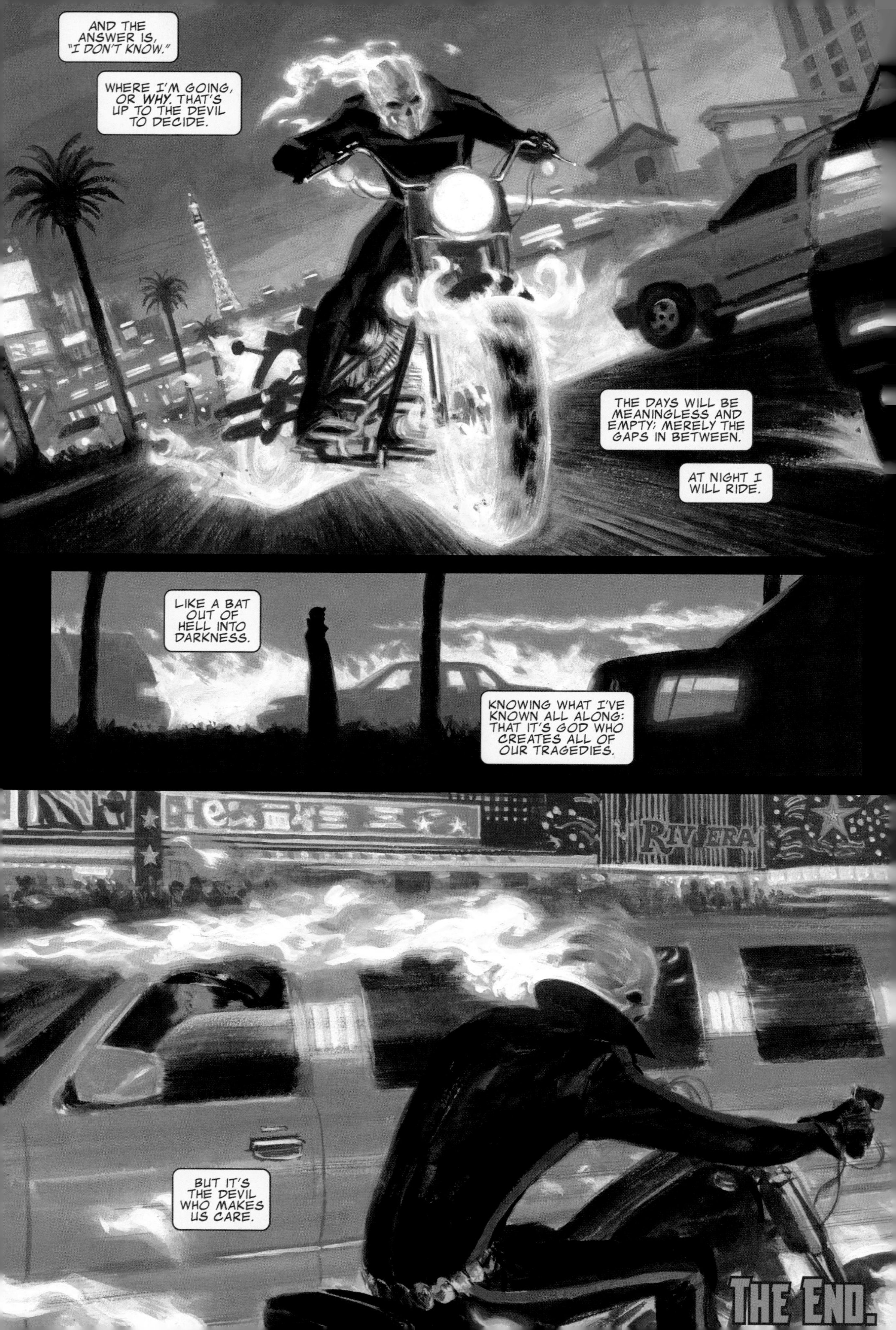
AND THE ANSWER IS, "I DON'T KNOW."
WHERE I'M GOING, OR WHY. THAT'S UP TO THE DEVIL TO DECIDE.
THE DAYS WILL BE MEANINGLESS AND EMPTY; MERELY THE GAPS IN BETWEEN.
AT NIGHT I WILL RIDE.
LIKE A BAT OUT OF HELL INTO DARKNESS.
KNOWING WHAT I'VE KNOWN ALL ALONG: THAT IT'S GOD WHO CREATES ALL OF OUR TRAGEDIES.
RIVIERA
BUT IT'S THE DEVIL WHO MAKES US CARE.
THE END.

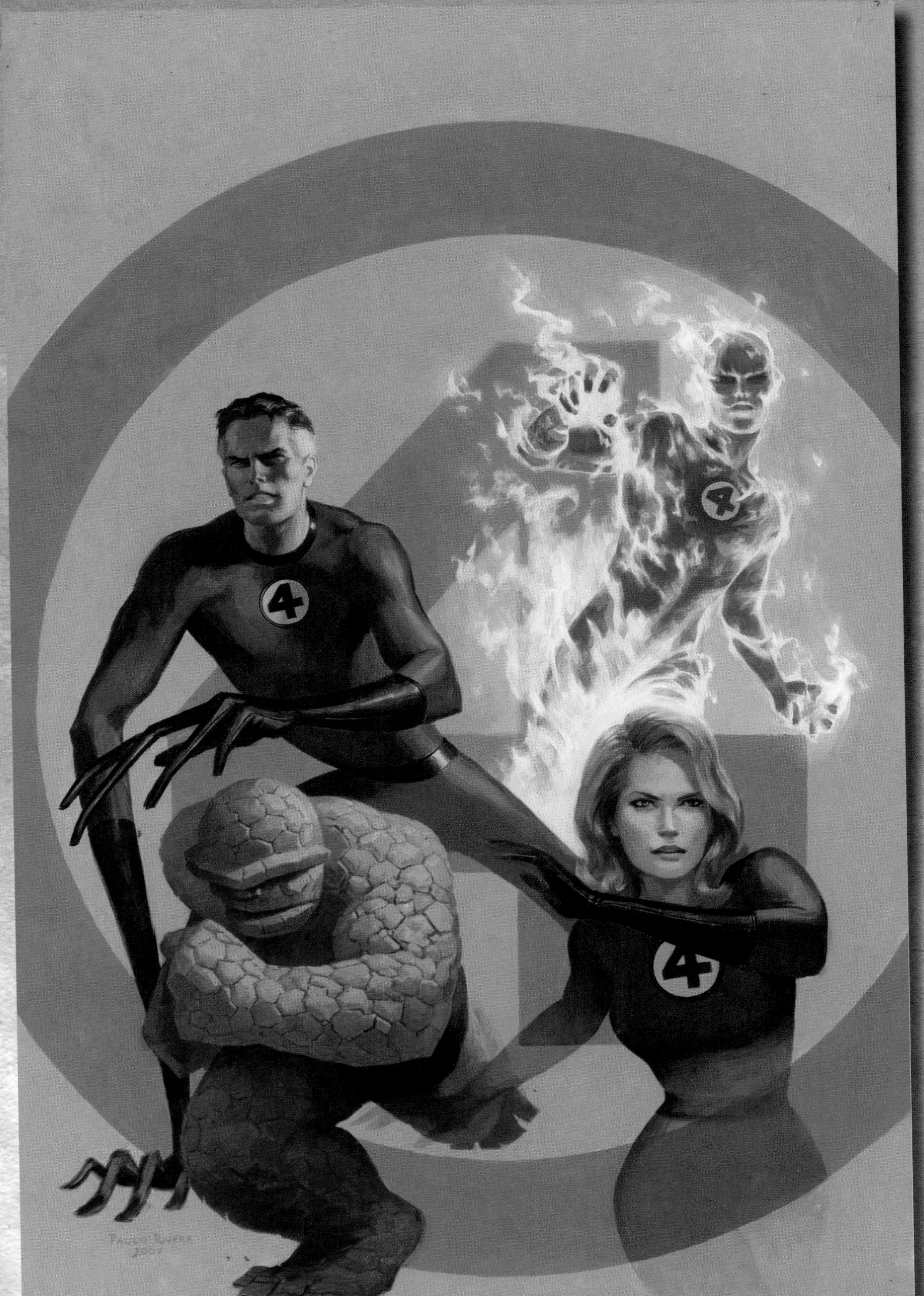
PAULO RIVERA
2007

- FANTASTIC FOUR -

MYTHOS

While testing an experimental spacecraft, Reed Richards, Ben Grimm, and Sue and Johnny Storm were exposed to a bombardment of mysterious cosmic rays. Upon their return to Earth, they found that they had gained wondrous abilities, the likes of which had never been seen before. Vowing to use these powers for good, they became…

THE Fantastic Four

| THE THING | MR. FANTASTIC | INVISIBLE WOMAN | HUMAN TORCH |
| BEN GRIMM | REED RICHARDS | SUE STORM | JOHNNY STORM |

Based on *Fantastic Four #1*, November 1961 by Stan Lee and Jack Kirby

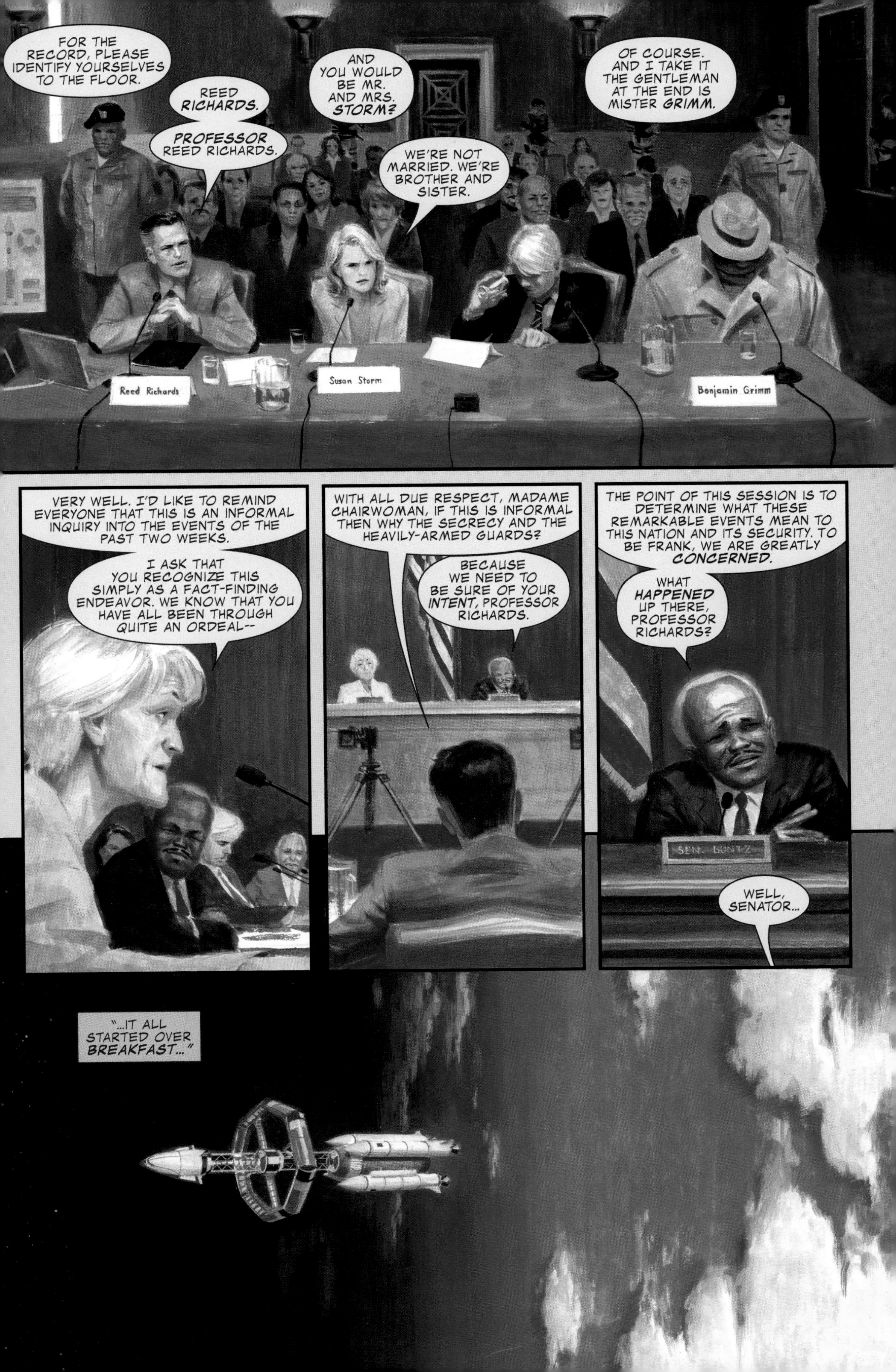

FOR THE RECORD, PLEASE IDENTIFY YOURSELVES TO THE FLOOR.
REED RICHARDS.
PROFESSOR REED RICHARDS.
AND YOU WOULD BE MR. AND MRS. STORM?
WE'RE NOT MARRIED. WE'RE BROTHER AND SISTER.
OF COURSE. AND I TAKE IT THE GENTLEMAN AT THE END IS MISTER GRIMM.
Reed Richards
Susan Storm
Benjamin Grimm
VERY WELL. I'D LIKE TO REMIND EVERYONE THAT THIS IS AN INFORMAL INQUIRY INTO THE EVENTS OF THE PAST TWO WEEKS.
I ASK THAT YOU RECOGNIZE THIS SIMPLY AS A FACT-FINDING ENDEAVOR. WE KNOW THAT YOU HAVE ALL BEEN THROUGH QUITE AN ORDEAL--
WITH ALL DUE RESPECT, MADAME CHAIRWOMAN, IF THIS IS INFORMAL THEN WHY THE SECRECY AND THE HEAVILY-ARMED GUARDS?
BECAUSE WE NEED TO BE SURE OF YOUR INTENT, PROFESSOR RICHARDS.
THE POINT OF THIS SESSION IS TO DETERMINE WHAT THESE REMARKABLE EVENTS MEAN TO THIS NATION AND ITS SECURITY. TO BE FRANK, WE ARE GREATLY CONCERNED.
WHAT HAPPENED UP THERE, PROFESSOR RICHARDS?
SEN. BUNTZ
WELL, SENATOR...
"...IT ALL STARTED OVER BREAKFAST..."

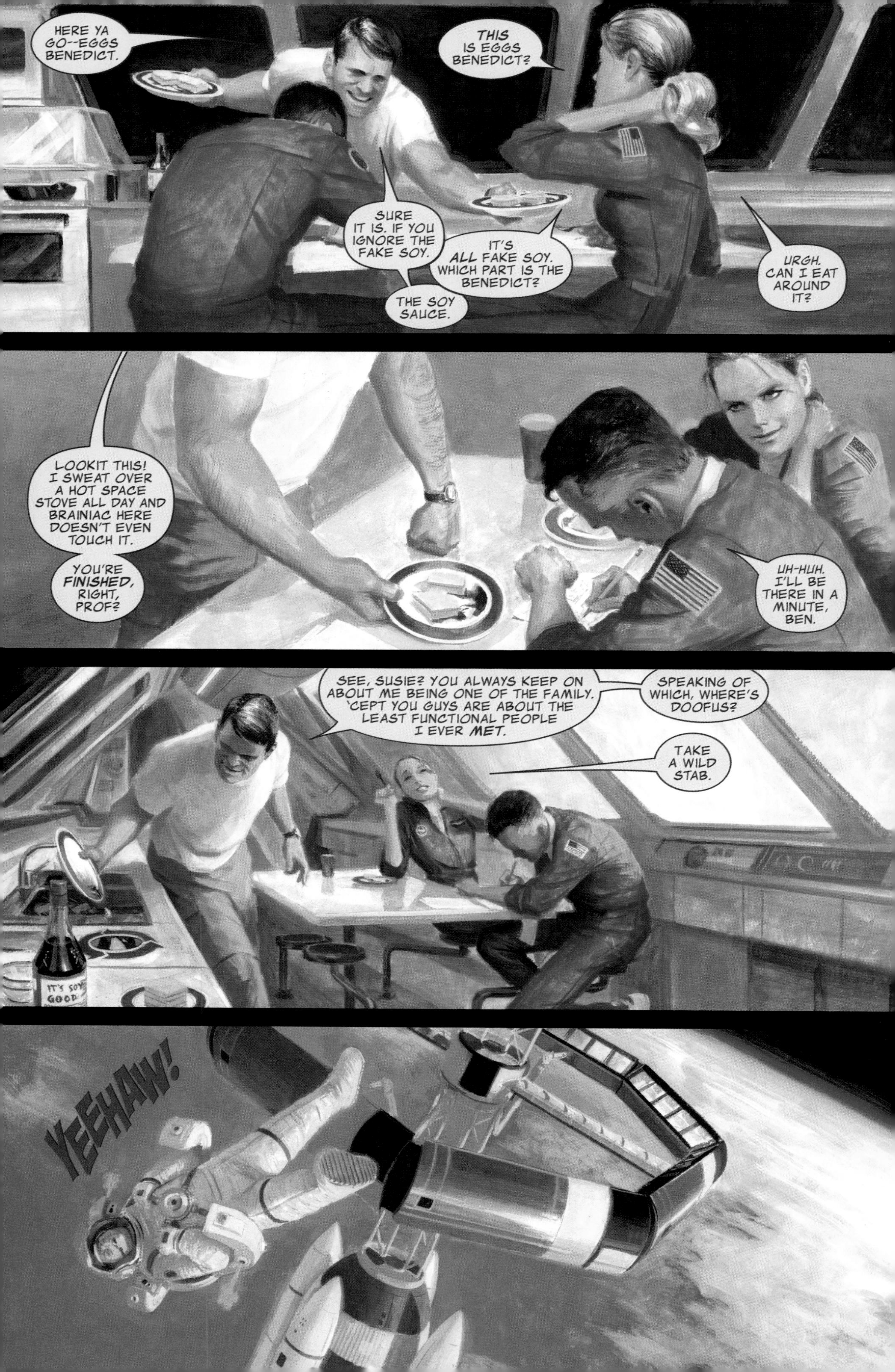
HERE YA GO--EGGS BENEDICT.
THIS IS EGGS BENEDICT?
SURE IT IS. IF YOU IGNORE THE FAKE SOY.
IT'S ALL FAKE SOY. WHICH PART IS THE BENEDICT?
THE SOY SAUCE.
URGH. CAN I EAT AROUND IT?
LOOKIT THIS! I SWEAT OVER A HOT SPACE STOVE ALL DAY AND BRAINIAC HERE DOESN'T EVEN TOUCH IT.
YOU'RE FINISHED, RIGHT, PROF?
UH-HUH. I'LL BE THERE IN A MINUTE, BEN.
SEE, SUSIE? YOU ALWAYS KEEP ON ABOUT ME BEING ONE OF THE FAMILY. 'CEPT YOU GUYS ARE ABOUT THE LEAST FUNCTIONAL PEOPLE I EVER MET.
SPEAKING OF WHICH, WHERE'S DOOFUS?
TAKE A WILD STAB.
IT'S SOY GOOD
YEEHAW!

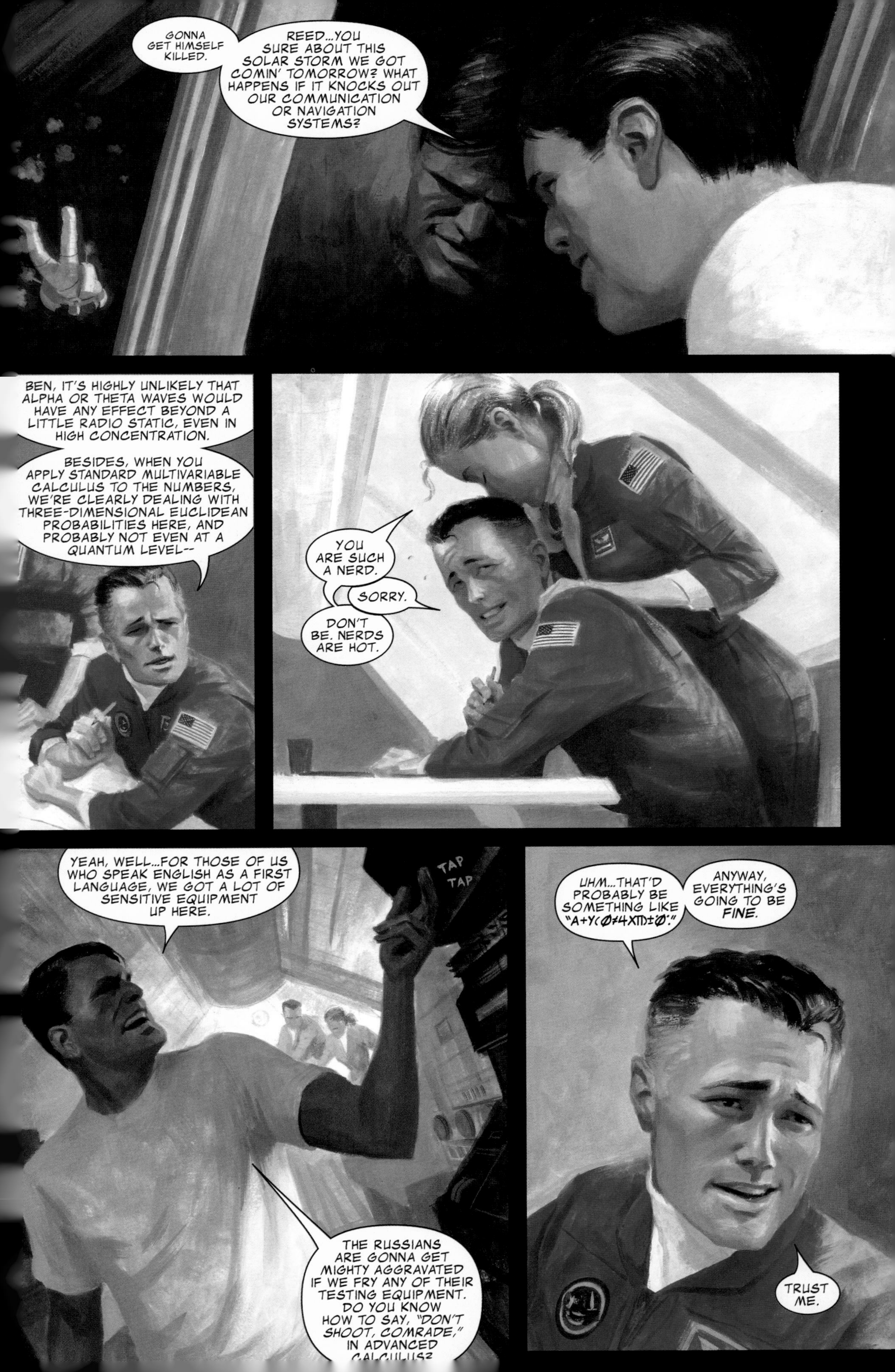
GONNA GET HIMSELF KILLED.
REED...YOU SURE ABOUT THIS SOLAR STORM WE GOT COMIN' TOMORROW? WHAT HAPPENS IF IT KNOCKS OUT OUR COMMUNICATION OR NAVIGATION SYSTEMS?
BEN, IT'S HIGHLY UNLIKELY THAT ALPHA OR THETA WAVES WOULD HAVE ANY EFFECT BEYOND A LITTLE RADIO STATIC, EVEN IN HIGH CONCENTRATION.
BESIDES, WHEN YOU APPLY STANDARD MULTIVARIABLE CALCULUS TO THE NUMBERS, WE'RE CLEARLY DEALING WITH THREE-DIMENSIONAL EUCLIDEAN PROBABILITIES HERE, AND PROBABLY NOT EVEN AT A QUANTUM LEVEL--
YOU ARE SUCH A NERD.
SORRY.
DON'T BE. NERDS ARE HOT.
YEAH, WELL...FOR THOSE OF US WHO SPEAK ENGLISH AS A FIRST LANGUAGE, WE GOT A LOT OF SENSITIVE EQUIPMENT UP HERE.
TAP TAP
THE RUSSIANS ARE GONNA GET MIGHTY AGGRAVATED IF WE FRY ANY OF THEIR TESTING EQUIPMENT. DO YOU KNOW HOW TO SAY, "DON'T SHOOT, COMRADE," IN ADVANCED
UHM...THAT'D PROBABLY BE SOMETHING LIKE "A+Y(Ø≠4XΠ)±Ø."
ANYWAY, EVERYTHING'S GOING TO BE *FINE*.
TRUST ME.

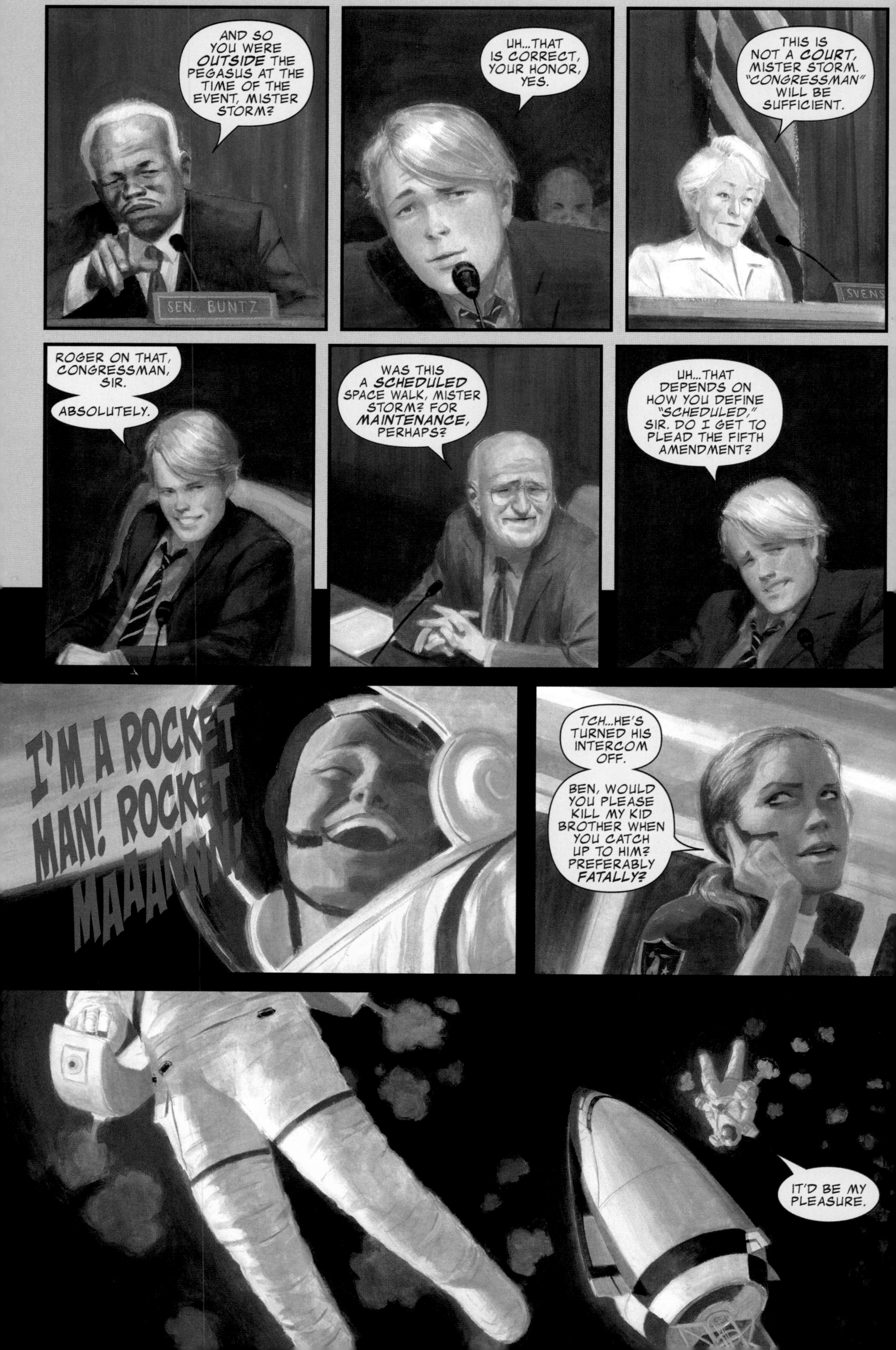
AND SO YOU WERE OUTSIDE THE PEGASUS AT THE TIME OF THE EVENT, MISTER STORM?
SEN. BUNTZ
UH...THAT IS CORRECT, YOUR HONOR, YES.
THIS IS NOT A COURT, MISTER STORM. "CONGRESSMAN" WILL BE SUFFICIENT.
SVENS
ROGER ON THAT, CONGRESSMAN, SIR.
ABSOLUTELY.
WAS THIS A SCHEDULED SPACE WALK, MISTER STORM? FOR MAINTENANCE, PERHAPS?
UH...THAT DEPENDS ON HOW YOU DEFINE "SCHEDULED," SIR. DO I GET TO PLEAD THE FIFTH AMENDMENT?
I'M A ROCKET MAN! ROCKET MAN! ROCKET MAAANNN!
TCH...HE'S TURNED HIS INTERCOM OFF.
BEN, WOULD YOU PLEASE KILL MY KID BROTHER WHEN YOU CATCH UP TO HIM? PREFERABLY FATALLY?
IT'D BE MY PLEASURE.

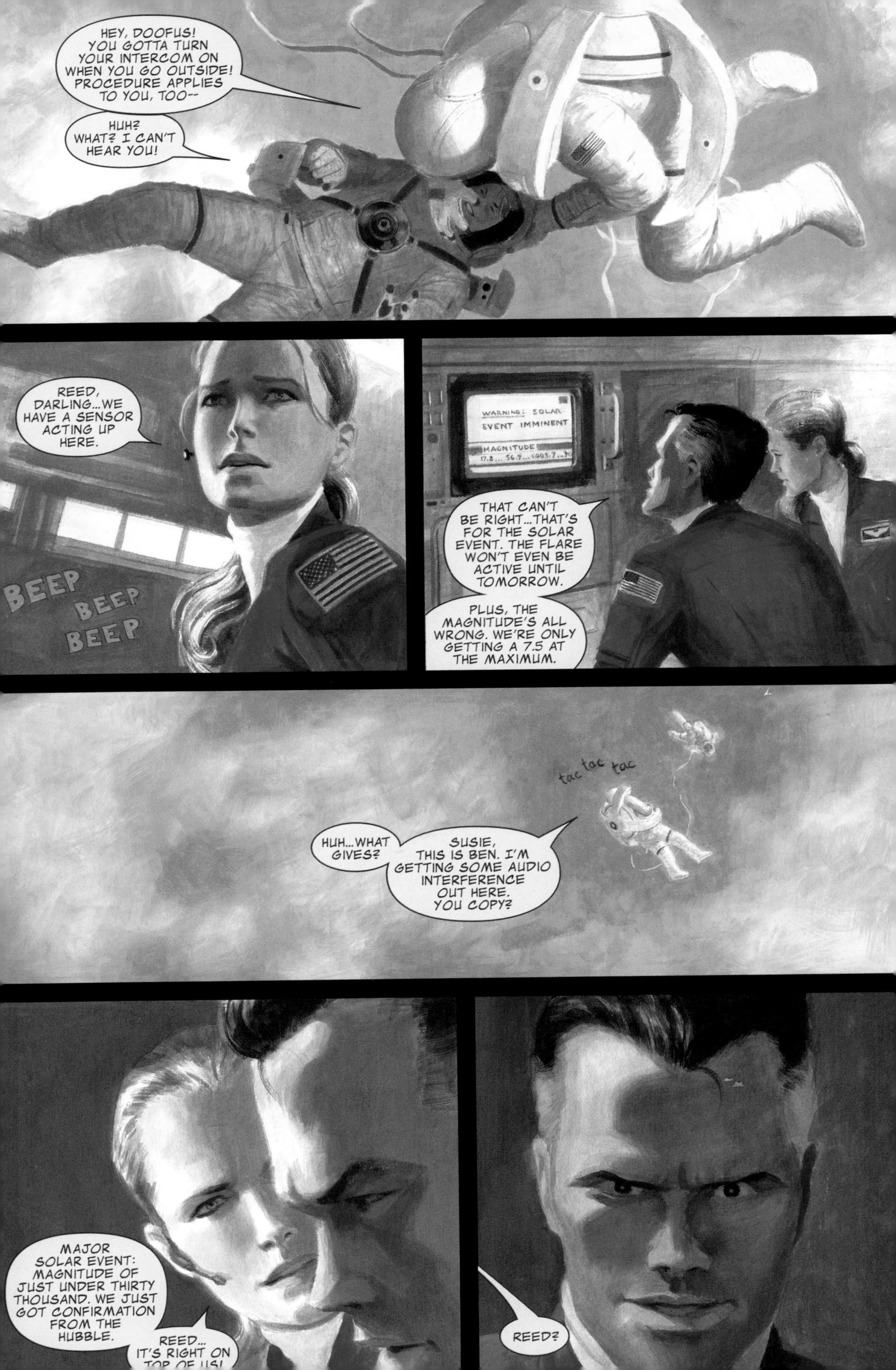
HEY, DOOFUS! YOU GOTTA TURN YOUR INTERCOM ON WHEN YOU GO OUTSIDE! PROCEDURE APPLIES TO YOU, TOO--
HUH? WHAT? I CAN'T HEAR YOU!
REED, DARLING...WE HAVE A SENSOR ACTING UP HERE.
BEEP BEEP BEEP
WARNING: SOLAR EVENT IMMINENT
MAGNITUDE
THAT CAN'T BE RIGHT...THAT'S FOR THE SOLAR EVENT. THE FLARE WON'T EVEN BE ACTIVE UNTIL TOMORROW.
PLUS, THE MAGNITUDE'S ALL WRONG. WE'RE ONLY GETTING A 7.5 AT THE MAXIMUM.
tac tac tac
HUH...WHAT GIVES?
SUSIE, THIS IS BEN. I'M GETTING SOME AUDIO INTERFERENCE OUT HERE. YOU COPY?
MAJOR SOLAR EVENT: MAGNITUDE OF JUST UNDER THIRTY THOUSAND. WE JUST GOT CONFIRMATION FROM THE HUBBLE.
REED... IT'S RIGHT ON TOP OF US!
REED?

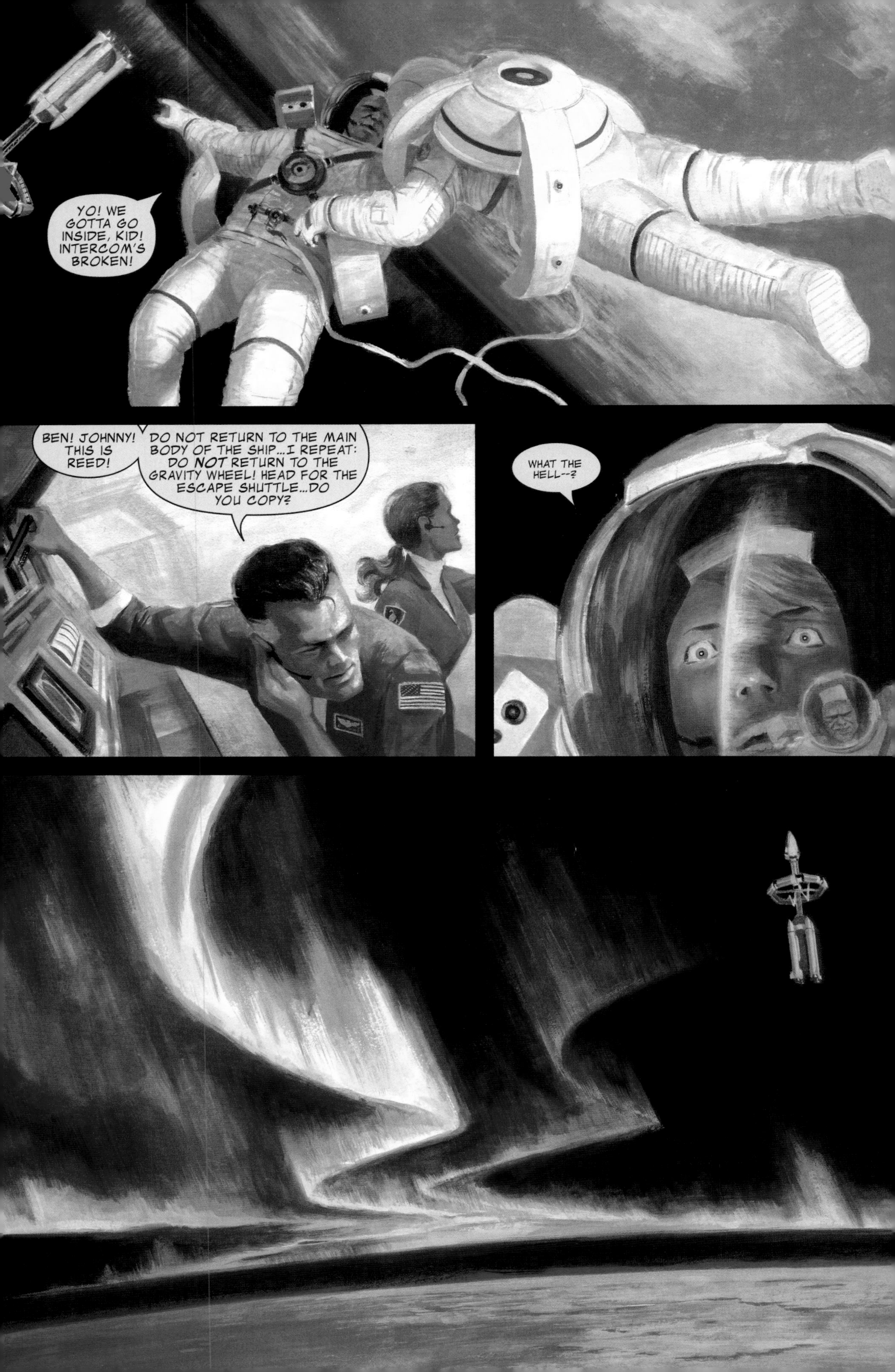
YO! WE GOTTA GO INSIDE, KID! INTERCOM'S BROKEN!
BEN! JOHNNY! THIS IS REED!
DO NOT RETURN TO THE MAIN BODY OF THE SHIP...I REPEAT: DO **NOT** RETURN TO THE GRAVITY WHEEL! HEAD FOR THE ESCAPE SHUTTLE...DO YOU COPY?
WHAT THE HELL--?

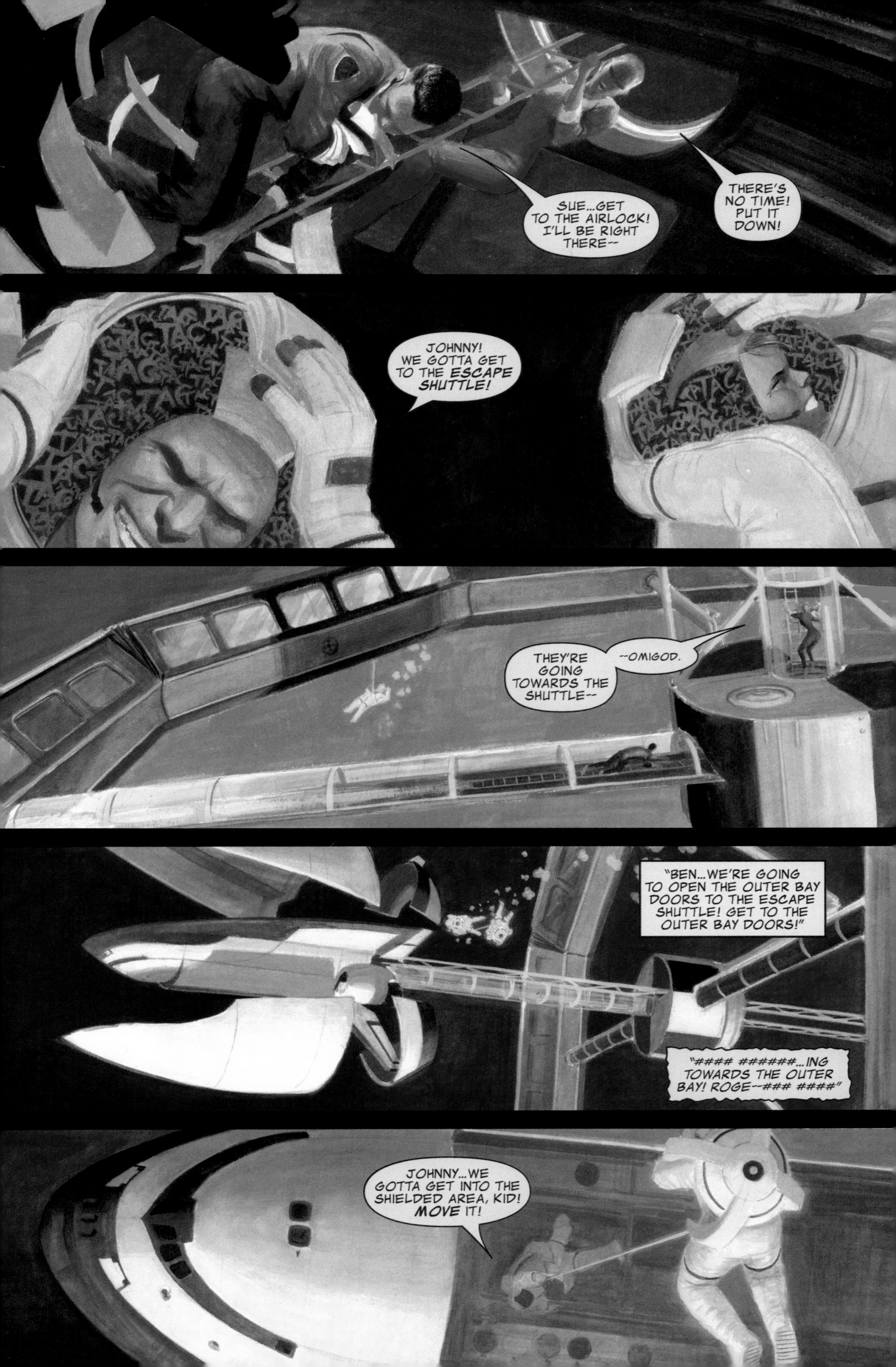
SUE...GET TO THE AIRLOCK! I'LL BE RIGHT THERE--
THERE'S NO TIME! PUT IT DOWN!
JOHNNY! WE GOTTA GET TO THE ESCAPE SHUTTLE!
THEY'RE GOING TOWARDS THE SHUTTLE--
--OMIGOD.
"BEN...WE'RE GOING TO OPEN THE OUTER BAY DOORS TO THE ESCAPE SHUTTLE! GET TO THE OUTER BAY DOORS!"
"#### ######...ING TOWARDS THE OUTER BAY! ROGE--### ####"
JOHNNY...WE GOTTA GET INTO THE SHIELDED AREA, KID! MOVE IT!

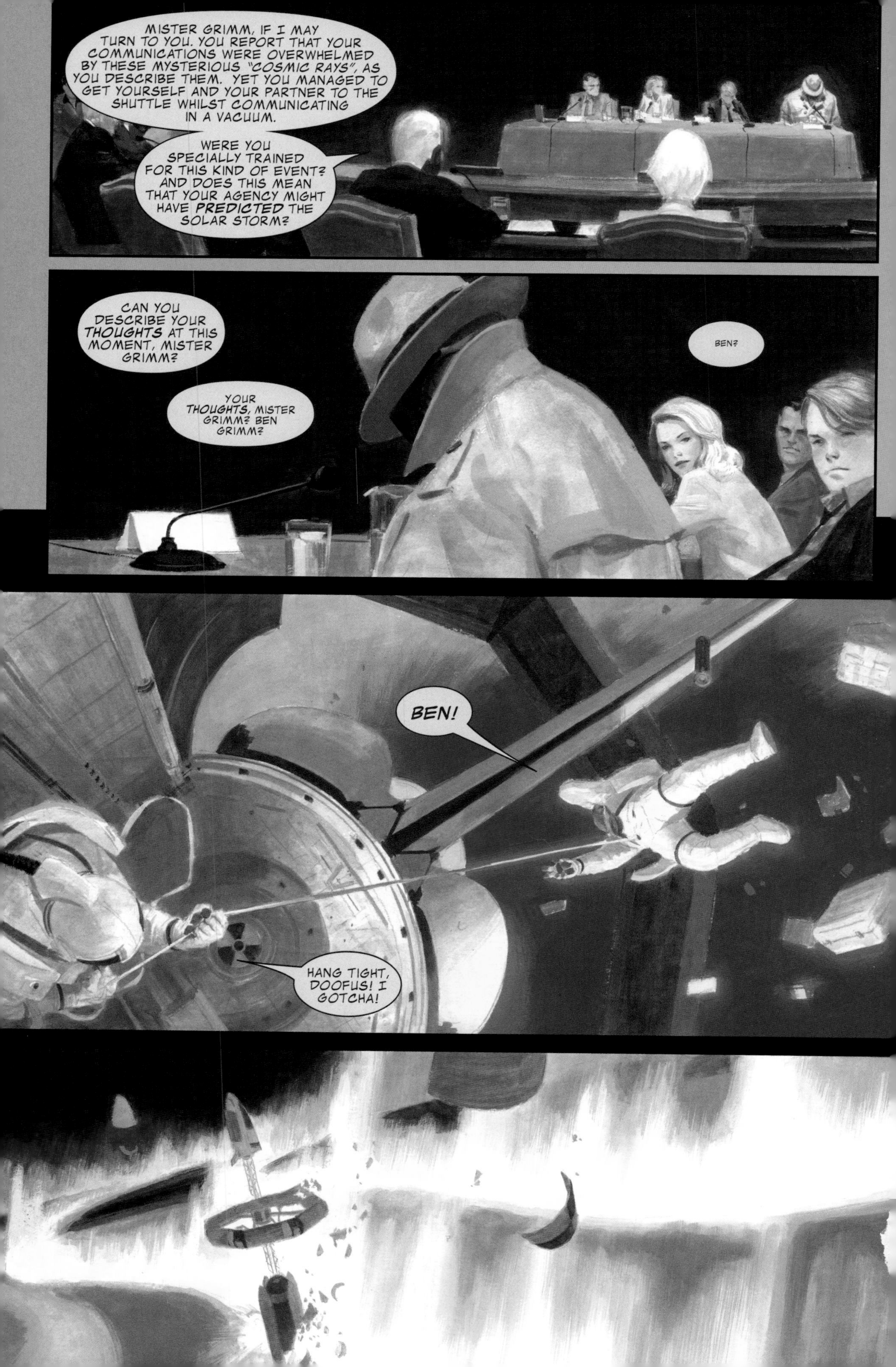
MISTER GRIMM, IF I MAY TURN TO YOU. YOU REPORT THAT YOUR COMMUNICATIONS WERE OVERWHELMED BY THESE MYSTERIOUS "COSMIC RAYS", AS YOU DESCRIBE THEM. YET YOU MANAGED TO GET YOURSELF AND YOUR PARTNER TO THE SHUTTLE WHILST COMMUNICATING IN A VACUUM.
WERE YOU SPECIALLY TRAINED FOR THIS KIND OF EVENT? AND DOES THIS MEAN THAT YOUR AGENCY MIGHT HAVE *PREDICTED* THE SOLAR STORM?
CAN YOU DESCRIBE YOUR *THOUGHTS* AT THIS MOMENT, MISTER GRIMM?
BEN?
YOUR *THOUGHTS*, MISTER GRIMM? BEN GRIMM?
BEN!
HANG TIGHT, DOOFUS! I GOTCHA!

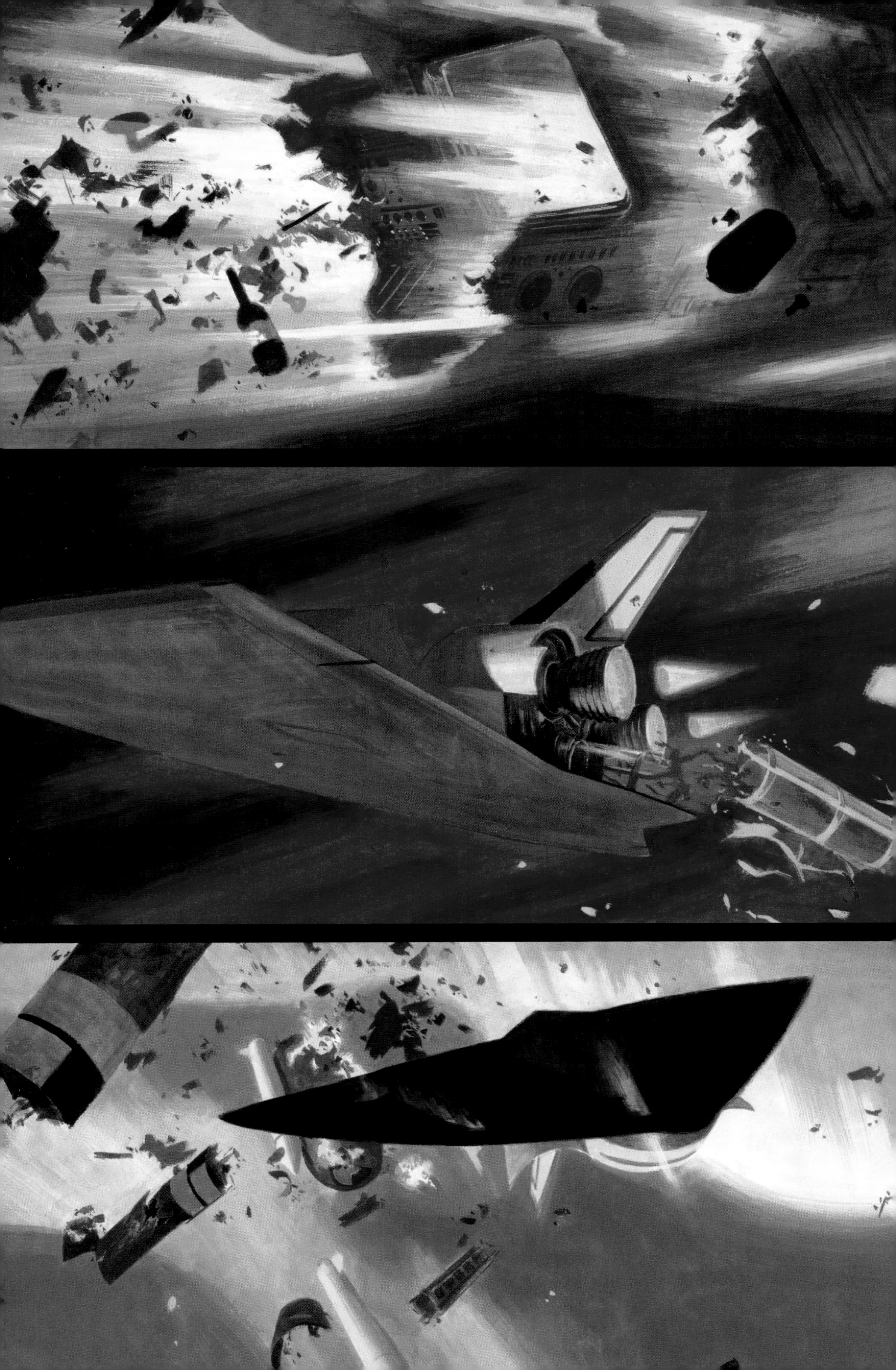

...YOUR THOUGHTS...
...CAN YOU DESCRIBE...
...THOUGHTS...
...I WAS SCARED... I REMEMBER...
...I WANTED TO HIDE...
...MAKE MYSELF DISAPPEAR...
...YOUR THOUGHTS...
...CAN YOU DESCRIBE...
...THOUGHTS...
...I THOUGHT I WOULD LOSE THE WOMAN I LOVE...
...I REMEMBER TRYING TO REACH HER...
...YOUR THOUGHTS...
...CAN YOU DESCRIBE...
...THOUGHTS...
...I WUZ ANGRY...
...DIDN'T WANNA DIE LIKE THIS...
...YOUR THOUGHTS...
...CAN YOU DESCRIBE...
...THOUGHTS...
...IT WAS HOT...

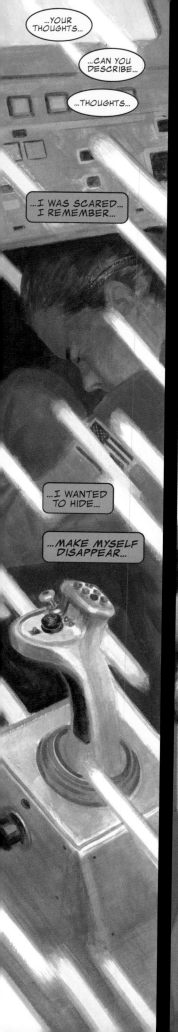

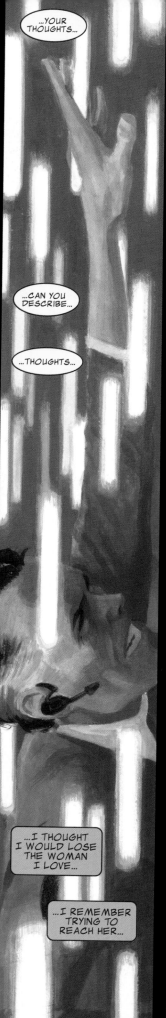

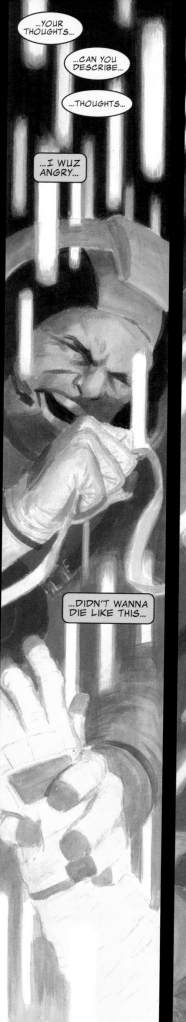

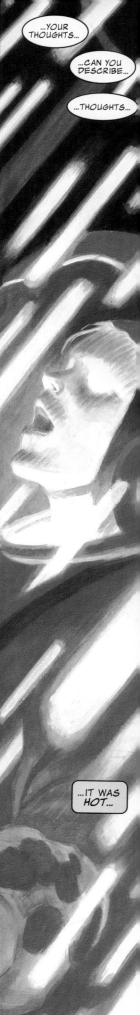

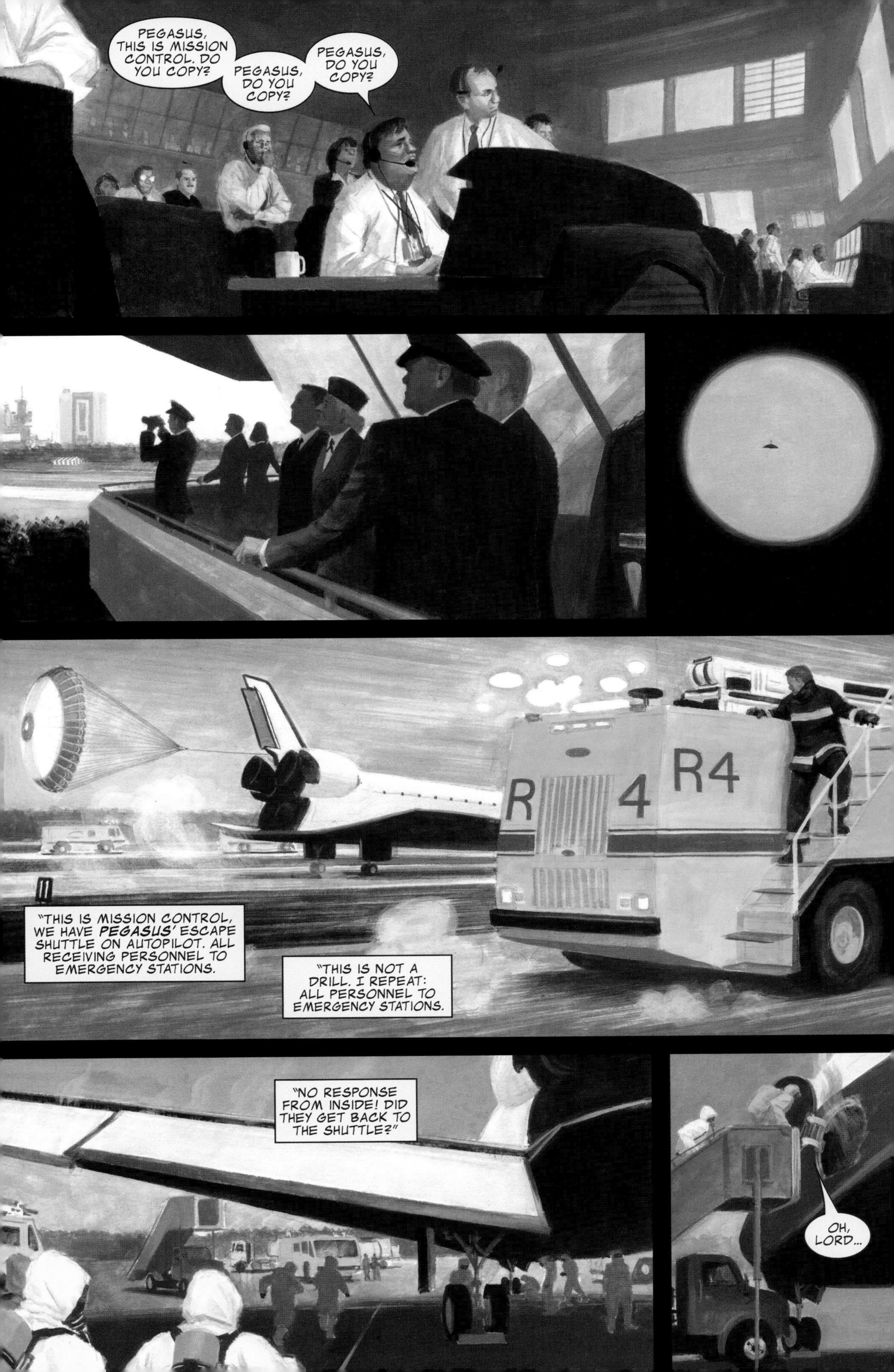
PEGASUS, THIS IS MISSION CONTROL. DO YOU COPY?
PEGASUS, DO YOU COPY?
PEGASUS, DO YOU COPY?
R4
R 4
"THIS IS MISSION CONTROL, WE HAVE PEGASUS' ESCAPE SHUTTLE ON AUTOPILOT. ALL RECEIVING PERSONNEL TO EMERGENCY STATIONS.
"THIS IS NOT A DRILL. I REPEAT: ALL PERSONNEL TO EMERGENCY STATIONS.
"NO RESPONSE FROM INSIDE! DID THEY GET BACK TO THE SHUTTLE?"
OH, LORD...

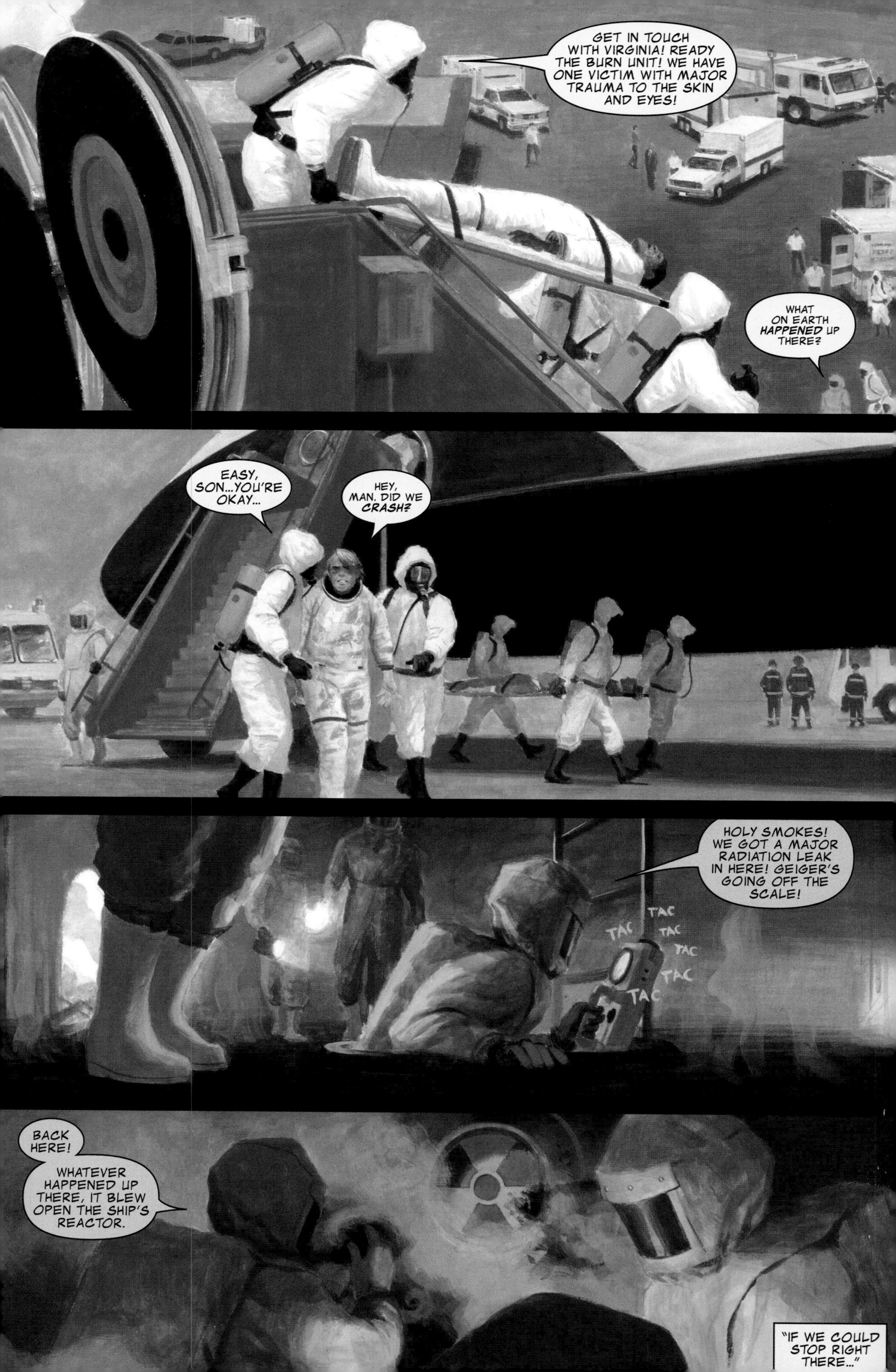
GET IN TOUCH WITH VIRGINIA! READY THE BURN UNIT! WE HAVE ONE VICTIM WITH MAJOR TRAUMA TO THE SKIN AND EYES!
WHAT ON EARTH HAPPENED UP THERE?
EASY, SON...YOU'RE OKAY...
HEY, MAN. DID WE CRASH?
HOLY SMOKES! WE GOT A MAJOR RADIATION LEAK IN HERE! GEIGER'S GOING OFF THE SCALE!
TAC TAC TAC TAC TAC TAC
BACK HERE!
WHATEVER HAPPENED UP THERE, IT BLEW OPEN THE SHIP'S REACTOR.
"IF WE COULD STOP RIGHT THERE..."

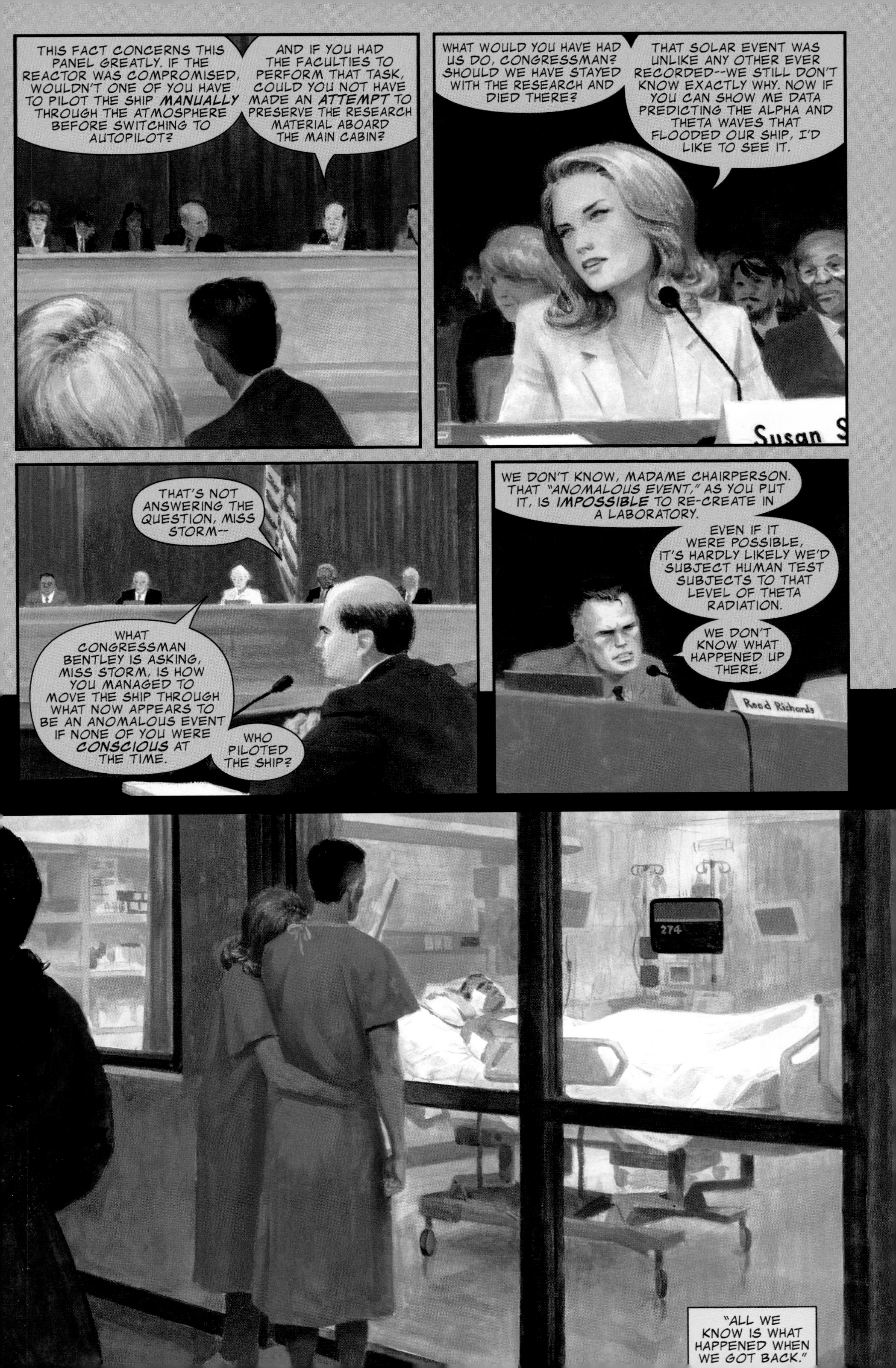

THIS FACT CONCERNS THIS PANEL GREATLY. IF THE REACTOR WAS COMPROMISED, WOULDN'T ONE OF YOU HAVE TO PILOT THE SHIP MANUALLY THROUGH THE ATMOSPHERE BEFORE SWITCHING TO AUTOPILOT?
AND IF YOU HAD THE FACULTIES TO PERFORM THAT TASK, COULD YOU NOT HAVE MADE AN ATTEMPT TO PRESERVE THE RESEARCH MATERIAL ABOARD THE MAIN CABIN?
WHAT WOULD YOU HAVE HAD US DO, CONGRESSMAN? SHOULD WE HAVE STAYED WITH THE RESEARCH AND DIED THERE?
THAT SOLAR EVENT WAS UNLIKE ANY OTHER EVER RECORDED--WE STILL DON'T KNOW EXACTLY WHY. NOW IF YOU CAN SHOW ME DATA PREDICTING THE ALPHA AND THETA WAVES THAT FLOODED OUR SHIP, I'D LIKE TO SEE IT.
Susan S
THAT'S NOT ANSWERING THE QUESTION, MISS STORM--
WHAT CONGRESSMAN BENTLEY IS ASKING, MISS STORM, IS HOW YOU MANAGED TO MOVE THE SHIP THROUGH WHAT NOW APPEARS TO BE AN ANOMALOUS EVENT IF NONE OF YOU WERE CONSCIOUS AT THE TIME.
WHO PILOTED THE SHIP?
WE DON'T KNOW, MADAME CHAIRPERSON. THAT "ANOMALOUS EVENT," AS YOU PUT IT, IS IMPOSSIBLE TO RE-CREATE IN A LABORATORY.
EVEN IF IT WERE POSSIBLE, IT'S HARDLY LIKELY WE'D SUBJECT HUMAN TEST SUBJECTS TO THAT LEVEL OF THETA RADIATION.
WE DON'T KNOW WHAT HAPPENED UP THERE.
Reed Richards
274
"ALL WE KNOW IS WHAT HAPPENED WHEN WE GOT BACK."

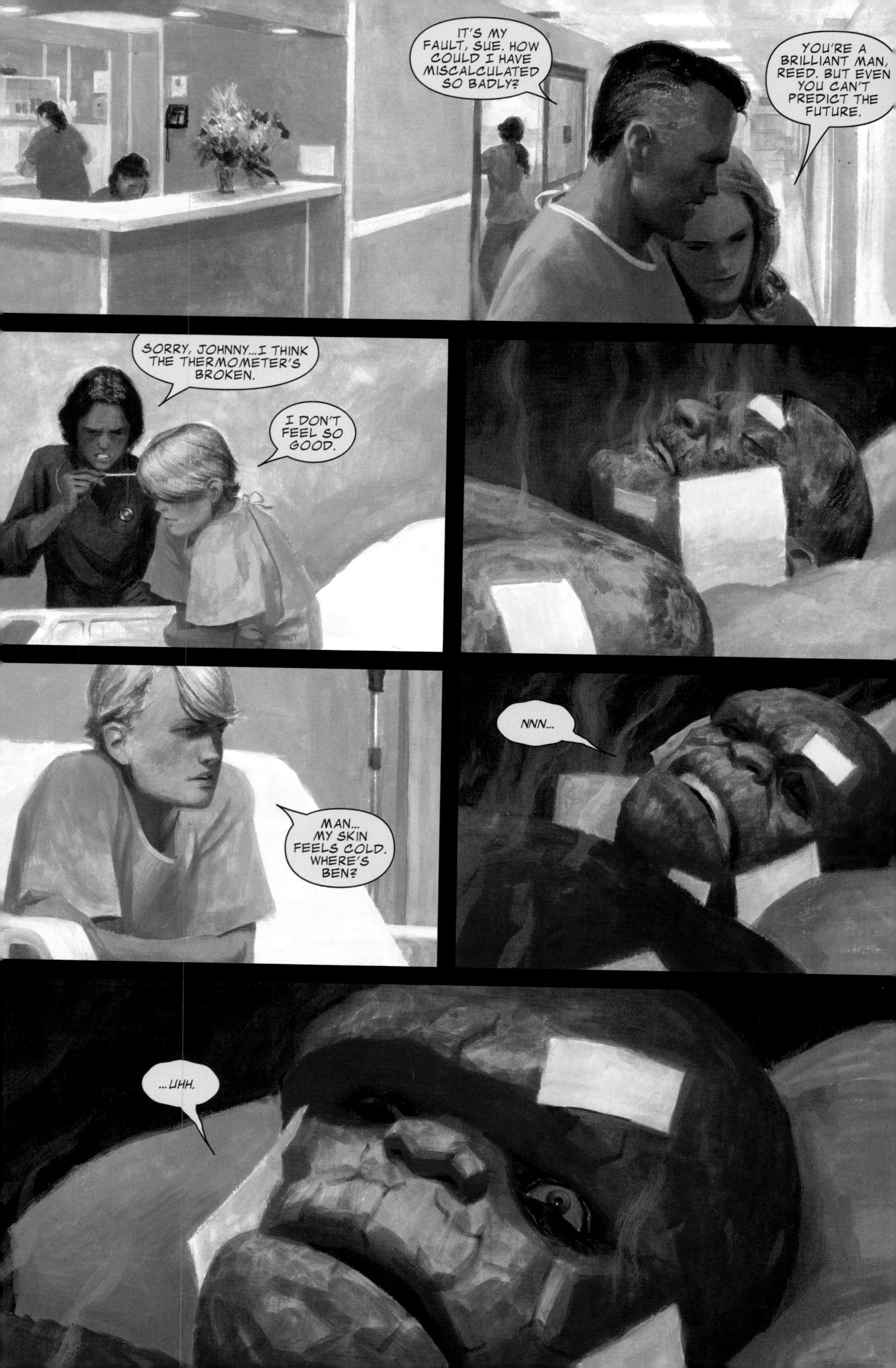
IT'S MY FAULT, SUE. HOW COULD I HAVE MISCALCULATED SO BADLY?
YOU'RE A BRILLIANT MAN, REED. BUT EVEN YOU CAN'T PREDICT THE FUTURE.
SORRY, JOHNNY...I THINK THE THERMOMETER'S BROKEN.
I DON'T FEEL SO GOOD.
MAN... MY SKIN FEELS COLD. WHERE'S BEN?
NNN...
...UHH.

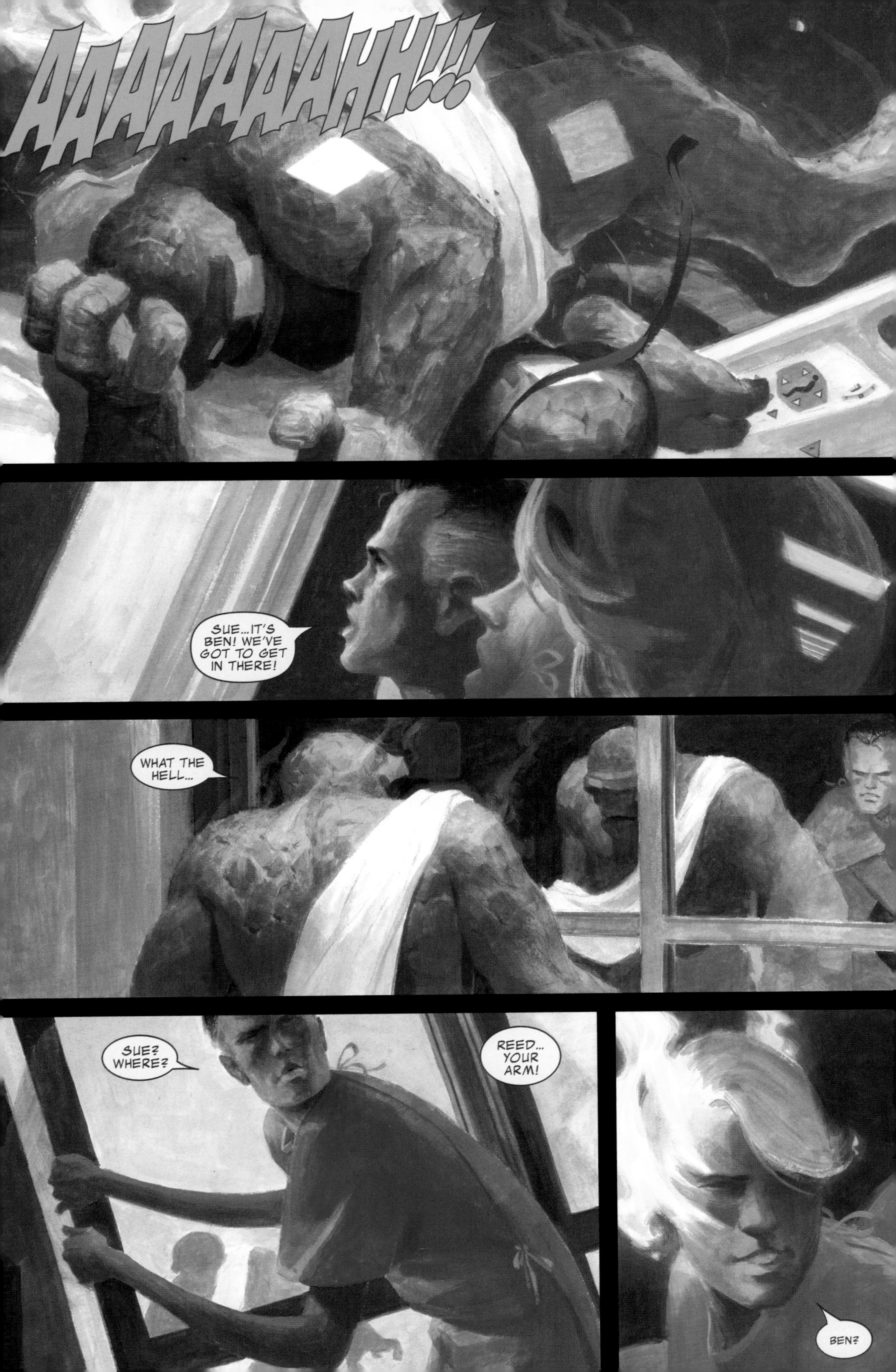
AAAAAAAAHH!!!
SUE...IT'S BEN! WE'VE GOT TO GET IN THERE!
WHAT THE HELL...
SUE? WHERE?
REED... YOUR ARM!
BEN?

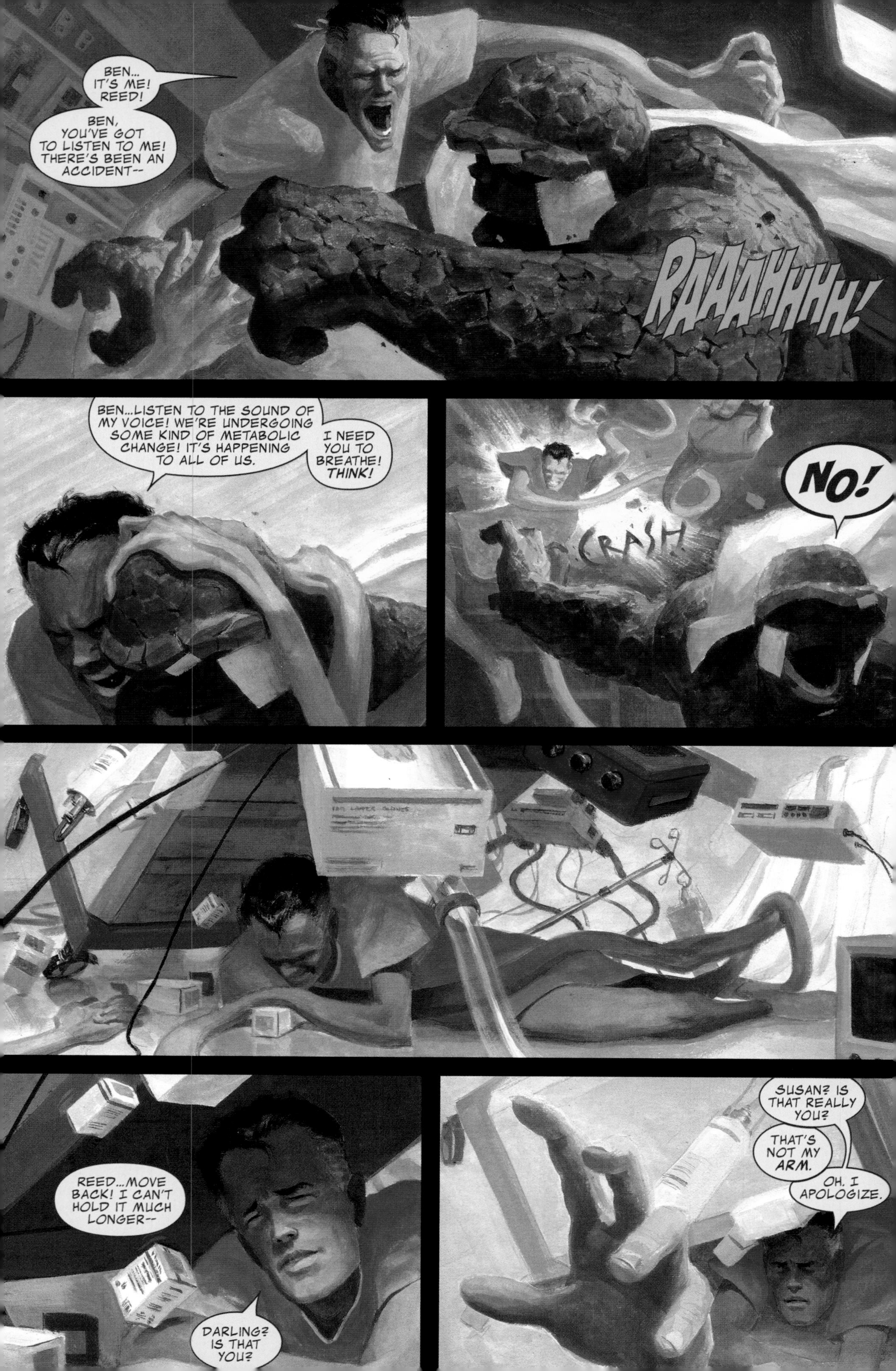
BEN... IT'S ME! REED!
BEN, YOU'VE GOT TO LISTEN TO ME! THERE'S BEEN AN ACCIDENT--
RAAAHHHH!
BEN...LISTEN TO THE SOUND OF MY VOICE! WE'RE UNDERGOING SOME KIND OF METABOLIC CHANGE! IT'S HAPPENING TO ALL OF US.
I NEED YOU TO BREATHE! *THINK!*
CRASH
NO!
REED...MOVE BACK! I CAN'T HOLD IT MUCH LONGER--
DARLING? IS THAT YOU?
SUSAN? IS THAT REALLY YOU?
THAT'S NOT MY *ARM*.
OH. I APOLOGIZE.

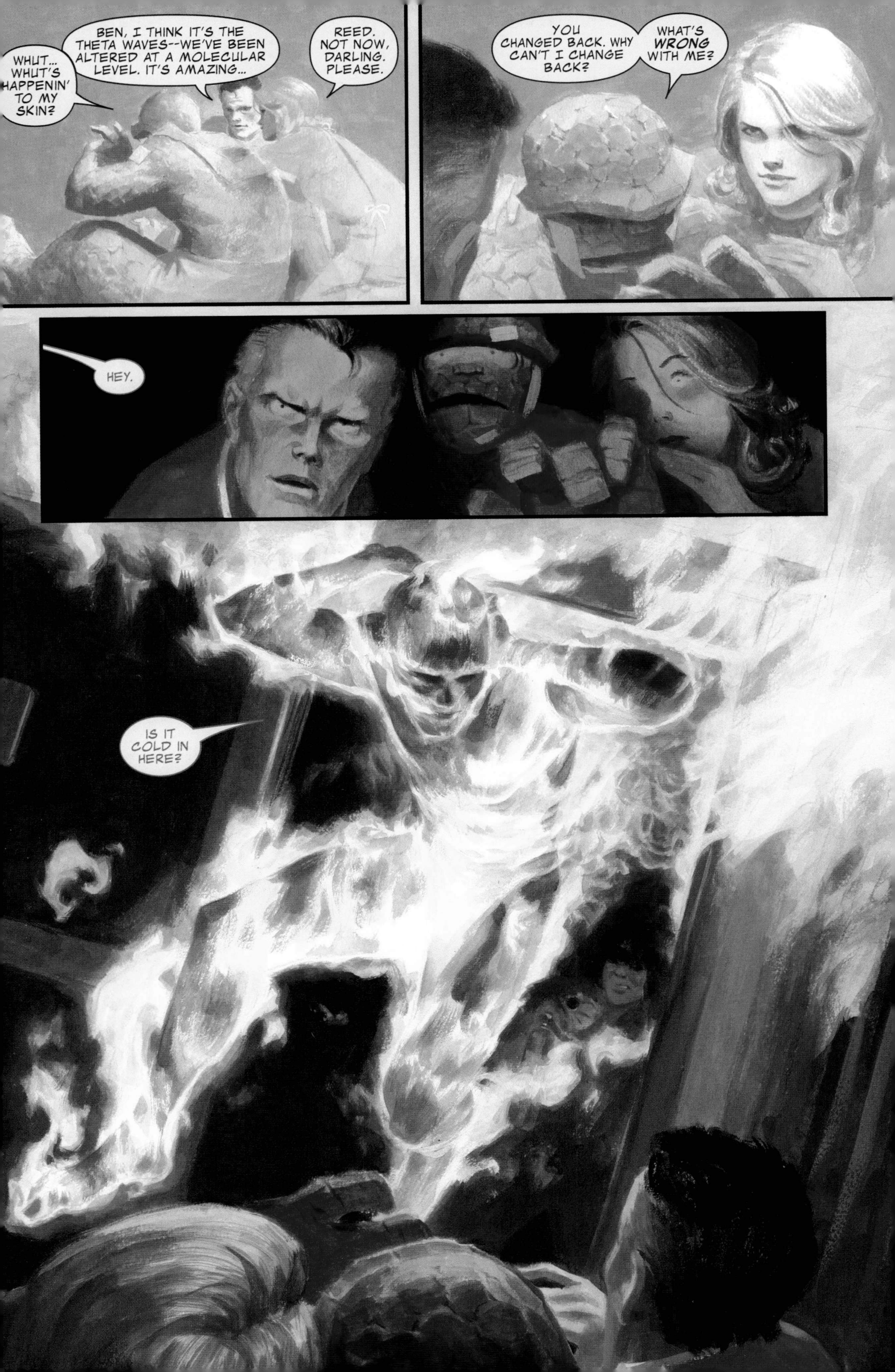

WHUT... WHUT'S HAPPENIN' TO MY SKIN?
BEN, I THINK IT'S THE THETA WAVES--WE'VE BEEN ALTERED AT A MOLECULAR LEVEL. IT'S AMAZING...
REED. NOT NOW, DARLING. PLEASE.
YOU CHANGED BACK. WHY CAN'T I CHANGE BACK?
WHAT'S WRONG WITH ME?
HEY.
IS IT COLD IN HERE?

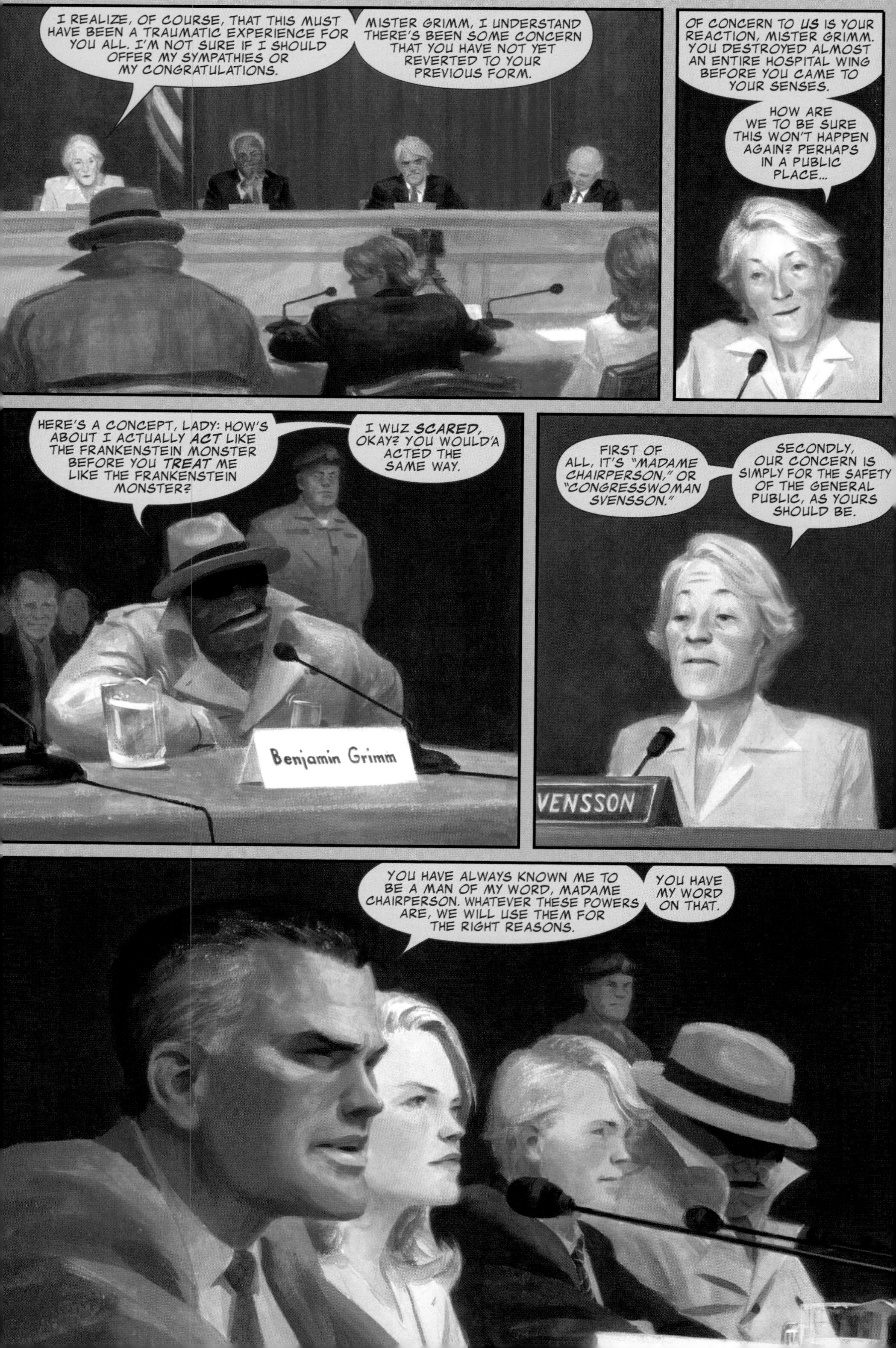
I REALIZE, OF COURSE, THAT THIS MUST HAVE BEEN A TRAUMATIC EXPERIENCE FOR YOU ALL. I'M NOT SURE IF I SHOULD OFFER MY SYMPATHIES OR MY CONGRATULATIONS.
MISTER GRIMM, I UNDERSTAND THERE'S BEEN SOME CONCERN THAT YOU HAVE NOT YET REVERTED TO YOUR PREVIOUS FORM.
OF CONCERN TO US IS YOUR REACTION, MISTER GRIMM. YOU DESTROYED ALMOST AN ENTIRE HOSPITAL WING BEFORE YOU CAME TO YOUR SENSES.
HOW ARE WE TO BE SURE THIS WON'T HAPPEN AGAIN? PERHAPS IN A PUBLIC PLACE...
HERE'S A CONCEPT, LADY: HOW'S ABOUT I ACTUALLY ACT LIKE THE FRANKENSTEIN MONSTER BEFORE YOU TREAT ME LIKE THE FRANKENSTEIN MONSTER?
I WUZ SCARED, OKAY? YOU WOULD'A ACTED THE SAME WAY.
Benjamin Grimm
FIRST OF ALL, IT'S "MADAME CHAIRPERSON," OR "CONGRESSWOMAN SVENSSON."
SECONDLY, OUR CONCERN IS SIMPLY FOR THE SAFETY OF THE GENERAL PUBLIC, AS YOURS SHOULD BE.
VENSSON
YOU HAVE ALWAYS KNOWN ME TO BE A MAN OF MY WORD, MADAME CHAIRPERSON. WHATEVER THESE POWERS ARE, WE WILL USE THEM FOR THE RIGHT REASONS.
YOU HAVE MY WORD ON THAT.

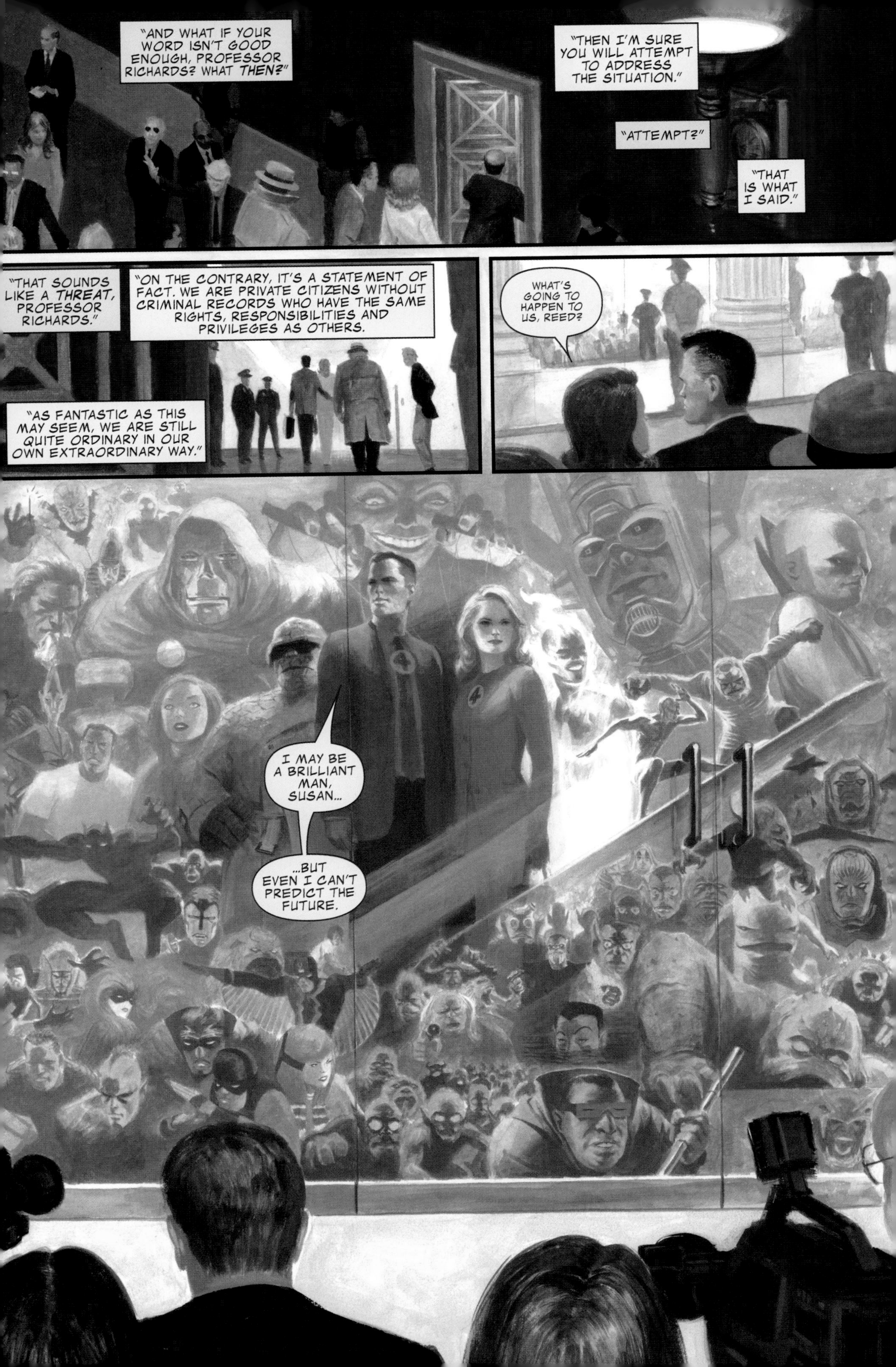
"AND WHAT IF YOUR WORD ISN'T GOOD ENOUGH, PROFESSOR RICHARDS? WHAT THEN?"
"THEN I'M SURE YOU WILL ATTEMPT TO ADDRESS THE SITUATION."
"ATTEMPT?"
"THAT IS WHAT I SAID."
"THAT SOUNDS LIKE A THREAT, PROFESSOR RICHARDS."
"ON THE CONTRARY, IT'S A STATEMENT OF FACT. WE ARE PRIVATE CITIZENS WITHOUT CRIMINAL RECORDS WHO HAVE THE SAME RIGHTS, RESPONSIBILITIES AND PRIVILEGES AS OTHERS.
"AS FANTASTIC AS THIS MAY SEEM, WE ARE STILL QUITE ORDINARY IN OUR OWN EXTRAORDINARY WAY."
WHAT'S GOING TO HAPPEN TO US, REED?
I MAY BE A BRILLIANT MAN, SUSAN...
...BUT EVEN I CAN'T PREDICT THE FUTURE.

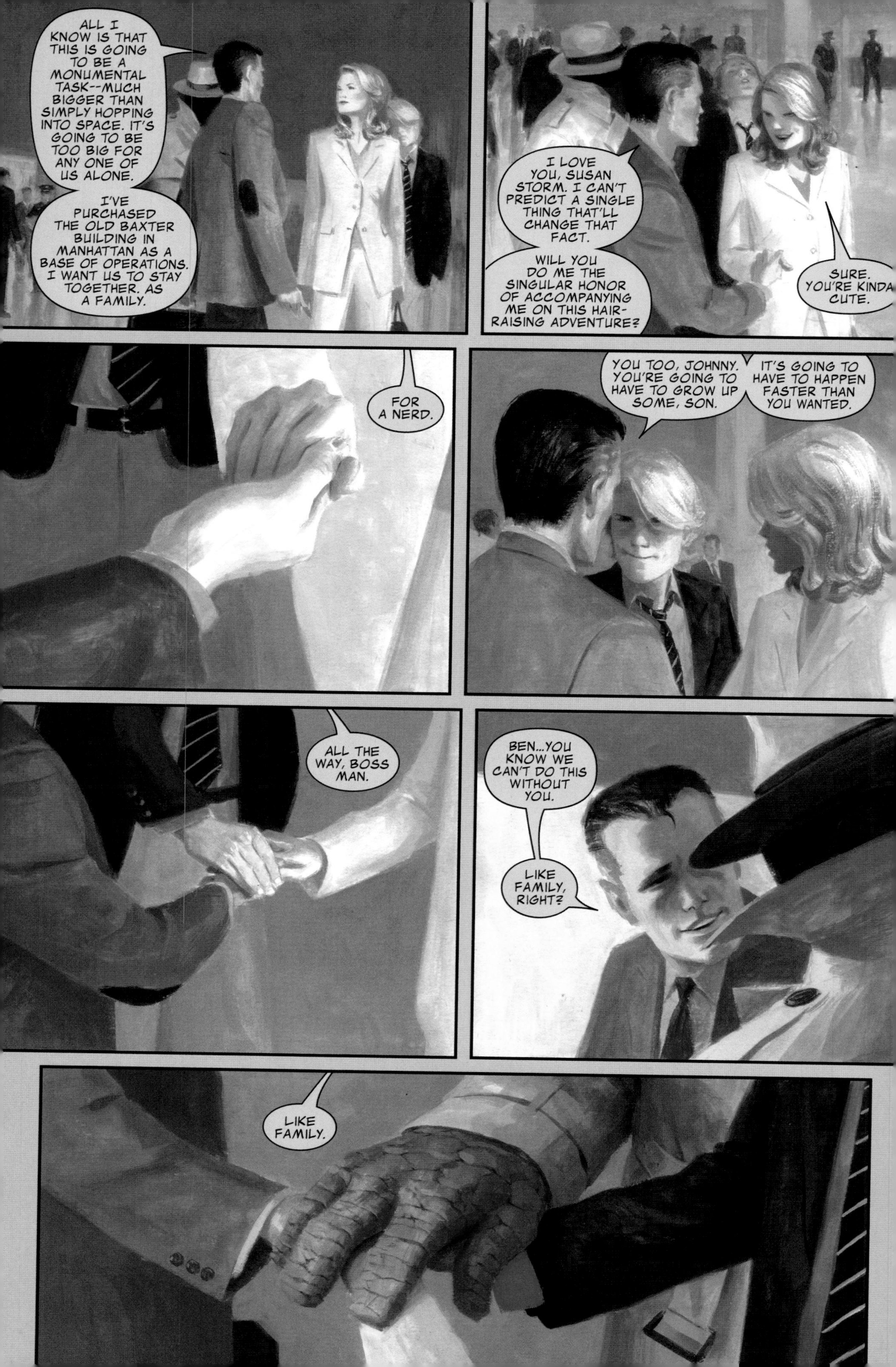
ALL I KNOW IS THAT THIS IS GOING TO BE A MONUMENTAL TASK--MUCH BIGGER THAN SIMPLY HOPPING INTO SPACE. IT'S GOING TO BE TOO BIG FOR ANY ONE OF US ALONE.
I'VE PURCHASED THE OLD BAXTER BUILDING IN MANHATTAN AS A BASE OF OPERATIONS. I WANT US TO STAY TOGETHER. AS A FAMILY.
I LOVE YOU, SUSAN STORM. I CAN'T PREDICT A SINGLE THING THAT'LL CHANGE THAT FACT.
WILL YOU DO ME THE SINGULAR HONOR OF ACCOMPANYING ME ON THIS HAIR-RAISING ADVENTURE?
SURE. YOU'RE KINDA CUTE.
FOR A NERD.
YOU TOO, JOHNNY. YOU'RE GOING TO HAVE TO GROW UP SOME, SON.
IT'S GOING TO HAVE TO HAPPEN FASTER THAN YOU WANTED.
ALL THE WAY, BOSS MAN.
BEN...YOU KNOW WE CAN'T DO THIS WITHOUT YOU.
LIKE FAMILY, RIGHT?
LIKE FAMILY.

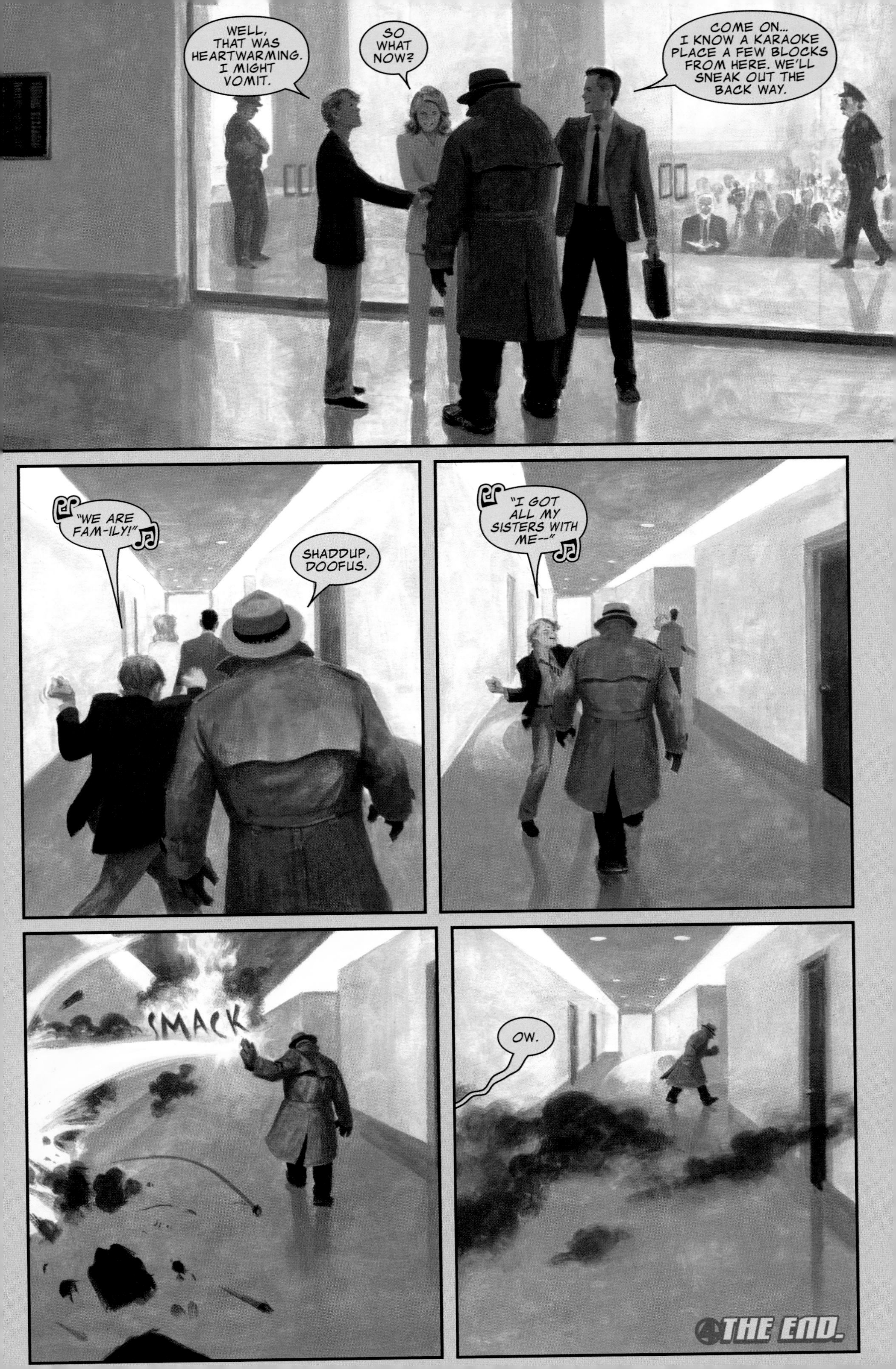
WELL, THAT WAS HEARTWARMING. I MIGHT VOMIT.
SO WHAT NOW?
COME ON... I KNOW A KARAOKE PLACE A FEW BLOCKS FROM HERE. WE'LL SNEAK OUT THE BACK WAY.
"WE ARE FAM-ILY!"
SHADDUP, DOOFUS.
"I GOT ALL MY SISTERS WITH ME--"
SMACK
OW.
THE END.

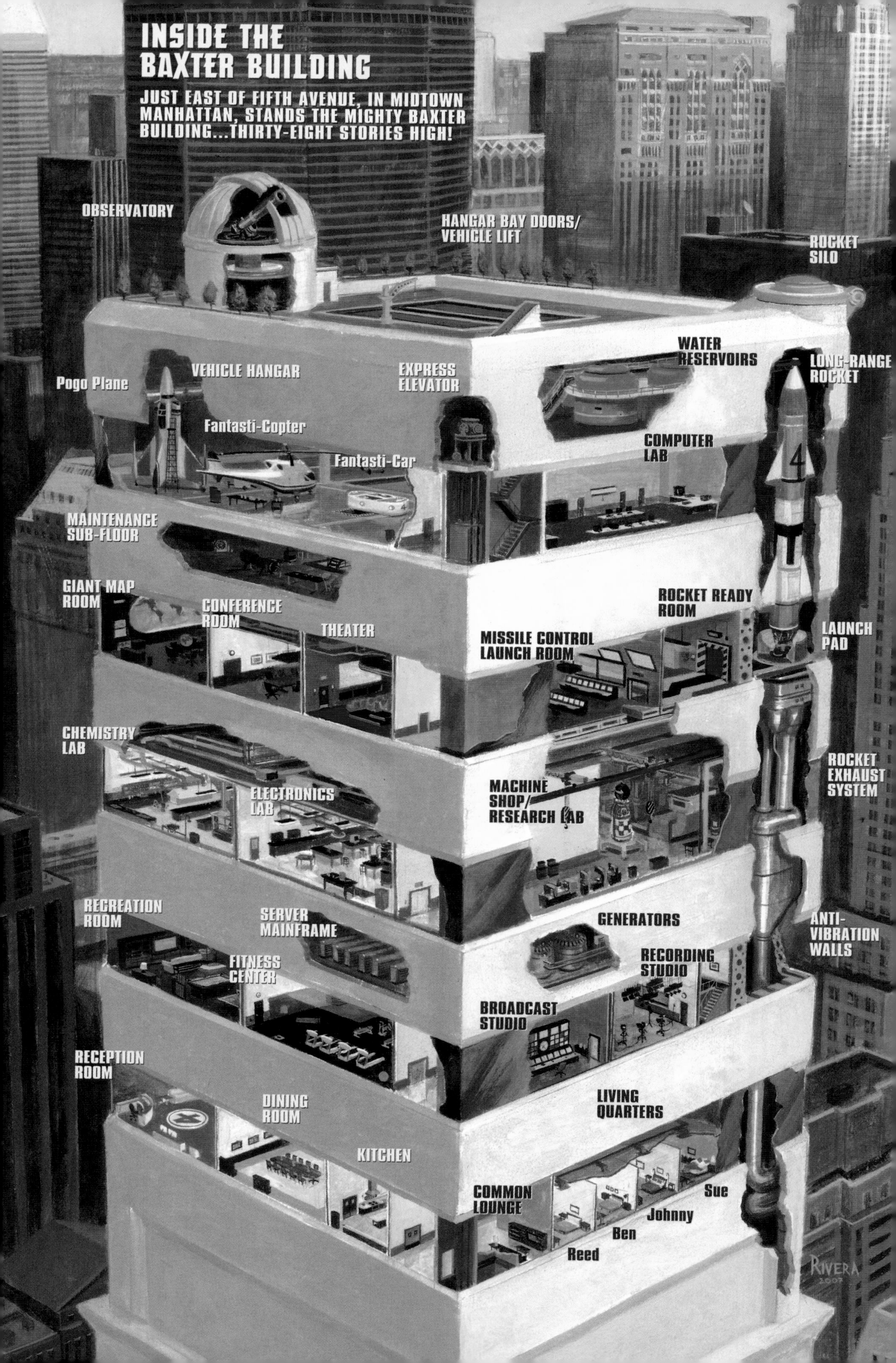
INSIDE THE BAXTER BUILDING
JUST EAST OF FIFTH AVENUE, IN MIDTOWN MANHATTAN, STANDS THE MIGHTY BAXTER BUILDING...THIRTY-EIGHT STORIES HIGH!
OBSERVATORY
HANGAR BAY DOORS/ VEHICLE LIFT
ROCKET SILO
WATER RESERVOIRS
LONG-RANGE ROCKET
Pogo Plane
VEHICLE HANGAR
EXPRESS ELEVATOR
Fantasti-Copter
Fantasti-Car
COMPUTER LAB
MAINTENANCE SUB-FLOOR
GIANT MAP ROOM
CONFERENCE ROOM
THEATER
ROCKET READY ROOM
MISSILE CONTROL LAUNCH ROOM
LAUNCH PAD
CHEMISTRY LAB
ELECTRONICS LAB
MACHINE SHOP/ RESEARCH LAB
ROCKET EXHAUST SYSTEM
RECREATION ROOM
SERVER MAINFRAME
GENERATORS
ANTI-VIBRATION WALLS
FITNESS CENTER
RECORDING STUDIO
BROADCAST STUDIO
RECEPTION ROOM
DINING ROOM
LIVING QUARTERS
KITCHEN
COMMON LOUNGE
Sue
Johnny
Ben
Reed
RIVERA 2007

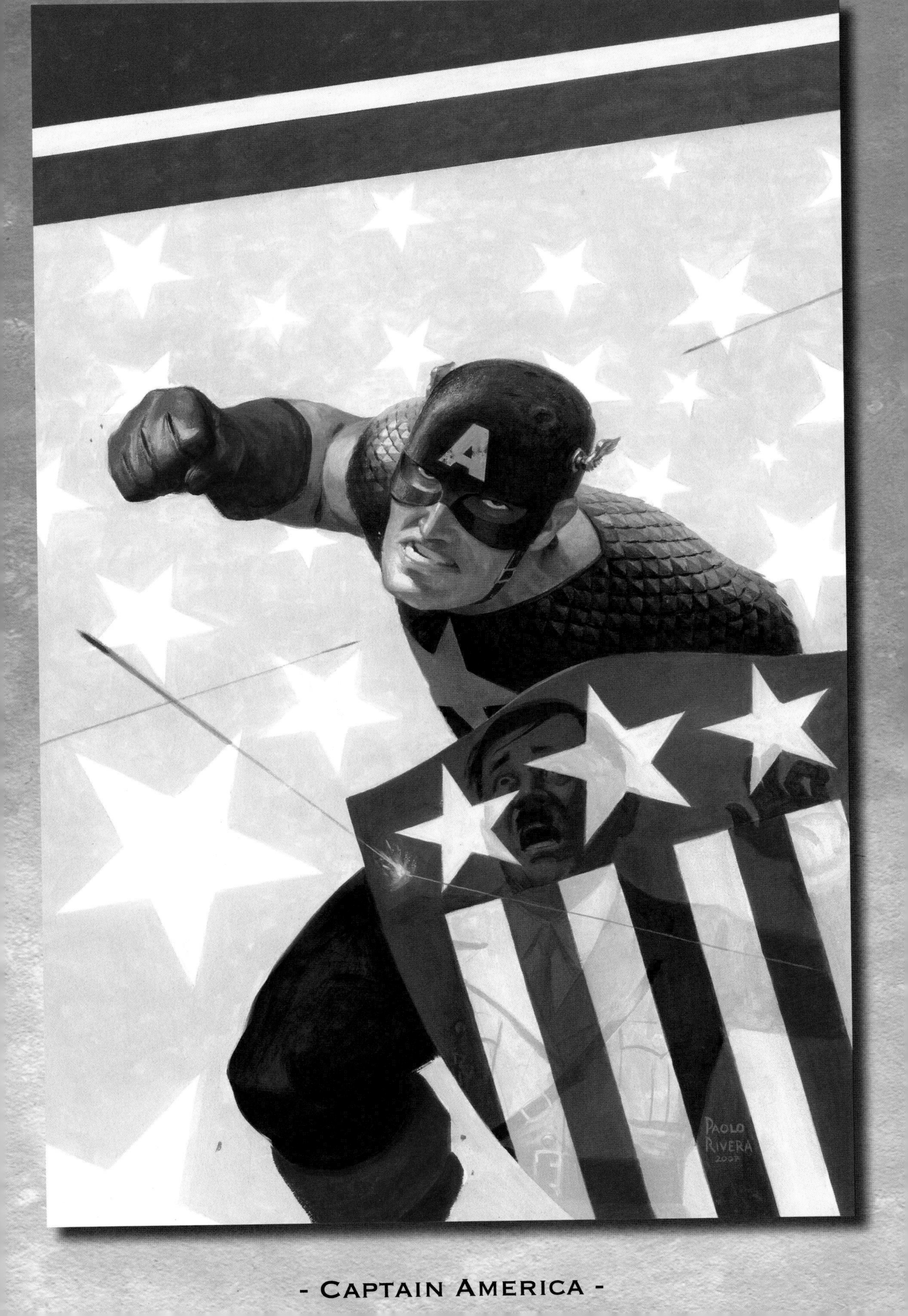
PAOLO
RIVERA
2007

- CAPTAIN AMERICA -

DON'T BE AFRAID, SON... YOU ARE ABOUT TO BECOME ONE OF AMERICA'S SAVIORS!

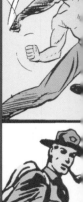

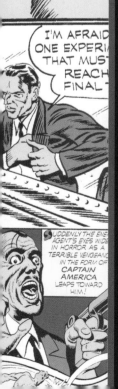

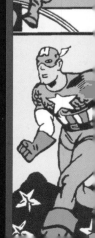

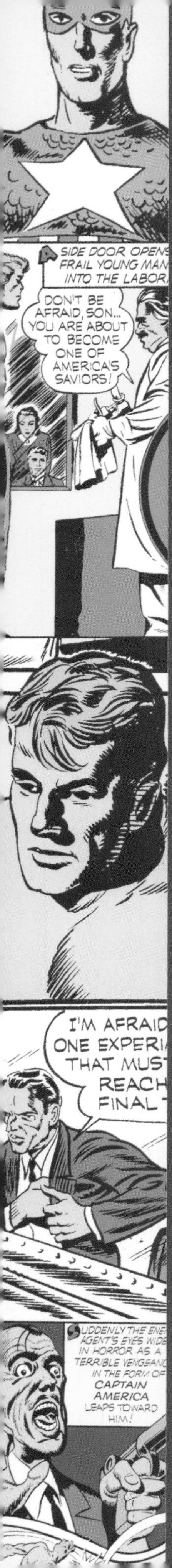

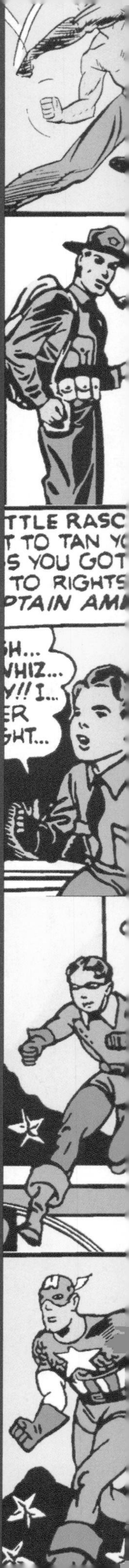

MYTHOS

1941! The World at War! And in a full-security laboratory, frail Steve Rogers became Captain America, the American super-soldier! For four thrilling years, he struck back at the Axis' treacherous attack – until a freak stroke of fate threw him into suspended animation…to awaken in the present day, a man out of his time! Since that day, Captain America has sought his destiny in this brave new world!

CAPTAIN AMERICA

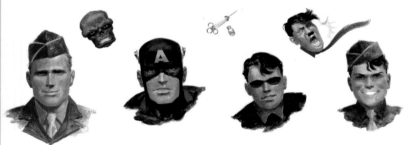

CAPTAIN AMERICA
STEVE ROGERS
BUCKY
JAMES BARNES

Based on *Captain America Comics #1, March 1941* by Joe Simon and Jack Kirby.
Captain America created by Joe Simon and Jack Kirby

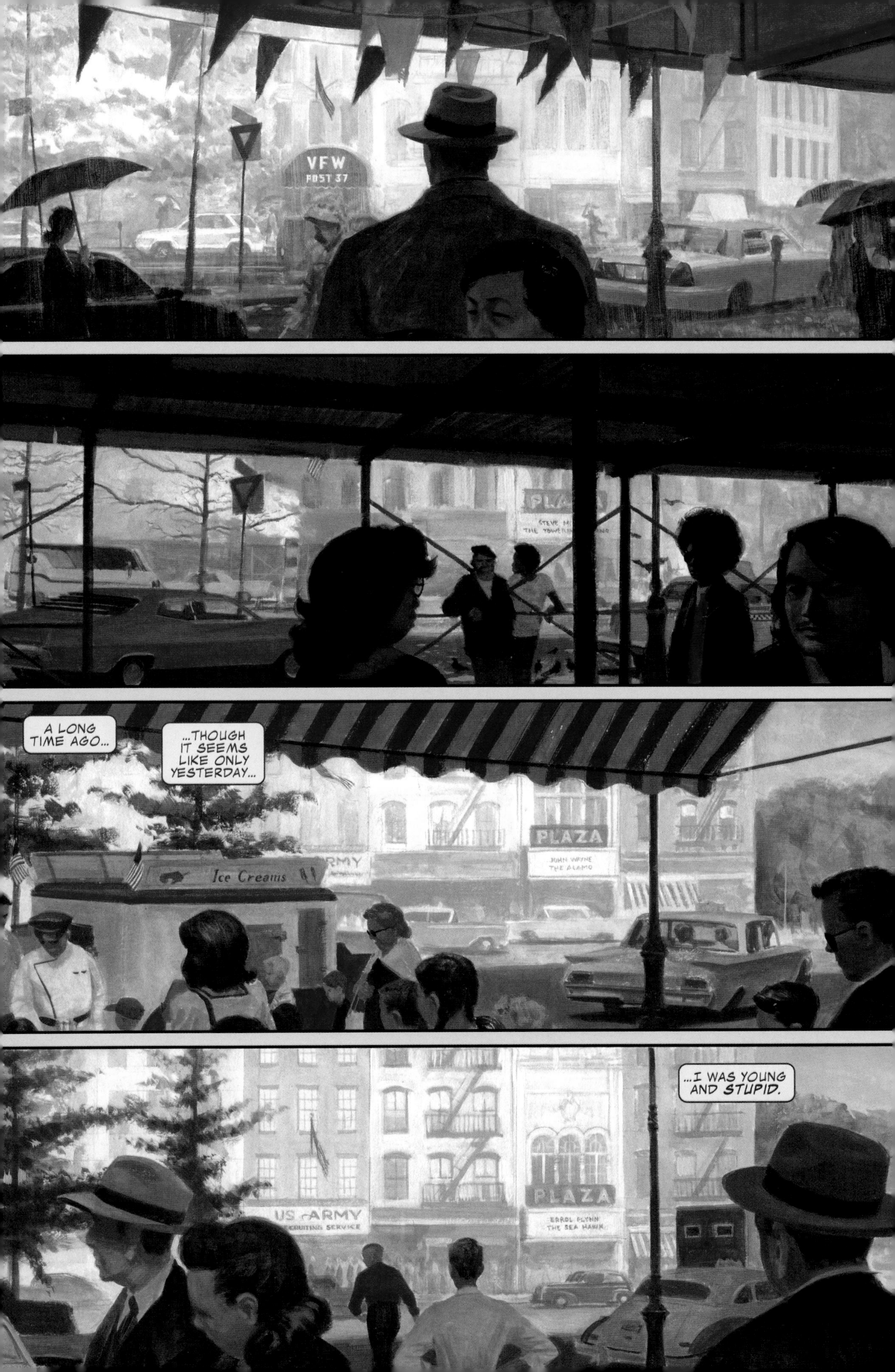
VFW
POST 37
PLAZA
A LONG TIME AGO...
...THOUGH IT SEEMS LIKE ONLY YESTERDAY...
Ice Creams
PLAZA
JOHN WAYNE
THE ALAMO
...I WAS YOUNG AND *STUPID.*
US ARMY
PLAZA
ERROL FLYNN
THE SEA HAWK

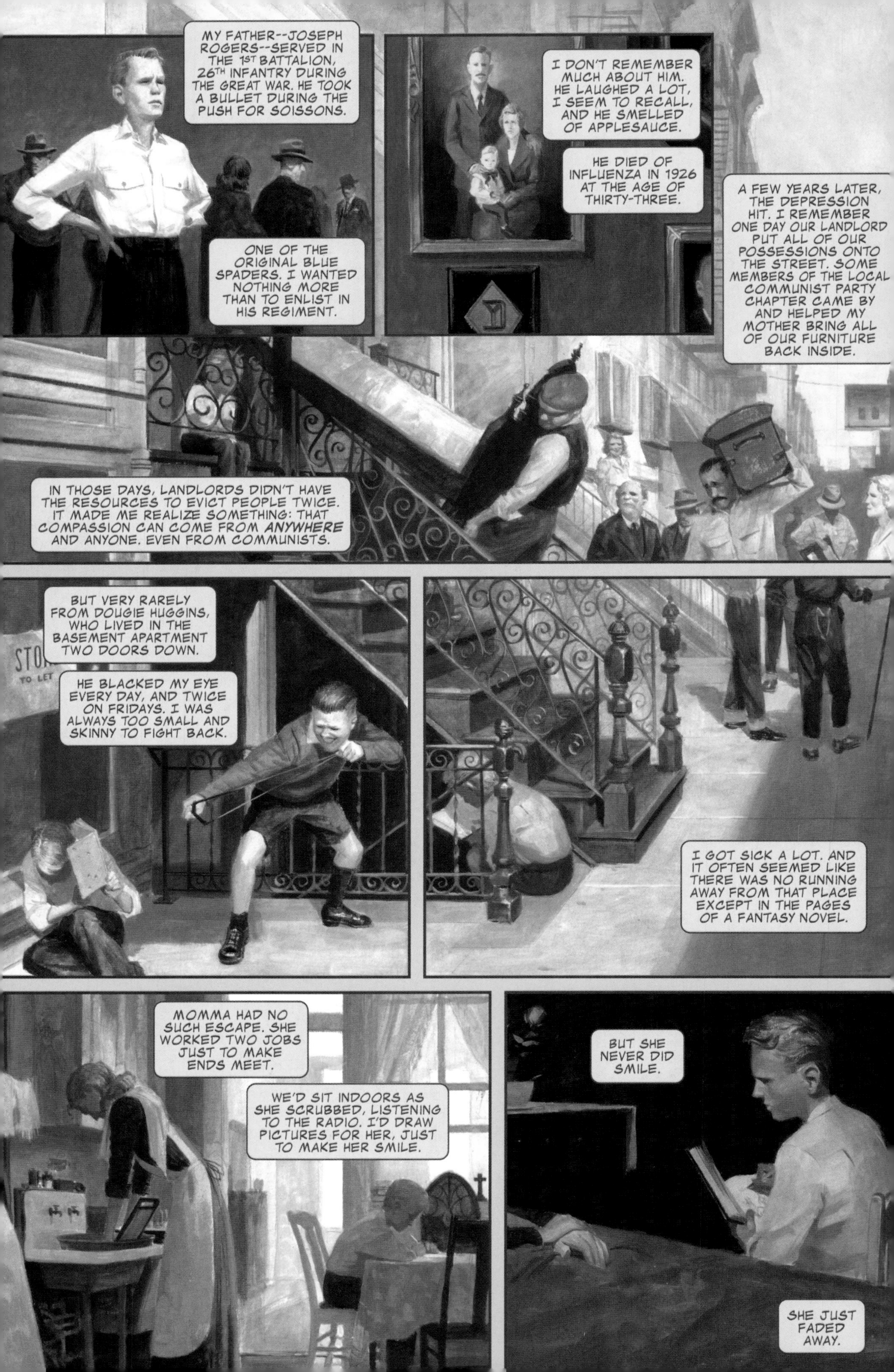
MY FATHER--JOSEPH ROGERS--SERVED IN THE 1ST BATTALION, 26TH INFANTRY DURING THE GREAT WAR. HE TOOK A BULLET DURING THE PUSH FOR SOISSONS.
ONE OF THE ORIGINAL BLUE SPADERS. I WANTED NOTHING MORE THAN TO ENLIST IN HIS REGIMENT.
I DON'T REMEMBER MUCH ABOUT HIM. HE LAUGHED A LOT, I SEEM TO RECALL, AND HE SMELLED OF APPLESAUCE.
HE DIED OF INFLUENZA IN 1926 AT THE AGE OF THIRTY-THREE.
A FEW YEARS LATER, THE DEPRESSION HIT. I REMEMBER ONE DAY OUR LANDLORD PUT ALL OF OUR POSSESSIONS ONTO THE STREET. SOME MEMBERS OF THE LOCAL COMMUNIST PARTY CHAPTER CAME BY AND HELPED MY MOTHER BRING ALL OF OUR FURNITURE BACK INSIDE.
IN THOSE DAYS, LANDLORDS DIDN'T HAVE THE RESOURCES TO EVICT PEOPLE TWICE. IT MADE ME REALIZE SOMETHING: THAT COMPASSION CAN COME FROM *ANYWHERE* AND ANYONE. EVEN FROM COMMUNISTS.
BUT VERY RARELY FROM DOUGIE HUGGINS, WHO LIVED IN THE BASEMENT APARTMENT TWO DOORS DOWN.
STO
TO LET
HE BLACKED MY EYE EVERY DAY, AND TWICE ON FRIDAYS. I WAS ALWAYS TOO SMALL AND SKINNY TO FIGHT BACK.
I GOT SICK A LOT. AND IT OFTEN SEEMED LIKE THERE WAS NO RUNNING AWAY FROM THAT PLACE EXCEPT IN THE PAGES OF A FANTASY NOVEL.
MOMMA HAD NO SUCH ESCAPE. SHE WORKED TWO JOBS JUST TO MAKE ENDS MEET.
WE'D SIT INDOORS AS SHE SCRUBBED, LISTENING TO THE RADIO. I'D DRAW PICTURES FOR HER, JUST TO MAKE HER SMILE.
BUT SHE NEVER DID SMILE.
SHE JUST FADED AWAY.

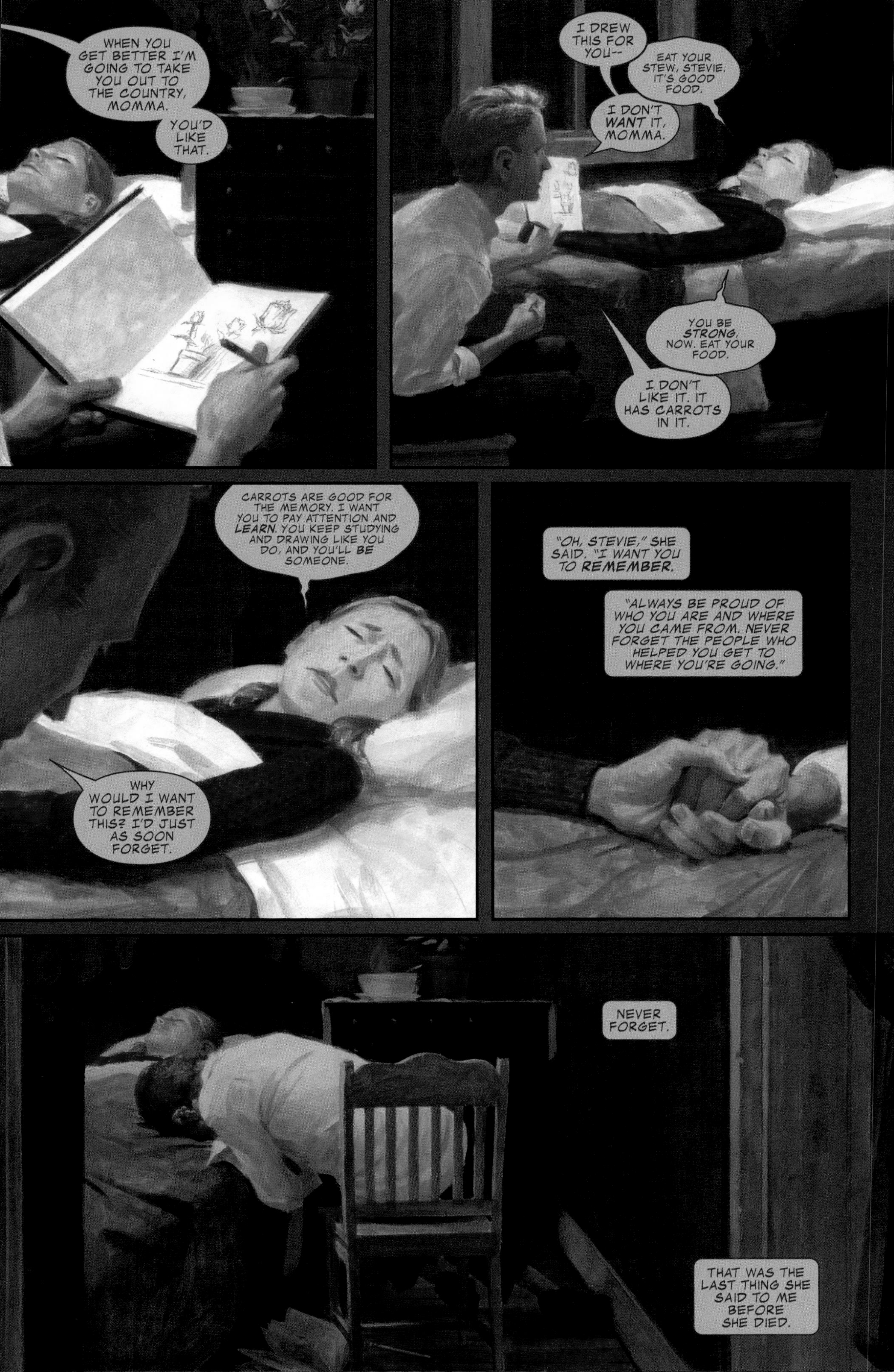
WHEN YOU GET BETTER I'M GOING TO TAKE YOU OUT TO THE COUNTRY, MOMMA.
YOU'D LIKE THAT.
I DREW THIS FOR YOU--
EAT YOUR STEW, STEVIE. IT'S GOOD FOOD.
I DON'T WANT IT, MOMMA.
YOU BE STRONG, NOW. EAT YOUR FOOD.
I DON'T LIKE IT. IT HAS CARROTS IN IT.
CARROTS ARE GOOD FOR THE MEMORY. I WANT YOU TO PAY ATTENTION AND LEARN. YOU KEEP STUDYING AND DRAWING LIKE YOU DO, AND YOU'LL BE SOMEONE.
WHY WOULD I WANT TO REMEMBER THIS? I'D JUST AS SOON FORGET.
"OH, STEVIE," SHE SAID. "I WANT YOU TO REMEMBER.
"ALWAYS BE PROUD OF WHO YOU ARE AND WHERE YOU CAME FROM. NEVER FORGET THE PEOPLE WHO HELPED YOU GET TO WHERE YOU'RE GOING."
NEVER FORGET.
THAT WAS THE LAST THING SHE SAID TO ME BEFORE SHE DIED.

I WAS ALONE...WISHING FOR ALL THE WORLD THAT I COULD BE ANYPLACE ELSE. BUT IF WISHES WERE NICKELS IN THOSE DAYS, WE'D ALL HAVE BEEN MILLIONAIRES.

AFTER SHE WAS GONE, I WORKED A DELIVERY TRUCK FOR A WHILE.

HERE I WAS, A NINETY-FIVE POUND TEENAGER UNLOADING TRUCKS FULL OF TOMATO PASTE THAT WEIGHED MORE THAN I DID.

DESPITE THE HARDSHIP, I FELT I HAD NO REASON TO COMPLAIN. THERE WERE OTHERS WORSE OFF THAN I.

ACROSS THE SEA IN EUROPE, A STORM GATHERED. NAZI GERMANY INVADED POLAND. BRITAIN AND FRANCE THEN DECLARED WAR ON THEM.

WE WATCHED IN HORROR AS HITLER'S WAR MACHINE GROUND COUNTRIES INTO DUST.

THE NIGHTMARE OF HIS THIRD REICH BECAME A REALITY. AN ENTIRE NATION FELL INTO MADNESS. ITALY FOLLOWED SUIT. IMPERIAL JAPAN BEGAN TO STIR.

"REMEMBER THIS MOMENT," MY MOTHER WOULD HAVE SAID. "NEVER FORGET THE EVENTS THAT SHAPE YOU."

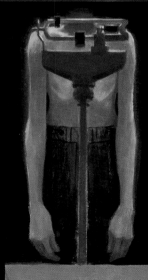

WE KNEW WAR WOULD EVENTUALLY COME TO US IF WE DIDN'T GO TO IT. DOUGIE HUGGINS AND I WENT TOGETHER TO ENLIST: ME, TO JOIN MY FATHER'S REGIMENT...HE, BECAUSE HE WAS BORED.

SHE WOULD HAVE BEEN WRONG.

I WAS CLASSIFIED 4-F, AND REJECTED FOR MILITARY SERVICE.

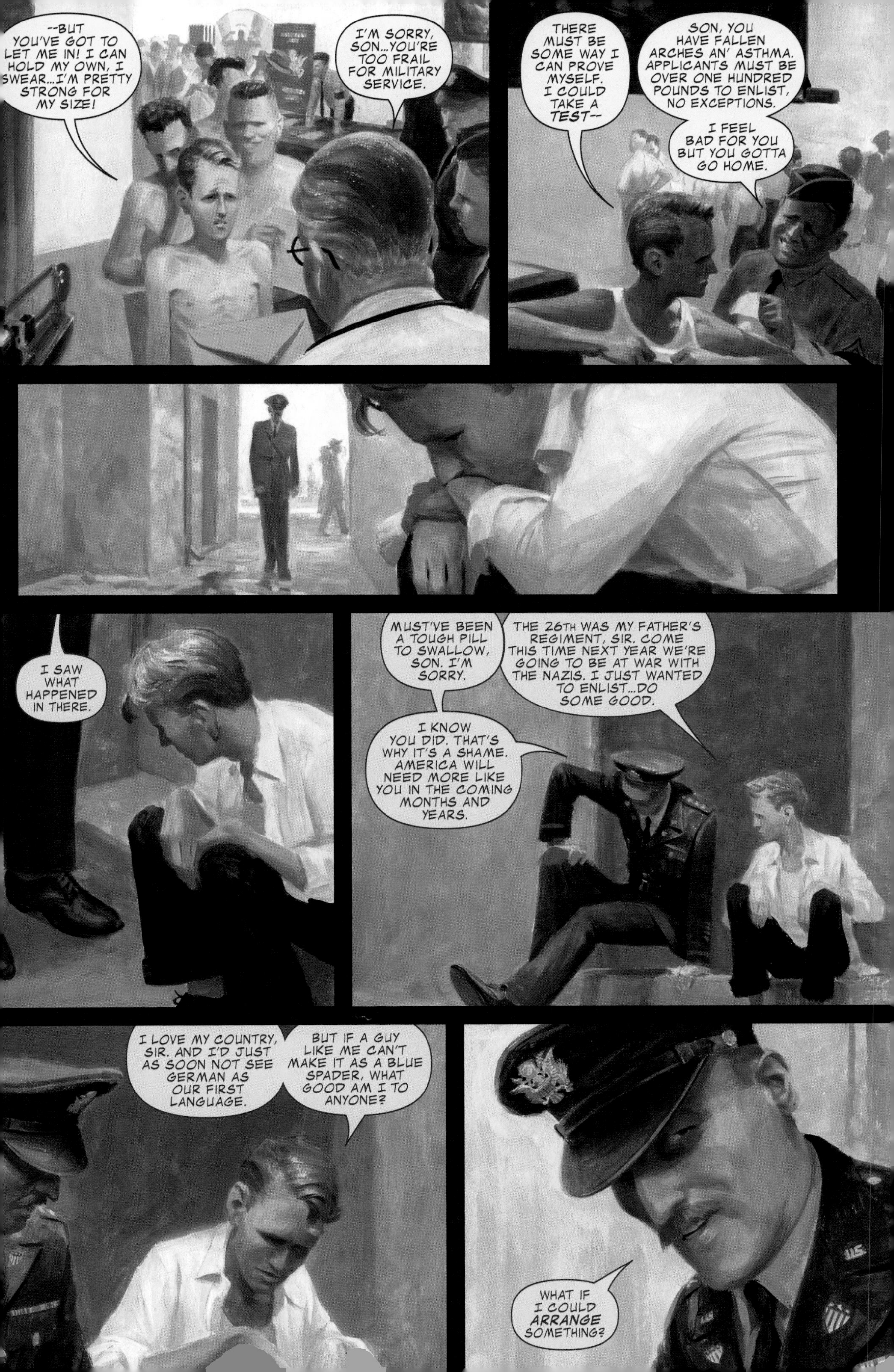
--BUT YOU'VE GOT TO LET ME IN! I CAN HOLD MY OWN, I SWEAR...I'M PRETTY STRONG FOR MY SIZE!
I'M SORRY, SON...YOU'RE TOO FRAIL FOR MILITARY SERVICE.
THERE MUST BE SOME WAY I CAN PROVE MYSELF. I COULD TAKE A TEST--
SON, YOU HAVE FALLEN ARCHES AN' ASTHMA. APPLICANTS MUST BE OVER ONE HUNDRED POUNDS TO ENLIST, NO EXCEPTIONS.
I FEEL BAD FOR YOU BUT YOU GOTTA GO HOME.
I SAW WHAT HAPPENED IN THERE.
I KNOW YOU DID. THAT'S WHY IT'S A SHAME. AMERICA WILL NEED MORE LIKE YOU IN THE COMING MONTHS AND YEARS.
THE 26TH WAS MY FATHER'S REGIMENT, SIR. COME THIS TIME NEXT YEAR WE'RE GOING TO BE AT WAR WITH THE NAZIS. I JUST WANTED TO ENLIST...DO SOME GOOD.
MUST'VE BEEN A TOUGH PILL TO SWALLOW, SON. I'M SORRY.
I LOVE MY COUNTRY, SIR. AND I'D JUST AS SOON NOT SEE GERMAN AS OUR FIRST LANGUAGE.
BUT IF A GUY LIKE ME CAN'T MAKE IT AS A BLUE SPADER, WHAT GOOD AM I TO ANYONE?
WHAT IF I COULD ARRANGE SOMETHING?

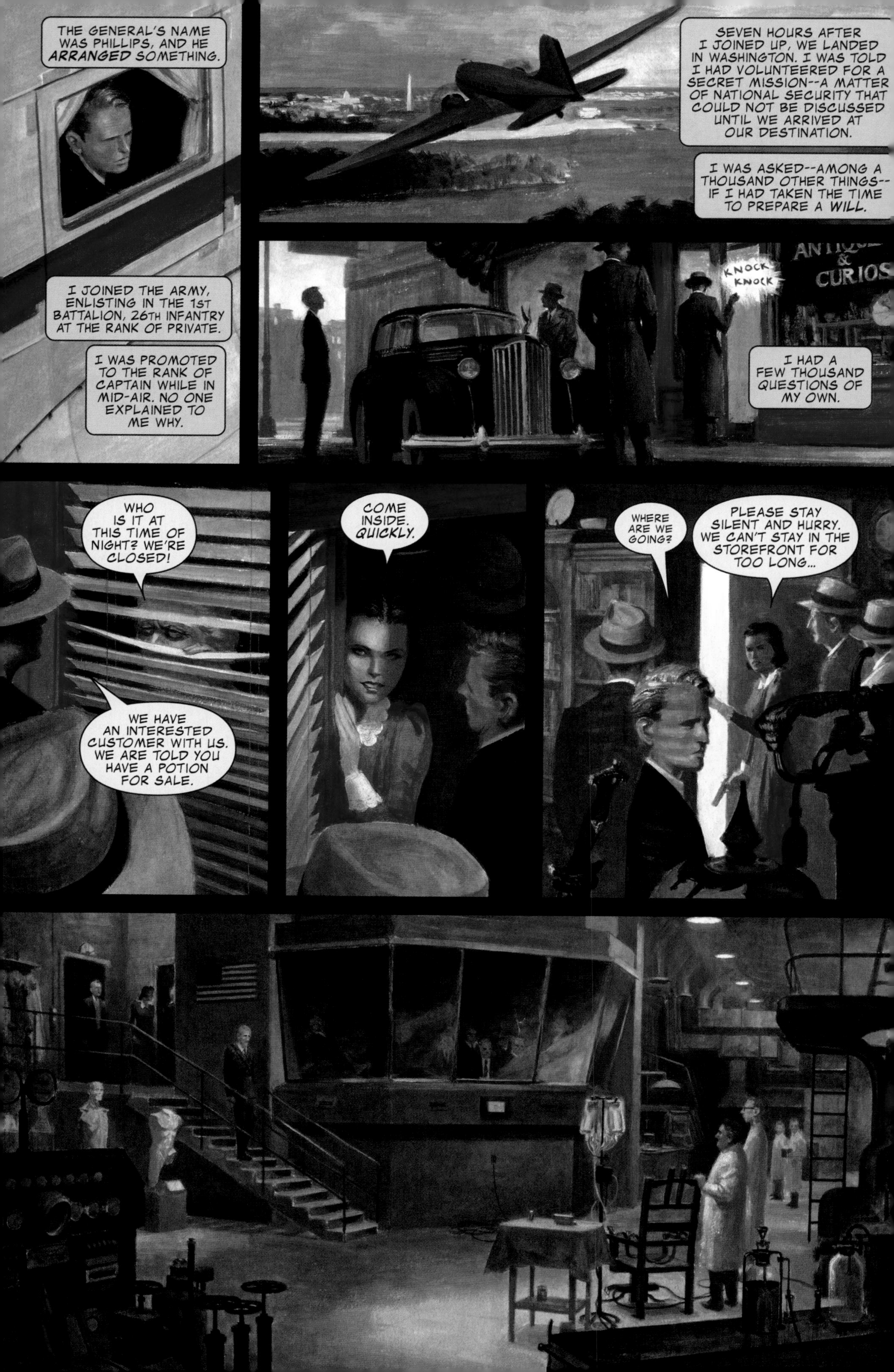
THE GENERAL'S NAME WAS PHILLIPS, AND HE ARRANGED SOMETHING.
I JOINED THE ARMY, ENLISTING IN THE 1ST BATTALION, 26TH INFANTRY AT THE RANK OF PRIVATE.
I WAS PROMOTED TO THE RANK OF CAPTAIN WHILE IN MID-AIR. NO ONE EXPLAINED TO ME WHY.
SEVEN HOURS AFTER I JOINED UP, WE LANDED IN WASHINGTON. I WAS TOLD I HAD VOLUNTEERED FOR A SECRET MISSION--A MATTER OF NATIONAL SECURITY THAT COULD NOT BE DISCUSSED UNTIL WE ARRIVED AT OUR DESTINATION.
I WAS ASKED--AMONG A THOUSAND OTHER THINGS--IF I HAD TAKEN THE TIME TO PREPARE A WILL.
ANTIQUES & CURIOS
KNOCK KNOCK
I HAD A FEW THOUSAND QUESTIONS OF MY OWN.
WHO IS IT AT THIS TIME OF NIGHT? WE'RE CLOSED!
WE HAVE AN INTERESTED CUSTOMER WITH US. WE ARE TOLD YOU HAVE A POTION FOR SALE.
COME INSIDE. QUICKLY.
WHERE ARE WE GOING?
PLEASE STAY SILENT AND HURRY. WE CAN'T STAY IN THE STOREFRONT FOR TOO LONG...

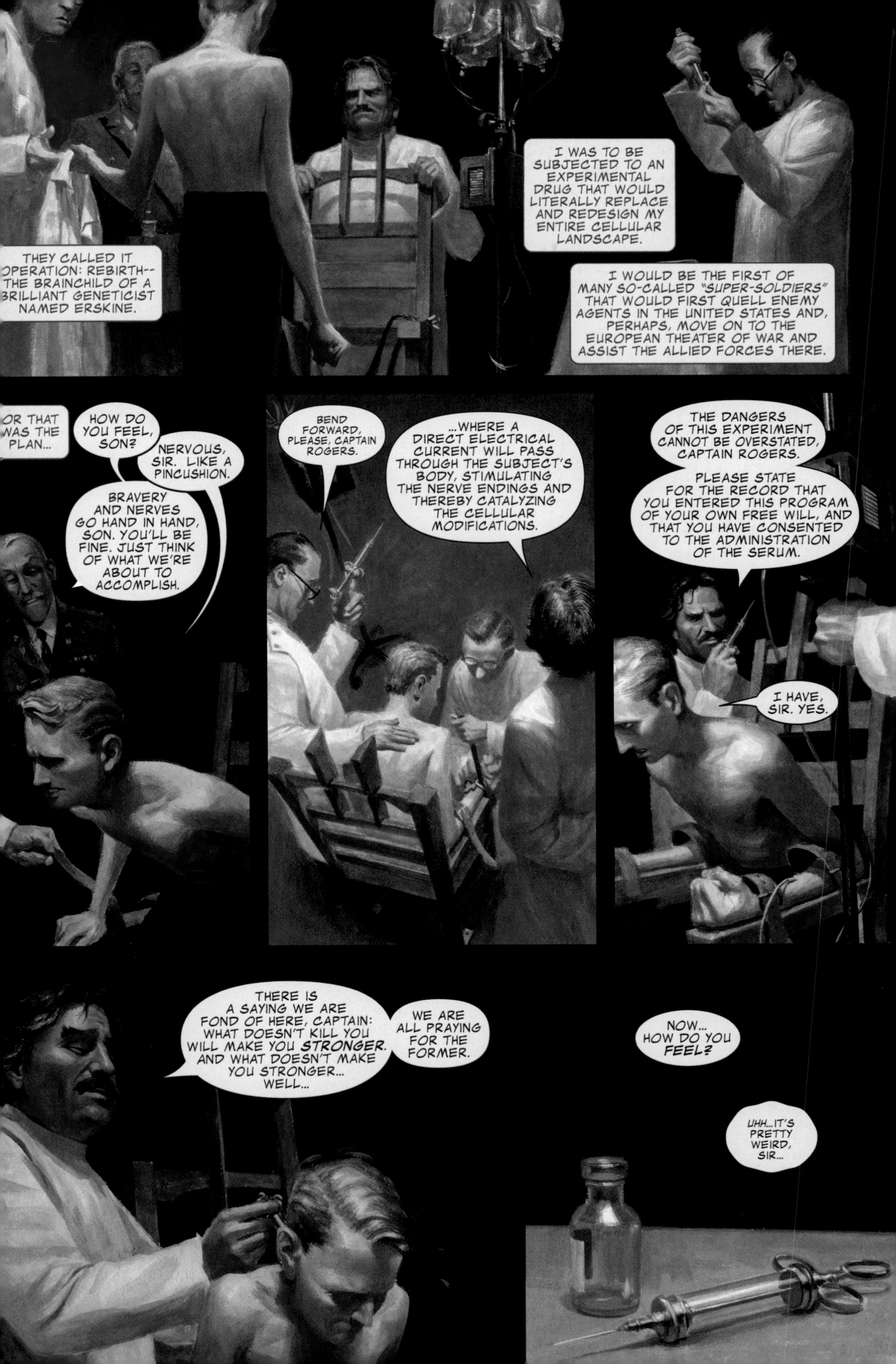
THEY CALLED IT OPERATION: REBIRTH-- THE BRAINCHILD OF A BRILLIANT GENETICIST NAMED ERSKINE.
I WAS TO BE SUBJECTED TO AN EXPERIMENTAL DRUG THAT WOULD LITERALLY REPLACE AND REDESIGN MY ENTIRE CELLULAR LANDSCAPE.
I WOULD BE THE FIRST OF MANY SO-CALLED "SUPER-SOLDIERS" THAT WOULD FIRST QUELL ENEMY AGENTS IN THE UNITED STATES AND, PERHAPS, MOVE ON TO THE EUROPEAN THEATER OF WAR AND ASSIST THE ALLIED FORCES THERE.
OR THAT WAS THE PLAN...
HOW DO YOU FEEL, SON?
NERVOUS, SIR. LIKE A PINCUSHION.
BRAVERY AND NERVES GO HAND IN HAND, SON. YOU'LL BE FINE. JUST THINK OF WHAT WE'RE ABOUT TO ACCOMPLISH.
BEND FORWARD, PLEASE, CAPTAIN ROGERS.
...WHERE A DIRECT ELECTRICAL CURRENT WILL PASS THROUGH THE SUBJECT'S BODY, STIMULATING THE NERVE ENDINGS AND THEREBY CATALYZING THE CELLULAR MODIFICATIONS.
THE DANGERS OF THIS EXPERIMENT CANNOT BE OVERSTATED, CAPTAIN ROGERS.
PLEASE STATE FOR THE RECORD THAT YOU ENTERED THIS PROGRAM OF YOUR OWN FREE WILL, AND THAT YOU HAVE CONSENTED TO THE ADMINISTRATION OF THE SERUM.
I HAVE, SIR. YES.
THERE IS A SAYING WE ARE FOND OF HERE, CAPTAIN: WHAT DOESN'T KILL YOU WILL MAKE YOU STRONGER. AND WHAT DOESN'T MAKE YOU STRONGER... WELL...
WE ARE ALL PRAYING FOR THE FORMER.
NOW... HOW DO YOU FEEL?
UHH...IT'S PRETTY WEIRD, SIR...

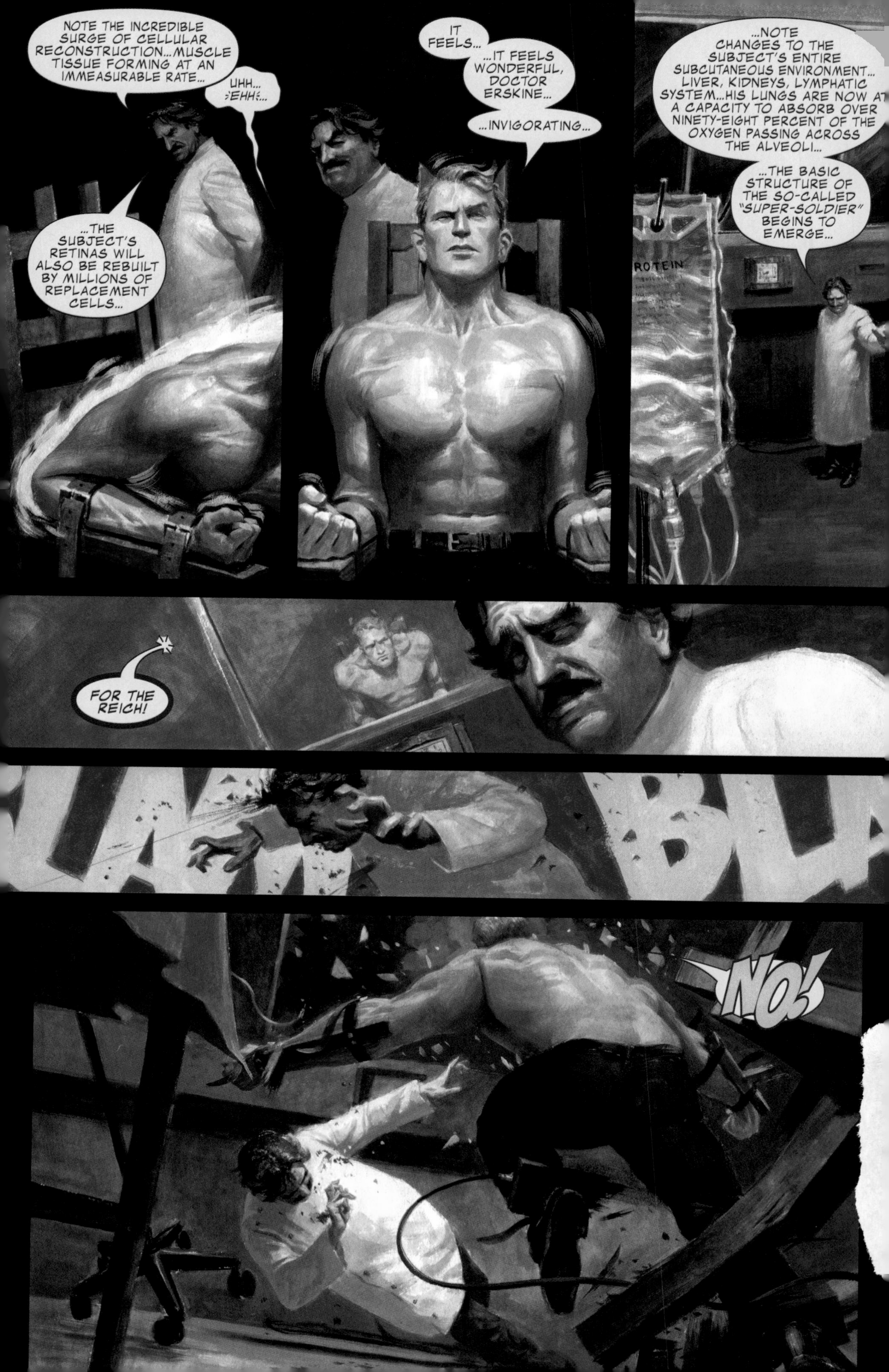
NOTE THE INCREDIBLE SURGE OF CELLULAR RECONSTRUCTION...MUSCLE TISSUE FORMING AT AN IMMEASURABLE RATE...
UHH... EHH...
...THE SUBJECT'S RETINAS WILL ALSO BE REBUILT BY MILLIONS OF REPLACEMENT CELLS...
IT FEELS...
...IT FEELS WONDERFUL, DOCTOR ERSKINE...
...INVIGORATING...
...NOTE CHANGES TO THE SUBJECT'S ENTIRE SUBCUTANEOUS ENVIRONMENT... LIVER, KIDNEYS, LYMPHATIC SYSTEM...HIS LUNGS ARE NOW AT A CAPACITY TO ABSORB OVER NINETY-EIGHT PERCENT OF THE OXYGEN PASSING ACROSS THE ALVEOLI...
...THE BASIC STRUCTURE OF THE SO-CALLED "SUPER-SOLDIER" BEGINS TO EMERGE...
PROTEIN
FOR THE REICH!
NO!

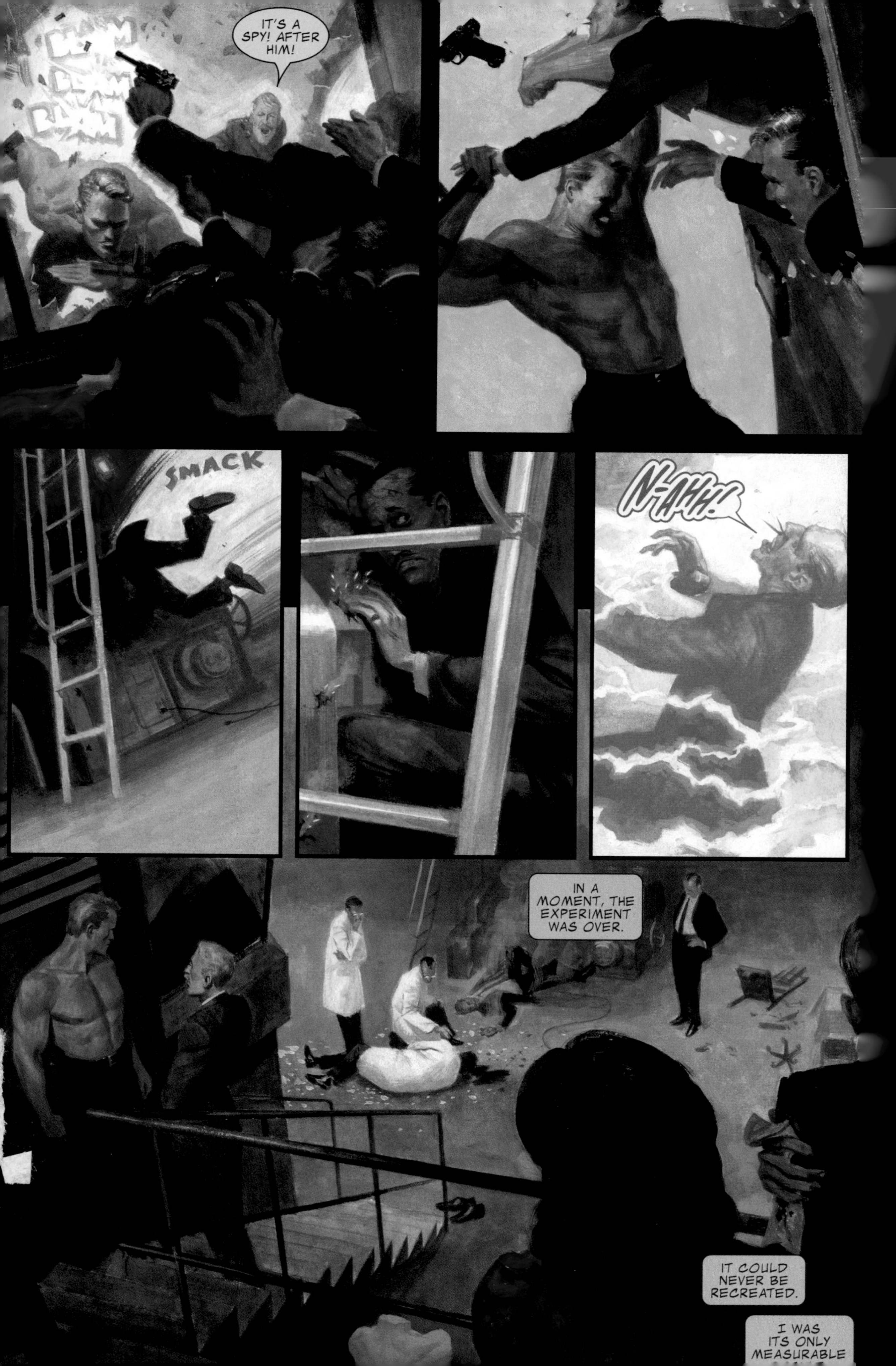
BLAM BLAM BLAM
IT'S A SPY! AFTER HIM!
SMACK
N-AHH!
IN A MOMENT, THE EXPERIMENT WAS OVER.
IT COULD NEVER BE RECREATED.
I WAS ITS ONLY MEASURABLE

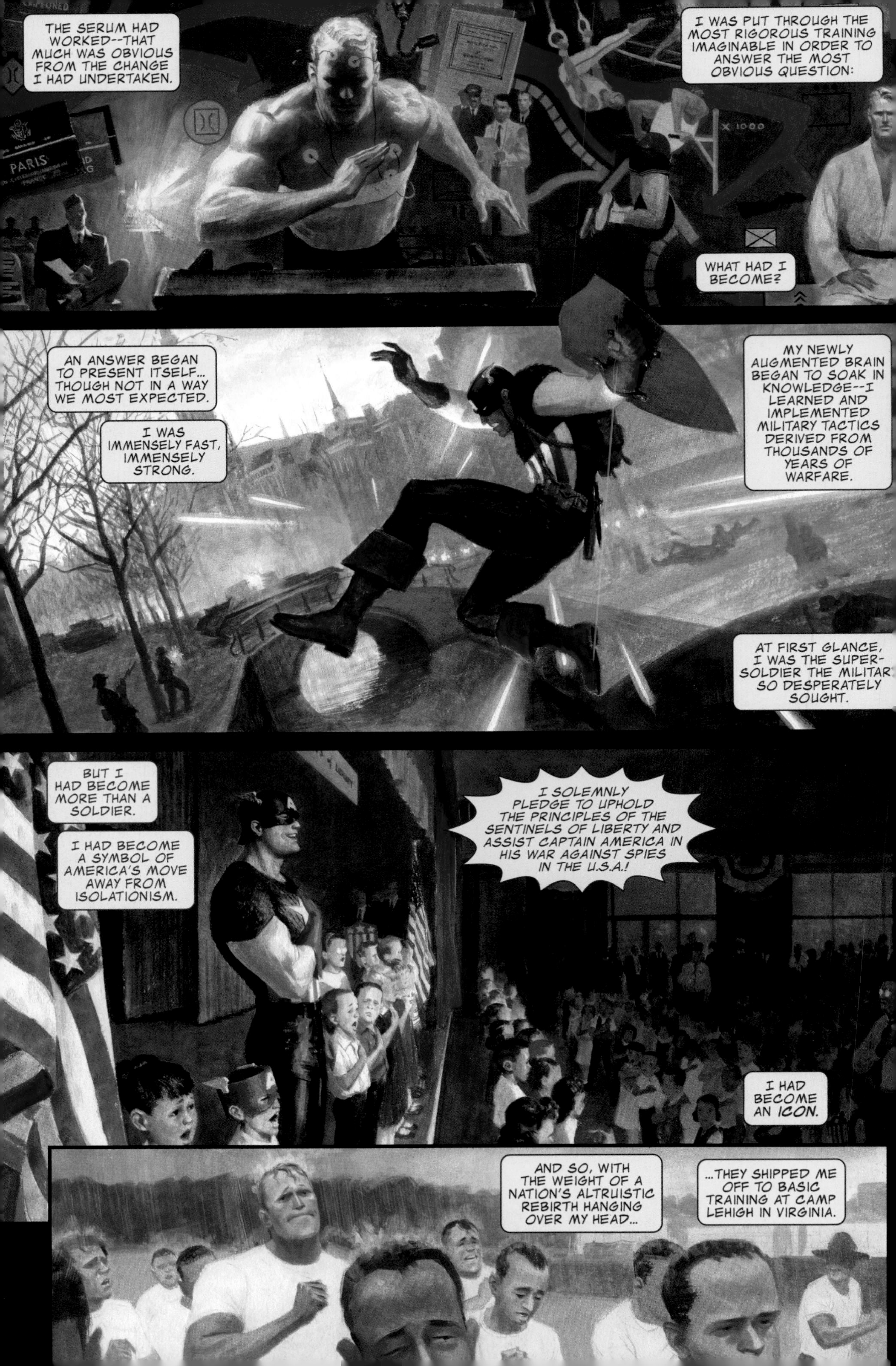
THE SERUM HAD WORKED--THAT MUCH WAS OBVIOUS FROM THE CHANGE I HAD UNDERTAKEN.
I WAS PUT THROUGH THE MOST RIGOROUS TRAINING IMAGINABLE IN ORDER TO ANSWER THE MOST OBVIOUS QUESTION:
PARIS
X 1000
WHAT HAD I BECOME?
AN ANSWER BEGAN TO PRESENT ITSELF... THOUGH NOT IN A WAY WE MOST EXPECTED.
I WAS IMMENSELY FAST, IMMENSELY STRONG.
MY NEWLY AUGMENTED BRAIN BEGAN TO SOAK IN KNOWLEDGE--I LEARNED AND IMPLEMENTED MILITARY TACTICS DERIVED FROM THOUSANDS OF YEARS OF WARFARE.
AT FIRST GLANCE, I WAS THE SUPER-SOLDIER THE MILITAR SO DESPERATELY SOUGHT.
BUT I HAD BECOME MORE THAN A SOLDIER.
I HAD BECOME A SYMBOL OF AMERICA'S MOVE AWAY FROM ISOLATIONISM.
I SOLEMNLY PLEDGE TO UPHOLD THE PRINCIPLES OF THE SENTINELS OF LIBERTY AND ASSIST CAPTAIN AMERICA IN HIS WAR AGAINST SPIES IN THE U.S.A.!
I HAD BECOME AN *ICON*.
AND SO, WITH THE WEIGHT OF A NATION'S ALTRUISTIC REBIRTH HANGING OVER MY HEAD...
...THEY SHIPPED ME OFF TO BASIC TRAINING AT CAMP LEHIGH IN VIRGINIA.

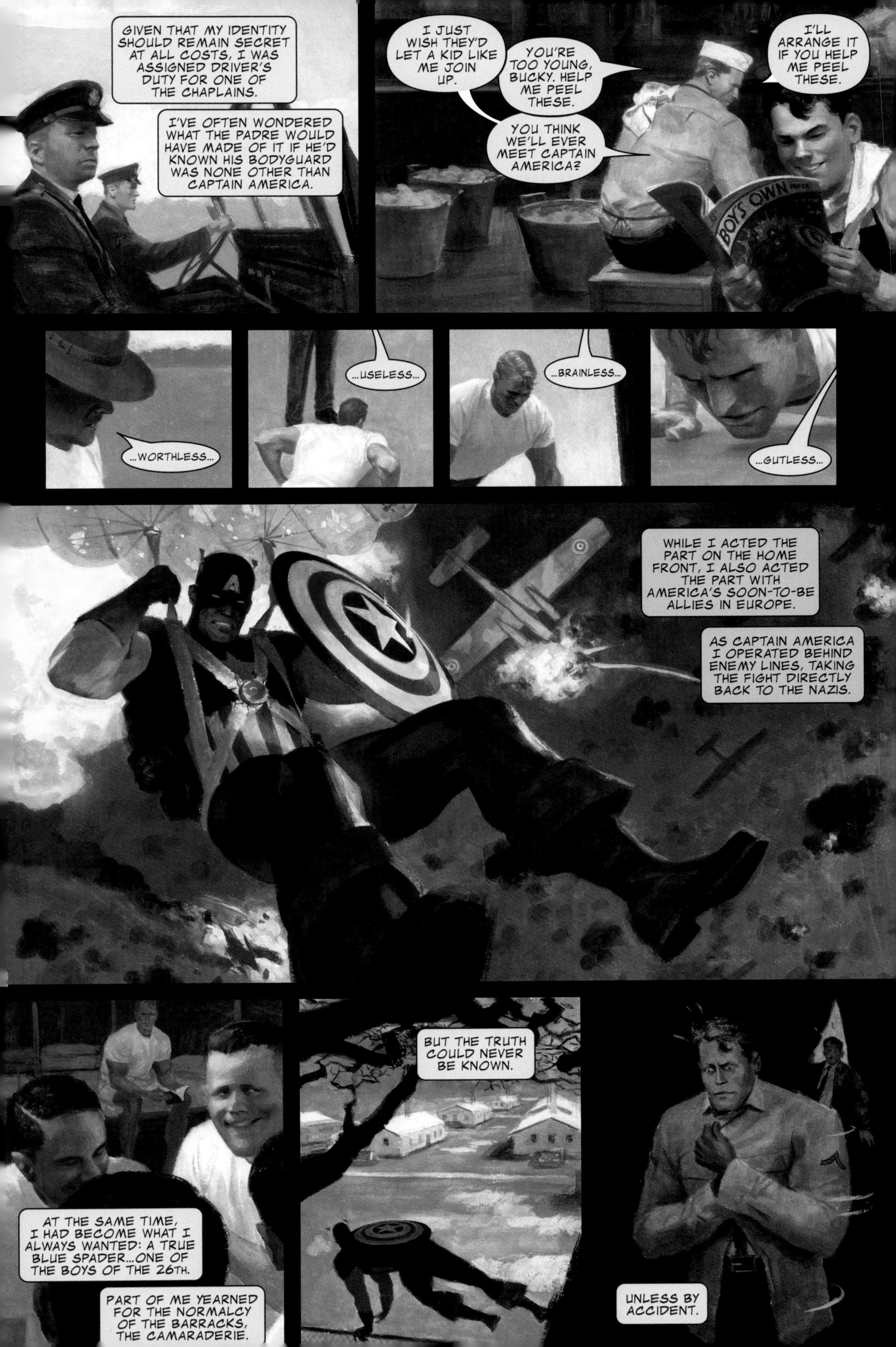
GIVEN THAT MY IDENTITY SHOULD REMAIN SECRET AT ALL COSTS, I WAS ASSIGNED DRIVER'S DUTY FOR ONE OF THE CHAPLAINS.
I'VE OFTEN WONDERED WHAT THE PADRE WOULD HAVE MADE OF IT IF HE'D KNOWN HIS BODYGUARD WAS NONE OTHER THAN CAPTAIN AMERICA.
I JUST WISH THEY'D LET A KID LIKE ME JOIN UP.
YOU'RE TOO YOUNG, BUCKY. HELP ME PEEL THESE.
YOU THINK WE'LL EVER MEET CAPTAIN AMERICA?
I'LL ARRANGE IT IF YOU HELP ME PEEL THESE.
BOYS OWN
...WORTHLESS...
...USELESS...
...BRAINLESS...
...GUTLESS...
WHILE I ACTED THE PART ON THE HOME FRONT, I ALSO ACTED THE PART WITH AMERICA'S SOON-TO-BE ALLIES IN EUROPE.
AS CAPTAIN AMERICA I OPERATED BEHIND ENEMY LINES, TAKING THE FIGHT DIRECTLY BACK TO THE NAZIS.
AT THE SAME TIME, I HAD BECOME WHAT I ALWAYS WANTED: A TRUE BLUE SPADER...ONE OF THE BOYS OF THE 26TH.
PART OF ME YEARNED FOR THE NORMALCY OF THE BARRACKS, THE CAMARADERIE.
BUT THE TRUTH COULD NEVER BE KNOWN.
UNLESS BY ACCIDENT.

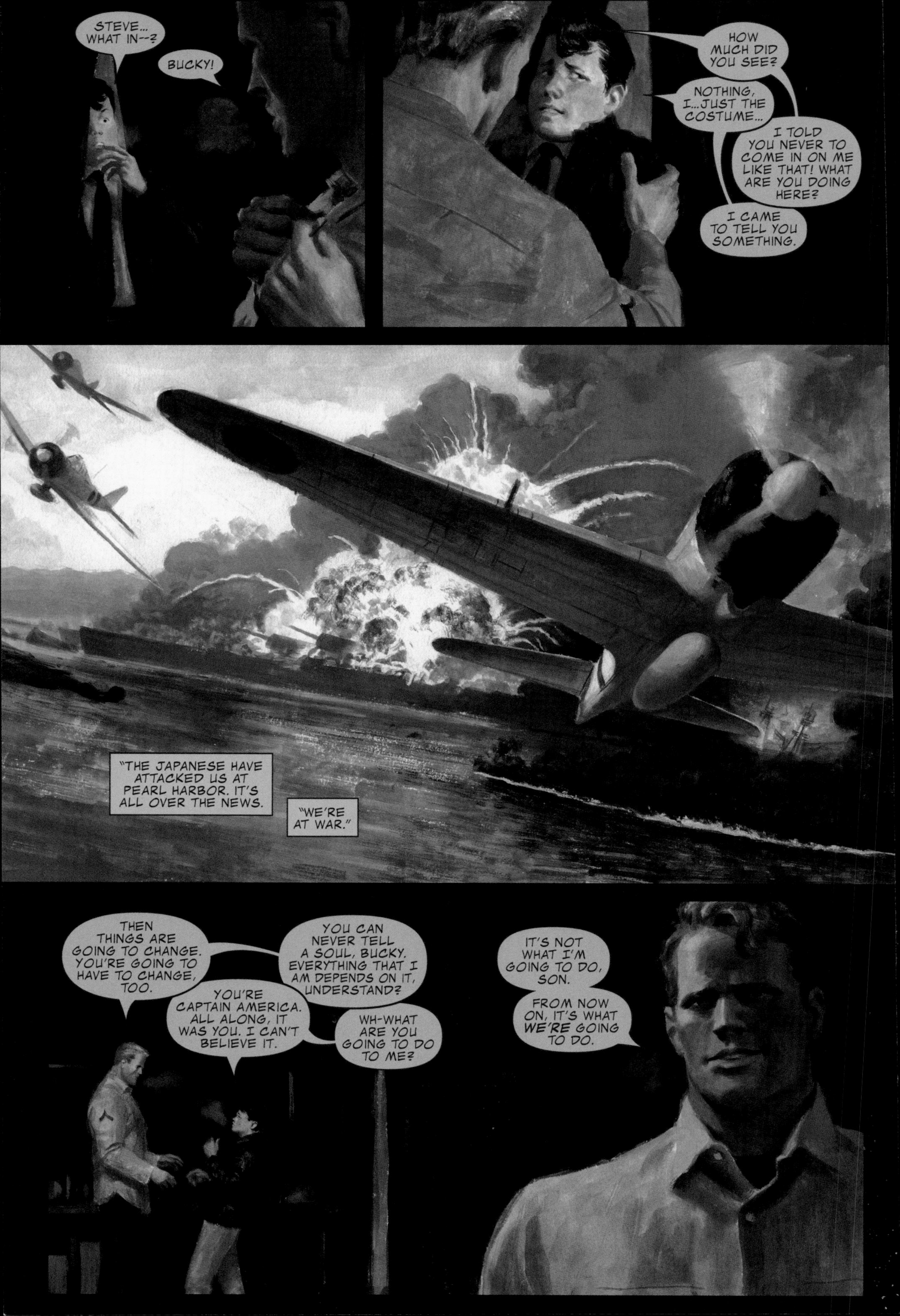
STEVE... WHAT IN--?
BUCKY!
HOW MUCH DID YOU SEE?
NOTHING, I...JUST THE COSTUME...
I TOLD YOU NEVER TO COME IN ON ME LIKE THAT! WHAT ARE YOU DOING HERE?
I CAME TO TELL YOU SOMETHING.
"THE JAPANESE HAVE ATTACKED US AT PEARL HARBOR. IT'S ALL OVER THE NEWS.
"WE'RE AT WAR."
THEN THINGS ARE GOING TO CHANGE. YOU'RE GOING TO HAVE TO CHANGE, TOO.
YOU'RE CAPTAIN AMERICA. ALL ALONG, IT WAS YOU. I CAN'T BELIEVE IT.
YOU CAN NEVER TELL A SOUL, BUCKY. EVERYTHING THAT I AM DEPENDS ON IT, UNDERSTAND?
WH-WHAT ARE YOU GOING TO DO TO ME?
IT'S NOT WHAT I'M GOING TO DO, SON.
FROM NOW ON, IT'S WHAT WE'RE GOING TO DO.

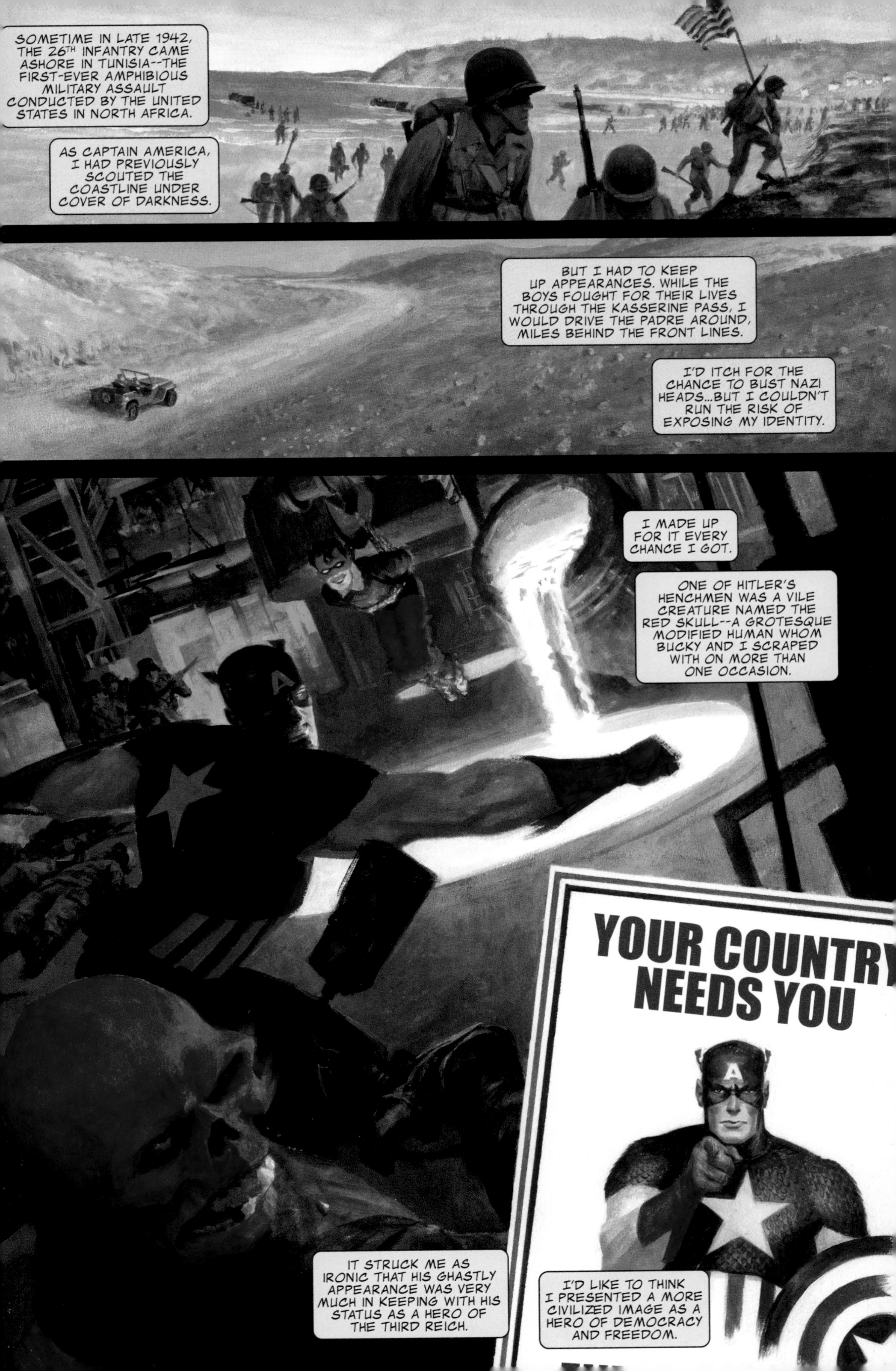
SOMETIME IN LATE 1942, THE 26TH INFANTRY CAME ASHORE IN TUNISIA--THE FIRST-EVER AMPHIBIOUS MILITARY ASSAULT CONDUCTED BY THE UNITED STATES IN NORTH AFRICA.
AS CAPTAIN AMERICA, I HAD PREVIOUSLY SCOUTED THE COASTLINE UNDER COVER OF DARKNESS.
BUT I HAD TO KEEP UP APPEARANCES. WHILE THE BOYS FOUGHT FOR THEIR LIVES THROUGH THE KASSERINE PASS, I WOULD DRIVE THE PADRE AROUND, MILES BEHIND THE FRONT LINES.
I'D ITCH FOR THE CHANCE TO BUST NAZI HEADS...BUT I COULDN'T RUN THE RISK OF EXPOSING MY IDENTITY.
I MADE UP FOR IT EVERY CHANCE I GOT.
ONE OF HITLER'S HENCHMEN WAS A VILE CREATURE NAMED THE RED SKULL--A GROTESQUE MODIFIED HUMAN WHOM BUCKY AND I SCRAPED WITH ON MORE THAN ONE OCCASION.
YOUR COUNTRY NEEDS YOU
IT STRUCK ME AS IRONIC THAT HIS GHASTLY APPEARANCE WAS VERY MUCH IN KEEPING WITH HIS STATUS AS A HERO OF THE THIRD REICH.
I'D LIKE TO THINK I PRESENTED A MORE CIVILIZED IMAGE AS A HERO OF DEMOCRACY AND FREEDOM.

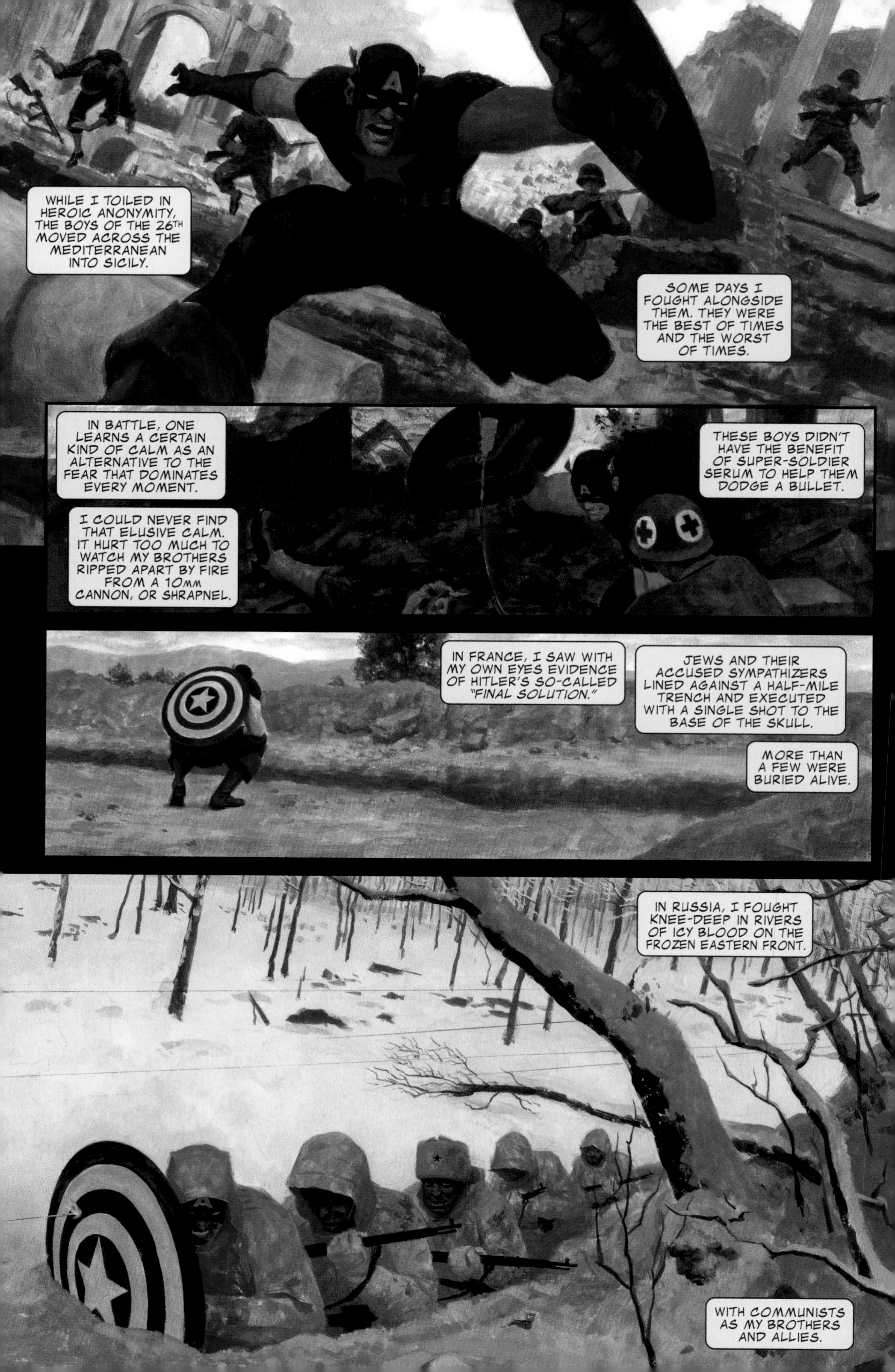
WHILE I TOILED IN HEROIC ANONYMITY, THE BOYS OF THE 26TH MOVED ACROSS THE MEDITERRANEAN INTO SICILY.
SOME DAYS I FOUGHT ALONGSIDE THEM. THEY WERE THE BEST OF TIMES AND THE WORST OF TIMES.
IN BATTLE, ONE LEARNS A CERTAIN KIND OF CALM AS AN ALTERNATIVE TO THE FEAR THAT DOMINATES EVERY MOMENT.
I COULD NEVER FIND THAT ELUSIVE CALM. IT HURT TOO MUCH TO WATCH MY BROTHERS RIPPED APART BY FIRE FROM A 10MM CANNON, OR SHRAPNEL.
THESE BOYS DIDN'T HAVE THE BENEFIT OF SUPER-SOLDIER SERUM TO HELP THEM DODGE A BULLET.
IN FRANCE, I SAW WITH MY OWN EYES EVIDENCE OF HITLER'S SO-CALLED *"FINAL SOLUTION."*
JEWS AND THEIR ACCUSED SYMPATHIZERS LINED AGAINST A HALF-MILE TRENCH AND EXECUTED WITH A SINGLE SHOT TO THE BASE OF THE SKULL.
MORE THAN A FEW WERE BURIED ALIVE.
IN RUSSIA, I FOUGHT KNEE-DEEP IN RIVERS OF ICY BLOOD ON THE FROZEN EASTERN FRONT.
WITH COMMUNISTS AS MY BROTHERS AND ALLIES.

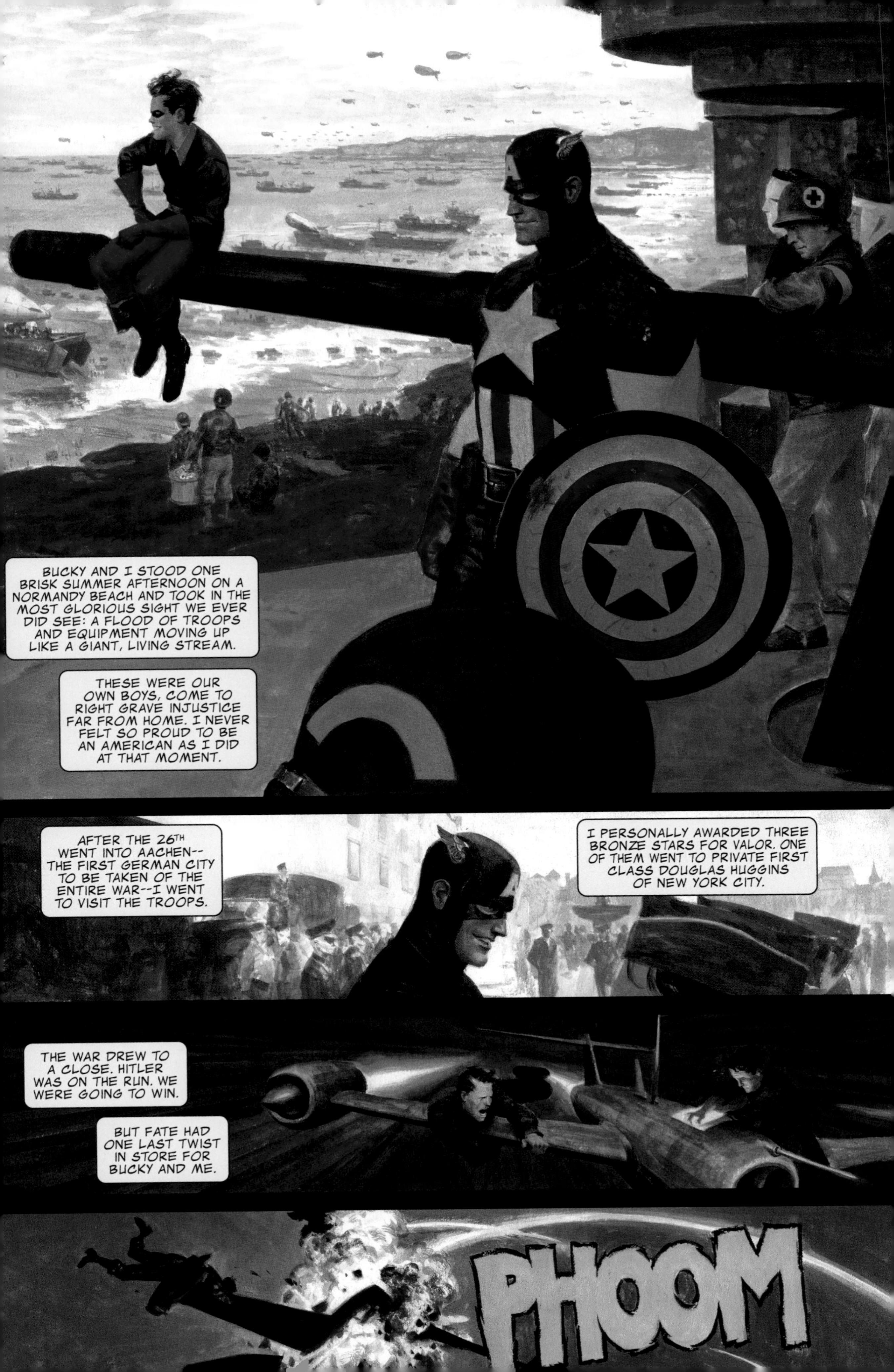
BUCKY AND I STOOD ONE BRISK SUMMER AFTERNOON ON A NORMANDY BEACH AND TOOK IN THE MOST GLORIOUS SIGHT WE EVER DID SEE: A FLOOD OF TROOPS AND EQUIPMENT MOVING UP LIKE A GIANT, LIVING STREAM.
THESE WERE OUR OWN BOYS, COME TO RIGHT GRAVE INJUSTICE FAR FROM HOME. I NEVER FELT SO PROUD TO BE AN AMERICAN AS I DID AT THAT MOMENT.
AFTER THE 26TH WENT INTO AACHEN-- THE FIRST GERMAN CITY TO BE TAKEN OF THE ENTIRE WAR--I WENT TO VISIT THE TROOPS.
I PERSONALLY AWARDED THREE BRONZE STARS FOR VALOR. ONE OF THEM WENT TO PRIVATE FIRST CLASS DOUGLAS HUGGINS OF NEW YORK CITY.
THE WAR DREW TO A CLOSE. HITLER WAS ON THE RUN. WE WERE GOING TO WIN.
BUT FATE HAD ONE LAST TWIST IN STORE FOR BUCKY AND ME.
PHOOM

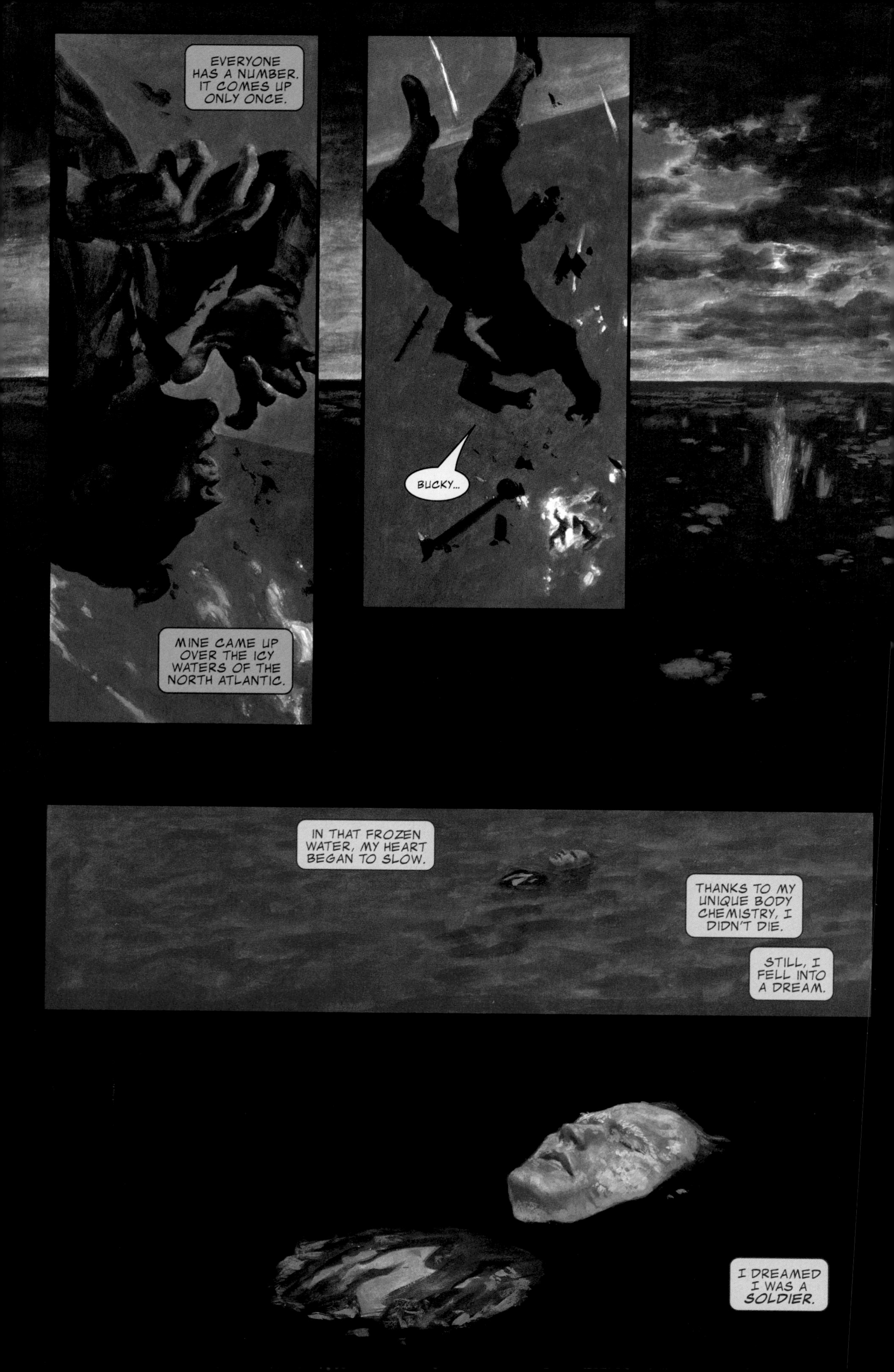
EVERYONE HAS A NUMBER. IT COMES UP ONLY ONCE.
MINE CAME UP OVER THE ICY WATERS OF THE NORTH ATLANTIC.
BUCKY...
IN THAT FROZEN WATER, MY HEART BEGAN TO SLOW.
THANKS TO MY UNIQUE BODY CHEMISTRY, I DIDN'T DIE.
STILL, I FELL INTO A DREAM.
I DREAMED I WAS A SOLDIER.

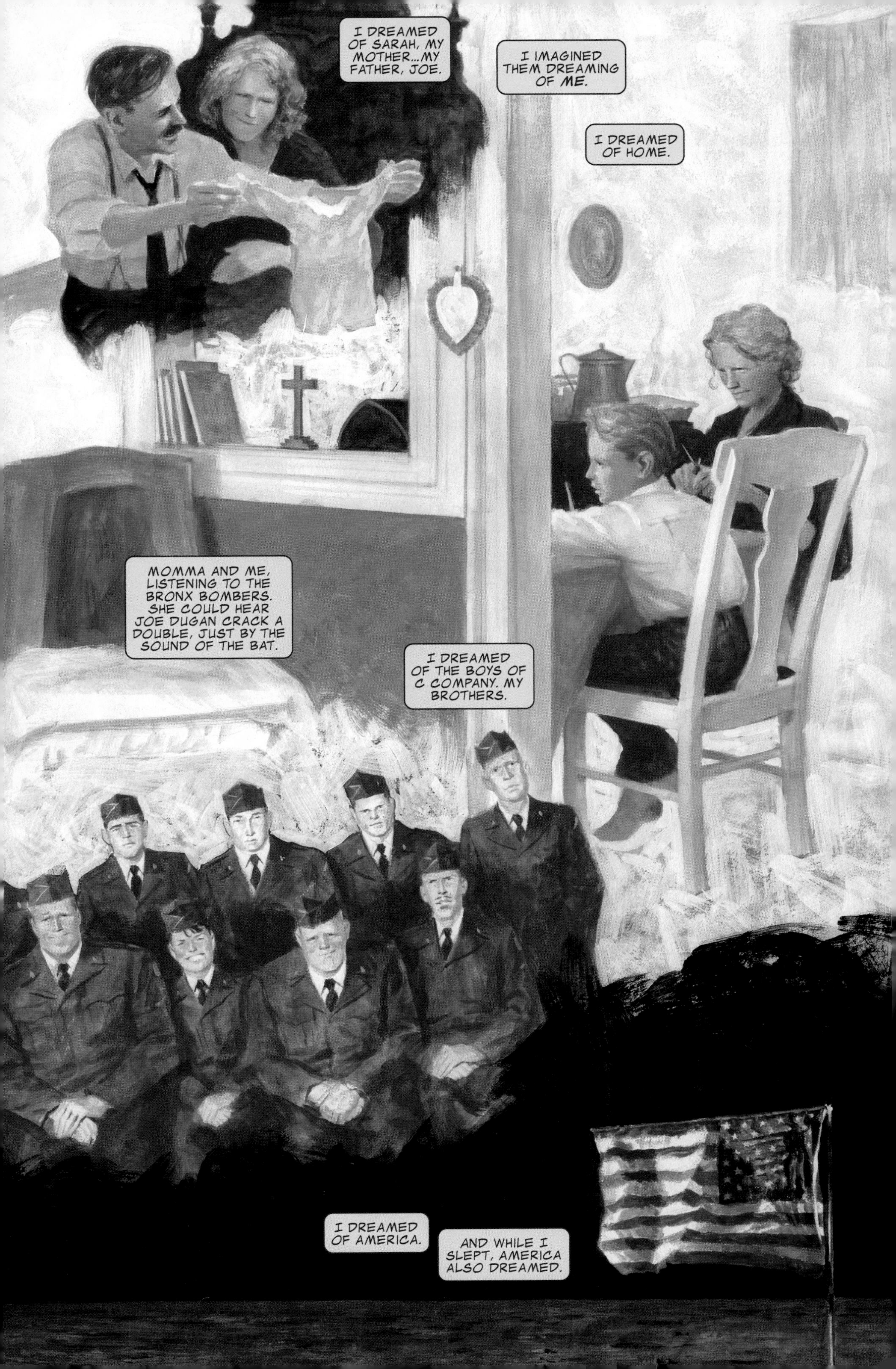
I DREAMED OF SARAH, MY MOTHER...MY FATHER, JOE.
I IMAGINED THEM DREAMING OF ME.
I DREAMED OF HOME.
MOMMA AND ME, LISTENING TO THE BRONX BOMBERS. SHE COULD HEAR JOE DUGAN CRACK A DOUBLE, JUST BY THE SOUND OF THE BAT.
I DREAMED OF THE BOYS OF C COMPANY. MY BROTHERS.
I DREAMED OF AMERICA.
AND WHILE I SLEPT, AMERICA ALSO DREAMED.

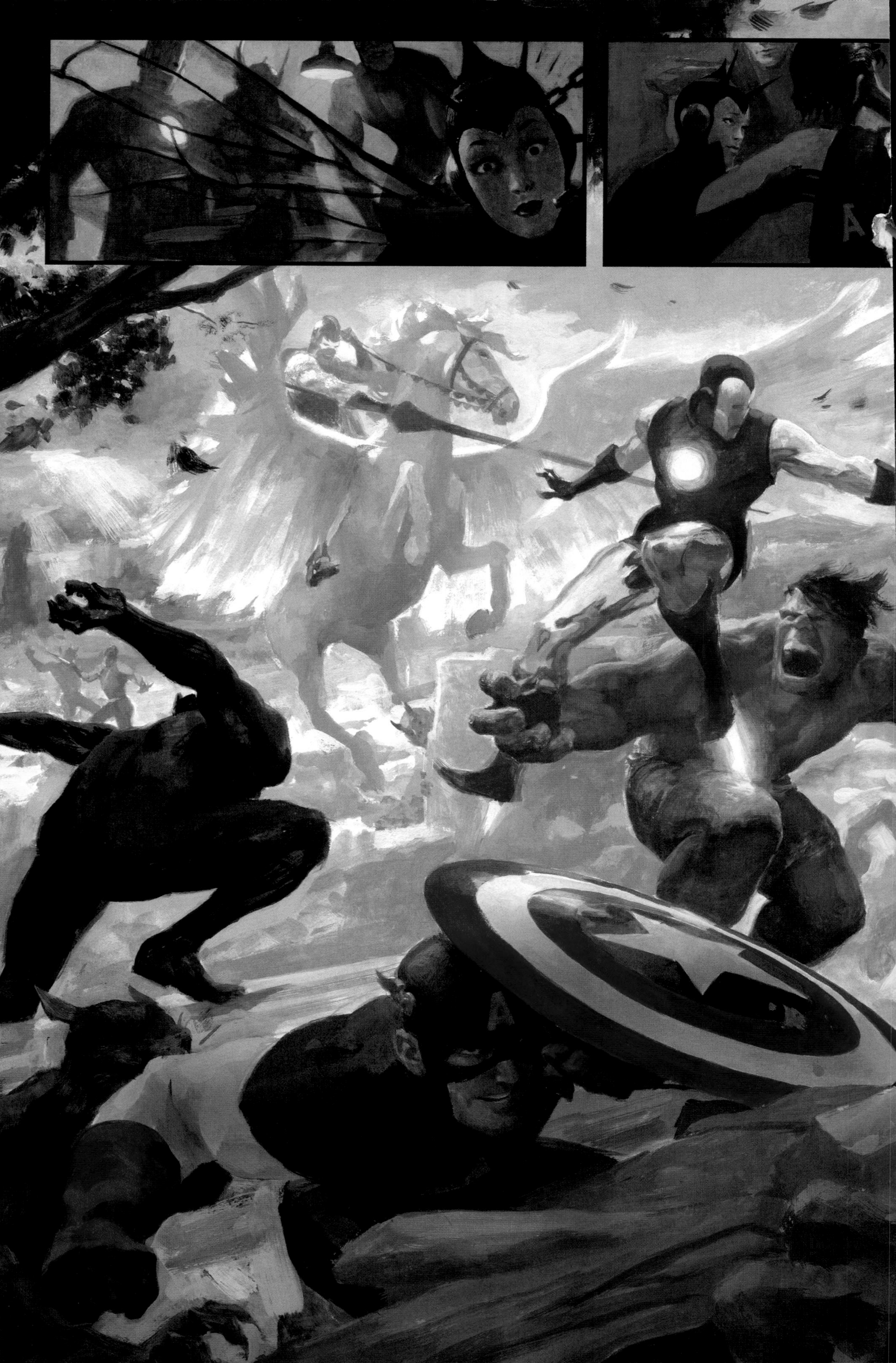

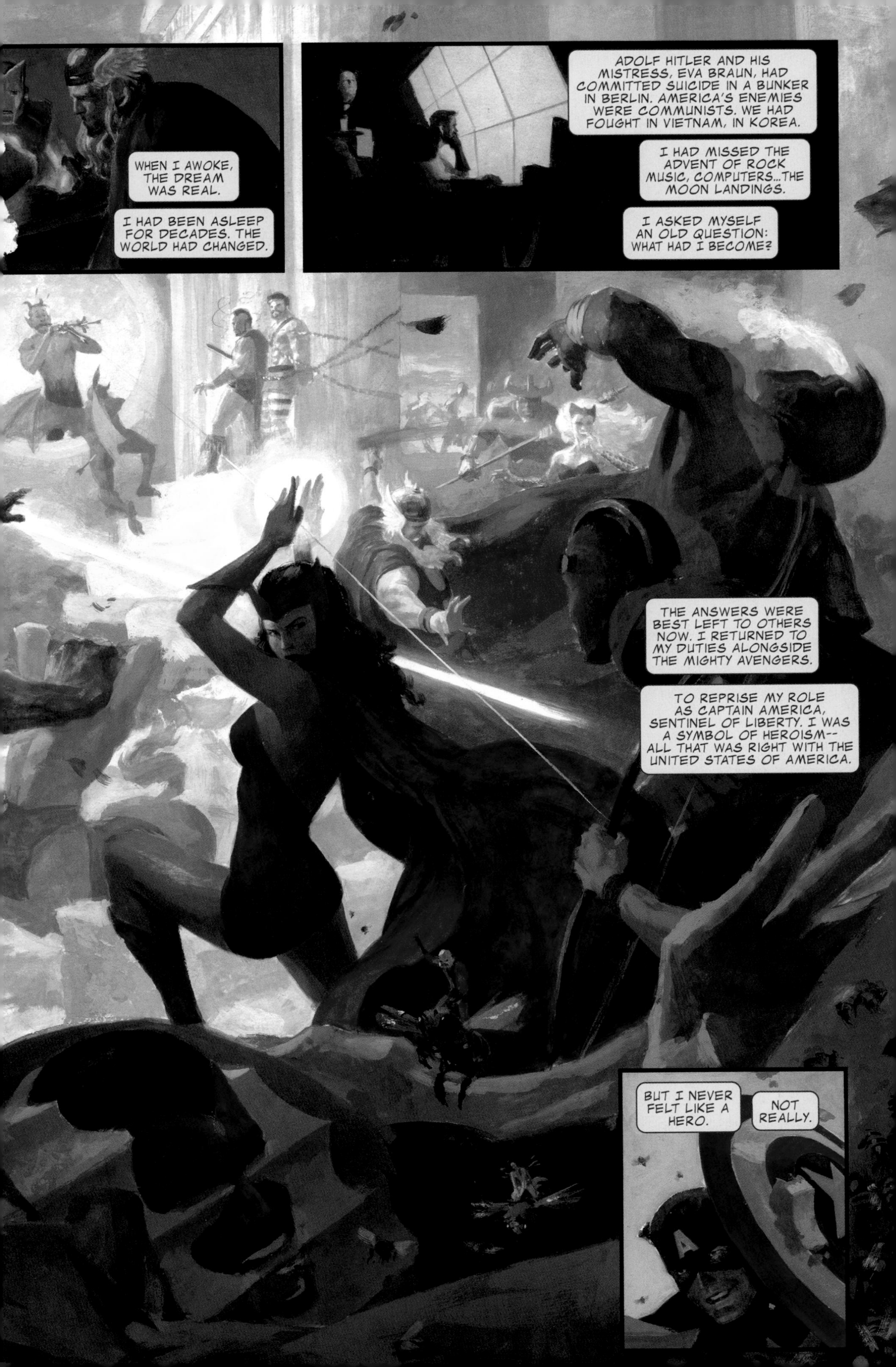
WHEN I AWOKE, THE DREAM WAS REAL.
I HAD BEEN ASLEEP FOR DECADES. THE WORLD HAD CHANGED.
ADOLF HITLER AND HIS MISTRESS, EVA BRAUN, HAD COMMITTED SUICIDE IN A BUNKER IN BERLIN. AMERICA'S ENEMIES WERE COMMUNISTS. WE HAD FOUGHT IN VIETNAM, IN KOREA.
I HAD MISSED THE ADVENT OF ROCK MUSIC, COMPUTERS...THE MOON LANDINGS.
I ASKED MYSELF AN OLD QUESTION: WHAT HAD I BECOME?
THE ANSWERS WERE BEST LEFT TO OTHERS NOW. I RETURNED TO MY DUTIES ALONGSIDE THE MIGHTY AVENGERS.
TO REPRISE MY ROLE AS CAPTAIN AMERICA, SENTINEL OF LIBERTY. I WAS A SYMBOL OF HEROISM--ALL THAT WAS RIGHT WITH THE UNITED STATES OF AMERICA.
BUT I NEVER FELT LIKE A HERO.
NOT REALLY.

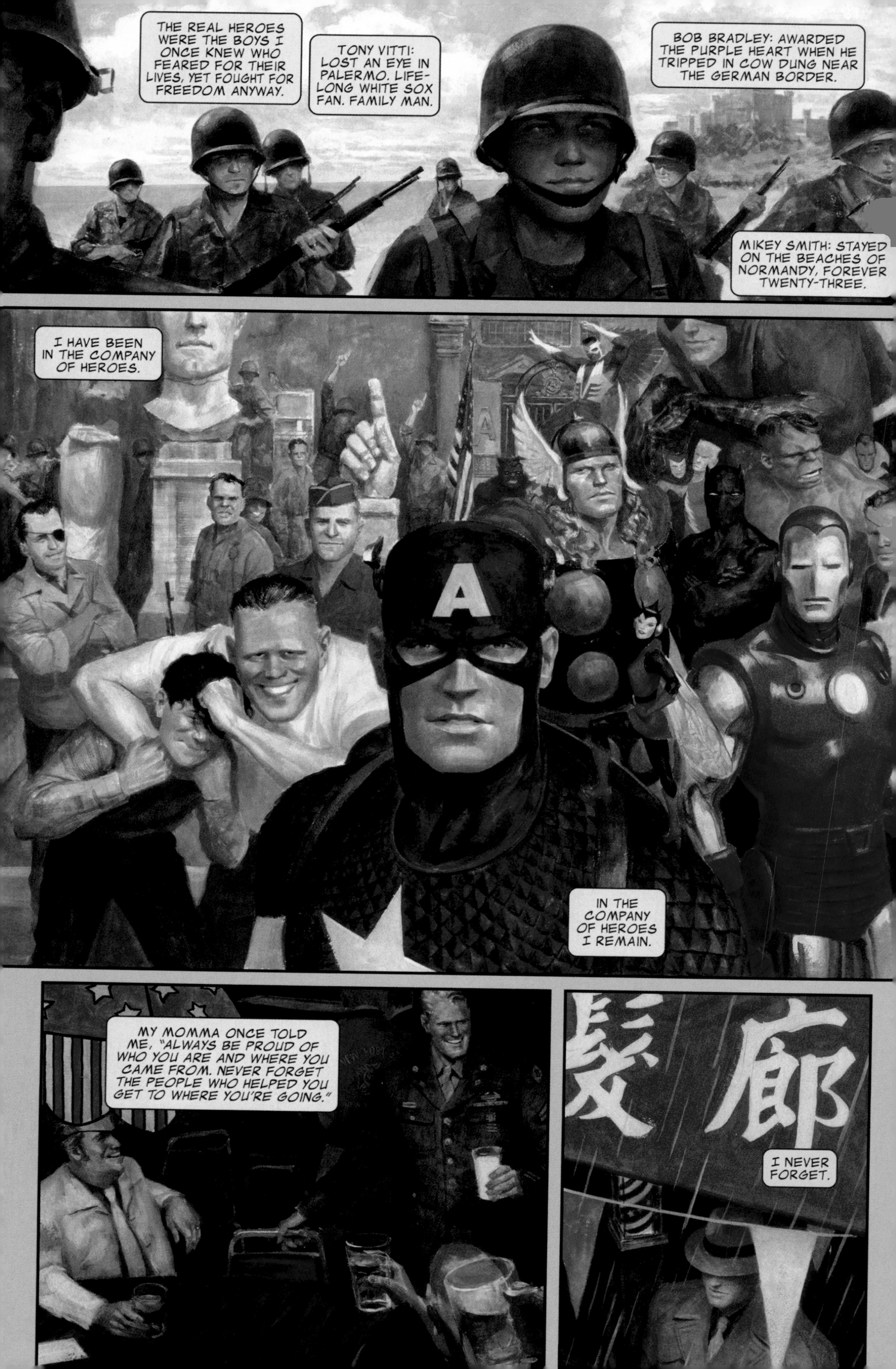
THE REAL HEROES WERE THE BOYS I ONCE KNEW WHO FEARED FOR THEIR LIVES, YET FOUGHT FOR FREEDOM ANYWAY.
TONY VITTI: LOST AN EYE IN PALERMO. LIFE-LONG WHITE SOX FAN. FAMILY MAN.
BOB BRADLEY: AWARDED THE PURPLE HEART WHEN HE TRIPPED IN COW DUNG NEAR THE GERMAN BORDER.
MIKEY SMITH: STAYED ON THE BEACHES OF NORMANDY, FOREVER TWENTY-THREE.
I HAVE BEEN IN THE COMPANY OF HEROES.
IN THE COMPANY OF HEROES I REMAIN.
MY MOMMA ONCE TOLD ME, "ALWAYS BE PROUD OF WHO YOU ARE AND WHERE YOU CAME FROM. NEVER FORGET THE PEOPLE WHO HELPED YOU GET TO WHERE YOU'RE GOING."
I NEVER FORGET.

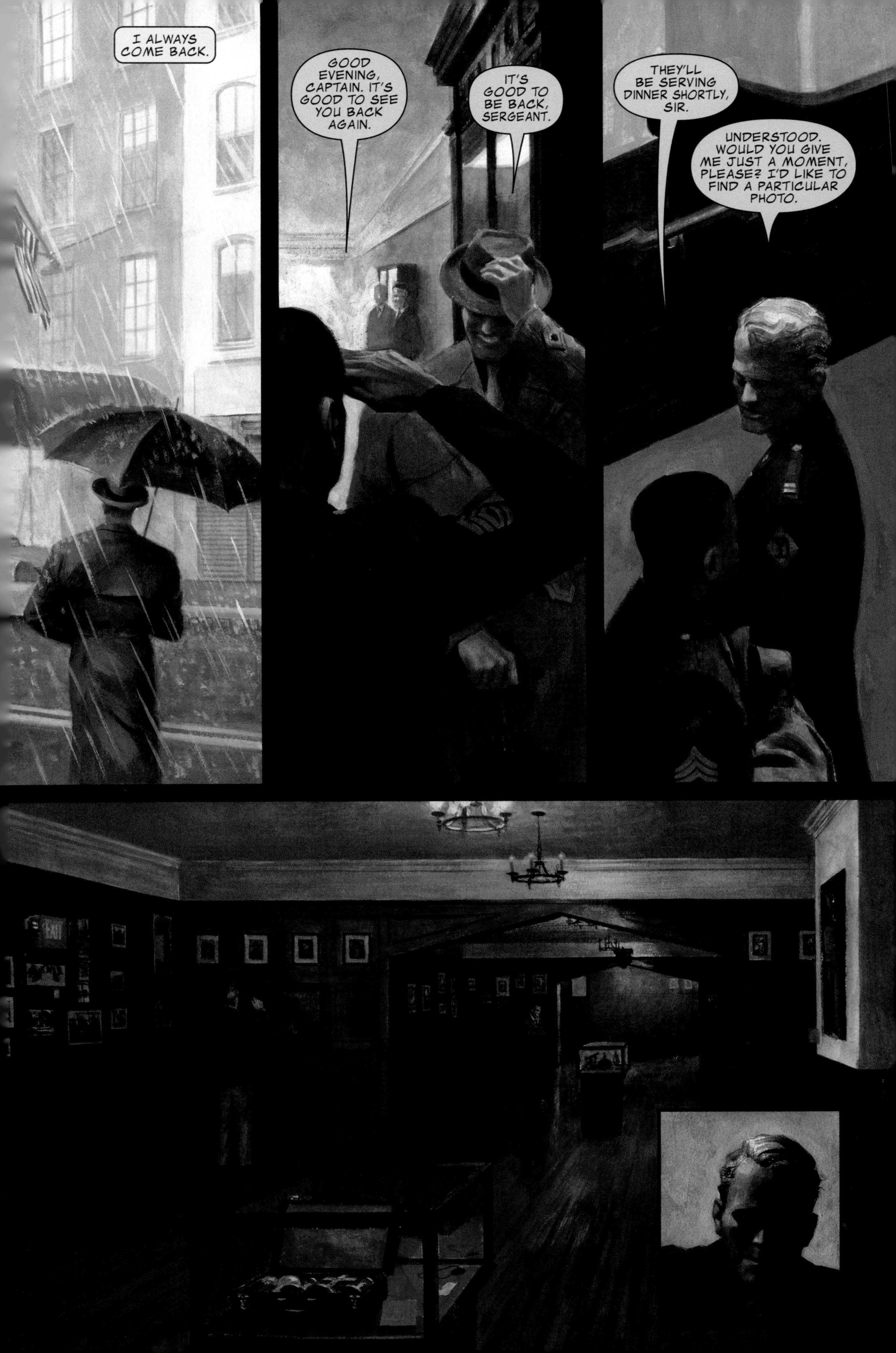
I ALWAYS COME BACK.
GOOD EVENING, CAPTAIN. IT'S GOOD TO SEE YOU BACK AGAIN.
IT'S GOOD TO BE BACK, SERGEANT.
THEY'LL BE SERVING DINNER SHORTLY, SIR.
UNDERSTOOD. WOULD YOU GIVE ME JUST A MOMENT, PLEASE? I'D LIKE TO FIND A PARTICULAR PHOTO.
EXIT

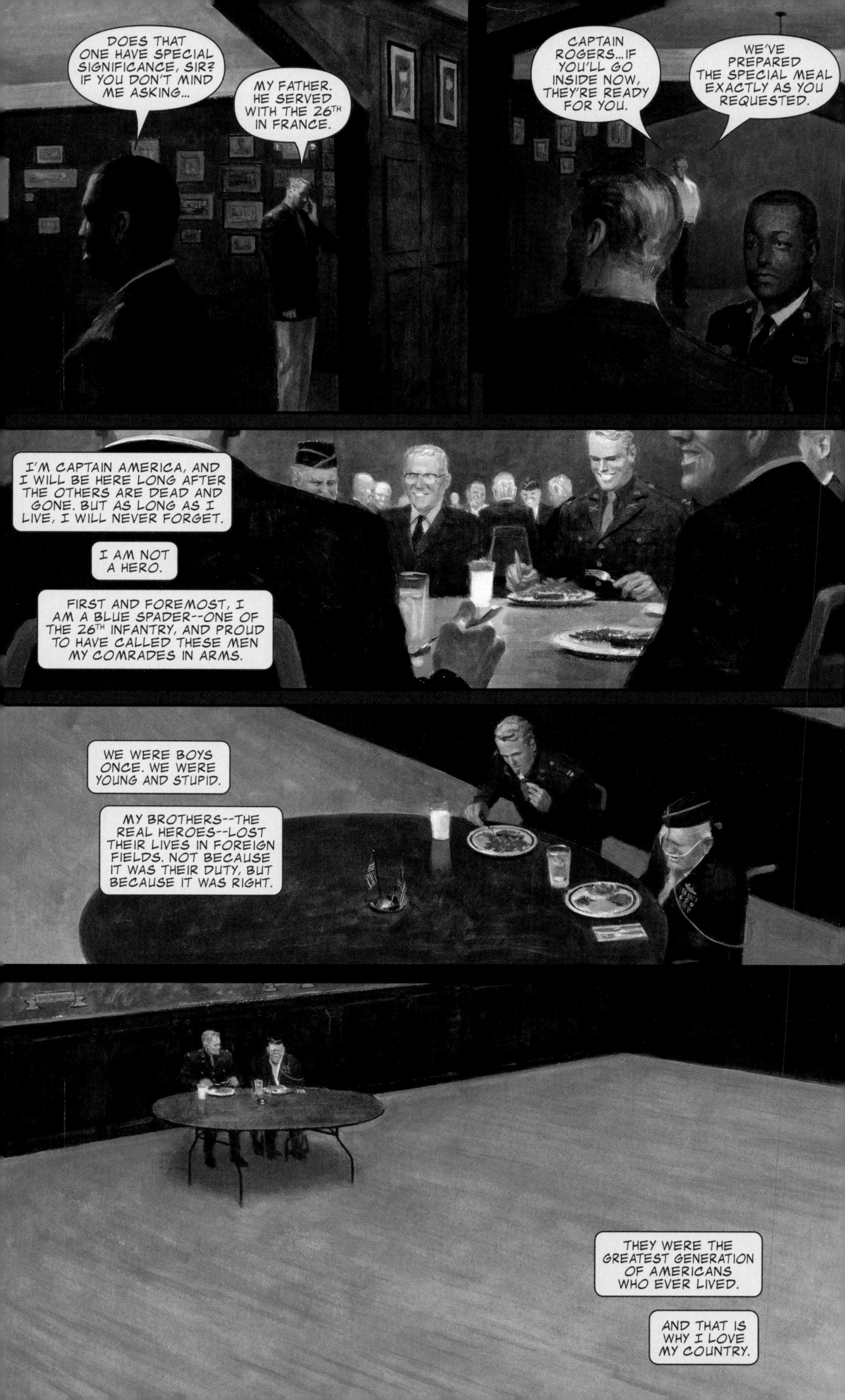
DOES THAT ONE HAVE SPECIAL SIGNIFICANCE, SIR? IF YOU DON'T MIND ME ASKING...
MY FATHER. HE SERVED WITH THE 26TH IN FRANCE.
CAPTAIN ROGERS...IF YOU'LL GO INSIDE NOW, THEY'RE READY FOR YOU.
WE'VE PREPARED THE SPECIAL MEAL EXACTLY AS YOU REQUESTED.
I'M CAPTAIN AMERICA, AND I WILL BE HERE LONG AFTER THE OTHERS ARE DEAD AND GONE. BUT AS LONG AS I LIVE, I WILL NEVER FORGET.
I AM NOT A HERO.
FIRST AND FOREMOST, I AM A BLUE SPADER--ONE OF THE 26TH INFANTRY, AND PROUD TO HAVE CALLED THESE MEN MY COMRADES IN ARMS.
WE WERE BOYS ONCE. WE WERE YOUNG AND STUPID.
MY BROTHERS--THE REAL HEROES--LOST THEIR LIVES IN FOREIGN FIELDS. NOT BECAUSE IT WAS THEIR DUTY, BUT BECAUSE IT WAS RIGHT.
THEY WERE THE GREATEST GENERATION OF AMERICANS WHO EVER LIVED.
AND THAT IS WHY I LOVE MY COUNTRY.